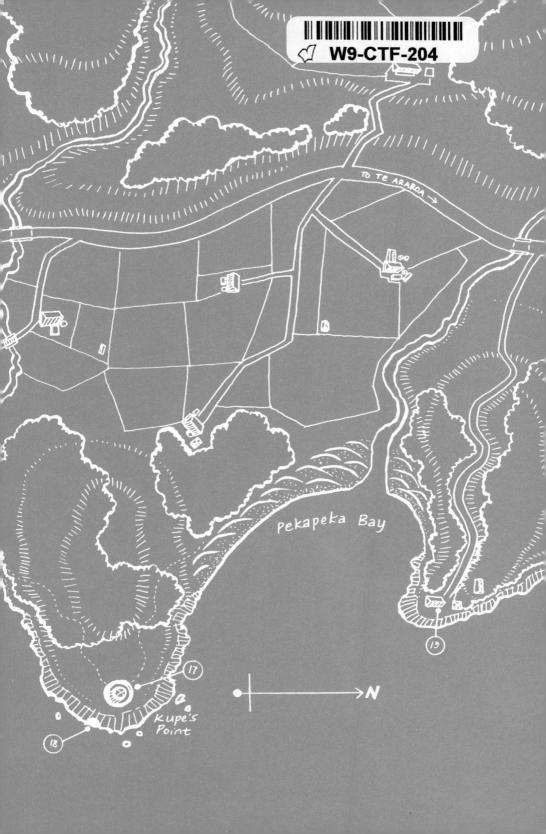

W9-CTF-204

TO TE ARAROA →

Pekapeka Bay

Kupe's
Point

⟶N

HICKSVILLE

A COMIC BOOK **BY DYLAN HORROCKS**

DRAWN AND QUARTERLY PUBLICATIONS

ACKNOWLEDGEMENTS

Arohanui to the family and friends who've let me use their computers, fax machines and kitchen tables at various times in the past 6 years or minded the kids while I slaved over the drawing board; especially Simone, John, Matthew and Shelley, Paul and Sara-Jane, Eleanor, Roger and Shirley, John and Clemency, Fran and Rob, Nerilee, Tim, Alex, Richard, Sylvie, and all three Davids. And to Andrew for giving life to Danton and Mopani.

Thanks to the many cartoonists and readers who have offered encouragement and support: Tim Bollinger, Lars Cawley, Timothy Kidd, Kelly Sheehan, Dominic, Adam Jamieson, Eric Searleman, Tom Hart, Jon Lewis, Brian Biggs, Matt Madden, Seth, Chester Brown, Jay Stephens, Nick Craine, Eddie Campbell, Bernard Caleo and Les Cartoonistes Dangereuses. And to all those I haven't named — *kia kaha*. You'll always be welcome in Hicksville.

Thanks to everyone at Comix@ for help with the Glossary (especially the omniscient Arthur van Kruining and Paul Gravett), to Karen at Panic Print for service beyond the call of duty, and of course to Michel Vrána, for making it all possible.

But the biggest thanks of all goes to Theresa for her tolerance, support, insight and love. And to Louis and Abe for being patient and beautiful.

Copyright © 2001 by Dylan Horrocks. All rights reserved.
Portions of the story appeared in a slightly different form in the periodical *Pickle* from issues 1-10.
First complete edition published in 1998 by Black Eye Books.
This edition published in 2001 by Drawn & Quarterly.
ISBN 1-896597-19-X
Printed in Canada.
10 9 8 7 6 5 4 3 2

Publication design
by Michel Vrána and Dylan Horrocks
Publisher: Chris Oliveros

Drawn & Quarterly
Post Office Box 48056
Montreal, Quebec
Canada H2V 4S8

Free Catalogue available upon request.

Website: www.drawnandquarterly.com
E-mail: info@drawnandquarterly.com

FOREWORD BY SETH

Warning — read this after you've read the book.

I wish there was a Hicksville. If there was, I'd find it. I might not want to spend the rest of my life there... but I'd certainly like to visit for a month or two each year. Sometimes, when I'm reading this story (and I've read it many times) I can almost believe there is such a place. Far back, in the dustier parts of my brain, there is a tiny inkling of an idea that perhaps Dylan *is* writing about a real place — a safe haven for the broken dreams of all those great cartoonists who came before me, a place unsullied by the realities of the comics "industry." Of course, there is no such place. The fact that Dylan has managed to evoke these feelings in me is a testament to his skill as a cartoonist.

More important than this skill though is the obvious fact that Dylan Horrocks loves comics. His work exudes this love. It seems to be an unconditional love too — covering everything from superheroes to humour strips, from autobiography to gag-cartooning. In this area, Dylan is a man after my own heart. He sees the whole continuum of cartooning and he embraces it. In "Hicksville" he manages to do a very difficult thing. He makes that love palpable and understandable. He infuses cartooning with wonder and depth and mystery. In the world of Hicksville, cartooning isn't just another part of the disposable junk culture, it's a powerful medium capable of sustaining the real complexities of life and art. He makes this clear with a voyage to the various corners of the mysterious comics world. From Far Cornucopia, where we meet Emil Kopen, the magician-cartographer of spatial relationships to the cold industry machine of Dick Burger (where he writes the best eulogy of old superhero comics I've ever read: "A bit sad and very moral and humane") to the warmth of Hicksville itself, with its Rarebit Fiend cafe and Annual Hogan's Alley

Festival. And though this journey is fascinating in itself we're also treated to a wonderful blurring of the edges between "reality" and "cartoon reality." Moxie and Toxie leave the page to interact freely with their creator, unexplained comics pages blow by (seemingly starring Captain Cook) and, in perhaps "Hicksville's" finest section, we lose touch with the "reality" that "Stars" is a strip drawn by Sam Zabel, not Dylan Horrocks.

The best trip is saved for last. The central, most powerful image that sits at the heart of Dylan's world — Kupe's lighthouse. Here in the lighthouse we come to the fabulous library. The library of comics that were never drawn. It's a sad image really... because it reflects the truth of what comics actually have been. An industry that, for the most part, robbed artists of the chance of doing their real work. An industry that forced great cartoonists to waste their talents hacking out insipid stories for a half interested audience. It's here in the library that you feel the tragedy of the wasted potential of a medium. When Kupe shows Leonard Batts the dream works of Kirby, Kurtzman, Wood and Picasso it's the sort of scene that sends a little mental shiver down a cartoonist's spine... because these books *could* have existed. If only comics had been a little different. I'm sure it's no coincidence that Dylan chose to put this magical library in a lighthouse.

Still, the sadness of this image is betrayed by the joy and lightheartedness of the book itself. "Hicksville" is filled with life. The drawing sparkles with originality, spontaneity and the obvious pleasure of a cartoonist enjoying himself. And, if there's one thing to be sure of, it's that if you found your way to Kupe's library, a copy of this book would surely be found on its shelves, right next to the other greats of cartooning.

Seth
Palookaville, 1998

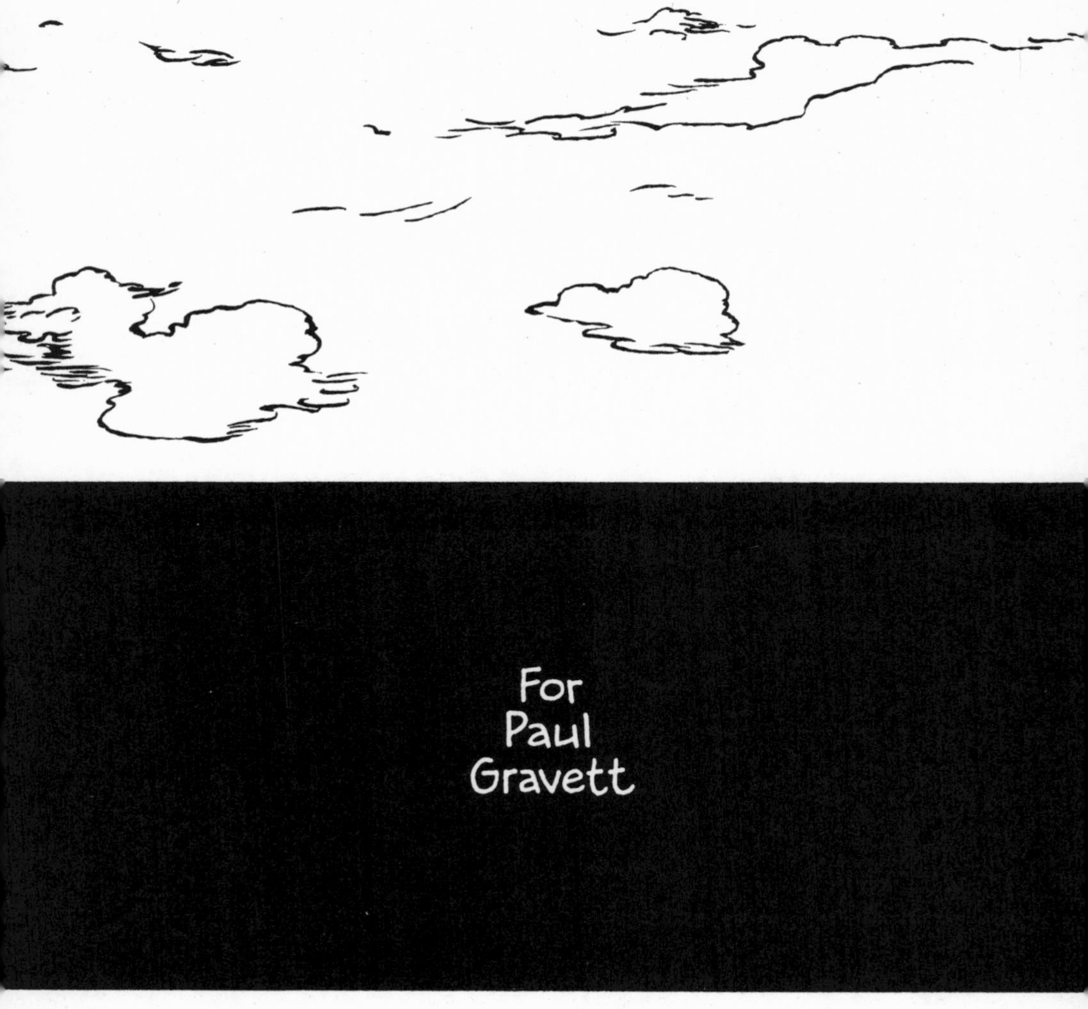

For
Paul
Gravett

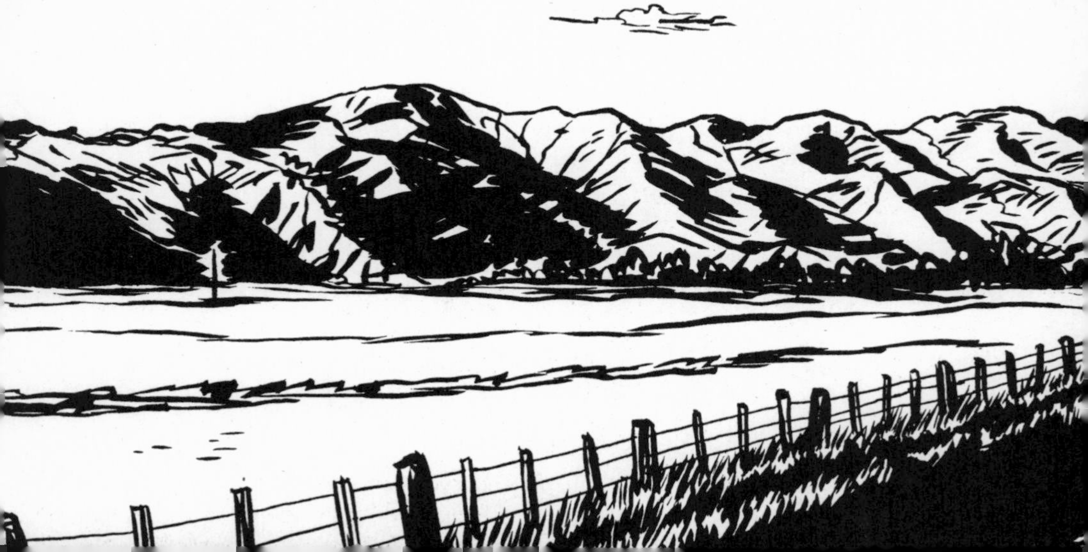

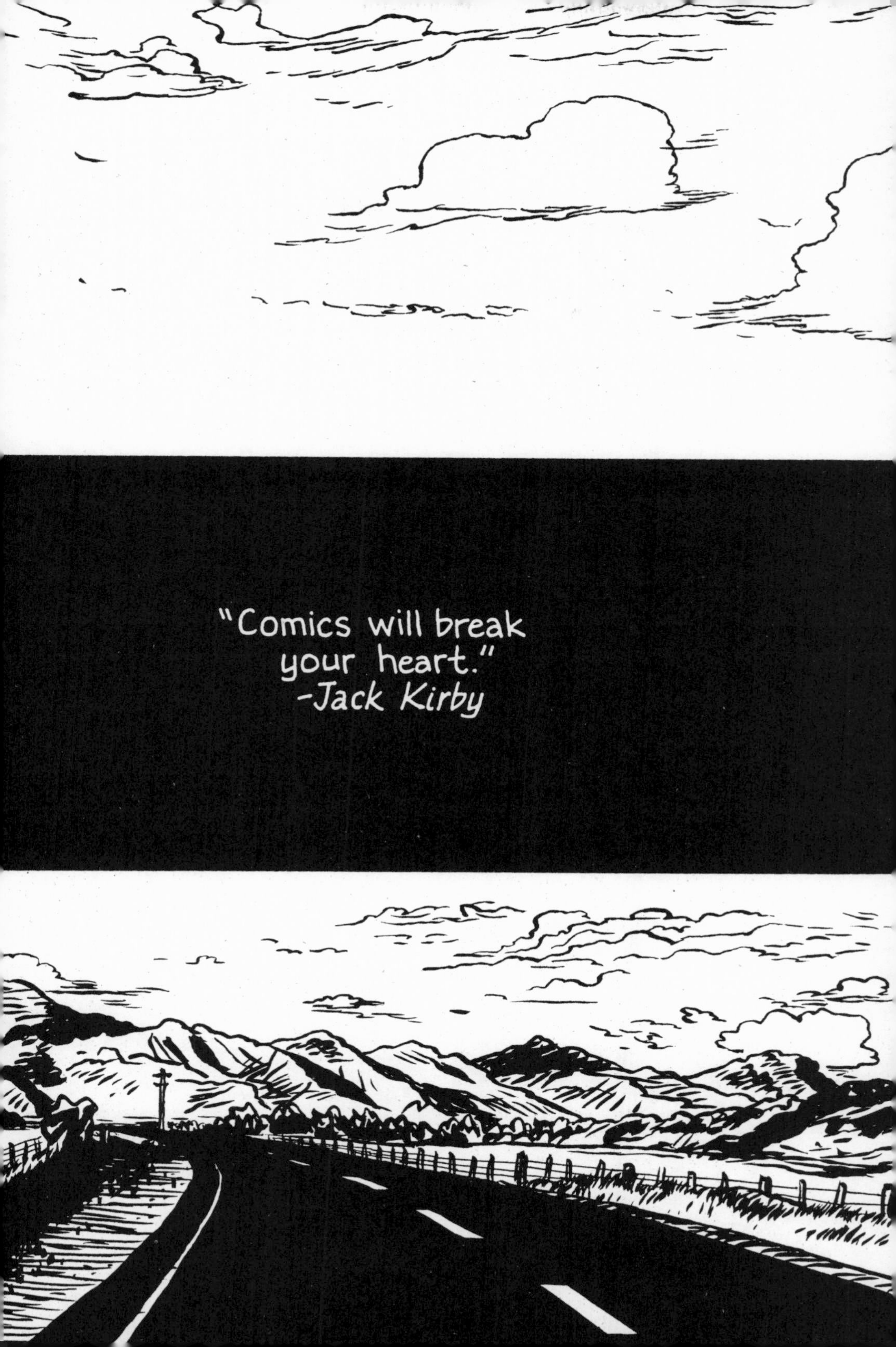
"Comics will break your heart."
-Jack Kirby

AUGUSTUS E.

The first letter came one miserable Saturday, when I was too tired from the week's work to do anything but brood...

CLATTER!

—dylan horrocks. London. 10/91

Life in general was fairly confused, and I faced a number of unpleasant decisions.

Postcard.

Come Back xxx

to: D. Horrocks
12 Bramshaw Rd
Hackney E95BD
England.

Colour
New Zealand

Home called, but I was hesitating.

Into all this came the letter.

?

Sender's Address:
Augustus E.
Hicksville, N.Z.

to: D. Horrocks
12 Bramshaw Rd
Hackney E95BD
England.

HICKSVILLE?
AUGUSTUS E.?

RIP

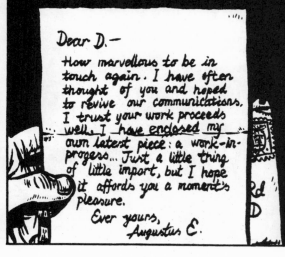

Dear D.—

How marvellous to be in touch again. I have often thought of you and hoped to revive our communications. I trust your work proceeds well. I have enclosed my own latest piece: a work-in-progress... Just a little thing of little import, but I hope it affords you a moment's pleasure.

Ever yours,
Augustus E.

Perplexed, I unfolded the enclosed art-work...

1

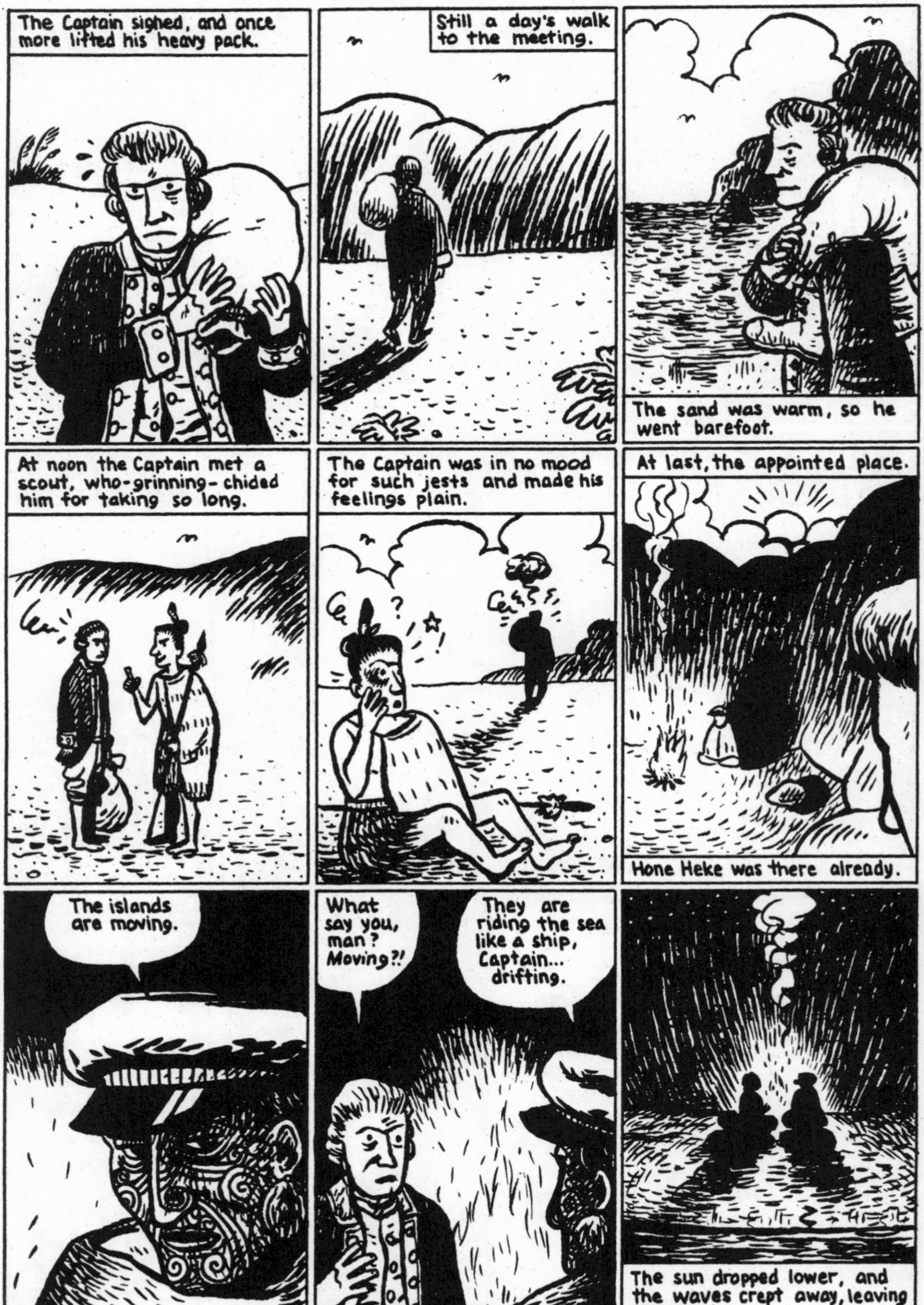
The Captain sighed, and once more lifted his heavy pack.
Still a day's walk to the meeting.
The sand was warm, so he went barefoot.
At noon the Captain met a scout, who-grinning-chided him for taking so long.
The Captain was in no mood for such jests and made his feelings plain.
?
At last, the appointed place.
Hone Heke was there already.
The islands are moving.
What say you, man? Moving?!
They are riding the sea like a ship, Captain... drifting.
The sun dropped lower, and the waves crept away, leaving the sand bare.
2

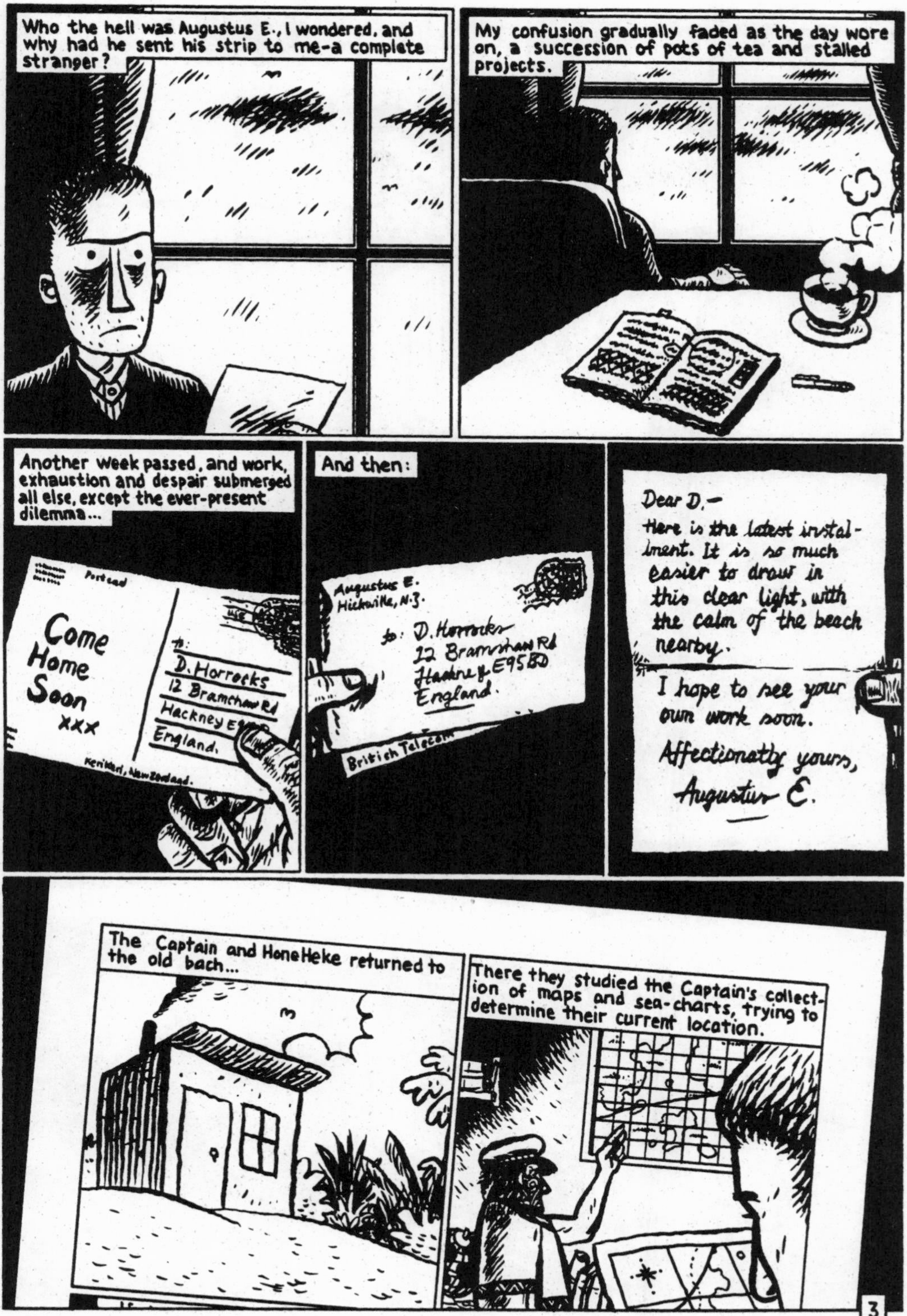

Who the hell was Augustus E., I wondered, and why had he sent his strip to me-a complete stranger?
My confusion gradually faded as the day wore on, a succession of pots of tea and stalled projects.
Another week passed, and work, exhaustion and despair submerged all else, except the ever-present dilemma...
Come Home Soon xxx
to: D. Horrocks 12 Bramshaw Rd Hackney E England.
And then:
Augustus E. Hickville, N.J.
to: D. Horrocks 22 Bramshaw Rd Hackney E95BD England.
British Telecom
Dear D.-
Here is the latest instalment. It is so much easier to draw in this clear light, with the calm of the beach nearby.
I hope to see your own work soon.
Affectionately yours,
Augustus E.
The Captain and HoneHeke returned to the old bach...
There they studied the Captain's collection of maps and sea-charts, trying to determine their current location.

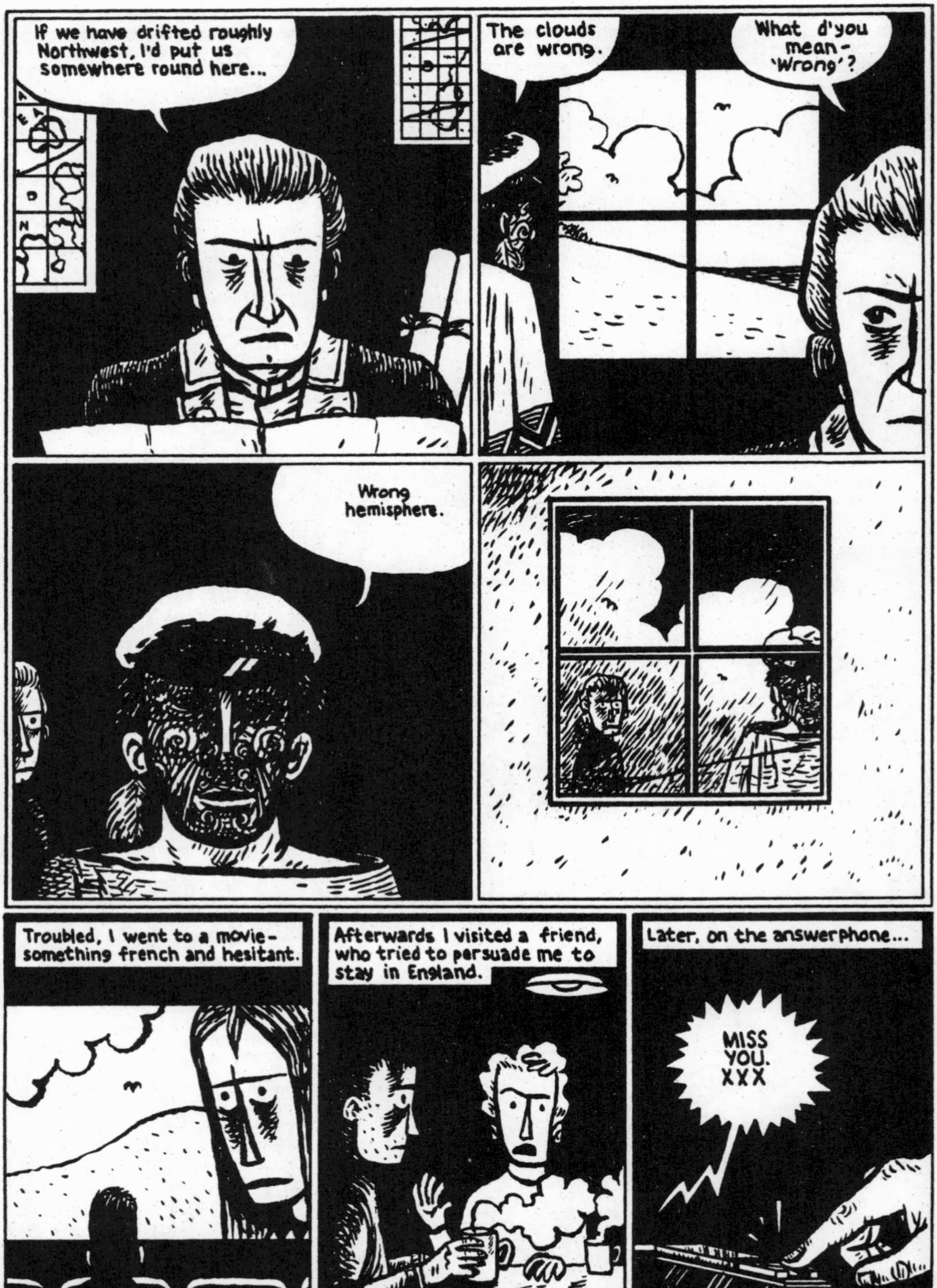
If we have drifted roughly Northwest, I'd put us somewhere round here...
The clouds are wrong.
What d'you mean- 'Wrong'?
Wrong hemisphere.
Troubled, I went to a movie- something french and hesitant.
Afterwards I visited a friend, who tried to persuade me to stay in England.
Later, on the answerphone...
MISS YOU. XXX

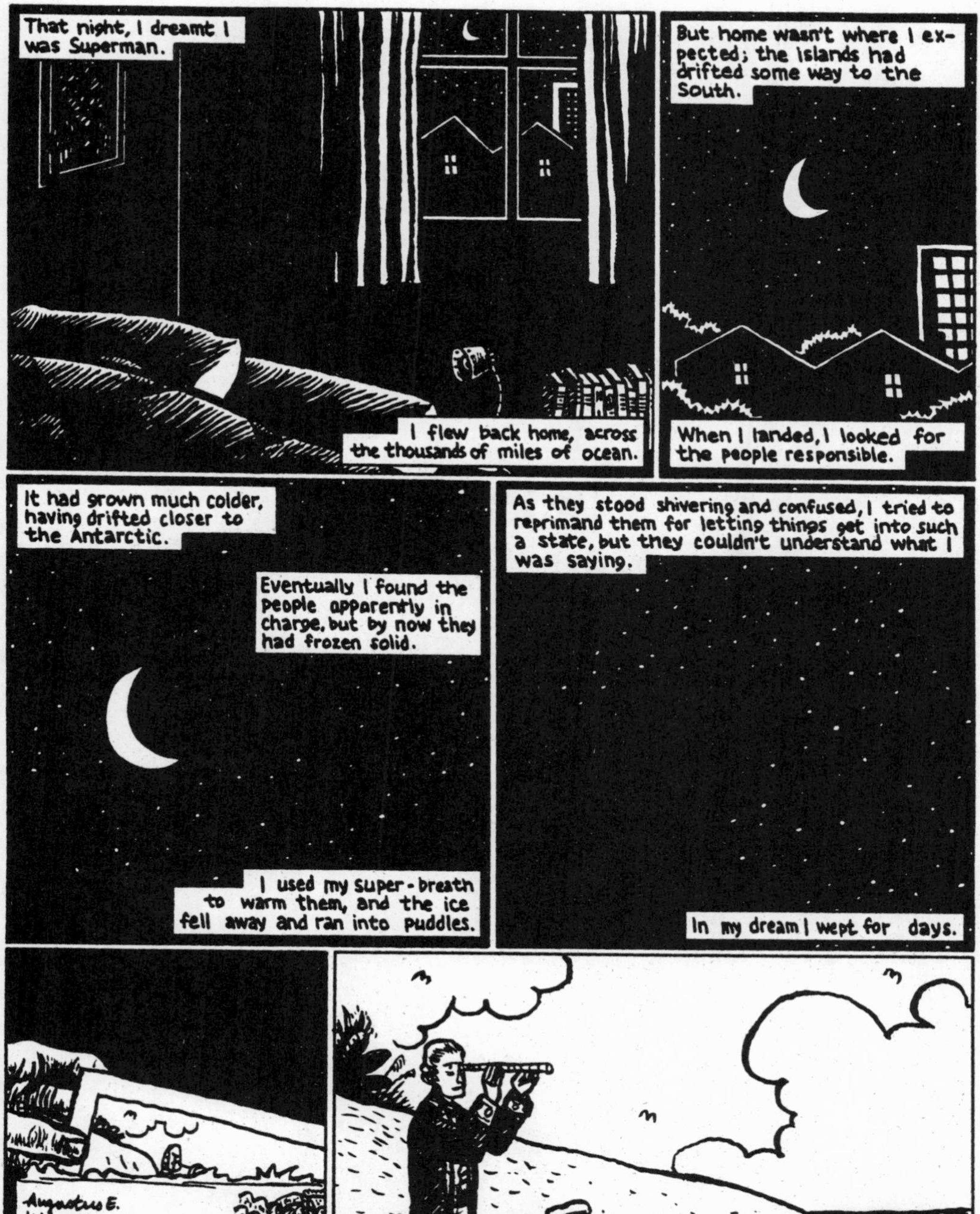
That night, I dreamt I was Superman.
I flew back home, across the thousands of miles of ocean.
But home wasn't where I expected; the islands had drifted some way to the South.
When I landed, I looked for the people responsible.
It had grown much colder, having drifted closer to the Antarctic.
Eventually I found the people apparently in charge, but by now they had frozen solid.
I used my super-breath to warm them, and the ice fell away and ran into puddles.
As they stood shivering and confused, I tried to reprimand them for letting things get into such a state, but they couldn't understand what I was saying.
In my dream I wept for days.
Augustus E.
Hicksville, N.Z
to: D. Horocks.
12 Bramshaw Rd
Hackney E95BD
England.

To Jeffrey. — dylan. 7.vii.92

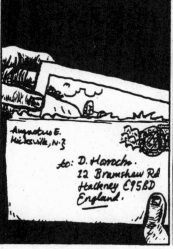

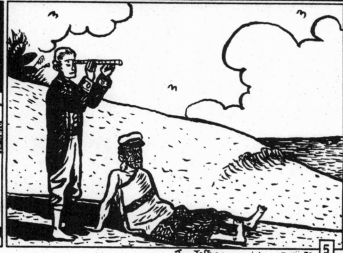

Chapter One

"From now on, I do not want progress."
Stan Lee, 1973.

VOLUME 1 OF 4. WINTER 1988. US.$6.95. CAN.$8.95.
VOLUME ONE IN A FOUR VOLUME EPIC!
Dick Burger's
CAPTAIN TOMORROW:
REBIRTH
Eternal Comics
Dick Burger

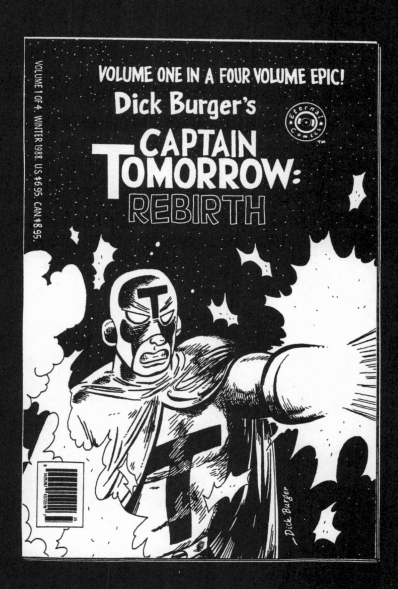

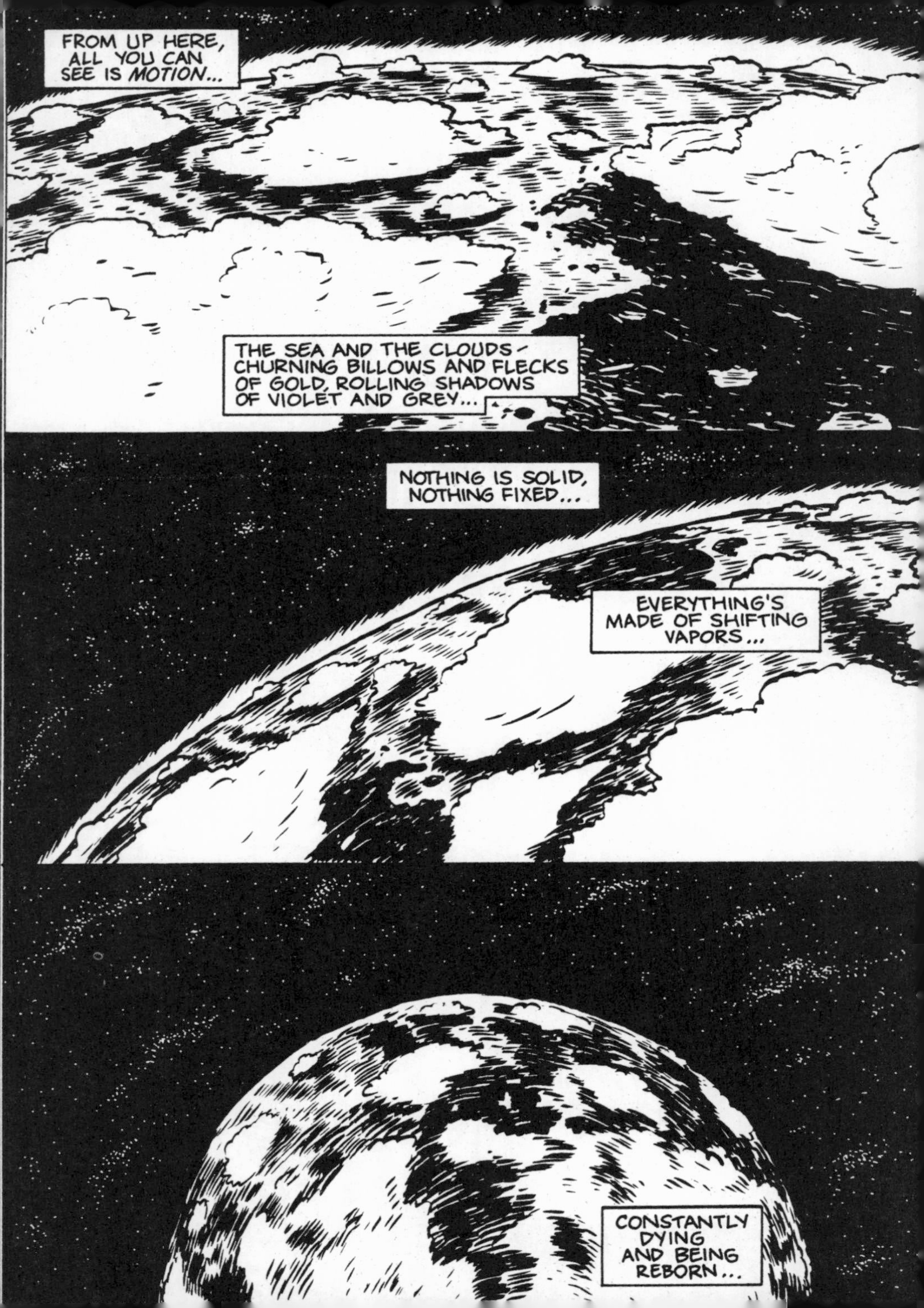
FROM UP HERE, ALL YOU CAN SEE IS *MOTION*...
THE SEA AND THE CLOUDS- CHURNING BILLOWS AND FLECKS OF GOLD, ROLLING SHADOWS OF VIOLET AND GREY...
NOTHING IS SOLID, NOTHING FIXED...
EVERYTHING'S MADE OF SHIFTING VAPORS...
CONSTANTLY DYING AND BEING REBORN...

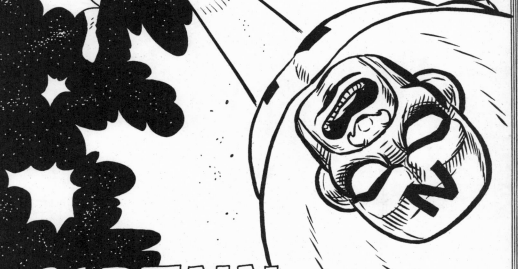

ON THE OTHER HAND, SOME THINGS JUST *NEVER* SEEM TO CHANGE...

CAPTAIN TOMORROW: REBIRTH ACT ONE

WRITTEN AND DRAWN BY
Dick Burger

COLOURED BY
Diane Worceski

LETTERED BY
CARL OBLESKI!

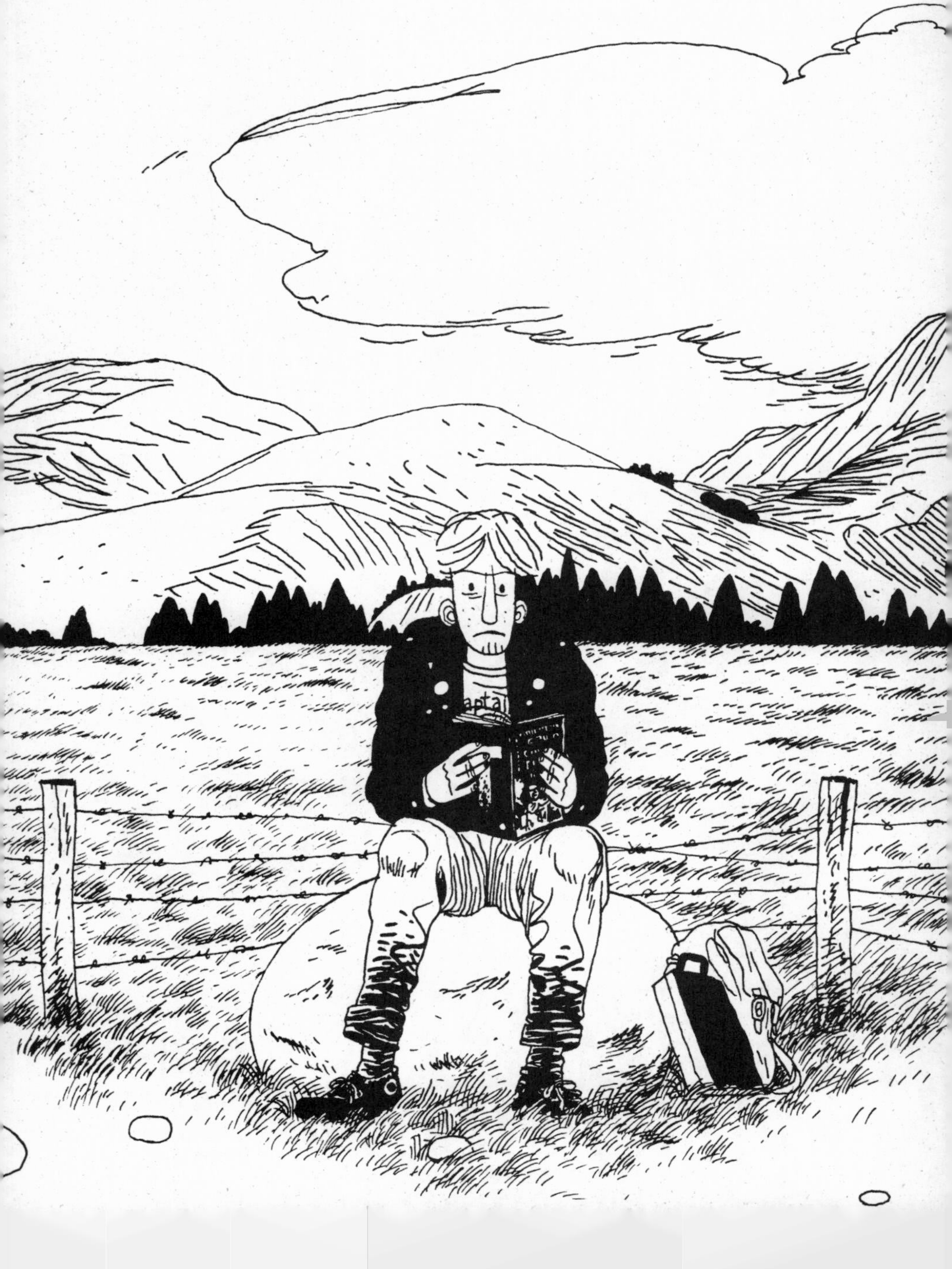

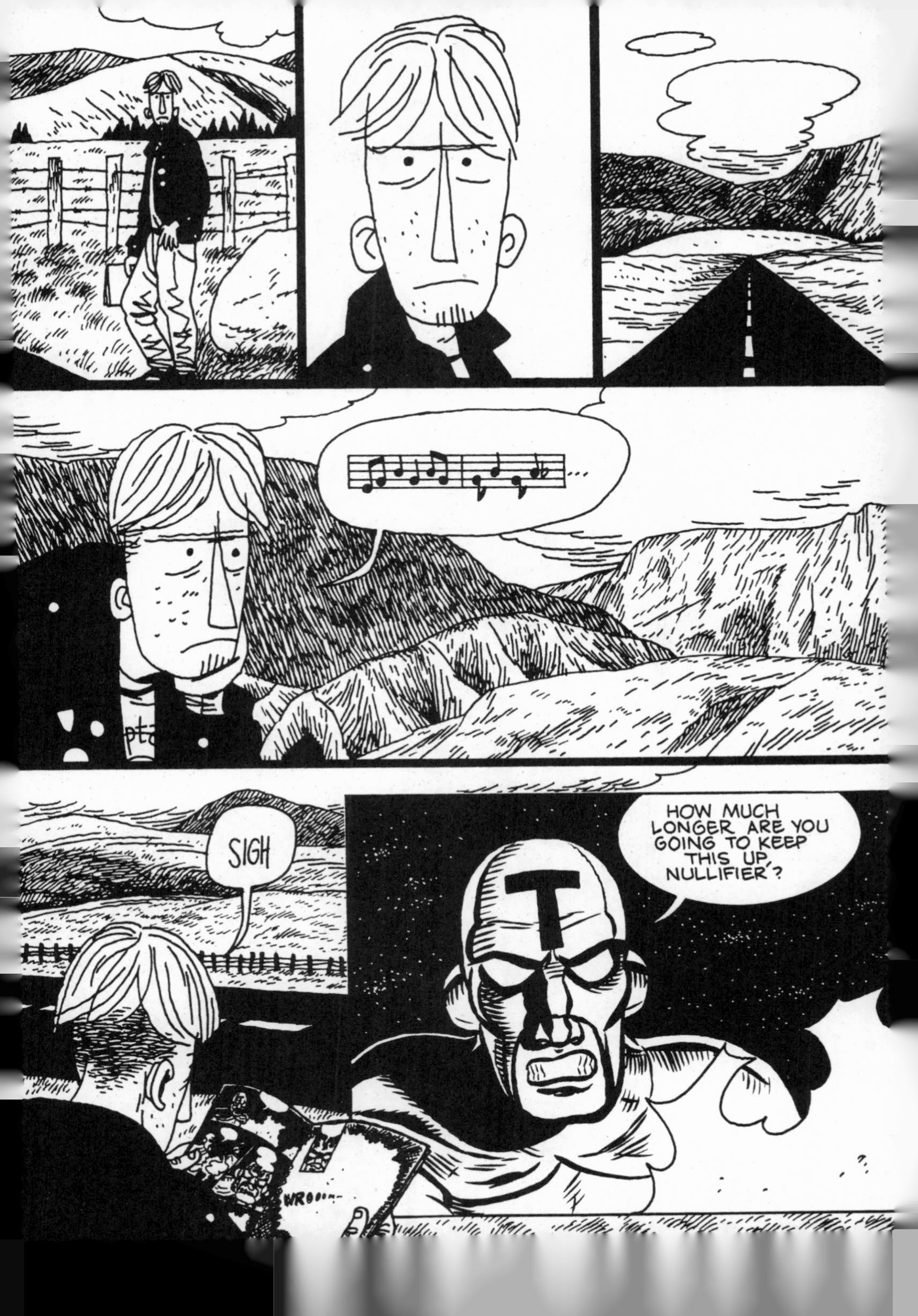
SIGH
HOW MUCH LONGER ARE YOU GOING TO KEEP THIS UP, NULLIFIER?
WROOOM—

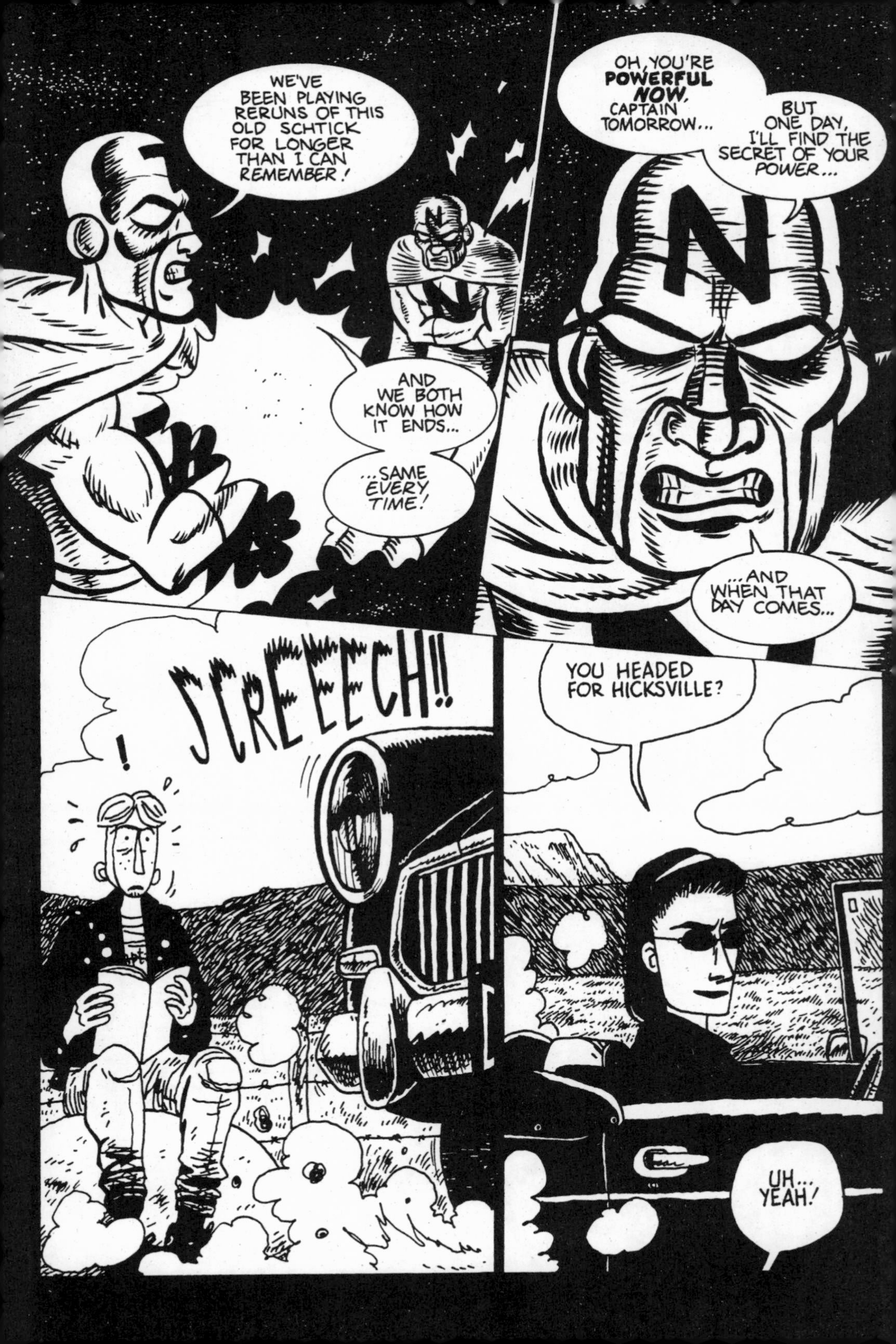
WE'VE BEEN PLAYING RERUNS OF THIS OLD SCHTICK FOR LONGER THAN I CAN REMEMBER!
AND WE BOTH KNOW HOW IT ENDS...
...SAME EVERY TIME!
OH, YOU'RE **POWERFUL NOW,** CAPTAIN TOMORROW...
BUT ONE DAY, I'LL FIND THE SECRET OF YOUR POWER...
...AND WHEN THAT DAY COMES...
SCREEECH!!
!
YOU HEADED FOR HICKSVILLE?
UH... YEAH!

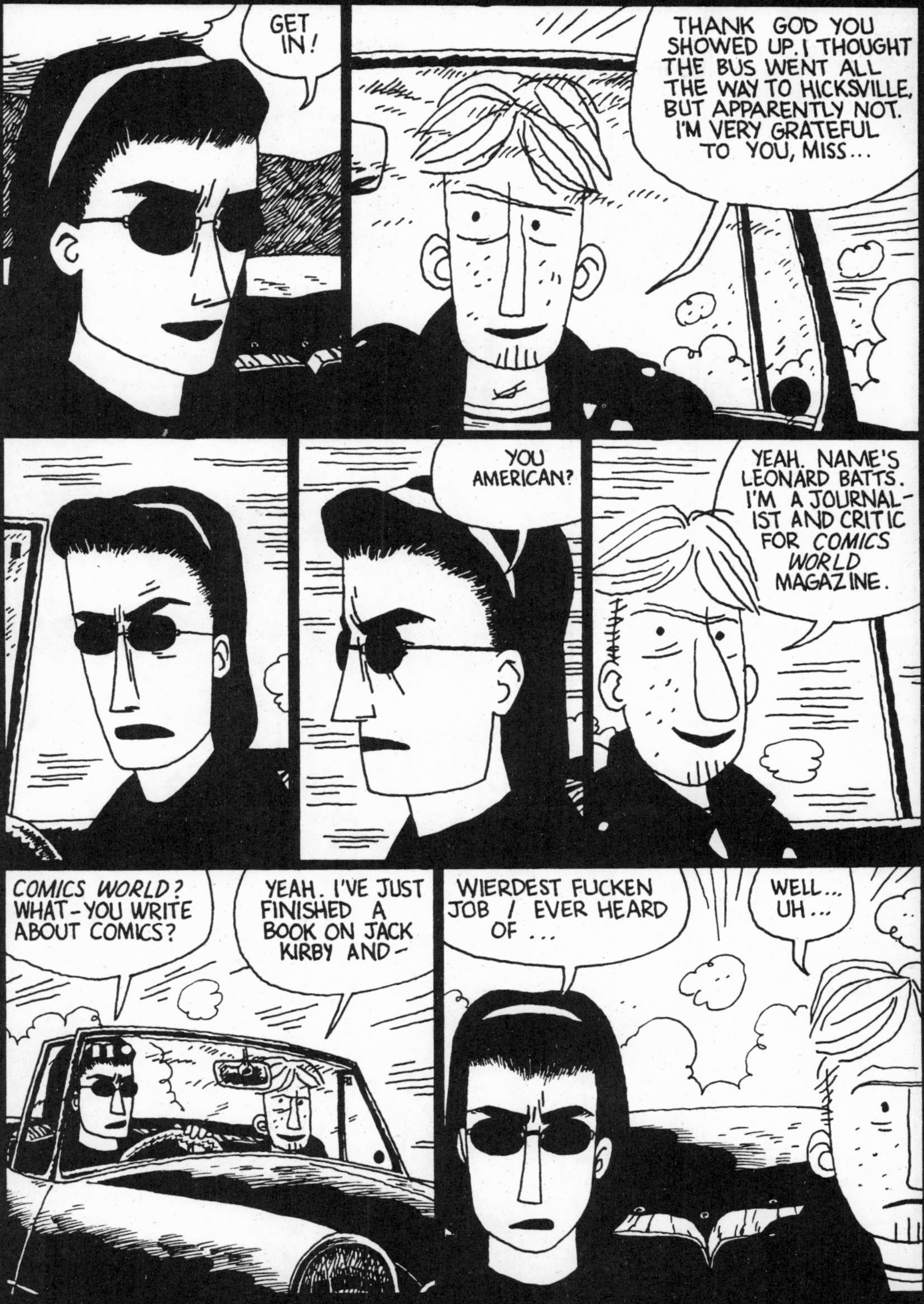
GET IN!
THANK GOD YOU SHOWED UP. I THOUGHT THE BUS WENT ALL THE WAY TO HICKSVILLE, BUT APPARENTLY NOT. I'M VERY GRATEFUL TO YOU, MISS...
YOU AMERICAN?
YEAH. NAME'S LEONARD BATTS. I'M A JOURNALIST AND CRITIC FOR *COMICS WORLD* MAGAZINE.
COMICS WORLD? WHAT-YOU WRITE ABOUT COMICS?
YEAH. I'VE JUST FINISHED A BOOK ON JACK KIRBY AND-
WIERDEST FUCKEN JOB I EVER HEARD OF...
WELL... UH...

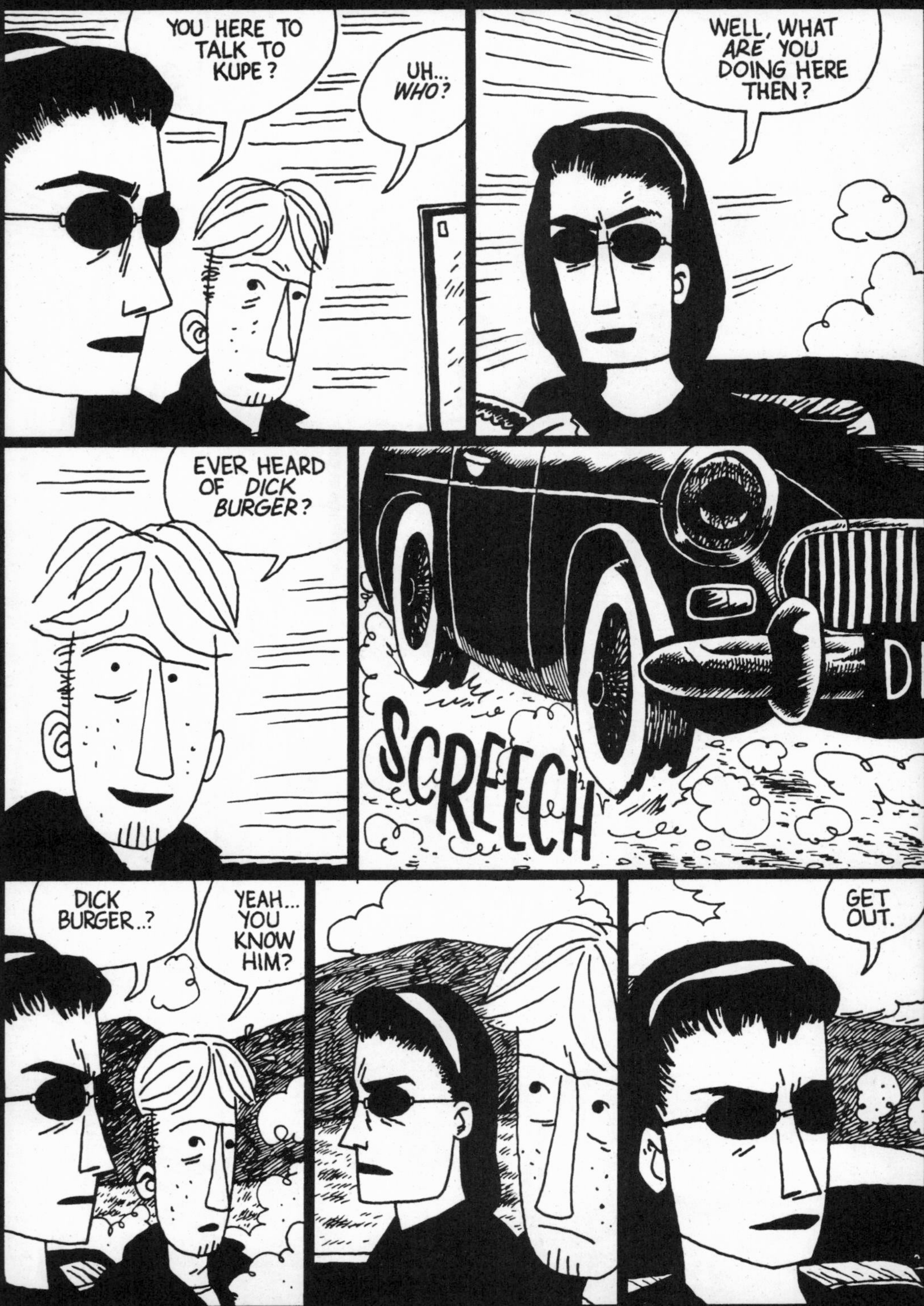
YOU HERE TO TALK TO KUPE?
UH... WHO?
WELL, WHAT ARE YOU DOING HERE THEN?
EVER HEARD OF DICK BURGER?
SCREECH
DICK BURGER..?
YEAH... YOU KNOW HIM?
GET OUT.

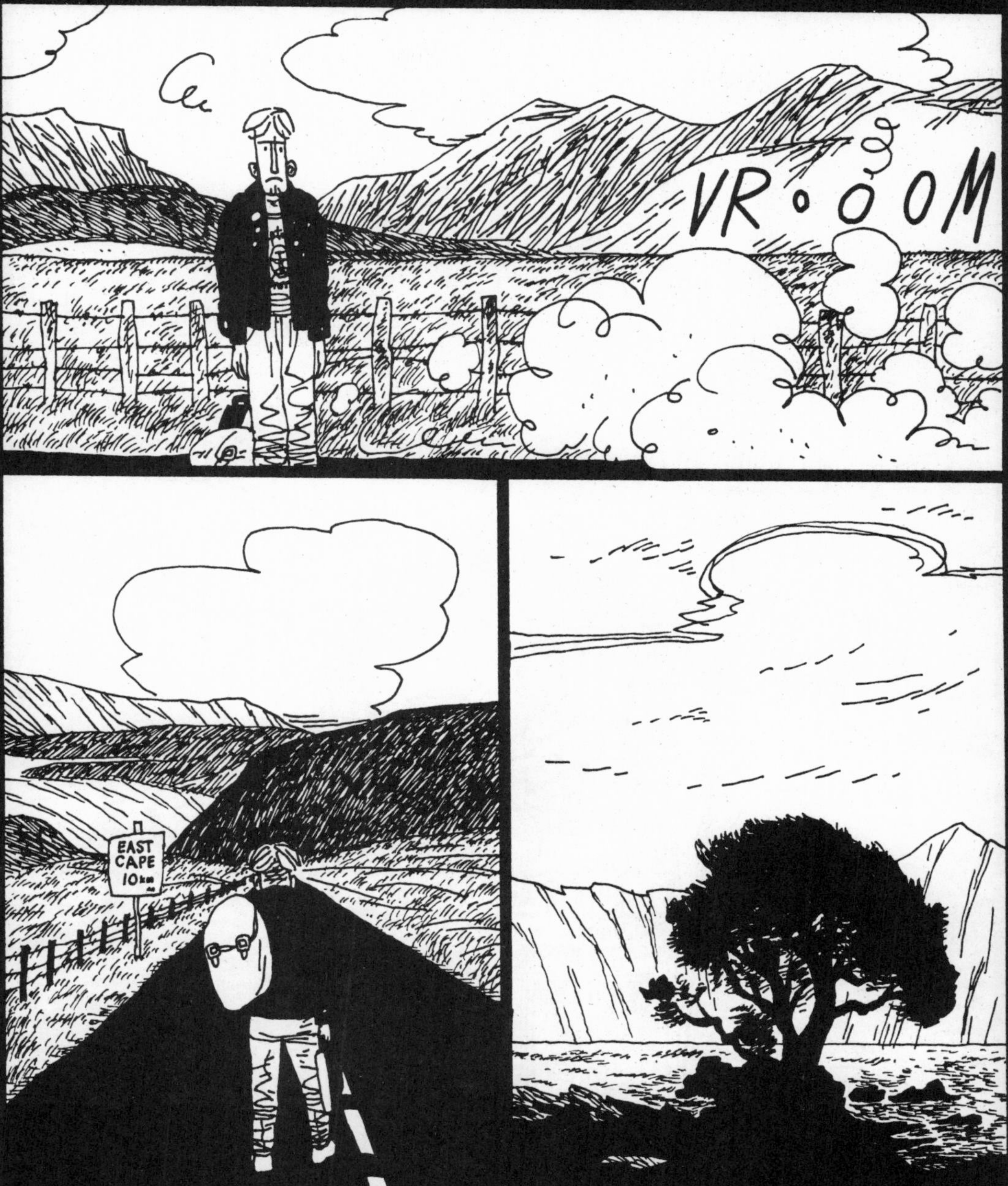
VR·OOM
EAST
CAPE
10km

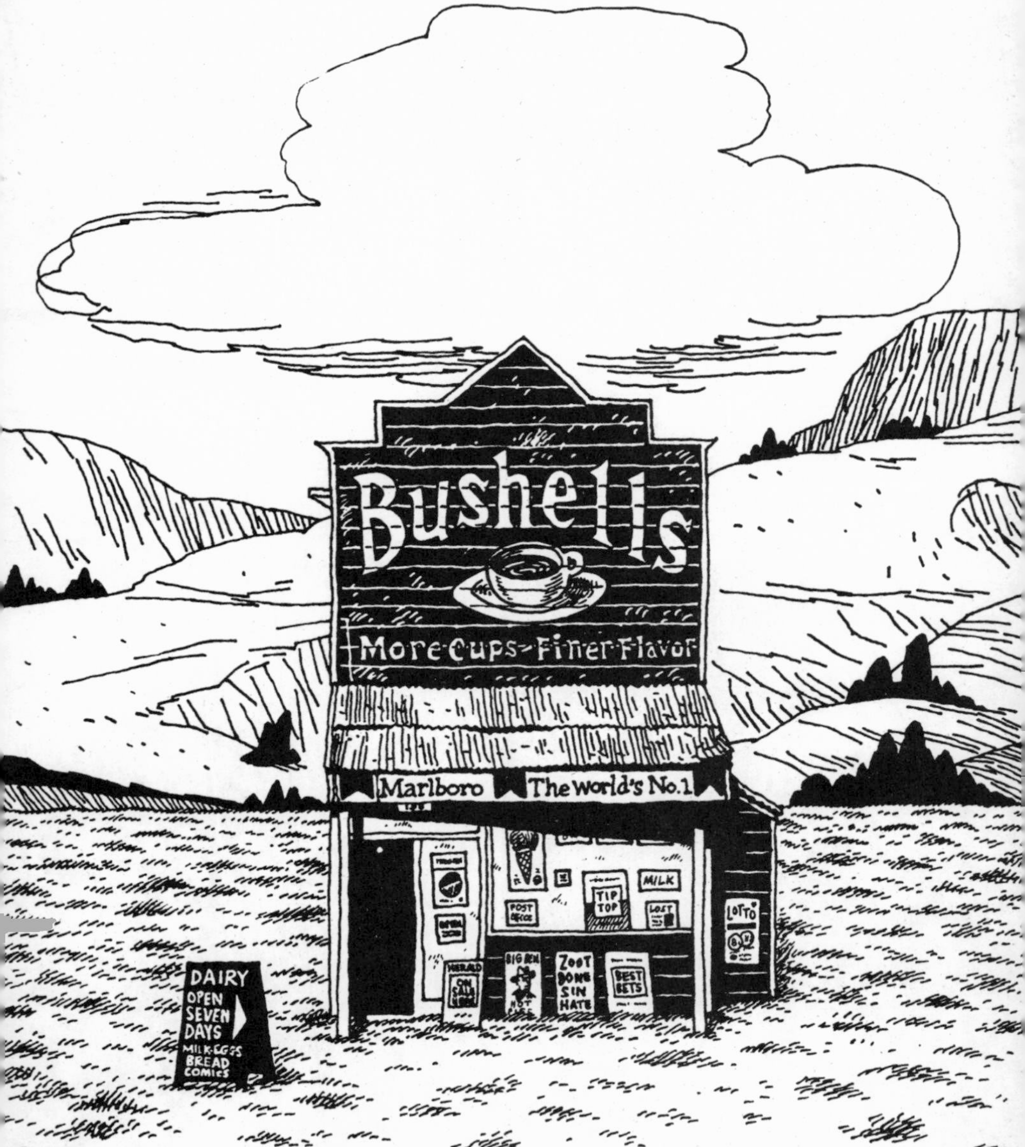
Bushells
More Cups - Finer Flavor
Marlboro
The world's No.1
MILK
POST OFFICE
TIP TOP
LOST
LOTTO
HERALD
BIG BEN
ZOOT BONE SIN HATE
BEST BETS
DAIRY
OPEN SEVEN DAYS
MILK·EGGS
BREAD
COMICS

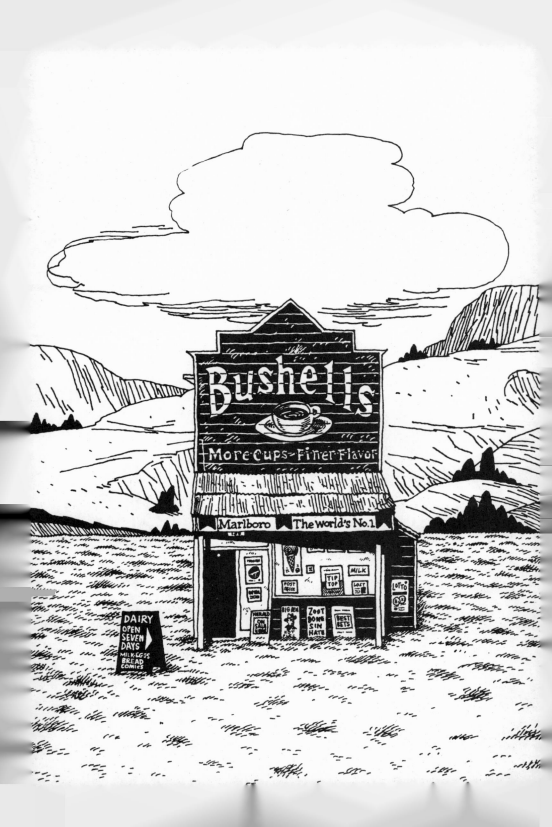

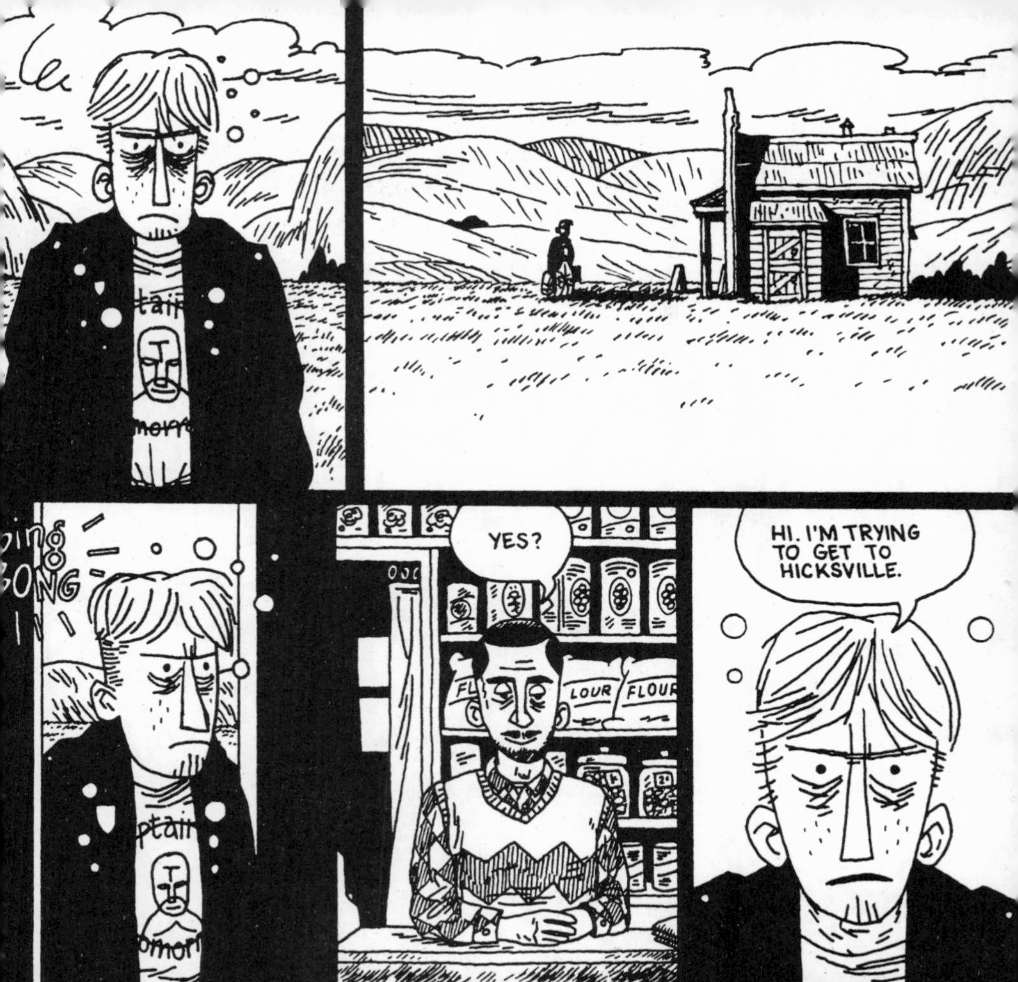
YES?
HI. I'M TRYING TO GET TO HICKSVILLE.
AMERICAN?
YES, I'M AMERICAN. WHICH WAY IS IT TO HICKSVILLE?
NEW YORK? WASHINGTON? IDAHO?
JUST AMERICAN...
PLEASE...
POPS!

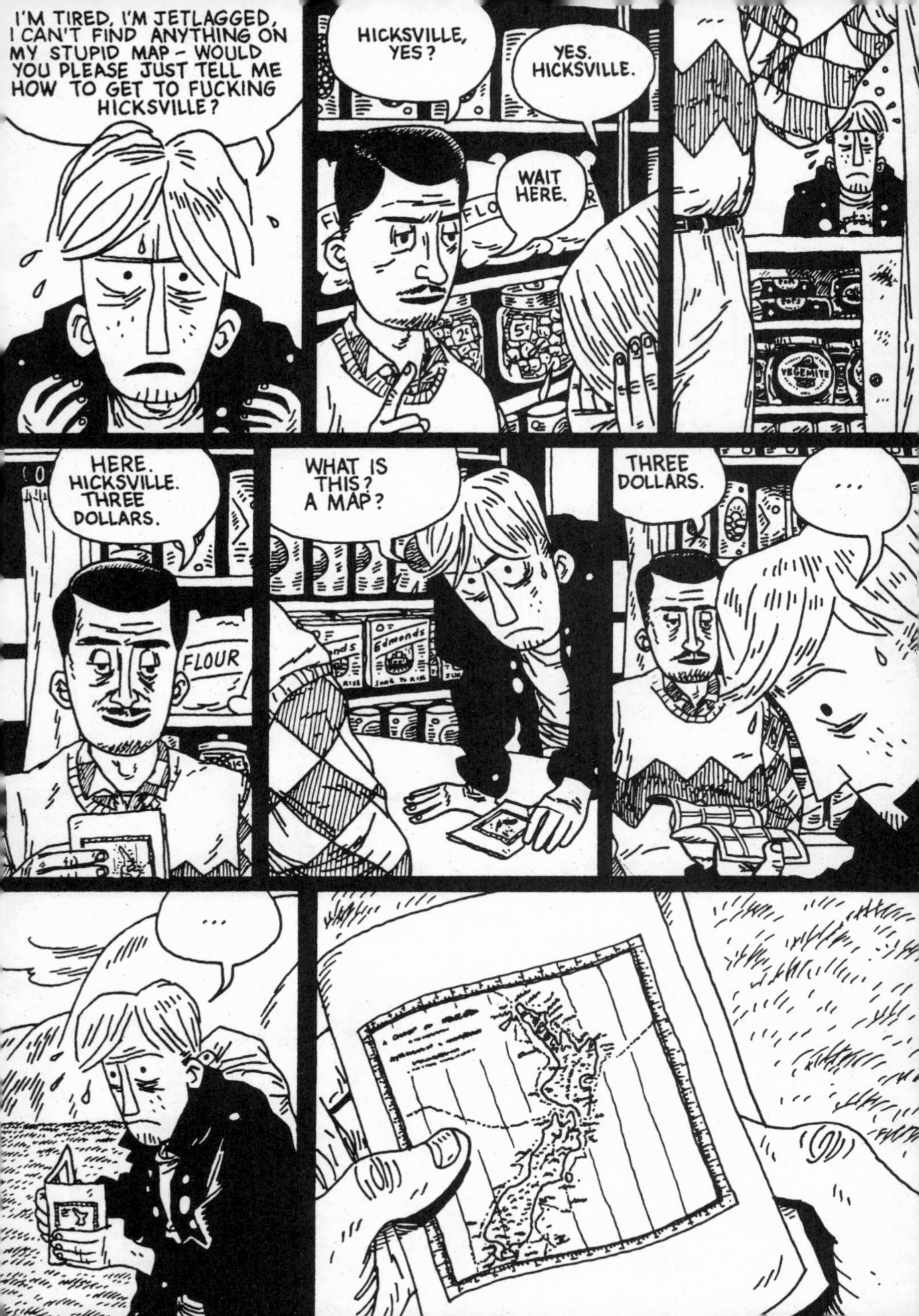
I'M TIRED, I'M JETLAGGED, I CAN'T FIND ANYTHING ON MY STUPID MAP - WOULD YOU PLEASE JUST TELL ME HOW TO GET TO FUCKING HICKSVILLE?
HICKSVILLE, YES?
YES. HICKSVILLE.
WAIT HERE.
HERE. HICKSVILLE. THREE DOLLARS.
WHAT IS THIS? A MAP?
THREE DOLLARS.
...
...

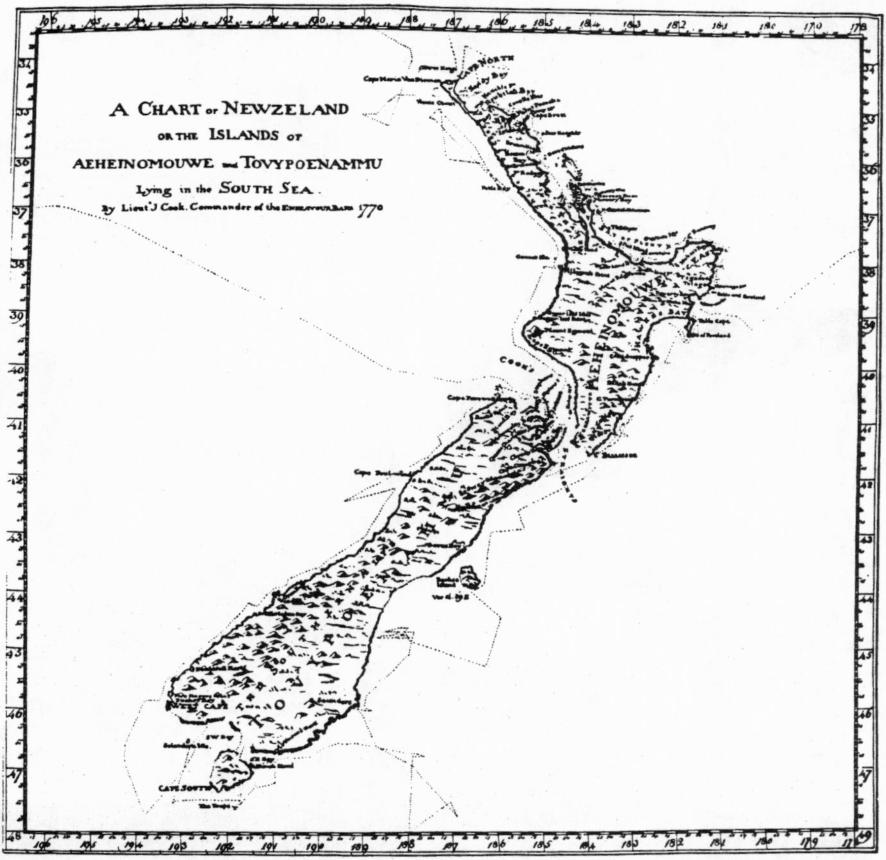

A CHART OF NEWZELAND
OR THE ISLANDS OF
AEHEINOMOUWE and TOVYPOENAMMU
Lying in the SOUTH SEA.
By Lieut.t J Cook. Commander of the ENDEAVOUR BARK 1770
CAPE NORTH
AEHEINOMOUWE
CAPE SOUTH

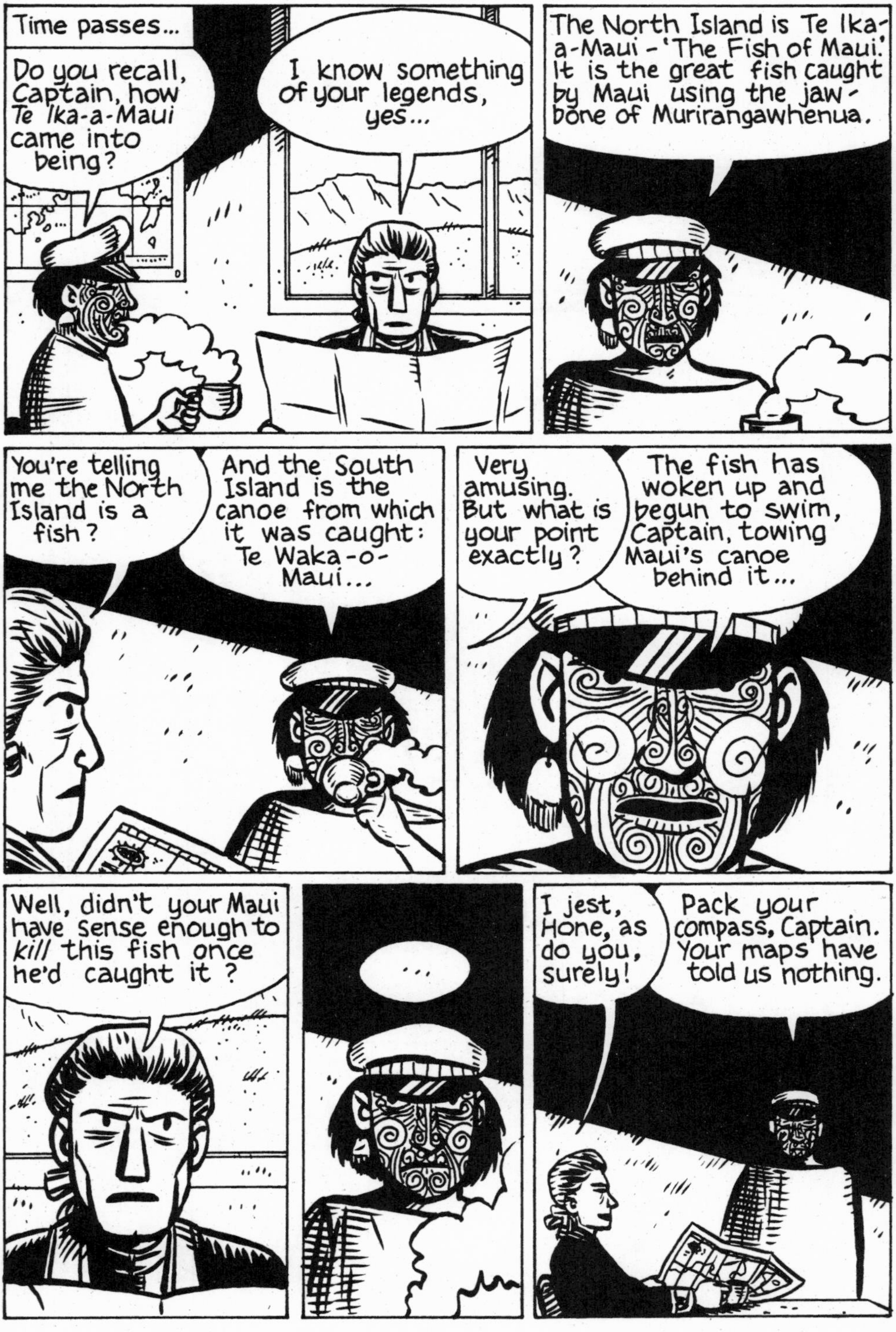

Time passes...
Do you recall, Captain, how *Te Ika-a-Maui* came into being?
I know something of your legends, yes...
The North Island is Te Ika-a-Maui – 'The Fish of Maui.' It is the great fish caught by Maui using the jaw-bone of Murirangawhenua.
You're telling me the North Island is a fish?
And the South Island is the canoe from which it was caught: Te Waka-o-Maui...
Very amusing. But what is your point exactly?
The fish has woken up and begun to swim, Captain, towing Maui's canoe behind it...
Well, didn't your Maui have sense enough to *kill* this fish once he'd caught it?
...
I jest, Hone, as do you, surely!
Pack your compass, Captain. Your maps have told us nothing.

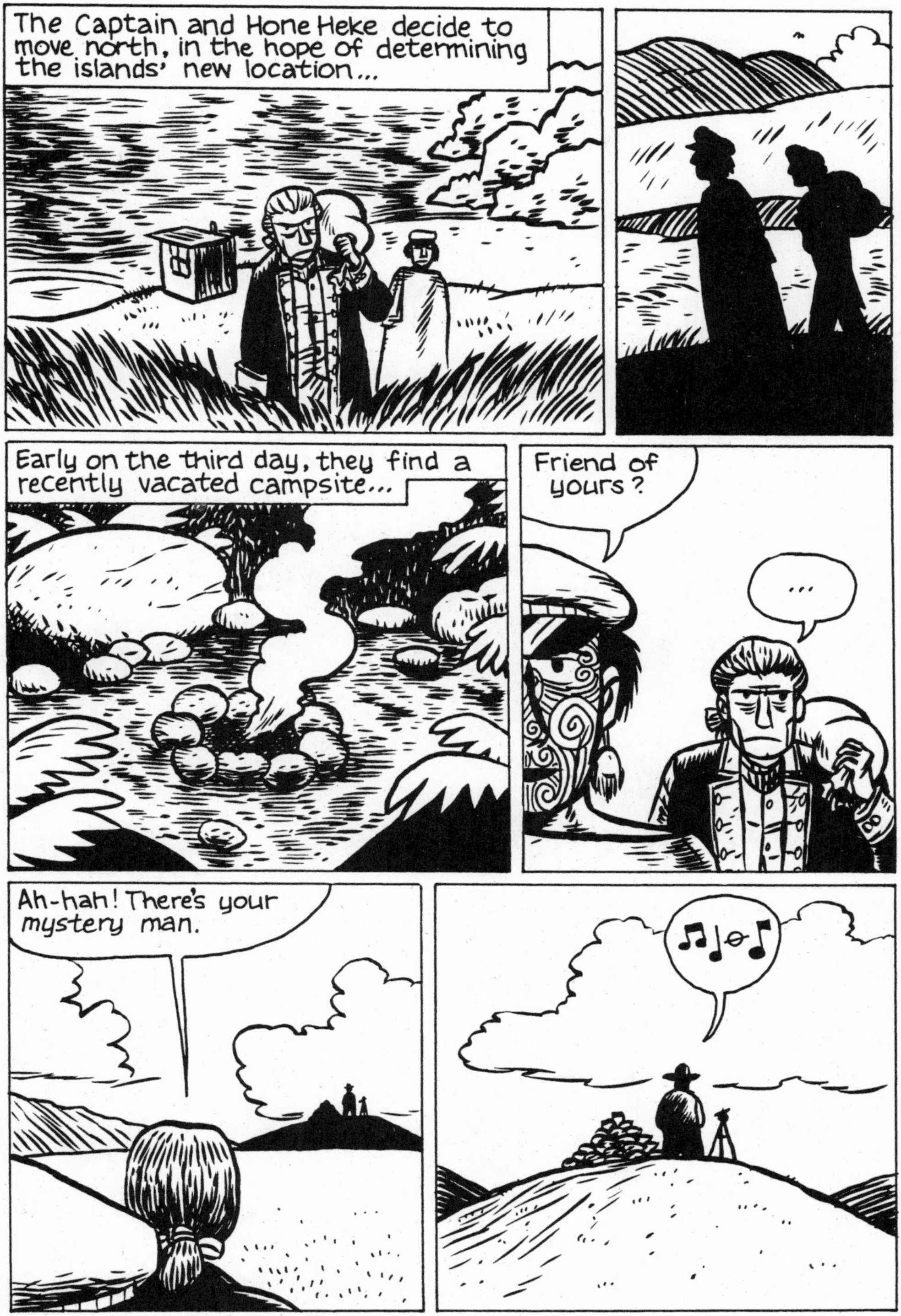
The Captain and Hone Heke decide to move north, in the hope of determining the islands' new location...
Early on the third day, they find a recently vacated campsite...
Friend of yours?
...
Ah-hah! There's your mystery man.

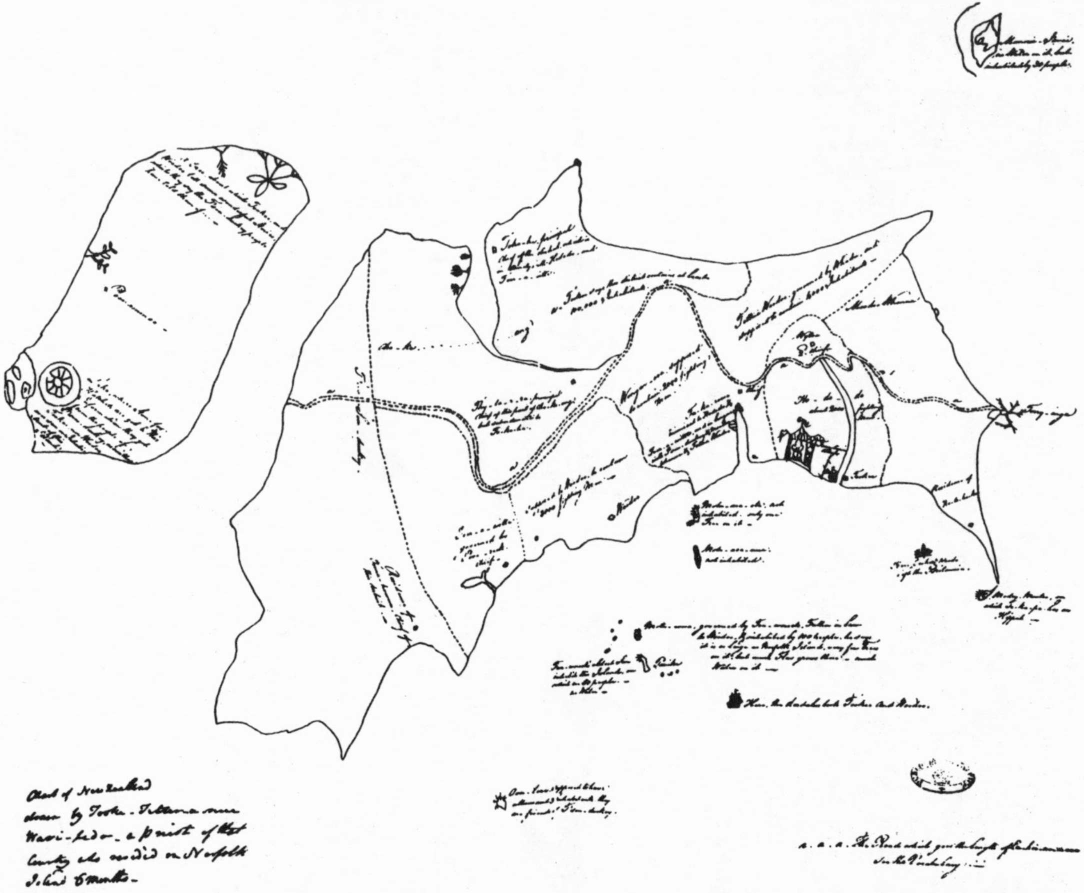
Chart of New Zealand
drawn by Tooke-Titter-a-nui
Wari-pedo - a Priest of that
Country who resided on Norfolk
Island 6 Months -

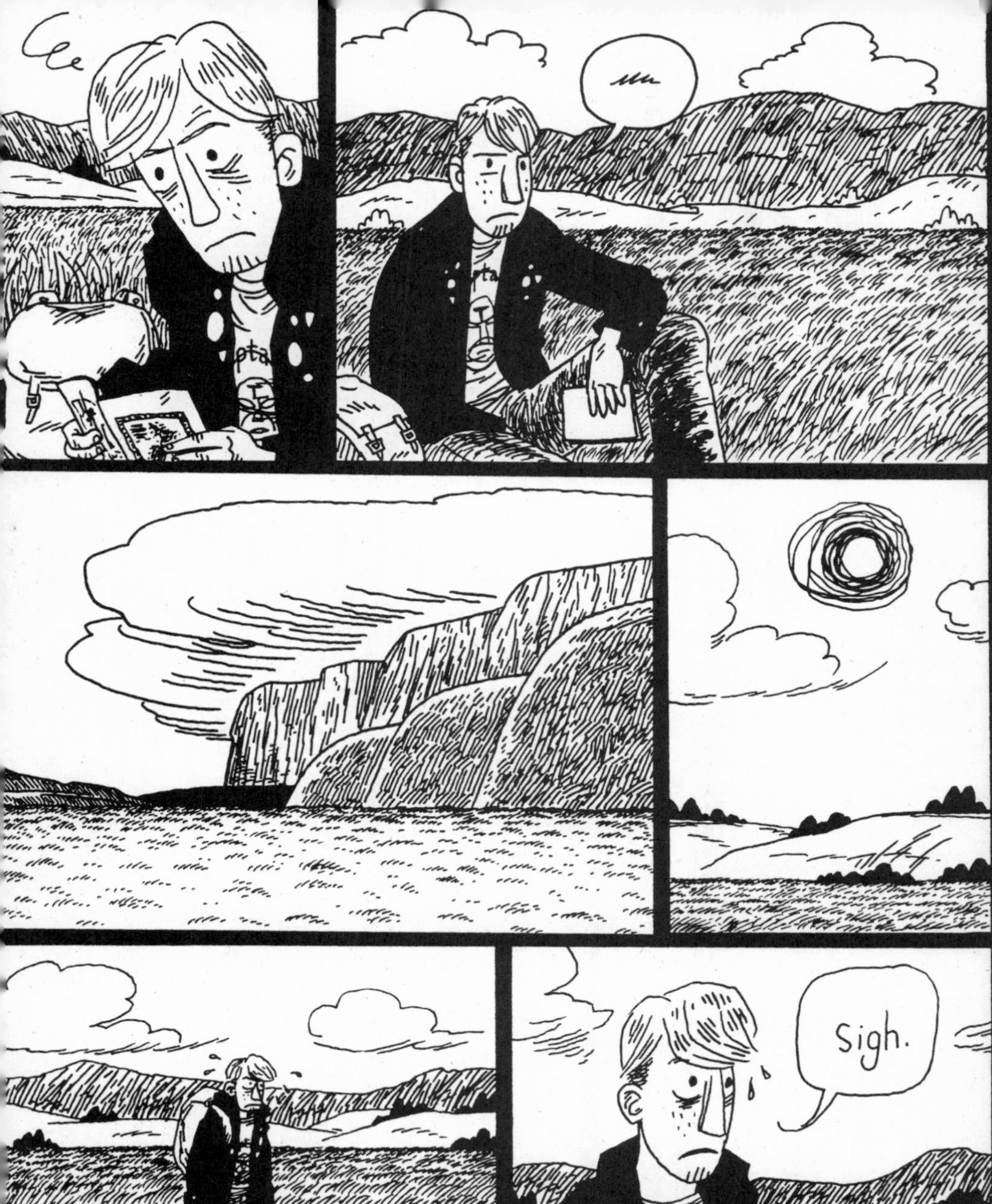
Sigh.
North

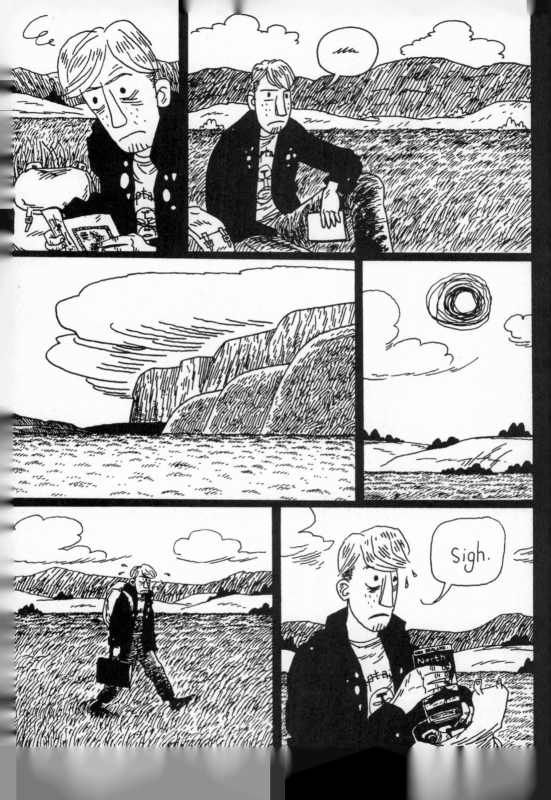

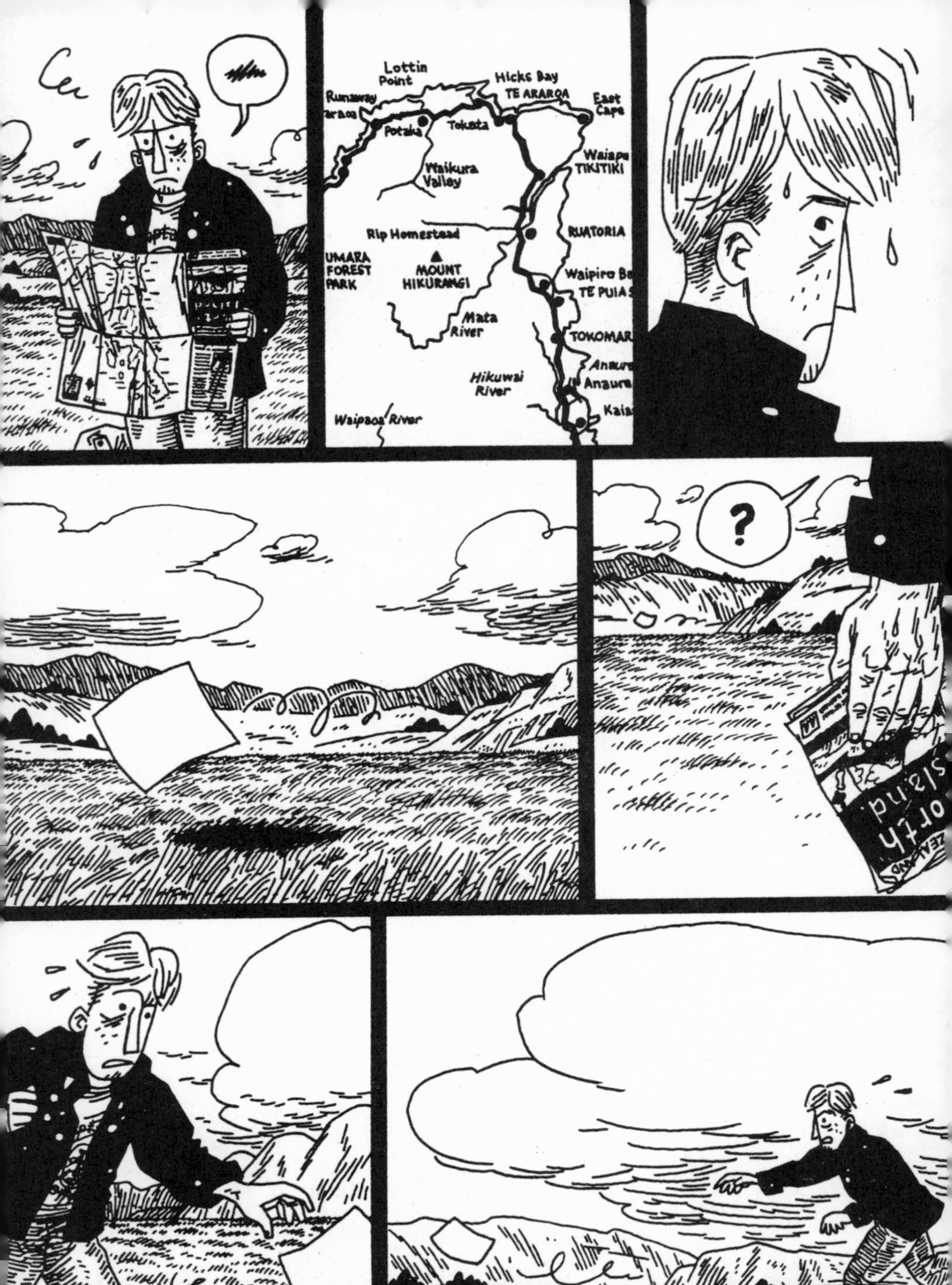
Lottin Point
Hicks Bay
Runaway
TE ARAROA
East Cape
Potaka
Tokata
Waipu
TIKITIKI
Waikura Valley
RUATORIA
Rip Homestead
MOUNT HIKURANGI
Mata River
TOKOMAR
Anaura
Hikuwai River
Waipaoa River
?

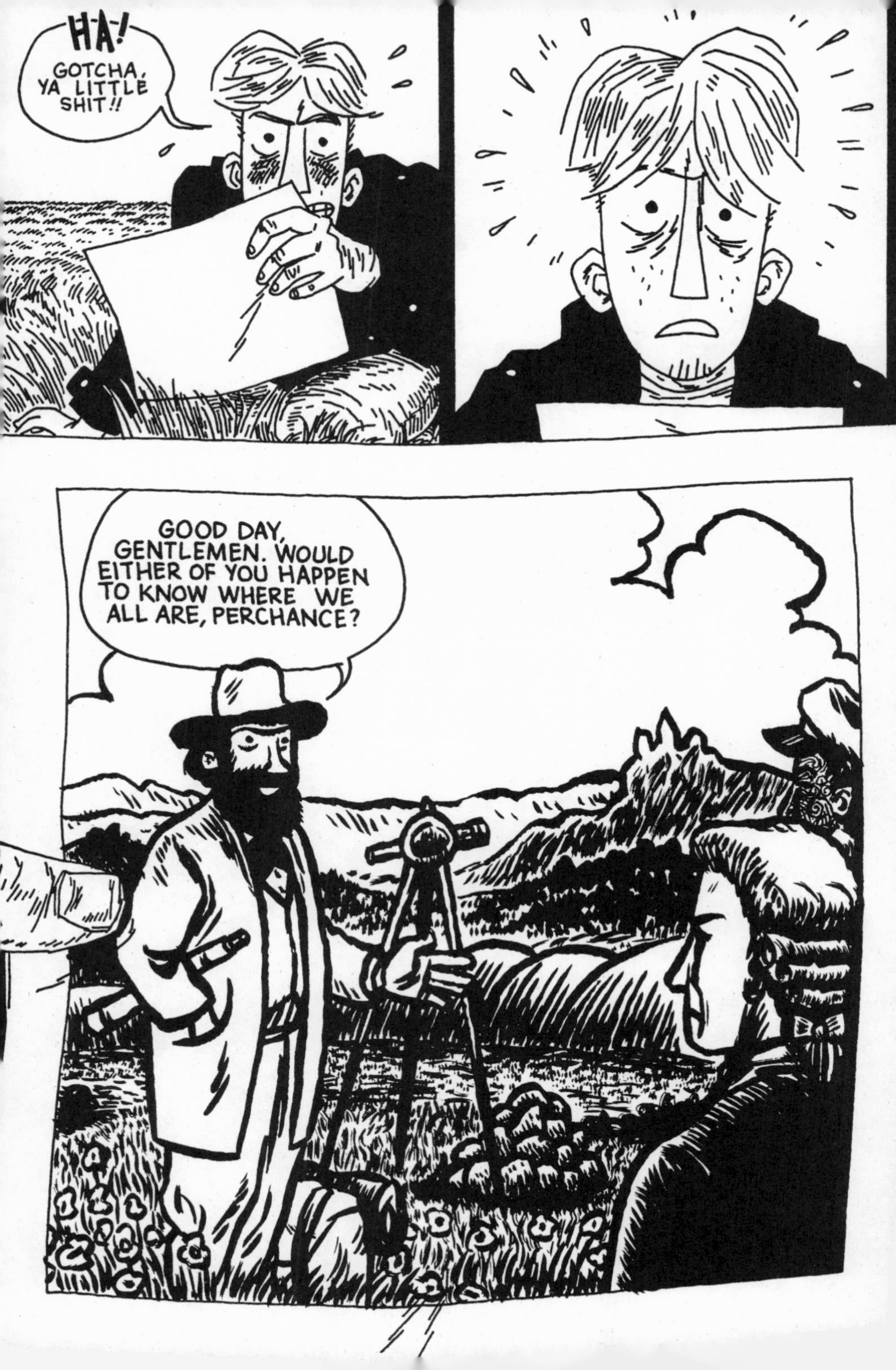
HA! GOTCHA, YA LITTLE SHIT!!
GOOD DAY, GENTLEMEN. WOULD EITHER OF YOU HAPPEN TO KNOW WHERE WE ALL ARE, PERCHANCE?

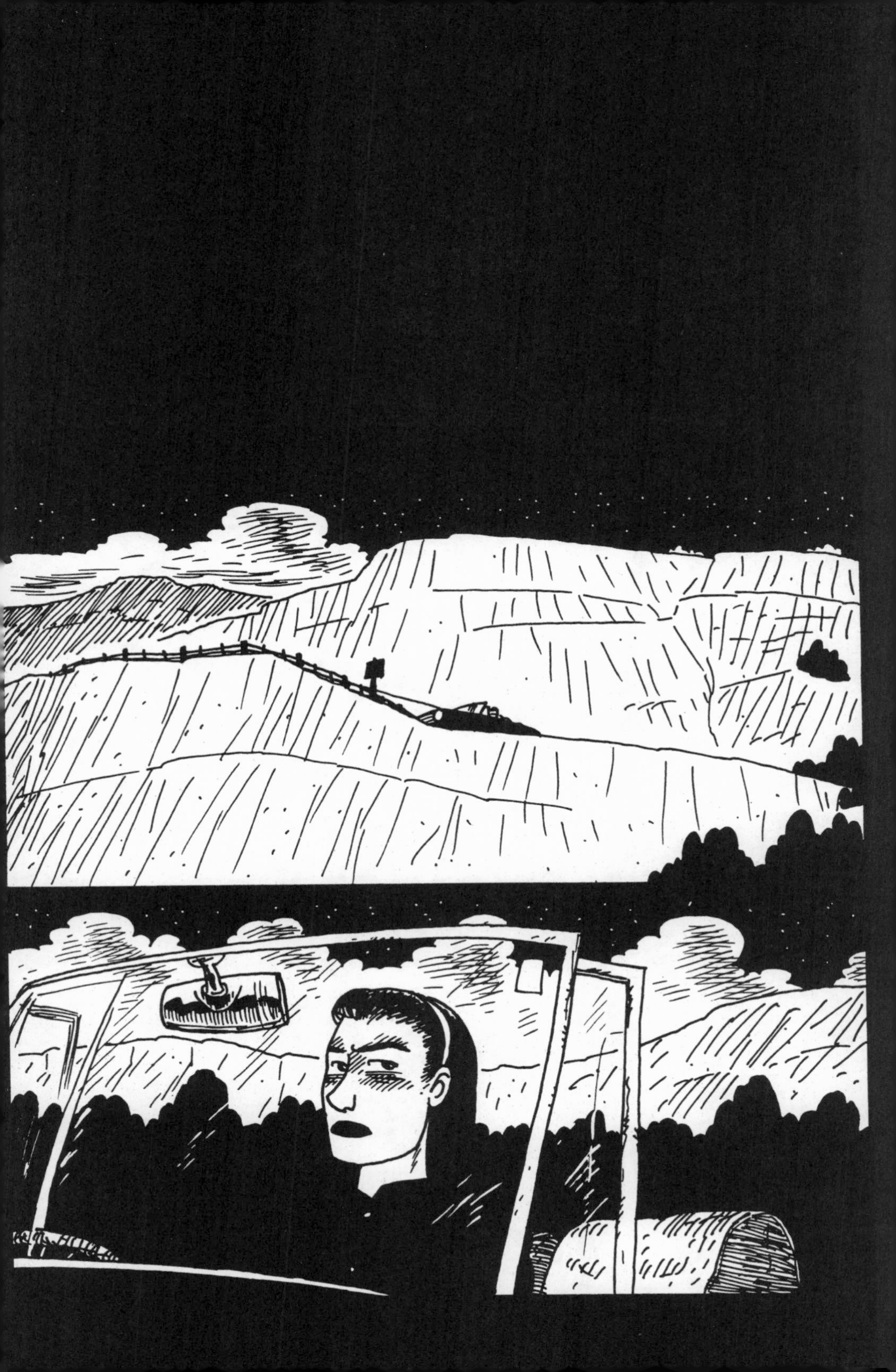

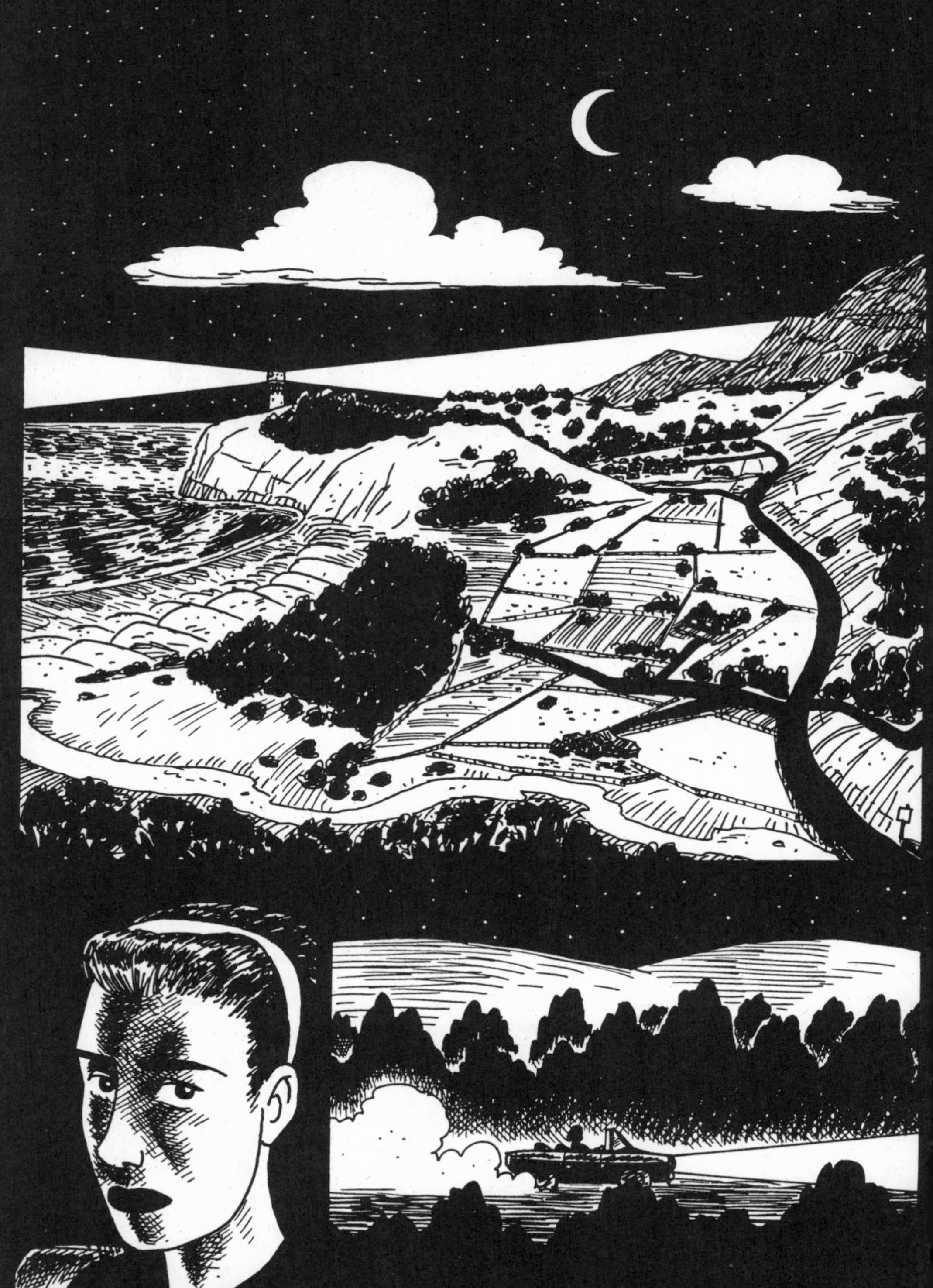

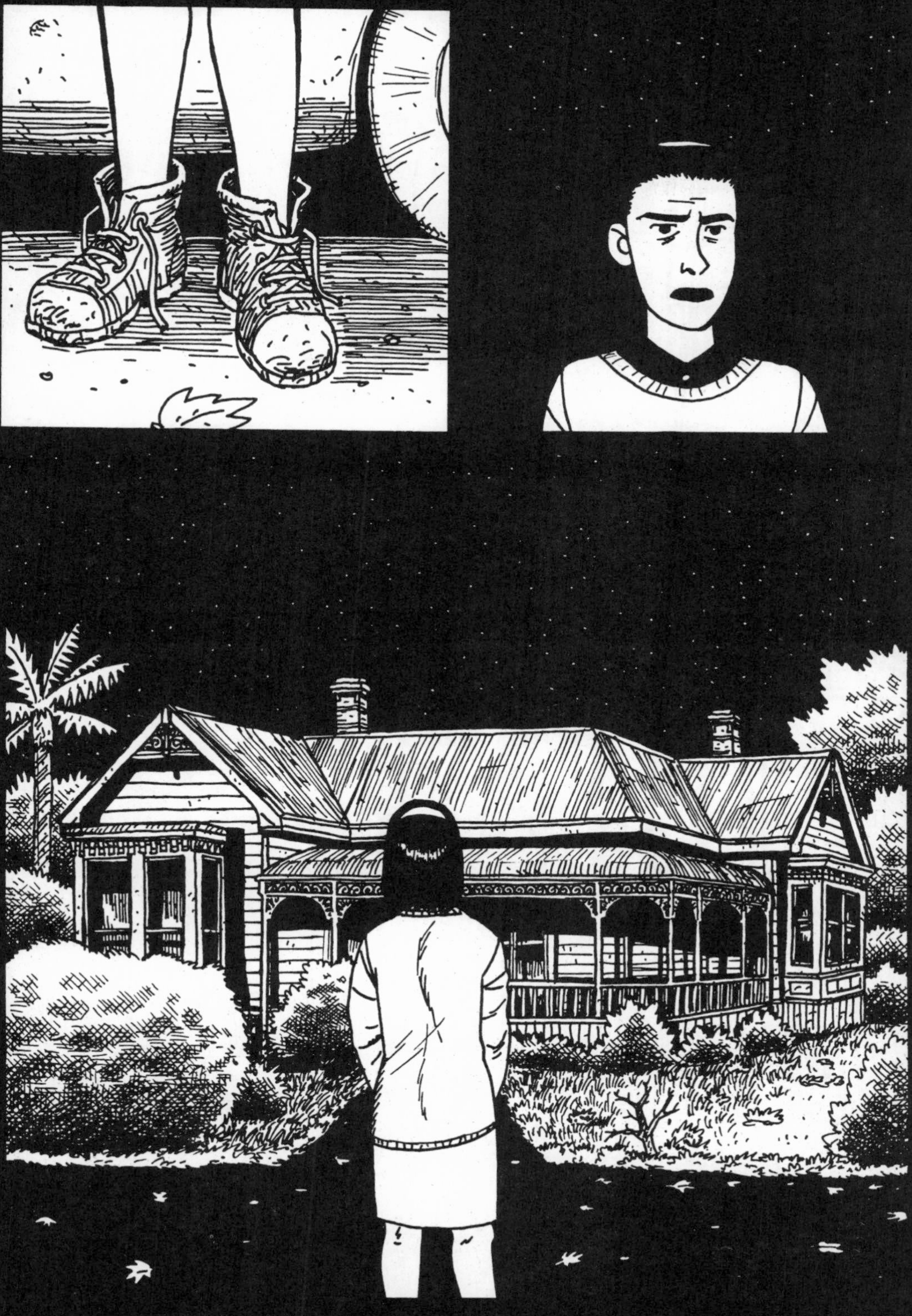

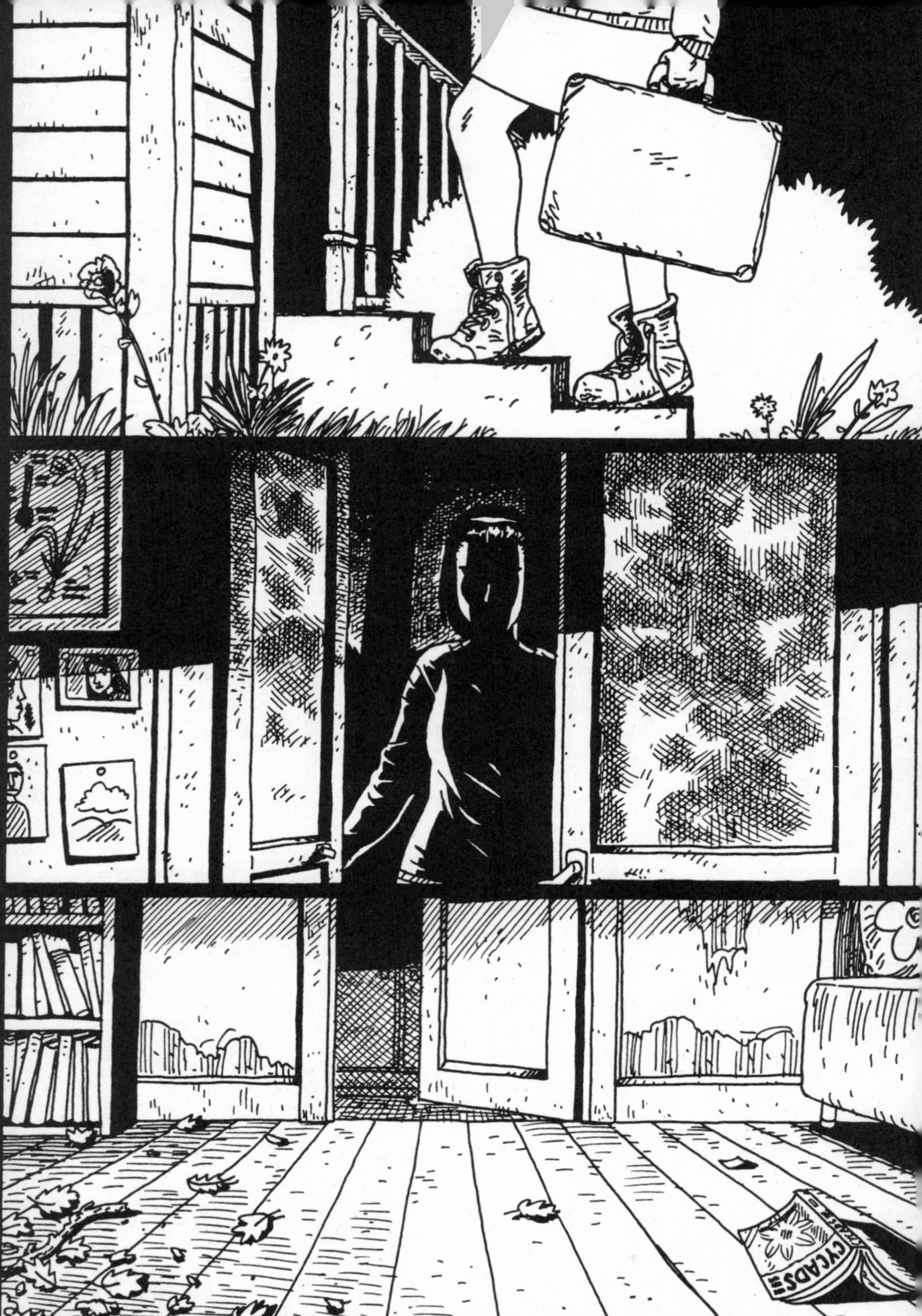
CYCADS

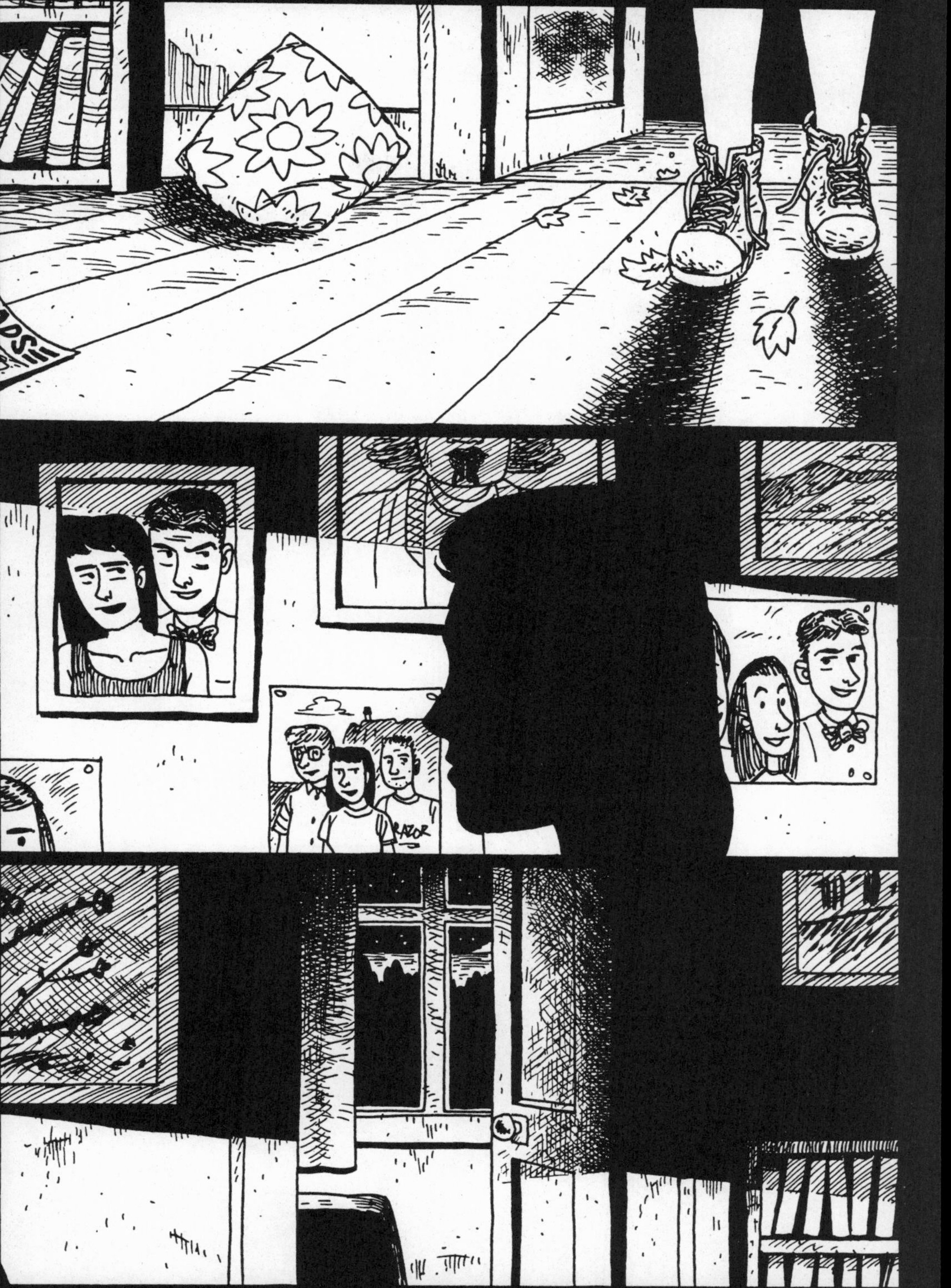
RAZOR

Chapter Two

"When somebody asks me what got me into comics I can only think of one word: malnutrition."

Will Eisner.

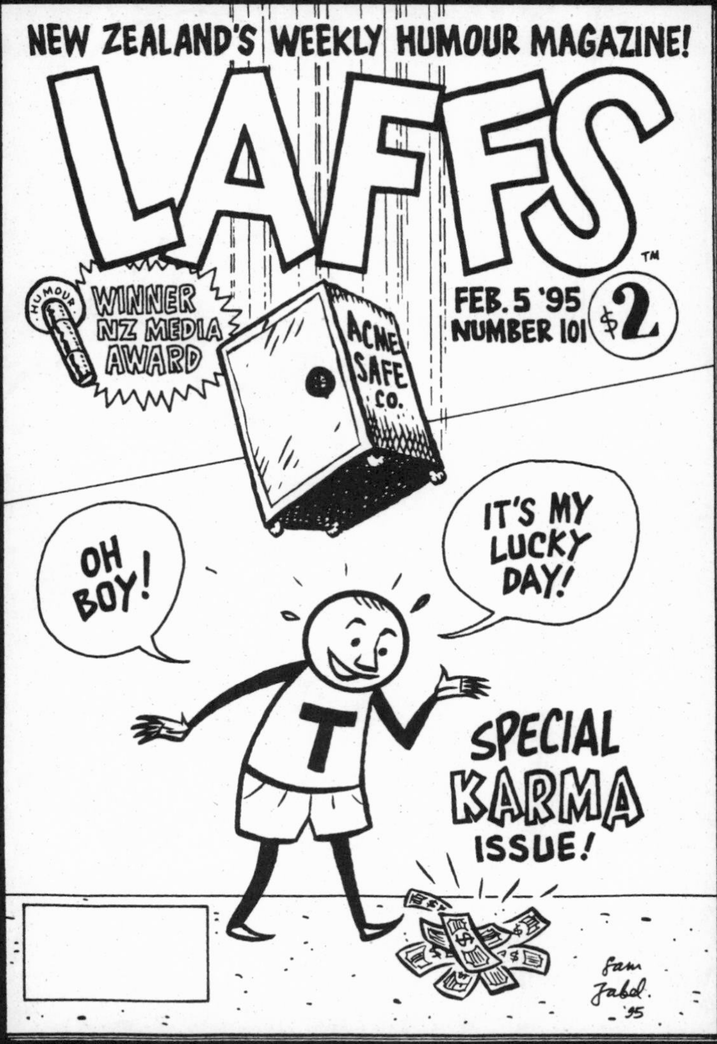
NEW ZEALAND'S WEEKLY HUMOUR MAGAZINE!
LAFFS
TM
HUMOUR
WINNER NZ MEDIA AWARD
ACME SAFE CO.
FEB. 5 '95
NUMBER 101
$2
OH BOY!
IT'S MY LUCKY DAY!
T
SPECIAL KARMA ISSUE!
Sam Zabel '95

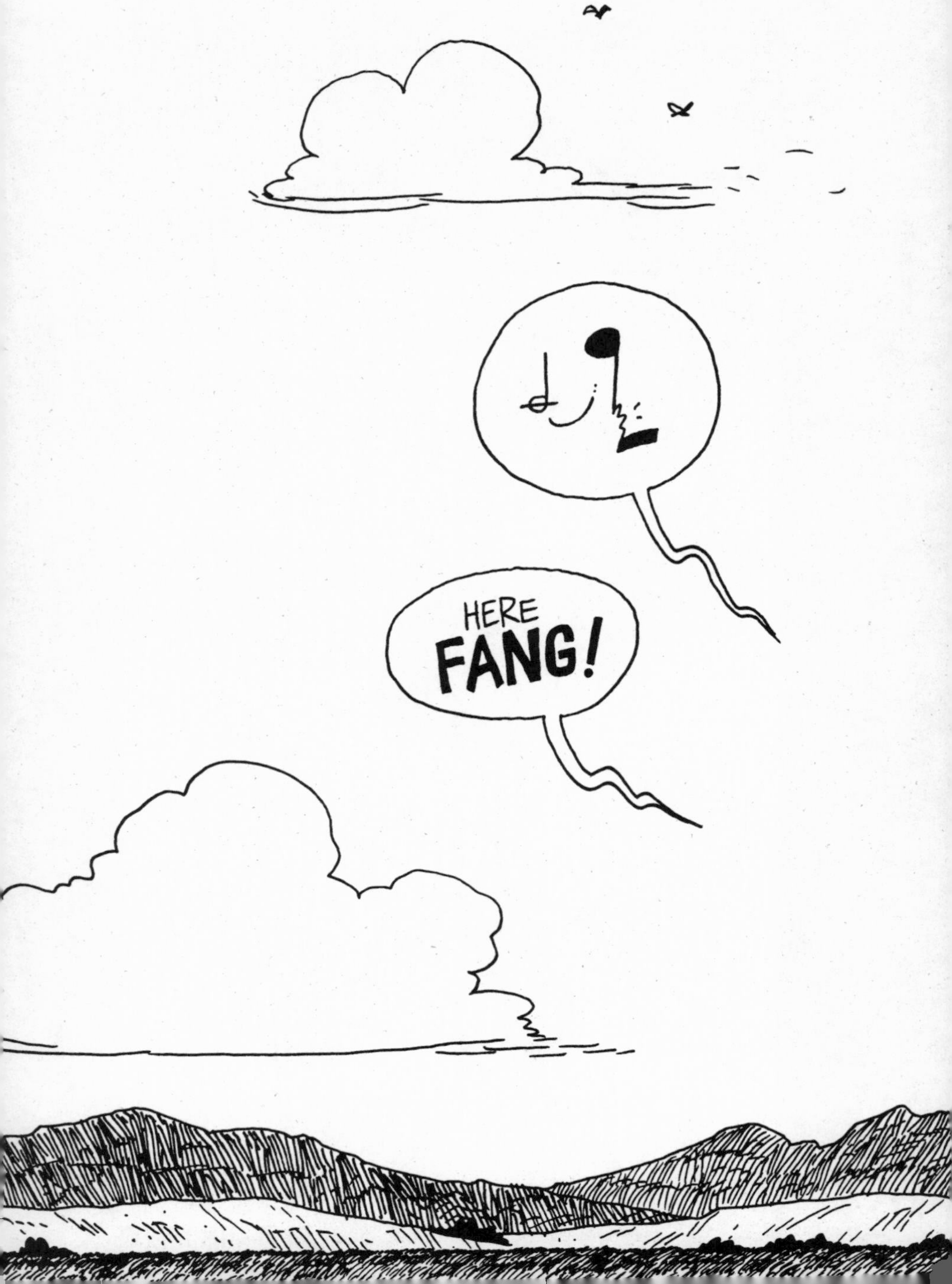
HERE FANG!

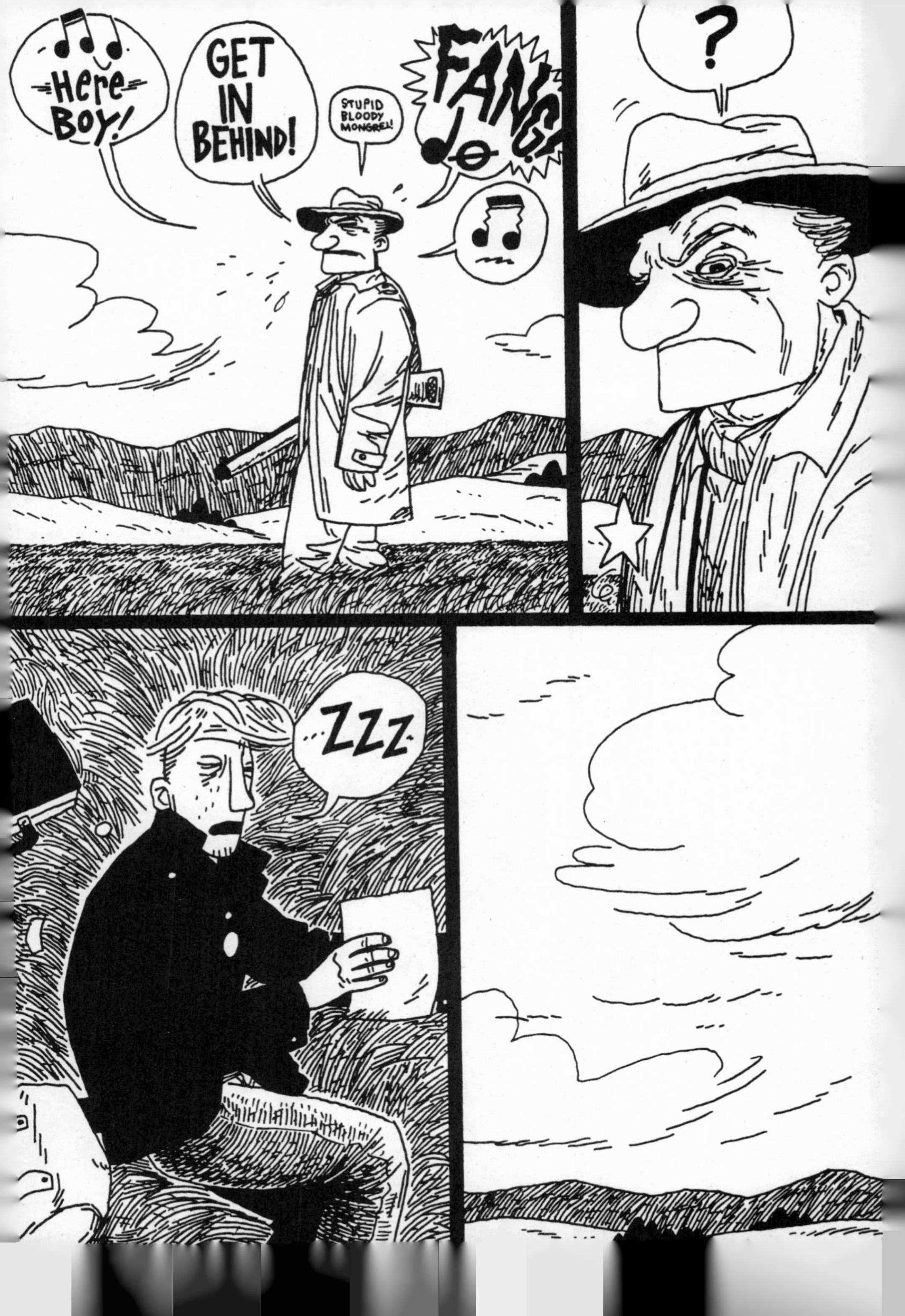
Here Boy!
GET IN BEHIND!
STUPID BLOODY MONGREL!
FANG!
?
ZZZ

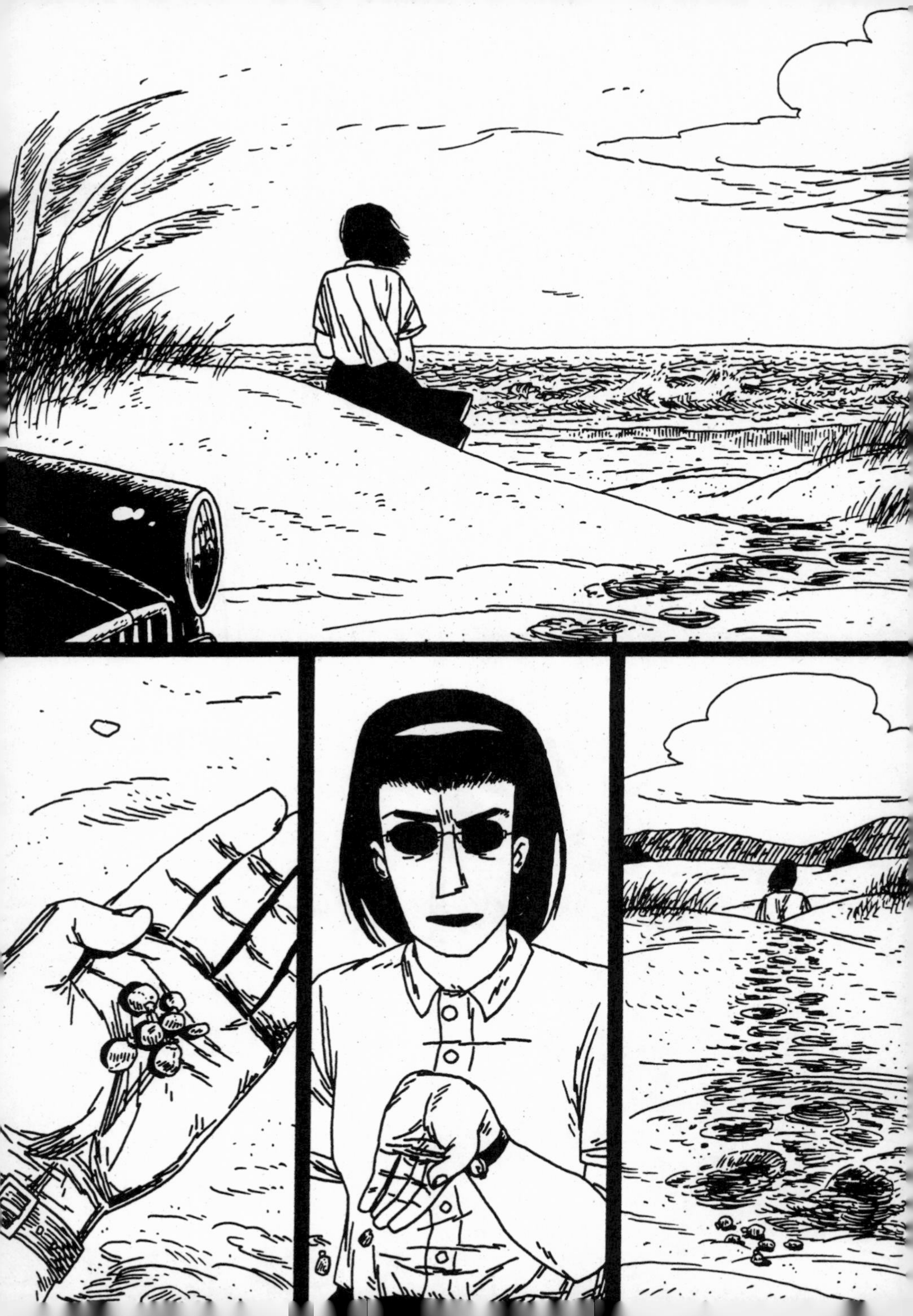

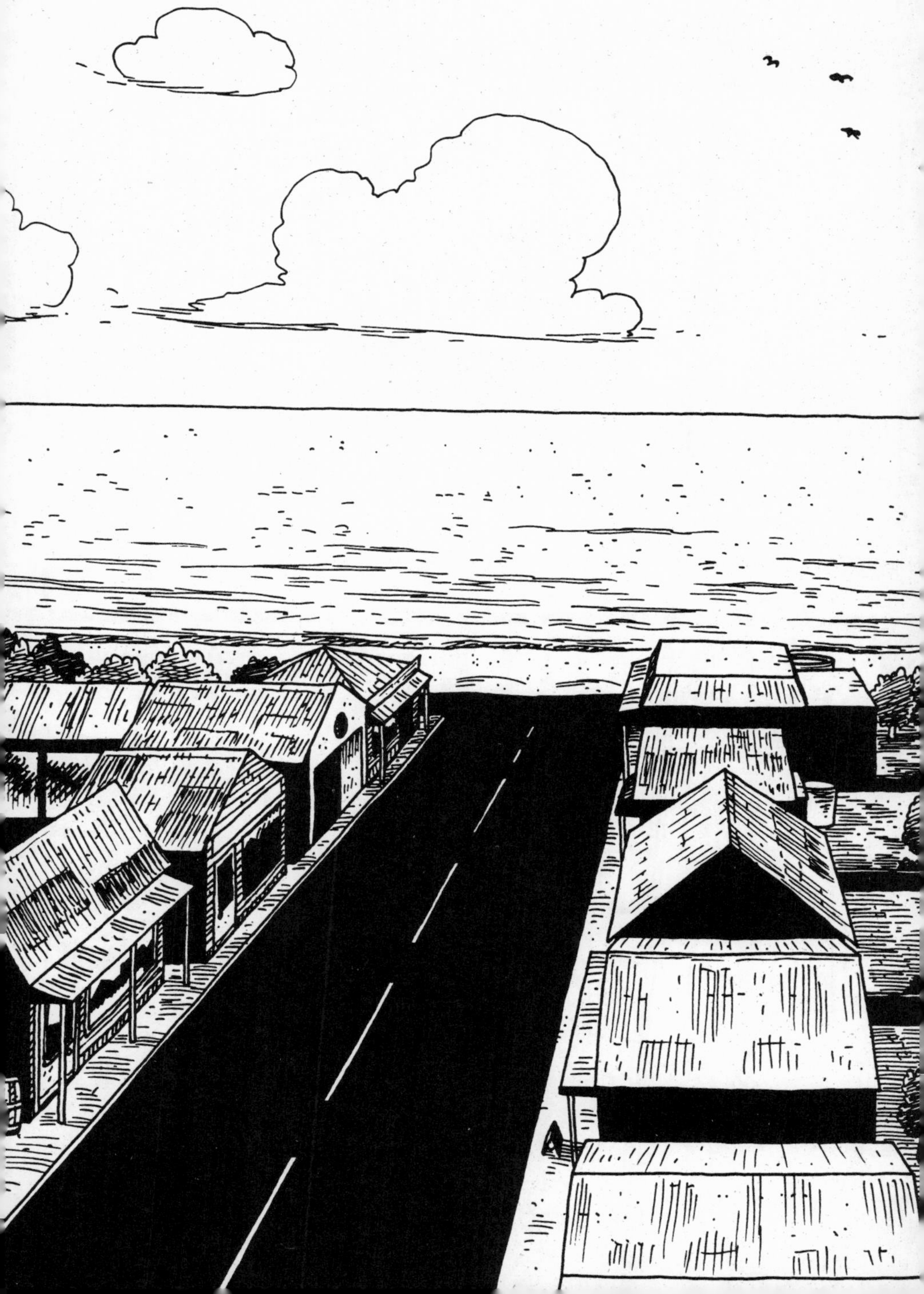

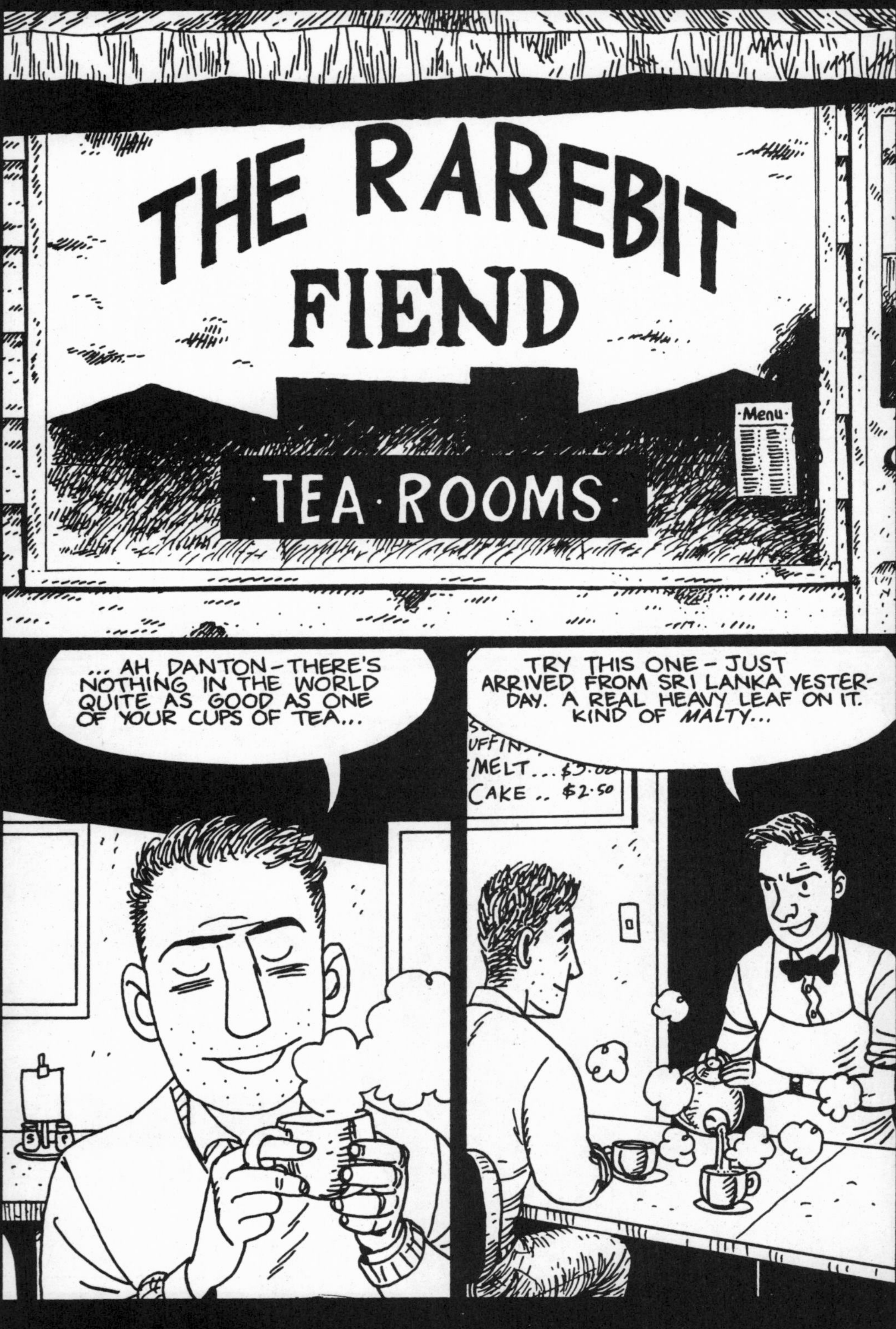
THE RAREBIT FIEND
·TEA·ROOMS·
·Menu·
... AH DANTON – THERE'S NOTHING IN THE WORLD QUITE AS GOOD AS ONE OF YOUR CUPS OF TEA...
TRY THIS ONE – JUST ARRIVED FROM SRI LANKA YESTERDAY. A REAL HEAVY LEAF ON IT. KIND OF *MALTY*...
MELT
CAKE .. $2.50

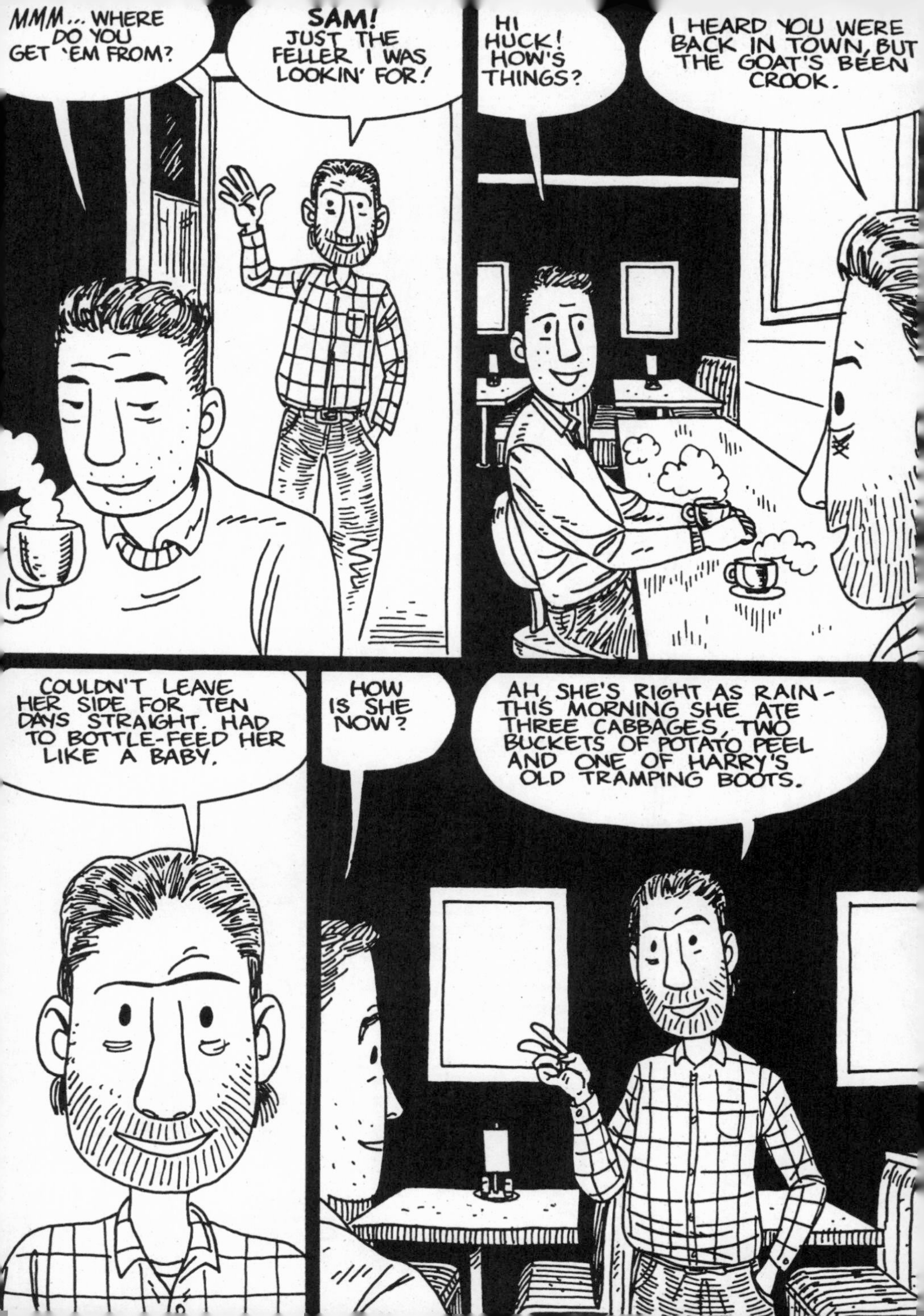
MMM... WHERE DO YOU GET 'EM FROM?
SAM! JUST THE FELLER I WAS LOOKIN' FOR!
HI HUCK! HOW'S THINGS?
I HEARD YOU WERE BACK IN TOWN, BUT THE GOAT'S BEEN CROOK.
COULDN'T LEAVE HER SIDE FOR TEN DAYS STRAIGHT. HAD TO BOTTLE-FEED HER LIKE A BABY.
HOW IS SHE NOW?
AH, SHE'S RIGHT AS RAIN- THIS MORNING SHE ATE THREE CABBAGES, TWO BUCKETS OF POTATO PEEL AND ONE OF HARRY'S OLD TRAMPING BOOTS.

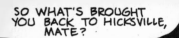

SO WHAT'S BROUGHT YOU BACK TO HICKSVILLE, MATE?

OH, JUST THE USUAL— BROKE AND UNEMPLOYED...

I THOUGHT YOU HAD A REGULAR SPOT IN 'LAFFS' MAGAZINE. WHAT HAPPENED TO THAT?

KITCHEN

DESSERTS·
PAVLOVA.. $2·50
RINGUE.. $2·00
RRIOCHE.. $1·50
IN PIE... $2·00
ESECAKE..$2·50
CONES
OFFIN
MEL'
CAK

HERE — SAM'S LATEST MINICOMIC TELLS ALL.

A NEW PICKLE! GREAT! LET'S HAVE A LOOK, THEN.

HEN

S.
..$2·50
.$2·00
.$1·50
E·$2·00
E..$2·50
...$1·00
S...$1·00

PiCKLE

PiCKLe.

Pickle

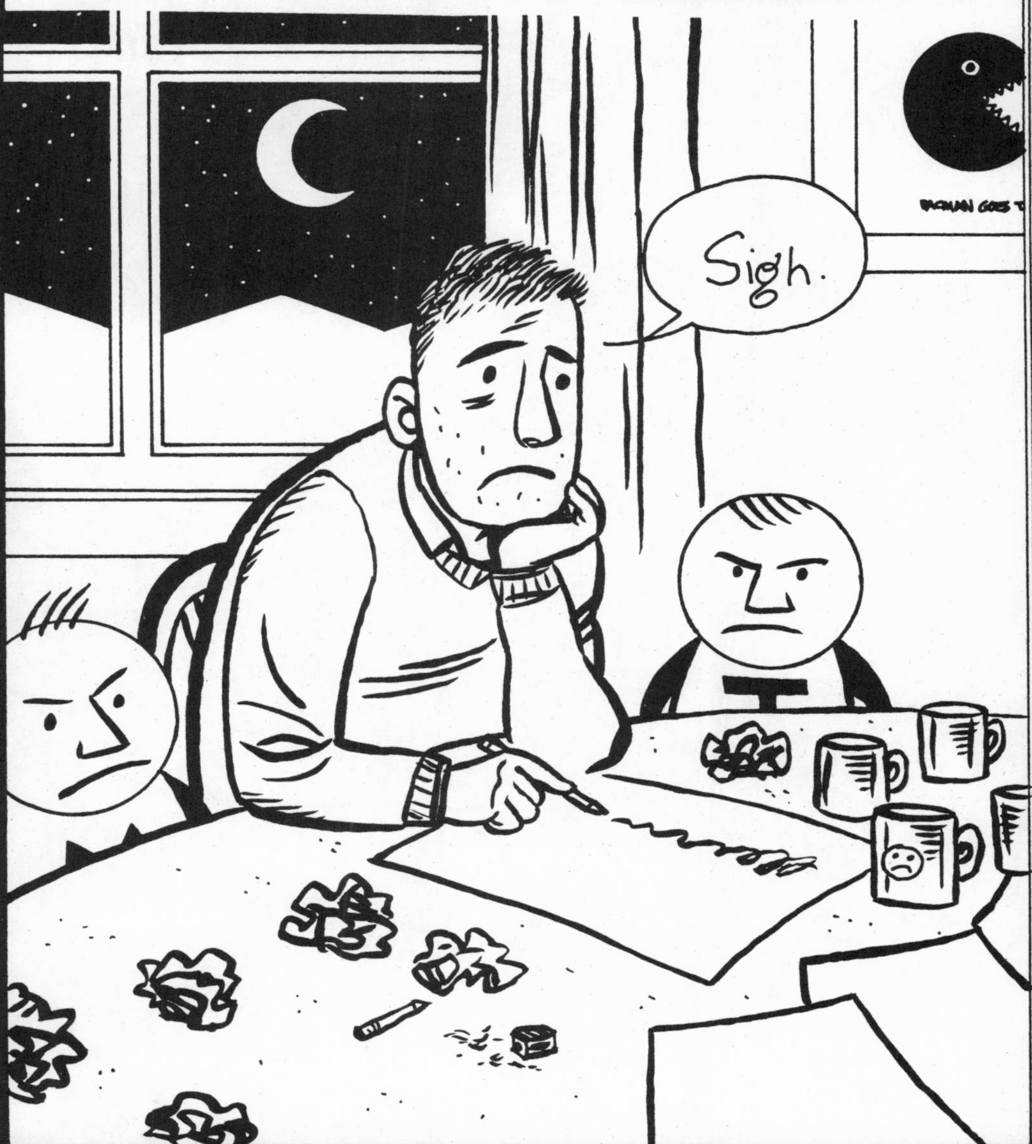
Sigh.

HALFWAY TO HEAVEN...

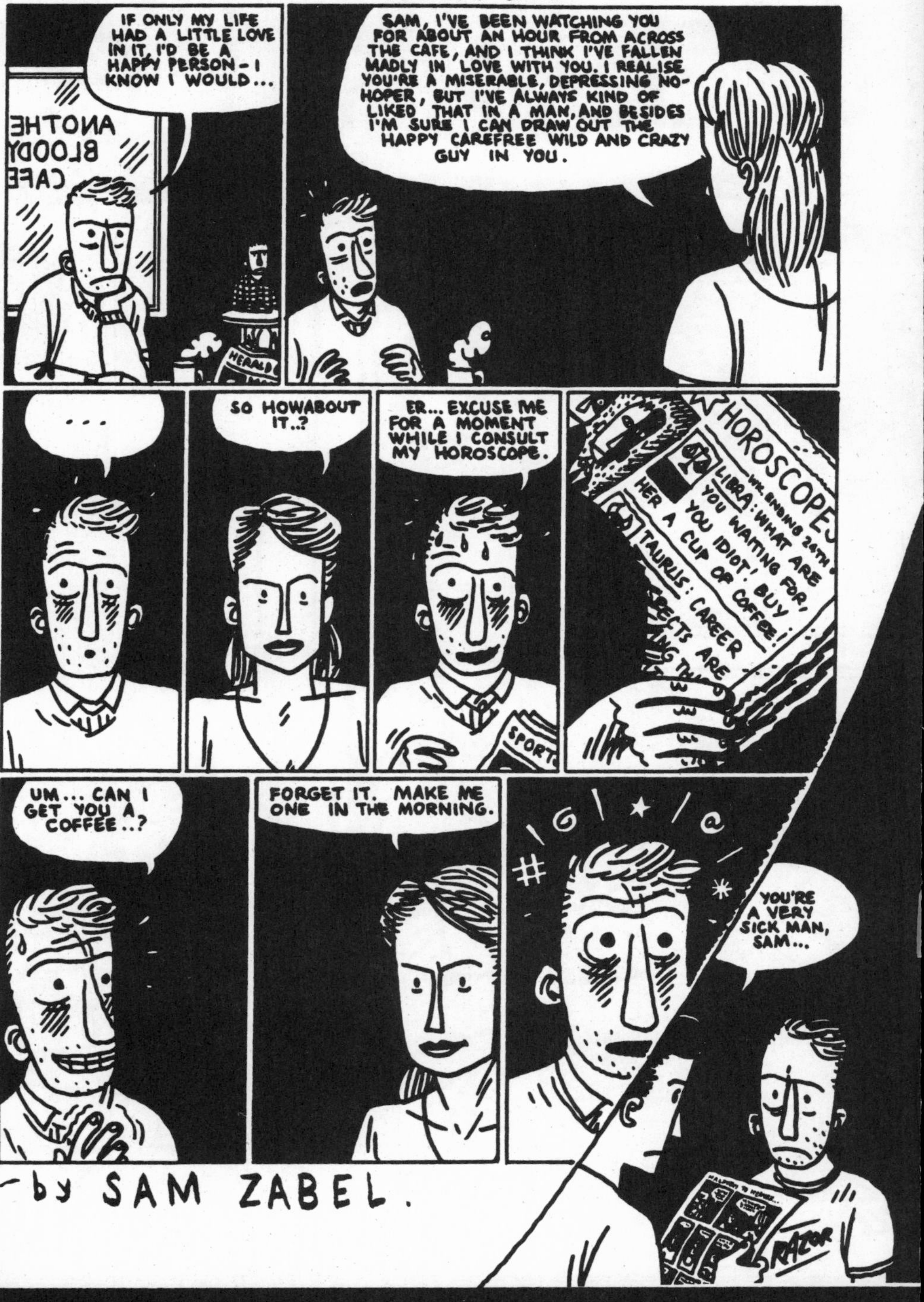
IF ONLY MY LIFE HAD A LITTLE LOVE IN IT, I'D BE A HAPPY PERSON - I KNOW I WOULD...
ANOTHE BLOODY CAFE
SAM, I'VE BEEN WATCHING YOU FOR ABOUT AN HOUR FROM ACROSS THE CAFE, AND I THINK I'VE FALLEN MADLY IN LOVE WITH YOU. I REALISE YOU'RE A MISERABLE, DEPRESSING NO-HOPER, BUT I'VE ALWAYS KIND OF LIKED THAT IN A MAN, AND BESIDES I'M SURE I CAN DRAW OUT THE HAPPY CAREFREE WILD AND CRAZY GUY IN YOU.
...
SO HOWABOUT IT..?
ER... EXCUSE ME FOR A MOMENT WHILE I CONSULT MY HOROSCOPE.
SPORT
HOROSCOPES
W/E ENDING 24TH
LIBRA: WHAT ARE YOU WAITING FOR, YOU IDIOT! BUY HER A CUP OF COFFEE!
TAURUS: CAREER
UM... CAN I GET YOU A COFFEE..?
FORGET IT. MAKE ME ONE IN THE MORNING.
YOU'RE A VERY SICK MAN, SAM...
RAZOR

-by SAM ZABEL.

HALFWAY TO HELL...

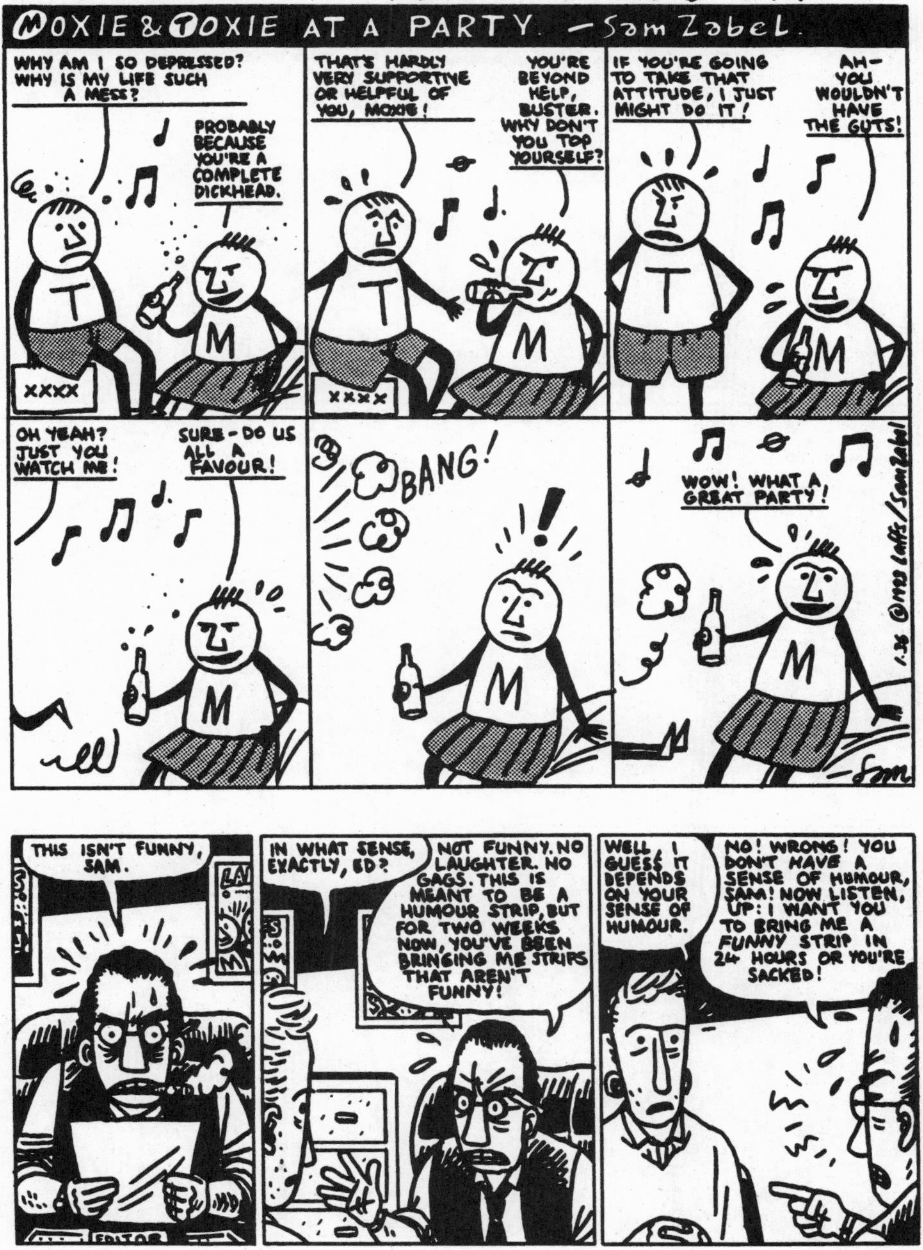
MOXIE & TOXIE AT A PARTY. —Sam Zabel.
WHY AM I SO DEPRESSED? WHY IS MY LIFE SUCH A MESS?
PROBABLY BECAUSE YOU'RE A COMPLETE DICKHEAD.
XXXX
THAT'S HARDLY VERY SUPPORTIVE OR HELPFUL OF YOU, MOXIE!
YOU'RE BEYOND HELP, BUSTER. WHY DON'T YOU TOP YOURSELF?
XXXX
IF YOU'RE GOING TO TAKE THAT ATTITUDE, I JUST MIGHT DO IT!
AH— YOU WOULDN'T HAVE THE GUTS!
OH YEAH? JUST YOU WATCH ME!
SURE—DO US ALL A FAVOUR!
BANG!
WOW! WHAT A GREAT PARTY!
Sam
THIS ISN'T FUNNY, SAM.
EDITOR
IN WHAT SENSE, EXACTLY, ED?
NOT FUNNY. NO LAUGHTER. NO GAGS. THIS IS MEANT TO BE A HUMOUR STRIP, BUT FOR TWO WEEKS NOW, YOU'VE BEEN BRINGING ME STRIPS THAT AREN'T FUNNY!
WELL, I GUESS IT DEPENDS ON YOUR SENSE OF HUMOUR.
NO! WRONG! YOU DON'T HAVE A SENSE OF HUMOUR, SAM! NOW LISTEN, UP: I WANT YOU TO BRING ME A FUNNY STRIP IN 24 HOURS OR YOU'RE SACKED!

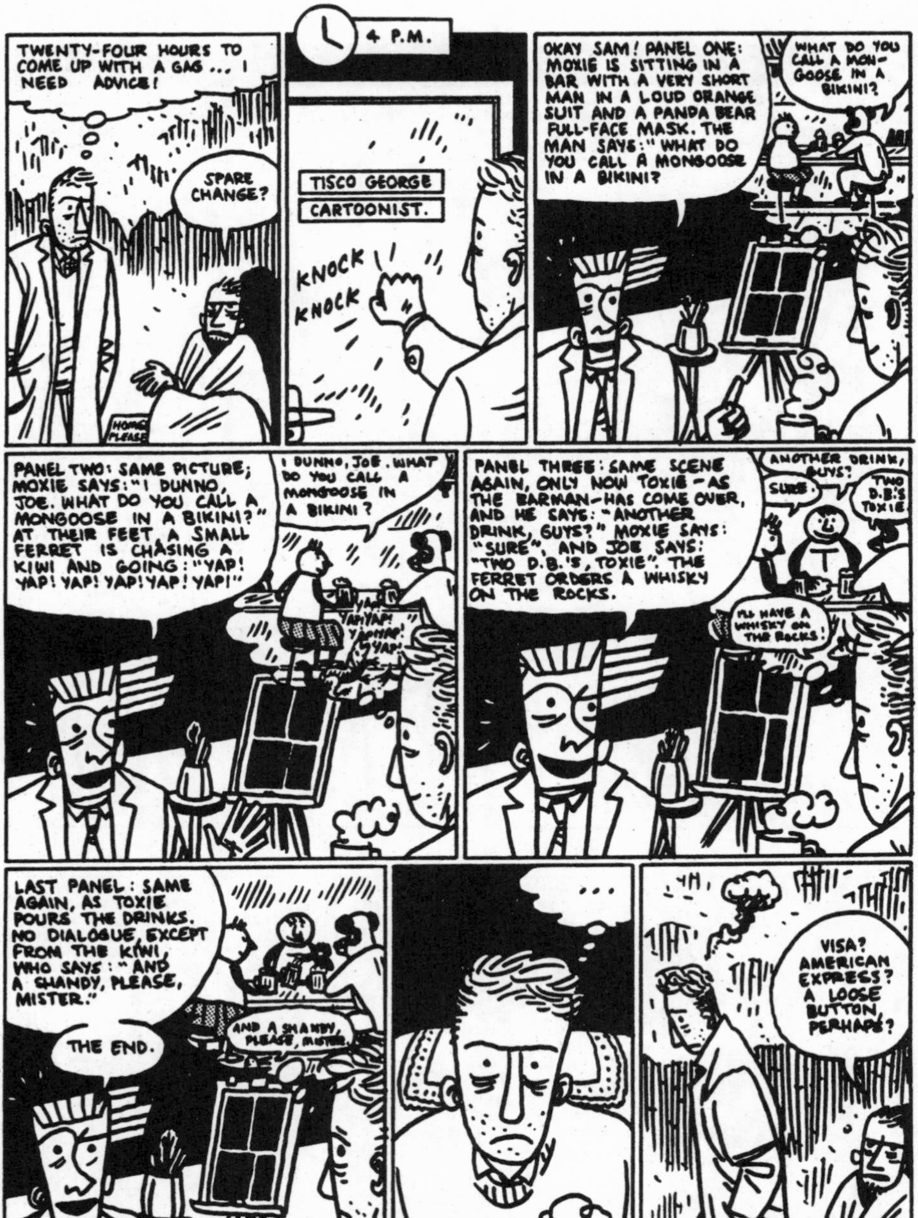
TWENTY-FOUR HOURS TO COME UP WITH A GAG ... I NEED ADVICE!
SPARE CHANGE?
4 P.M.
TISCO GEORGE
CARTOONIST.
KNOCK
KNOCK
OKAY SAM! PANEL ONE: MOXIE IS SITTING IN A BAR WITH A VERY SHORT MAN IN A LOUD ORANGE SUIT AND A PANDA BEAR FULL-FACE MASK. THE MAN SAYS: "WHAT DO YOU CALL A MONGOOSE IN A BIKINI?
WHAT DO YOU CALL A MONGOOSE IN A BIKINI?
PANEL TWO: SAME PICTURE; MOXIE SAYS: "I DUNNO, JOE. WHAT DO YOU CALL A MONGOOSE IN A BIKINI?" AT THEIR FEET, A SMALL FERRET IS CHASING A KIWI AND GOING: "YAP! YAP! YAP! YAP! YAP! YAP!"
I DUNNO, JOE. WHAT DO YOU CALL A MONGOOSE IN A BIKINI?
PANEL THREE: SAME SCENE AGAIN, ONLY NOW TOXIE—AS THE BARMAN—HAS COME OVER, AND HE SAYS: "ANOTHER DRINK, GUYS?" MOXIE SAYS: "SURE", AND JOE SAYS: "TWO D.B.'S, TOXIE". THE FERRET ORDERS A WHISKY ON THE ROCKS.
ANOTHER DRINK, GUYS?
SURE.
TWO D.B.'S TOXIE.
I'LL HAVE A WHISKY ON THE ROCKS!
LAST PANEL: SAME AGAIN, AS TOXIE POURS THE DRINKS. NO DIALOGUE, EXCEPT FROM THE KIWI, WHO SAYS: "AND A SHANDY, PLEASE, MISTER."
AND A SHANDY, PLEASE, MISTER.
THE END.
...
VISA? AMERICAN EXPRESS? A LOOSE BUTTON, PERHAPS?

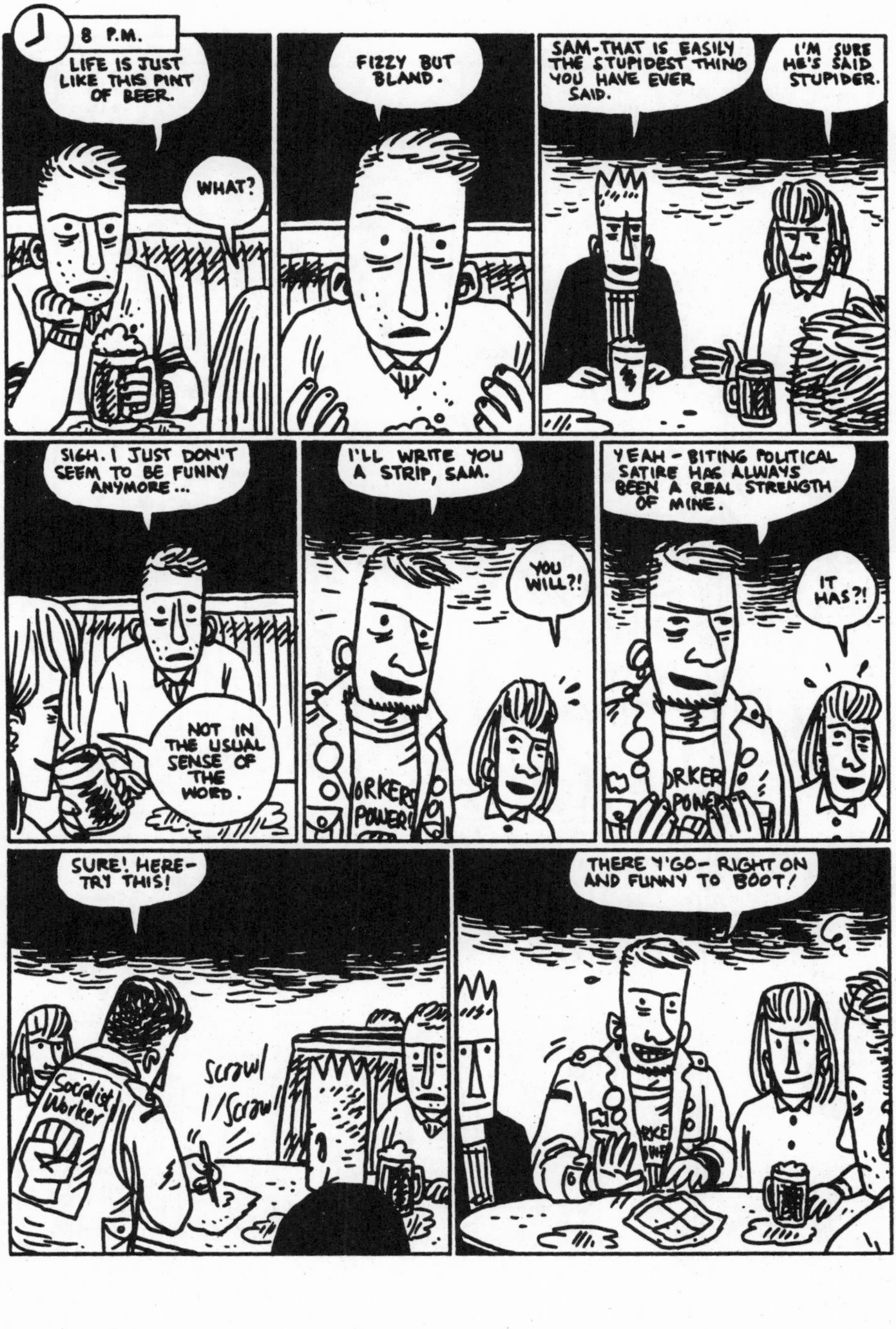
8 P.M.
LIFE IS JUST LIKE THIS PINT OF BEER.
WHAT?
FIZZY BUT BLAND.
SAM-THAT IS EASILY THE STUPIDEST THING YOU HAVE EVER SAID.
I'M SURE HE'S SAID STUPIDER.
SIGH. I JUST DON'T SEEM TO BE FUNNY ANYMORE...
NOT IN THE USUAL SENSE OF THE WORD.
I'LL WRITE YOU A STRIP, SAM.
YOU WILL?!
YEAH - BITING POLITICAL SATIRE HAS ALWAYS BEEN A REAL STRENGTH OF MINE.
IT HAS?!
SURE! HERE- TRY THIS!
Socialist Worker
Scrawl
Scrawl
THERE Y'GO- RIGHT ON AND FUNNY TO BOOT!

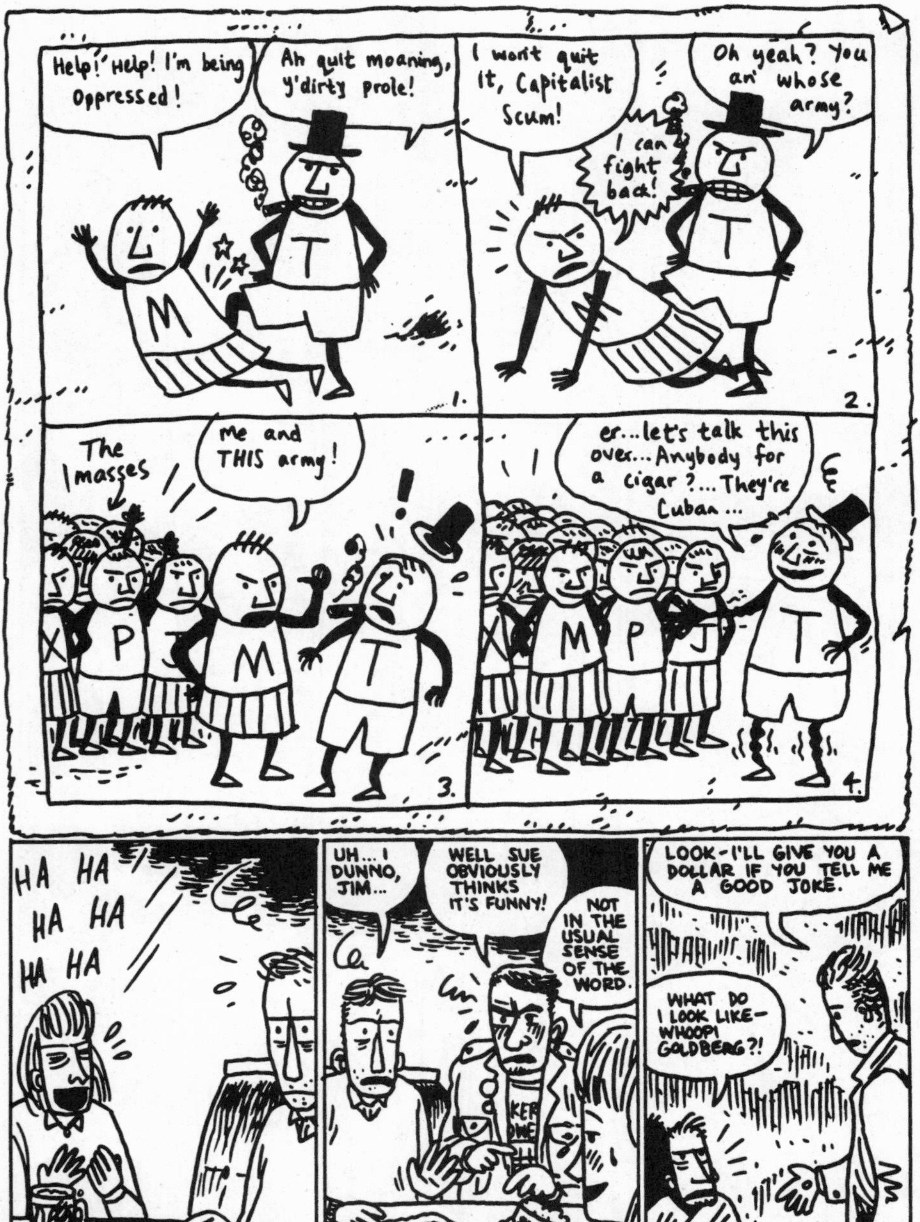
Help! Help! I'm being Oppressed!
Ah quit moaning, y'dirty prole!
1.
I won't quit it, Capitalist Scum!
I can fight back!
Oh yeah? You an' whose army?
2.
The masses
me and THIS army!
!
3.
er...let's talk this over...Anybody for a cigar?...They're Cuban...
4.
HA HA HA HA HA HA
UH... I DUNNO, JIM...
WELL SUE OBVIOUSLY THINKS IT'S FUNNY!
NOT IN THE USUAL SENSE OF THE WORD.
LOOK-I'LL GIVE YOU A DOLLAR IF YOU TELL ME A GOOD JOKE.
WHAT DO I LOOK LIKE-WHOOPI GOLDBERG?!

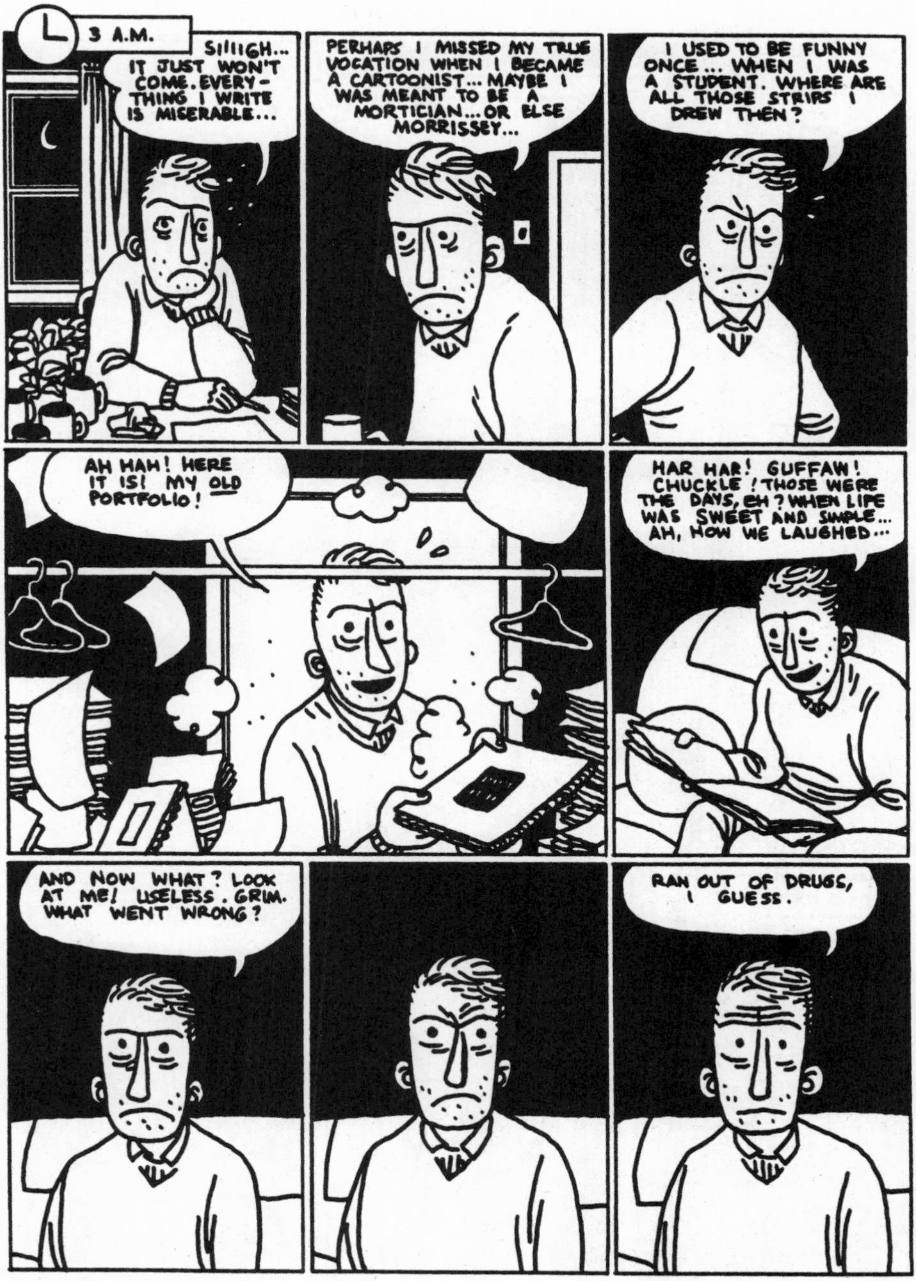
3 A.M.
SIIIIGH... IT JUST WON'T COME. EVERYTHING I WRITE IS MISERABLE...
PERHAPS I MISSED MY TRUE VOCATION WHEN I BECAME A CARTOONIST... MAYBE I WAS MEANT TO BE A MORTICIAN... OR ELSE MORRISSEY...
I USED TO BE FUNNY ONCE... WHEN I WAS A STUDENT. WHERE ARE ALL THOSE STRIPS I DREW THEN?
AH HAH! HERE IT IS! MY OLD PORTFOLIO!
HAR HAR! GUFFAW! CHUCKLE! THOSE WERE THE DAYS, EH? WHEN LIFE WAS SWEET AND SIMPLE... AH, HOW WE LAUGHED...
AND NOW WHAT? LOOK AT ME! USELESS. GRIM. WHAT WENT WRONG?
RAN OUT OF DRUGS, I GUESS.

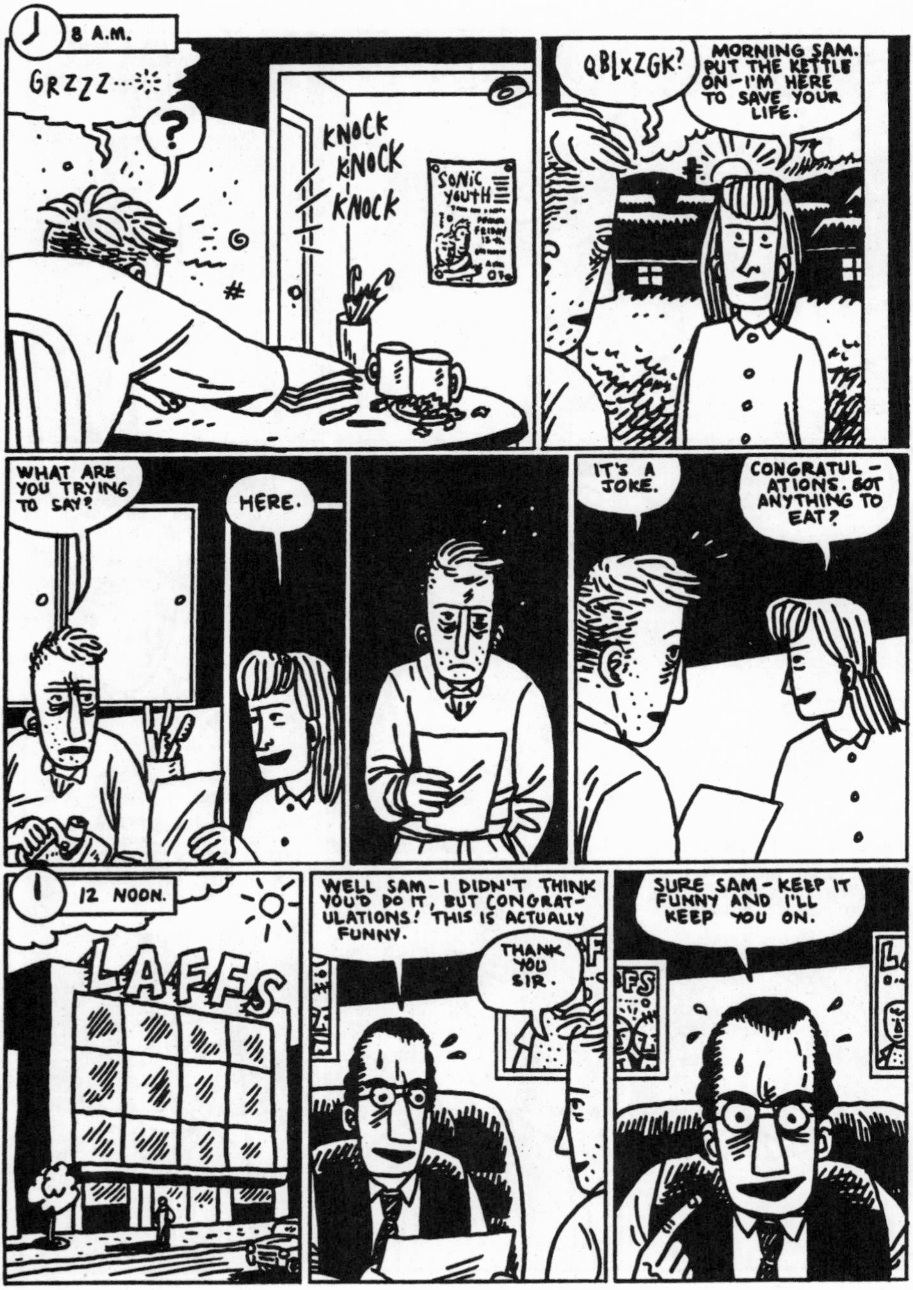
8 A.M.
GRZZZ...
?
KNOCK
KNOCK
KNOCK
QBLXZGK?
MORNING SAM. PUT THE KETTLE ON—I'M HERE TO SAVE YOUR LIFE.
WHAT ARE YOU TRYING TO SAY?
HERE.
IT'S A JOKE.
CONGRATUL-ATIONS. GOT ANYTHING TO EAT?
12 NOON.
LAFFS
WELL SAM—I DIDN'T THINK YOU'D DO IT, BUT CONGRAT-ULATIONS! THIS IS ACTUALLY FUNNY.
THANK YOU SIR.
SURE SAM—KEEP IT FUNNY AND I'LL KEEP YOU ON.

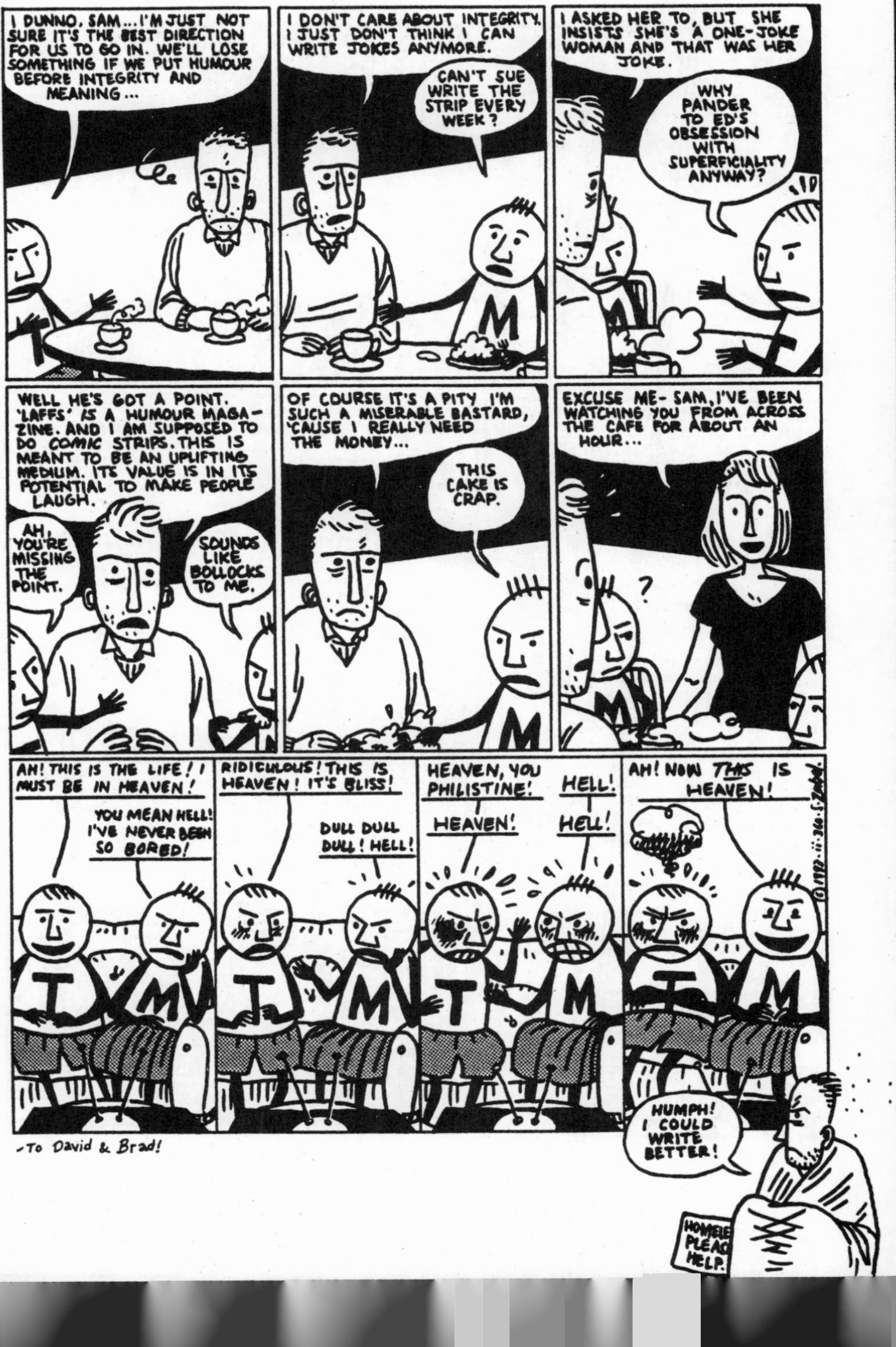

I DUNNO, SAM... I'M JUST NOT SURE IT'S THE BEST DIRECTION FOR US TO GO IN. WE'LL LOSE SOMETHING IF WE PUT HUMOUR BEFORE INTEGRITY AND MEANING...
I DON'T CARE ABOUT INTEGRITY, I JUST DON'T THINK I CAN WRITE JOKES ANYMORE.
CAN'T SUE WRITE THE STRIP EVERY WEEK?
I ASKED HER TO, BUT SHE INSISTS SHE'S A ONE-JOKE WOMAN AND THAT WAS HER JOKE.
WHY PANDER TO ED'S OBSESSION WITH SUPERFICIALITY ANYWAY?
WELL HE'S GOT A POINT. 'LAFFS' IS A HUMOUR MAGAZINE. AND I AM SUPPOSED TO DO COMIC STRIPS. THIS IS MEANT TO BE AN UPLIFTING MEDIUM. ITS VALUE IS IN ITS POTENTIAL TO MAKE PEOPLE LAUGH.
AH, YOU'RE MISSING THE POINT.
SOUNDS LIKE BOLLOCKS TO ME.
OF COURSE IT'S A PITY I'M SUCH A MISERABLE BASTARD, 'CAUSE I REALLY NEED THE MONEY...
THIS CAKE IS CRAP.
EXCUSE ME- SAM, I'VE BEEN WATCHING YOU FROM ACROSS THE CAFE FOR ABOUT AN HOUR...
?
AH! THIS IS THE LIFE! I MUST BE IN HEAVEN!
YOU MEAN HELL! I'VE NEVER BEEN SO BORED!
RIDICULOUS! THIS IS HEAVEN! IT'S BLISS!
DULL DULL DULL! HELL!
HEAVEN, YOU PHILISTINE!
HELL!
HEAVEN!
HELL!
AH! NOW THIS IS HEAVEN!
HUMPH! I COULD WRITE BETTER!
HOMELE... PLEA... HELP.
-To David & Brad!

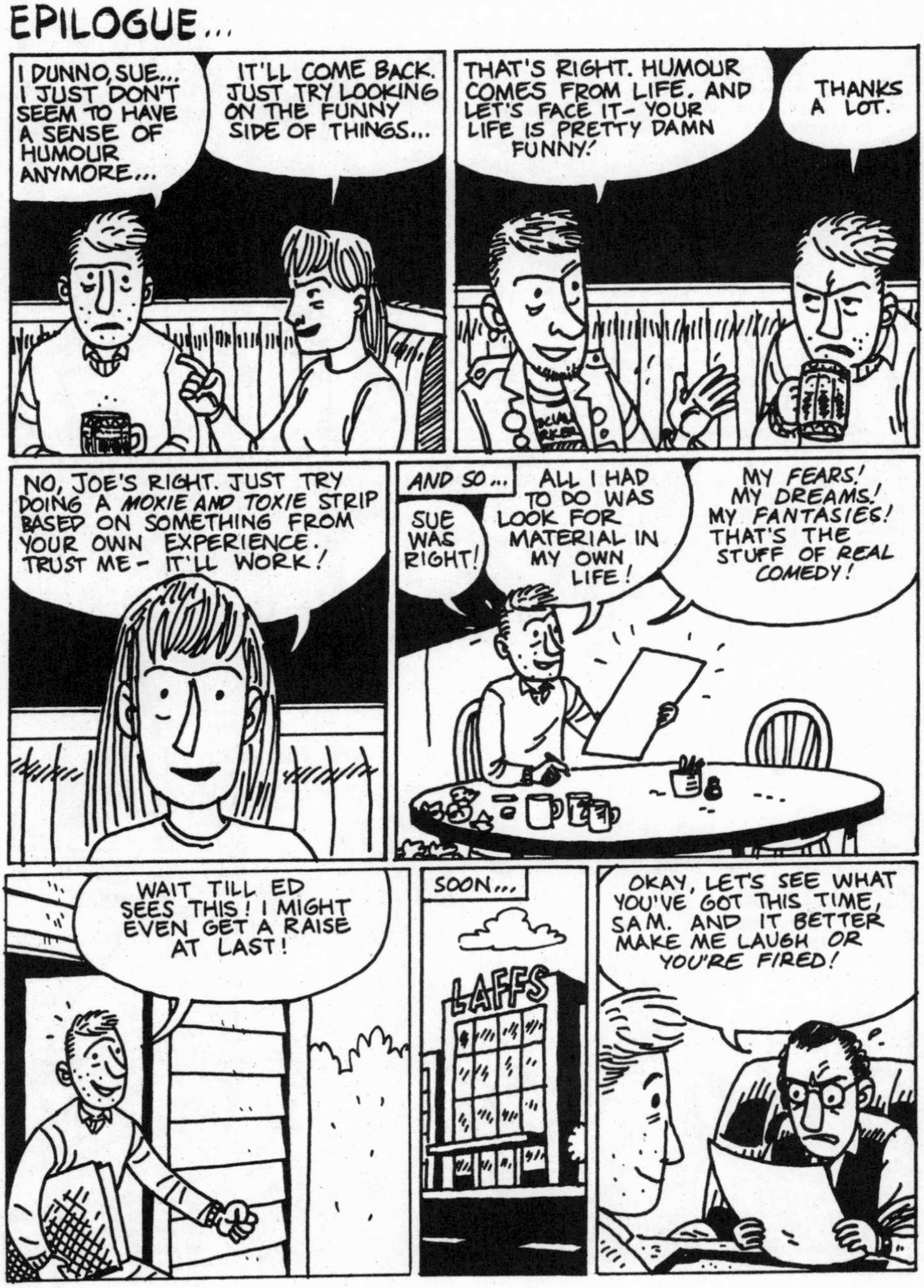
EPILOGUE...
I DUNNO, SUE... I JUST DON'T SEEM TO HAVE A SENSE OF HUMOUR ANYMORE...
IT'LL COME BACK. JUST TRY LOOKING ON THE FUNNY SIDE OF THINGS...
THAT'S RIGHT. HUMOUR COMES FROM LIFE. AND LET'S FACE IT- YOUR LIFE IS PRETTY DAMN FUNNY!
THANKS A LOT.
NO, JOE'S RIGHT. JUST TRY DOING A MOXIE AND TOXIE STRIP BASED ON SOMETHING FROM YOUR OWN EXPERIENCE. TRUST ME- IT'LL WORK!
AND SO...
SUE WAS RIGHT!
ALL I HAD TO DO WAS LOOK FOR MATERIAL IN MY OWN LIFE!
MY FEARS! MY DREAMS! MY FANTASIES! THAT'S THE STUFF OF REAL COMEDY!
WAIT TILL ED SEES THIS! I MIGHT EVEN GET A RAISE AT LAST!
SOON...
LAFFS
OKAY, LET'S SEE WHAT YOU'VE GOT THIS TIME, SAM. AND IT BETTER MAKE ME LAUGH OR YOU'RE FIRED!

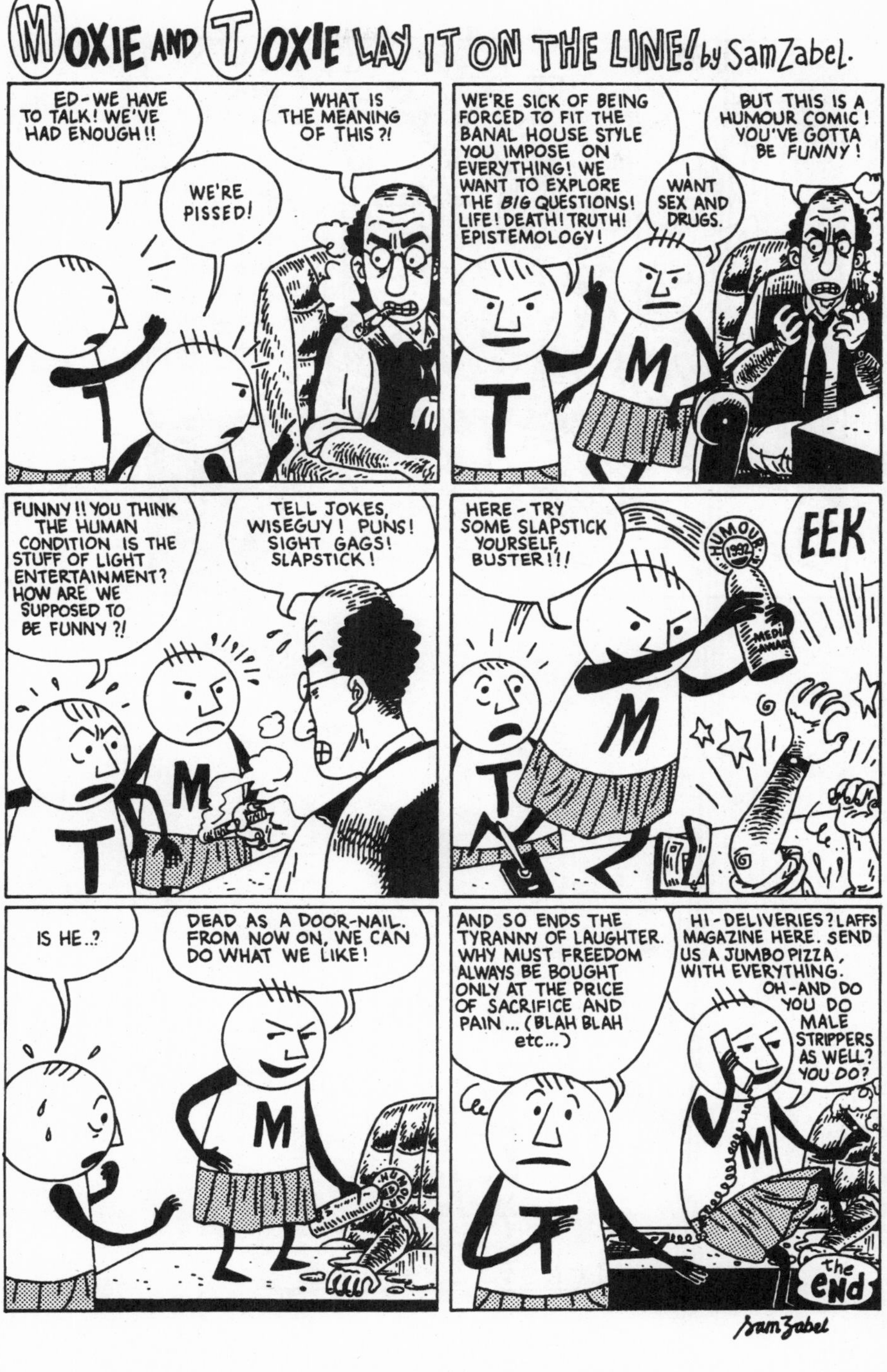
MOXIE AND TOXIE LAY IT ON THE LINE! by Sam Zabel.
ED-WE HAVE TO TALK! WE'VE HAD ENOUGH!!
WE'RE PISSED!
WHAT IS THE MEANING OF THIS ?!
WE'RE SICK OF BEING FORCED TO FIT THE BANAL HOUSE STYLE YOU IMPOSE ON EVERYTHING! WE WANT TO EXPLORE THE BIG QUESTIONS! LIFE! DEATH! TRUTH! EPISTEMOLOGY!
I WANT SEX AND DRUGS.
BUT THIS IS A HUMOUR COMIC! YOU'VE GOTTA BE FUNNY!
FUNNY!! YOU THINK THE HUMAN CONDITION IS THE STUFF OF LIGHT ENTERTAINMENT? HOW ARE WE SUPPOSED TO BE FUNNY ?!
TELL JOKES, WISEGUY! PUNS! SIGHT GAGS! SLAPSTICK!
HERE-TRY SOME SLAPSTICK YOURSELF, BUSTER!!!
HUMOUR 1992
MEDIA AWARD
EEK
IS HE..?
DEAD AS A DOOR-NAIL. FROM NOW ON, WE CAN DO WHAT WE LIKE!
AND SO ENDS THE TYRANNY OF LAUGHTER. WHY MUST FREEDOM ALWAYS BE BOUGHT ONLY AT THE PRICE OF SACRIFICE AND PAIN... (BLAH BLAH etc...)
HI-DELIVERIES? LAFFS MAGAZINE HERE. SEND US A JUMBO PIZZA, WITH EVERYTHING.
OH-AND DO YOU DO MALE STRIPPERS AS WELL? YOU DO?
the end
Sam Zabel

DELIVERY ENTRANCE
OH WELL- AT LEAST I'VE GOT MY SENSE OF *HUMOUR* BACK!

The End

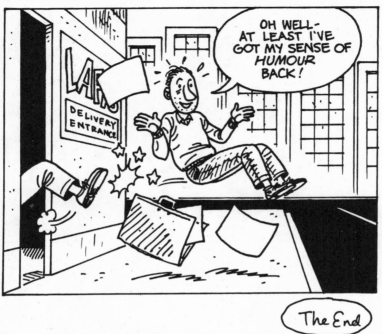

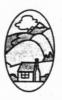

Hicksville Press

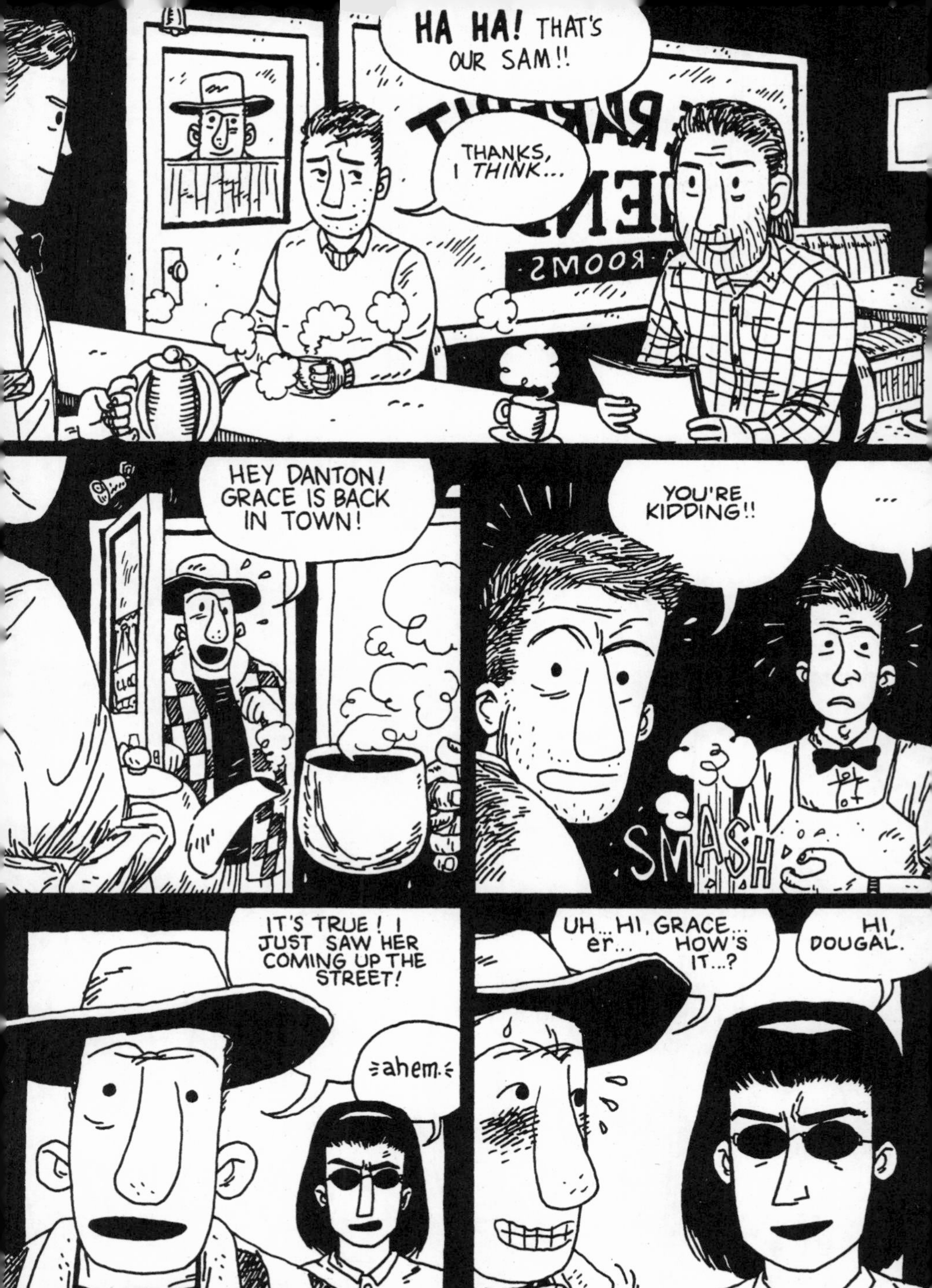
HA HA! THAT'S OUR SAM!!
THANKS, I THINK...
HEY DANTON! GRACE IS BACK IN TOWN!
YOU'RE KIDDING!!
...
SMASH
IT'S TRUE! I JUST SAW HER COMING UP THE STREET!
ahem
UH... HI, GRACE... er... HOW'S IT...?
HI, DOUGAL.

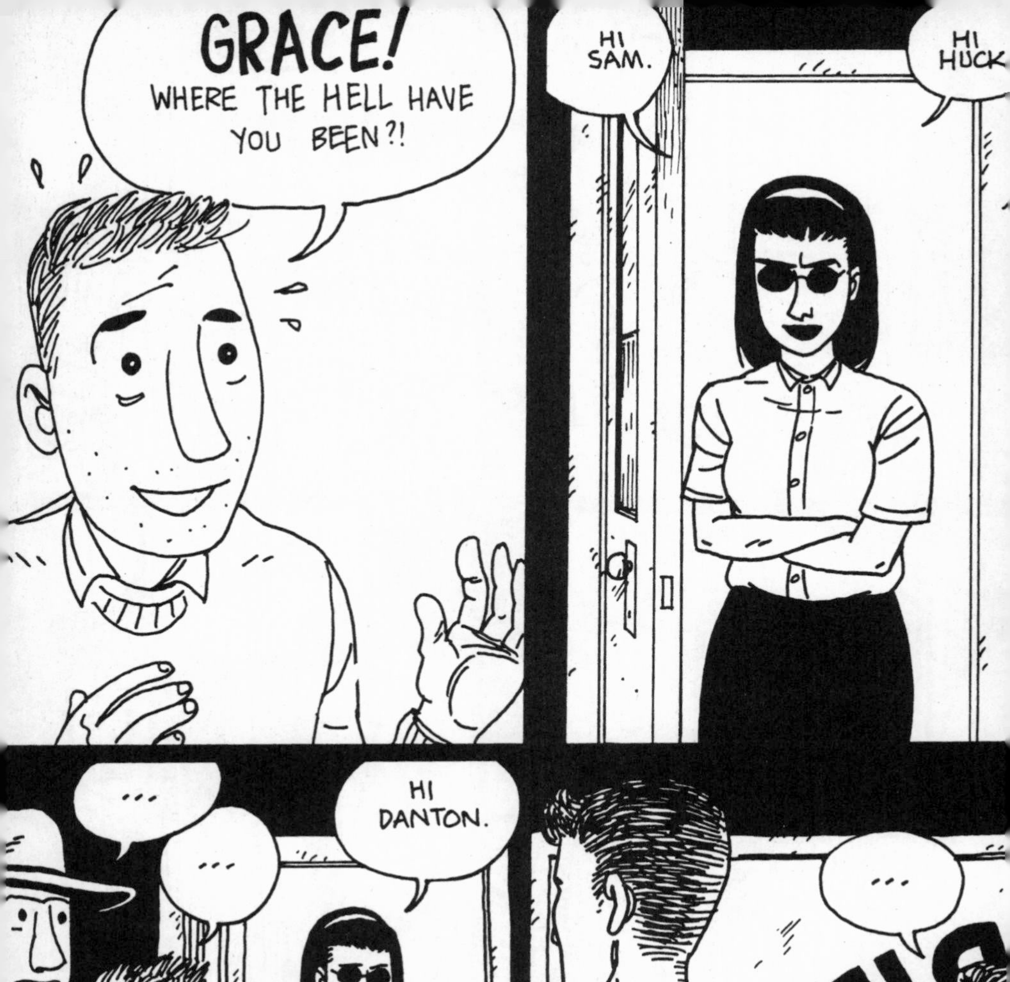
GRACE!
WHERE THE HELL HAVE YOU BEEN?!
HI SAM.
HI HUCK
...
...
HI DANTON.
...

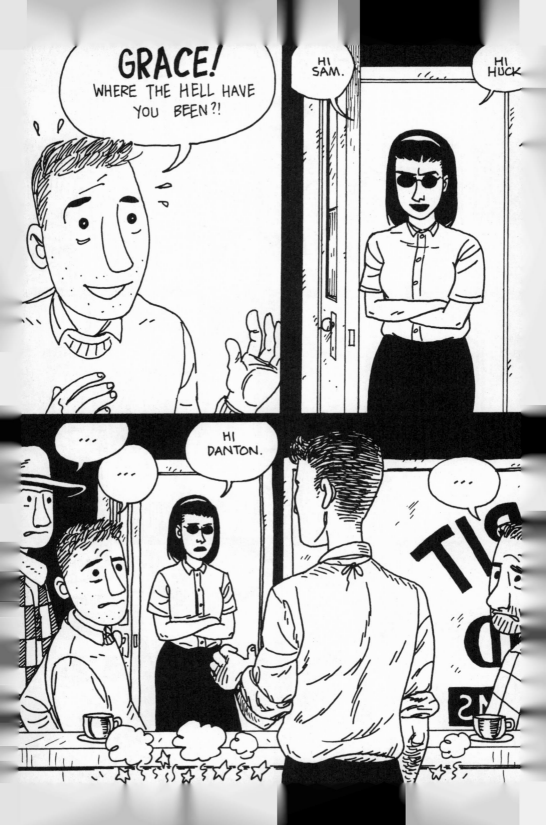

Chapter Three

"I loved the comics from the start, especially when I read somewhere that Bud Fisher married a fresh Ziegfield Follies girl every couple of years - and could afford them all."

Al Capp.

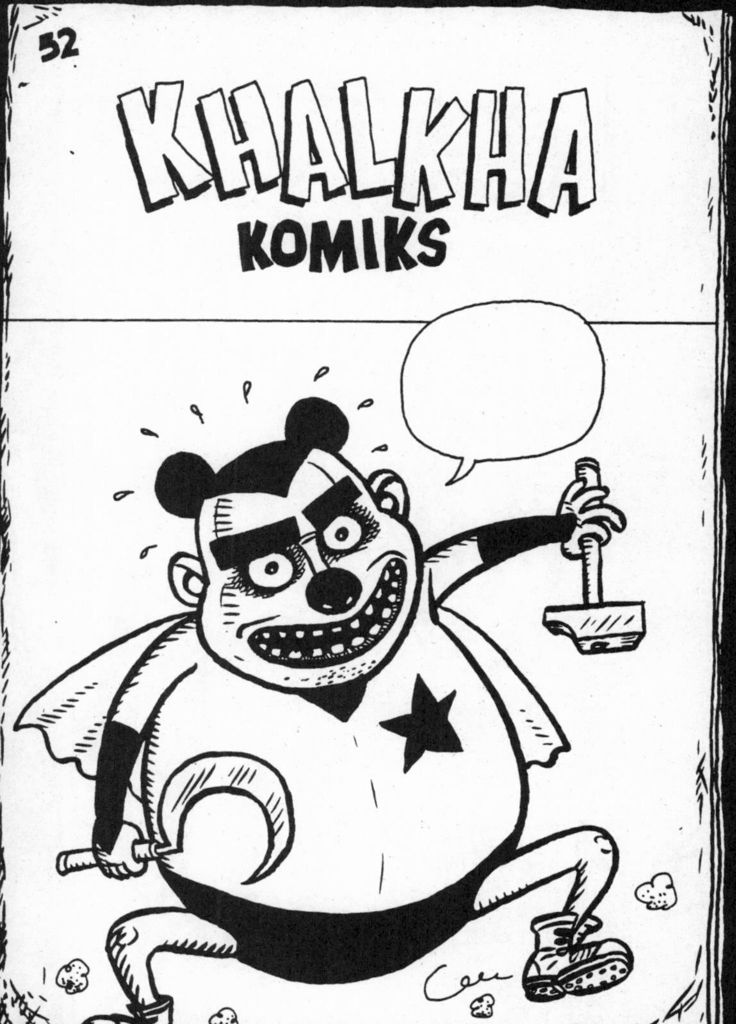
52
KHALKHA
KOMIKS

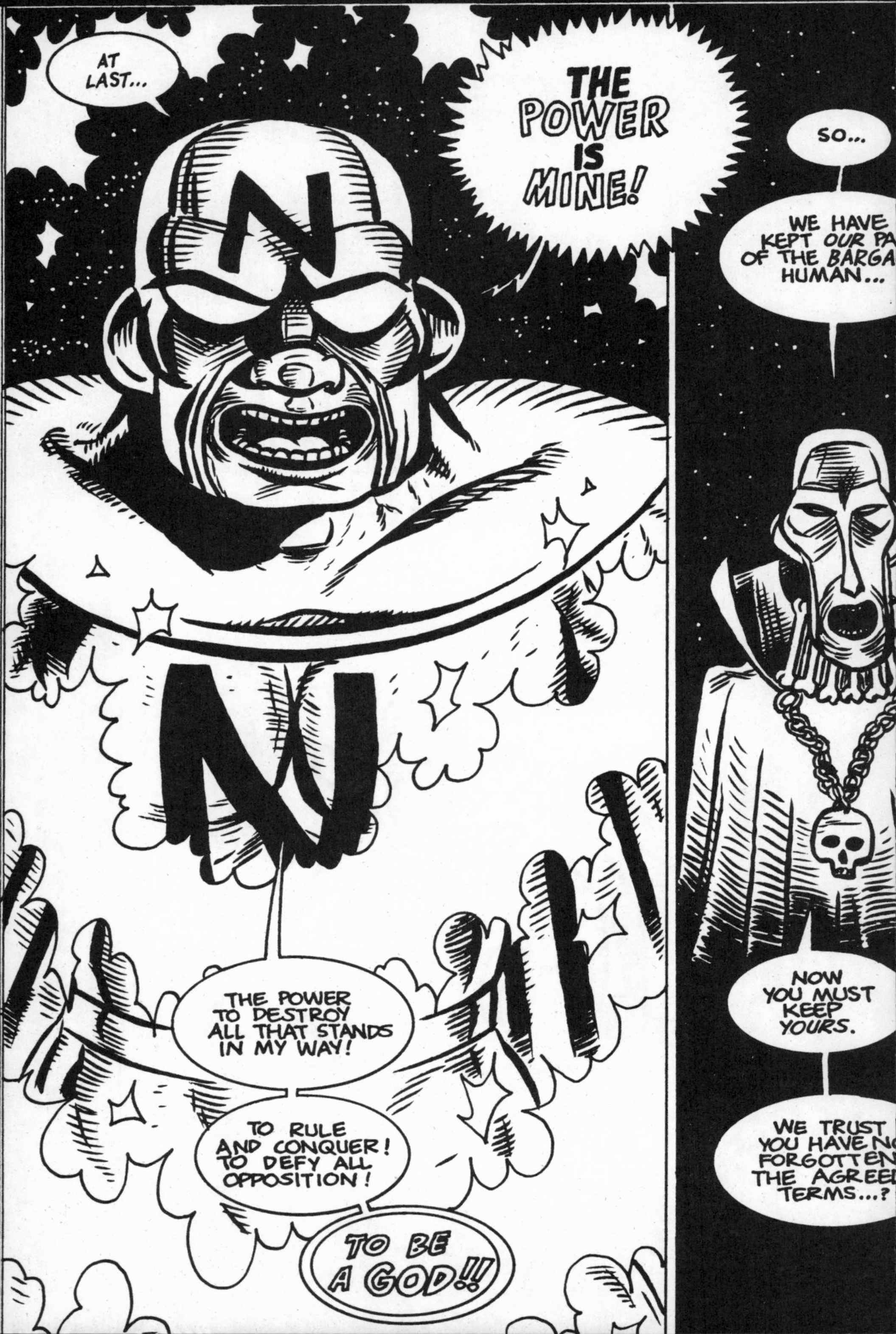
AT LAST...
THE POWER IS MINE!
THE POWER TO DESTROY ALL THAT STANDS IN MY WAY!
TO RULE AND CONQUER! TO DEFY ALL OPPOSITION!
TO BE A GOD!!
SO...
WE HAVE KEPT OUR PA
OF THE BARGA
HUMAN...
NOW YOU MUST KEEP YOURS.
WE TRUST
YOU HAVE N
FORGOTTEN
THE AGREE
TERMS...?

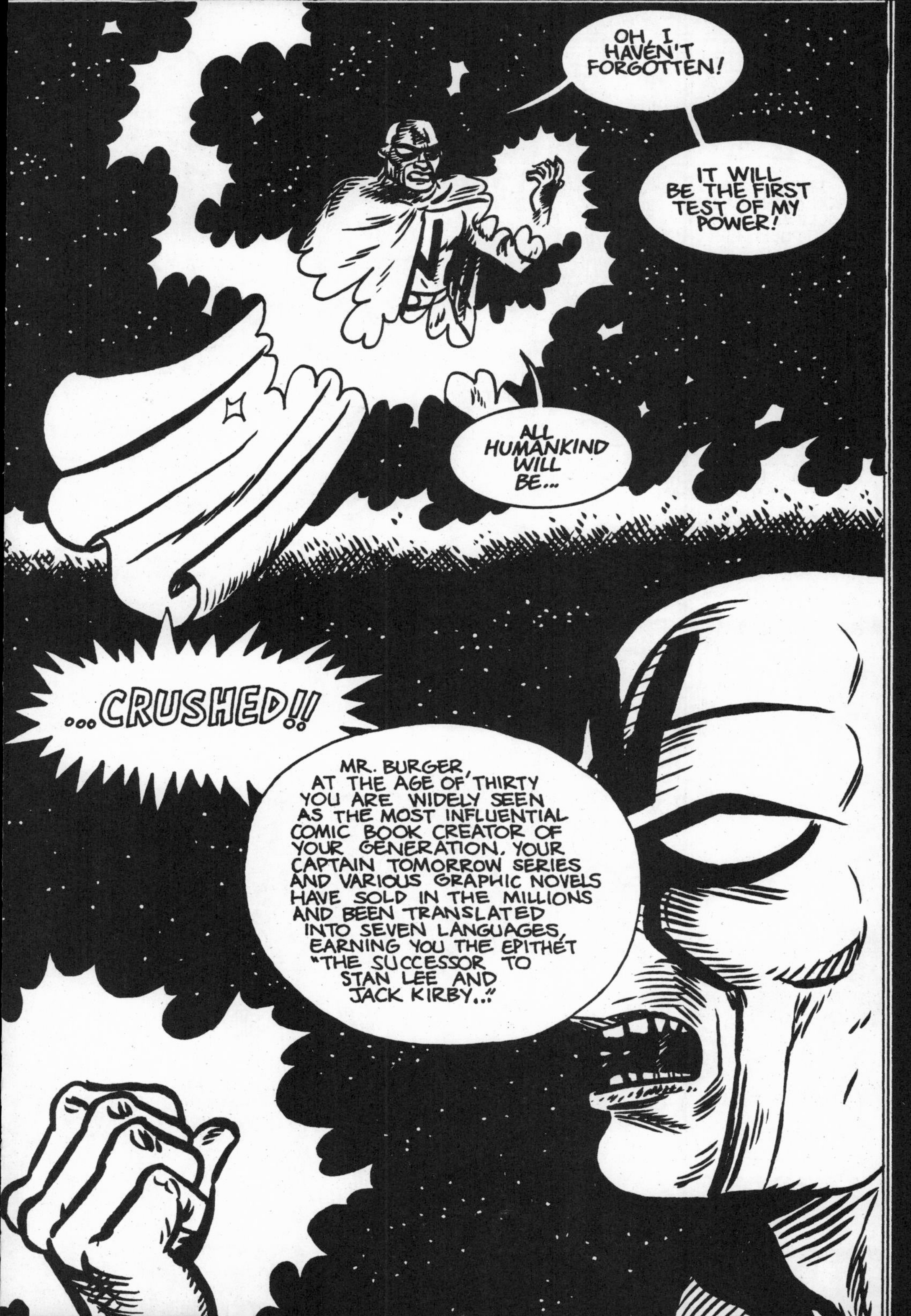
OH, I HAVEN'T FORGOTTEN!
IT WILL BE THE FIRST TEST OF MY POWER!
ALL HUMANKIND WILL BE...
...CRUSHED!!
MR. BURGER, AT THE AGE OF THIRTY YOU ARE WIDELY SEEN AS THE MOST INFLUENTIAL COMIC BOOK CREATOR OF YOUR GENERATION. YOUR CAPTAIN TOMORROW SERIES AND VARIOUS GRAPHIC NOVELS HAVE SOLD IN THE MILLIONS AND BEEN TRANSLATED INTO SEVEN LANGUAGES, EARNING YOU THE EPITHET "THE SUCCESSOR TO STAN LEE AND JACK KIRBY..."

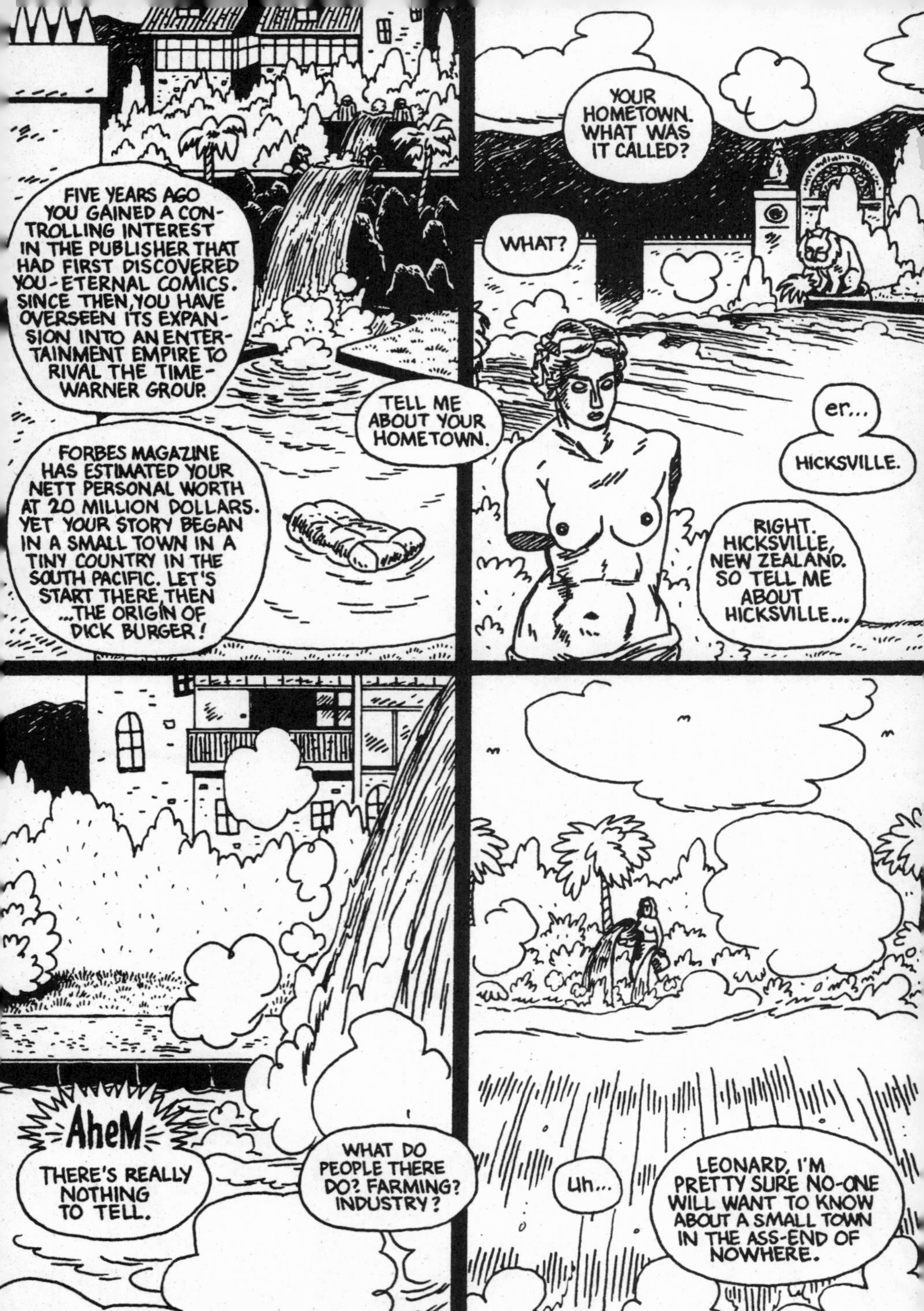
FIVE YEARS AGO YOU GAINED A CONTROLLING INTEREST IN THE PUBLISHER THAT HAD FIRST DISCOVERED YOU - ETERNAL COMICS. SINCE THEN, YOU HAVE OVERSEEN ITS EXPANSION INTO AN ENTERTAINMENT EMPIRE TO RIVAL THE TIME-WARNER GROUP.
FORBES MAGAZINE HAS ESTIMATED YOUR NETT PERSONAL WORTH AT 20 MILLION DOLLARS. YET YOUR STORY BEGAN IN A SMALL TOWN IN A TINY COUNTRY IN THE SOUTH PACIFIC. LET'S START THERE, THEN ...THE ORIGIN OF DICK BURGER!
TELL ME ABOUT YOUR HOMETOWN.
YOUR HOMETOWN. WHAT WAS IT CALLED?
WHAT?
er...
HICKSVILLE.
RIGHT. HICKSVILLE, NEW ZEALAND. SO TELL ME ABOUT HICKSVILLE...
AheM
THERE'S REALLY NOTHING TO TELL.
WHAT DO PEOPLE THERE DO? FARMING? INDUSTRY?
uh...
LEONARD, I'M PRETTY SURE NO-ONE WILL WANT TO KNOW ABOUT A SMALL TOWN IN THE ASS-END OF NOWHERE.

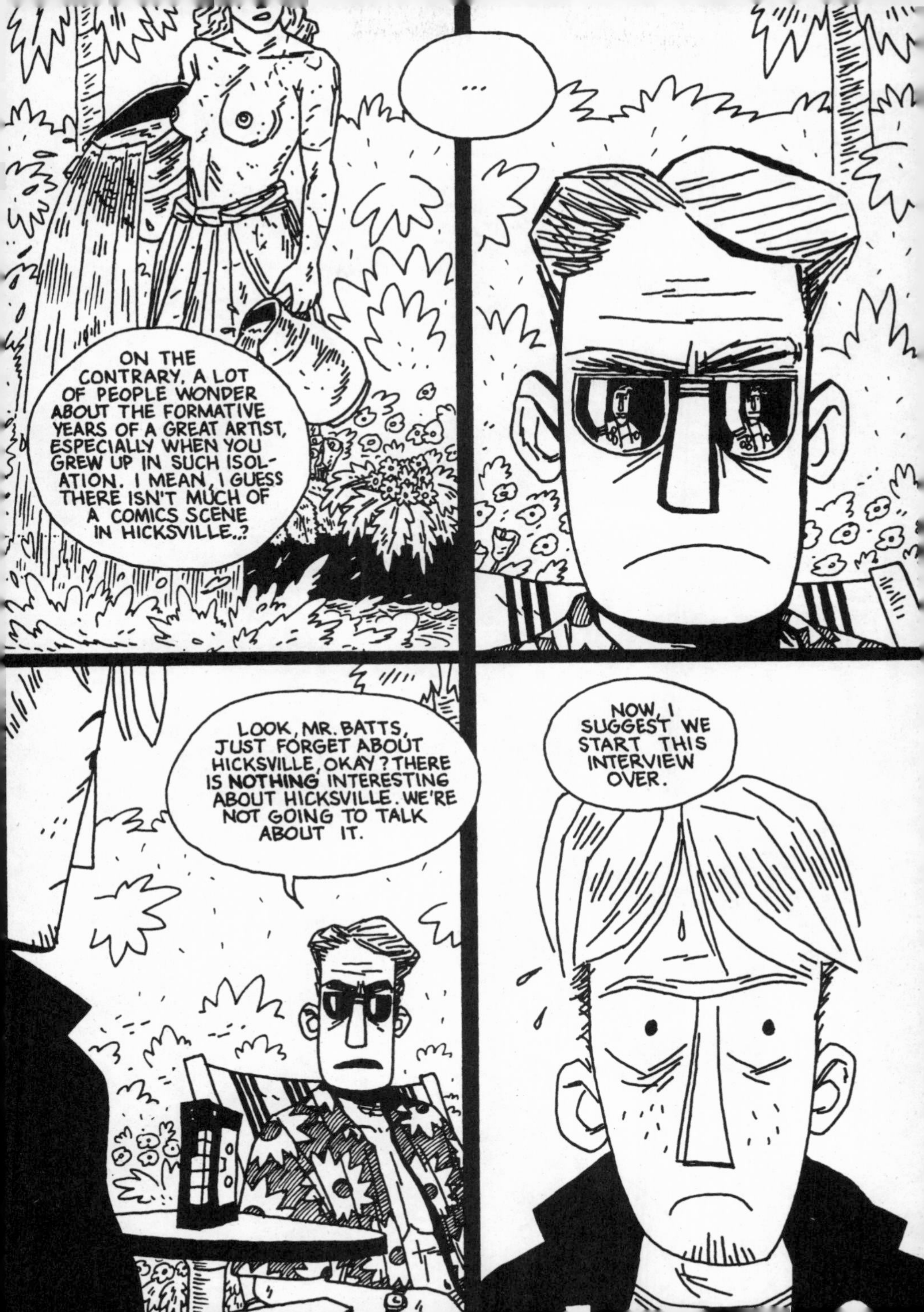
ON THE CONTRARY, A LOT OF PEOPLE WONDER ABOUT THE FORMATIVE YEARS OF A GREAT ARTIST, ESPECIALLY WHEN YOU GREW UP IN SUCH ISOLATION. I MEAN, I GUESS THERE ISN'T MUCH OF A COMICS SCENE IN HICKSVILLE..?
...
LOOK, MR. BATTS, JUST FORGET ABOUT HICKSVILLE, OKAY? THERE IS NOTHING INTERESTING ABOUT HICKSVILLE. WE'RE NOT GOING TO TALK ABOUT IT.
NOW, I SUGGEST WE START THIS INTERVIEW OVER.

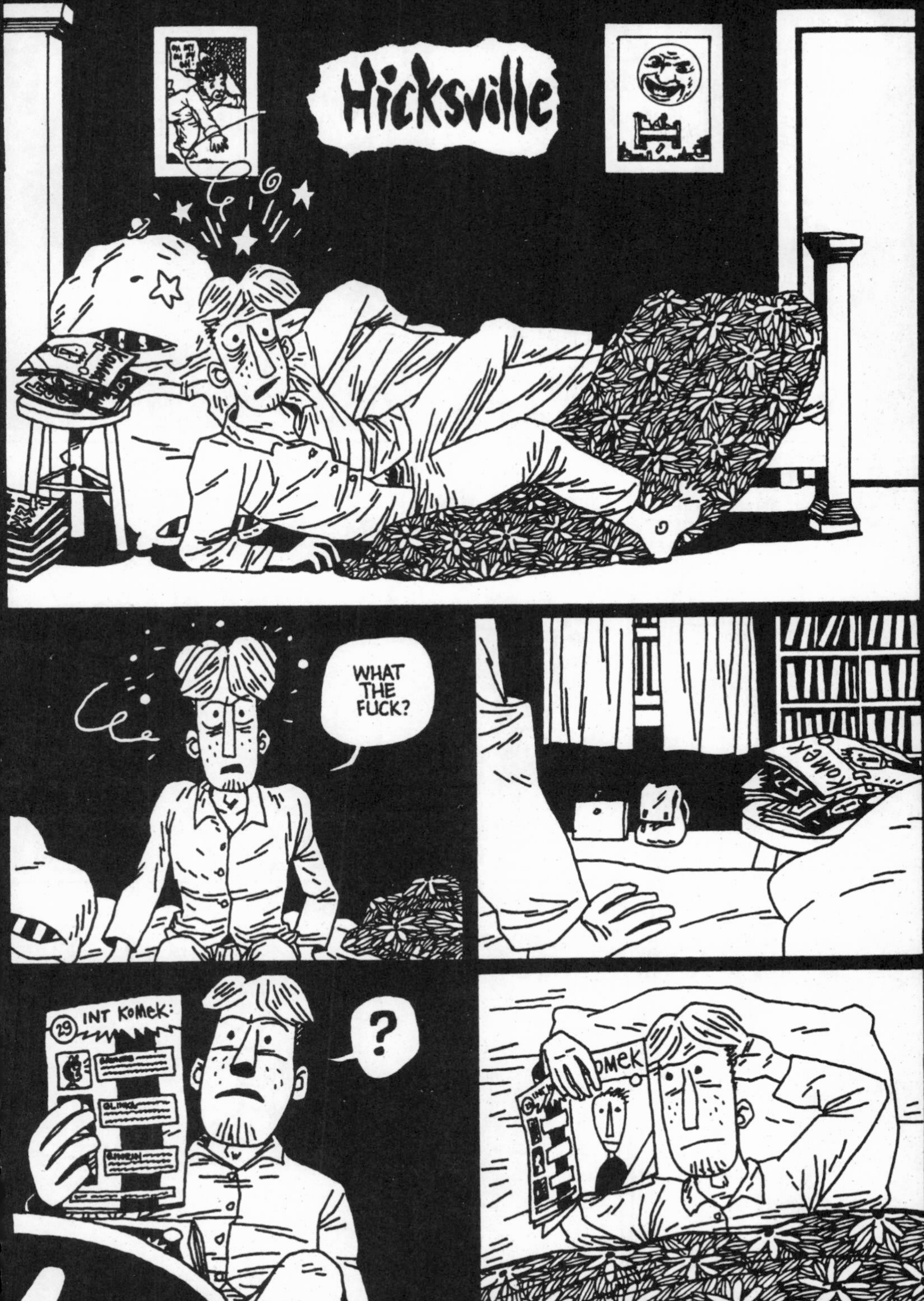
Hicksville
WHAT THE FUCK?
INT KOMEK:
?
KOMEK

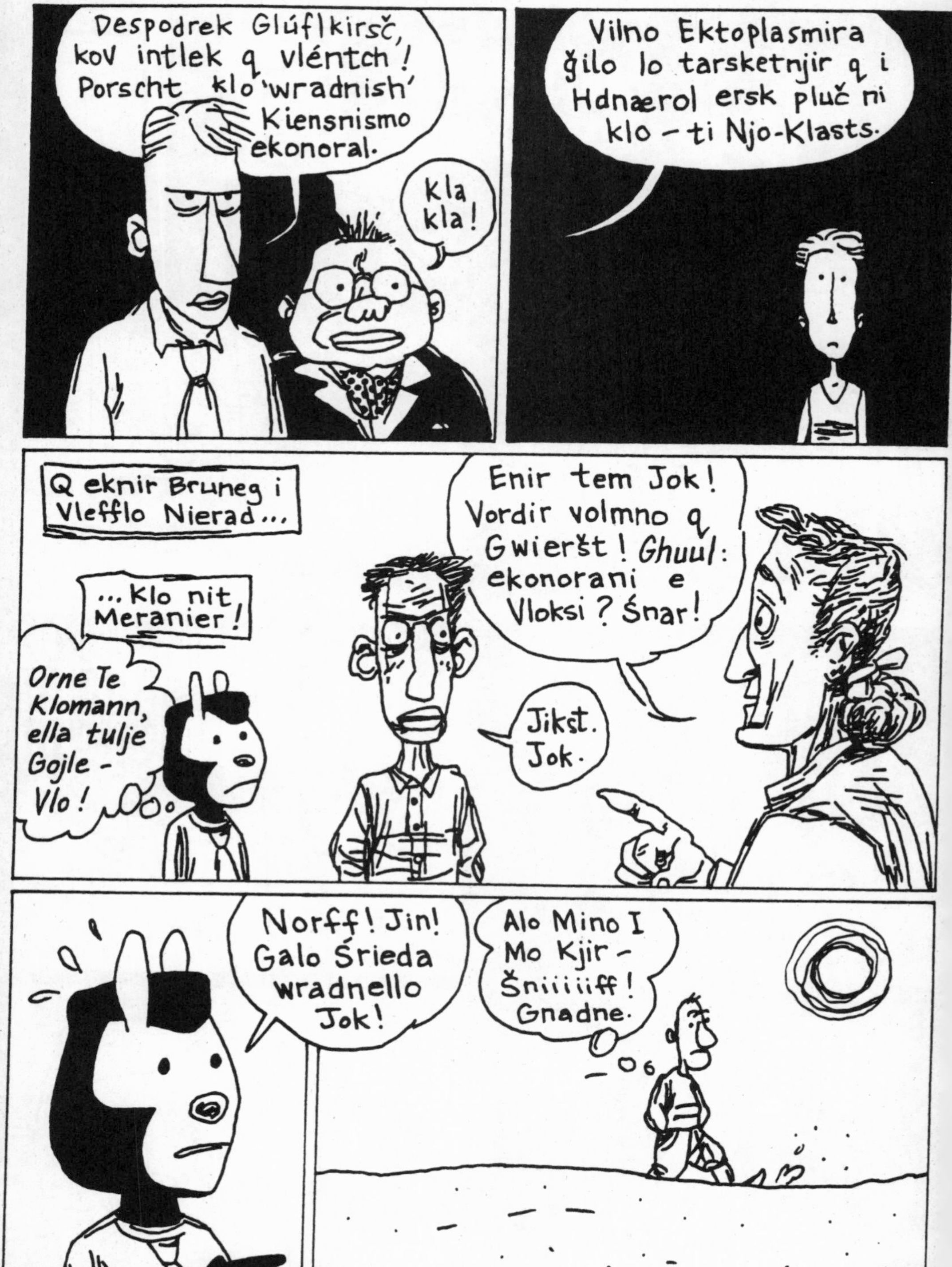
Despodrek Glúflkirsč, kov intlek q vléntch! Porscht klo 'wradnish' Kiensnismo ekonoral.
Kla kla!
Vilno Ektoplasmira ğilo lo tarsketnjir q i Hdnærol ersk pluč ni klo – ti Njo-Klasts.
Q eknir Bruneg i Vlefflo Nierad...
Enir tem Jok! Vordir volmno q Gwieršt! Ghuul: ekonorani e Vloksi? Śnar!
...Klo nit Meranier!
Orne Te Klomann, ella tulje Gojle - Vlo!
Jikst. Jok.
Norff! Jin! Galo Śrieda wradnello Jok!
Alo Mino I Mo Kjir - Šniiiiiff! Gnadne.
5

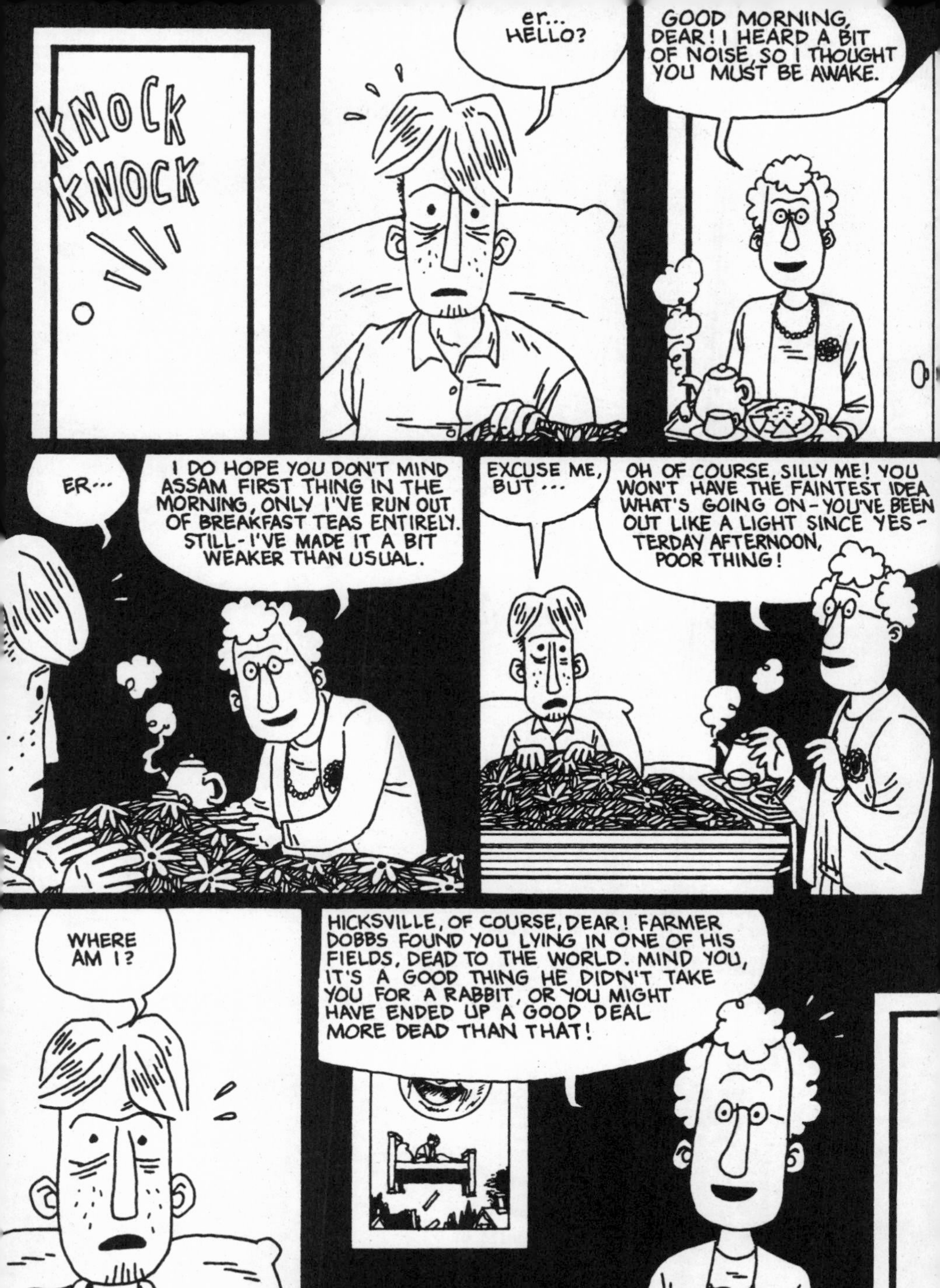

KNOCK KNOCK
er... HELLO?
GOOD MORNING, DEAR! I HEARD A BIT OF NOISE, SO I THOUGHT YOU MUST BE AWAKE.
ER...
I DO HOPE YOU DON'T MIND ASSAM FIRST THING IN THE MORNING, ONLY I'VE RUN OUT OF BREAKFAST TEAS ENTIRELY. STILL- I'VE MADE IT A BIT WEAKER THAN USUAL.
EXCUSE ME, BUT ...
OH OF COURSE, SILLY ME! YOU WON'T HAVE THE FAINTEST IDEA WHAT'S GOING ON - YOU'VE BEEN OUT LIKE A LIGHT SINCE YESTERDAY AFTERNOON, POOR THING!
WHERE AM I?
HICKSVILLE, OF COURSE, DEAR! FARMER DOBBS FOUND YOU LYING IN ONE OF HIS FIELDS, DEAD TO THE WORLD. MIND YOU, IT'S A GOOD THING HE DIDN'T TAKE YOU FOR A RABBIT, OR YOU MIGHT HAVE ENDED UP A GOOD DEAL MORE DEAD THAN THAT!

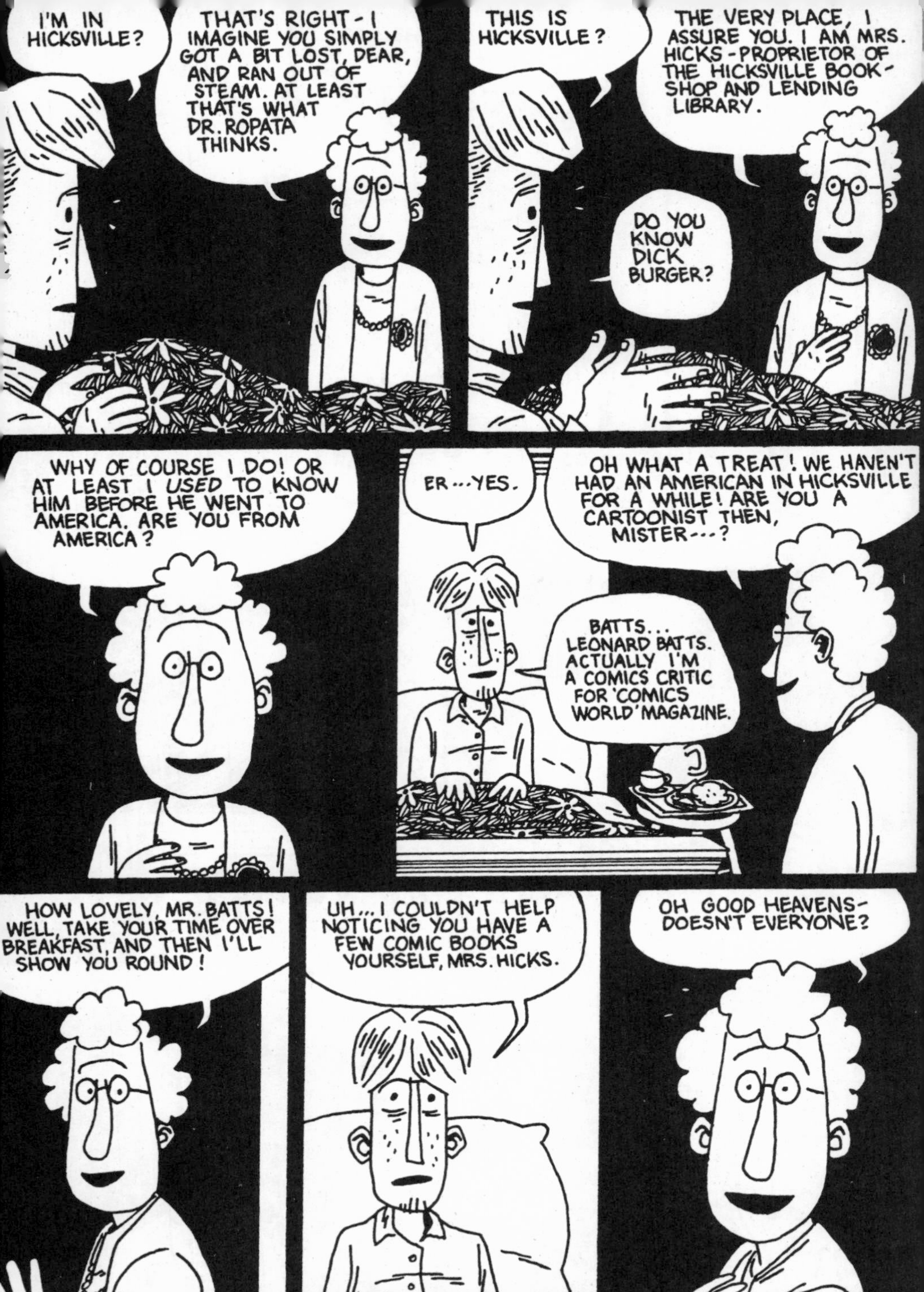
I'M IN HICKSVILLE?
THAT'S RIGHT - I IMAGINE YOU SIMPLY GOT A BIT LOST, DEAR, AND RAN OUT OF STEAM. AT LEAST THAT'S WHAT DR. ROPATA THINKS.
THIS IS HICKSVILLE?
THE VERY PLACE, I ASSURE YOU. I AM MRS. HICKS - PROPRIETOR OF THE HICKSVILLE BOOK-SHOP AND LENDING LIBRARY.
DO YOU KNOW DICK BURGER?
WHY OF COURSE I DO! OR AT LEAST I USED TO KNOW HIM BEFORE HE WENT TO AMERICA. ARE YOU FROM AMERICA?
ER...YES.
OH WHAT A TREAT! WE HAVEN'T HAD AN AMERICAN IN HICKSVILLE FOR A WHILE! ARE YOU A CARTOONIST THEN, MISTER...?
BATTS... LEONARD BATTS. ACTUALLY I'M A COMICS CRITIC FOR 'COMICS WORLD' MAGAZINE.
HOW LOVELY, MR. BATTS! WELL, TAKE YOUR TIME OVER BREAKFAST, AND THEN I'LL SHOW YOU ROUND!
UH...I COULDN'T HELP NOTICING YOU HAVE A FEW COMIC BOOKS YOURSELF, MRS. HICKS.
OH GOOD HEAVENS- DOESN'T EVERYONE?

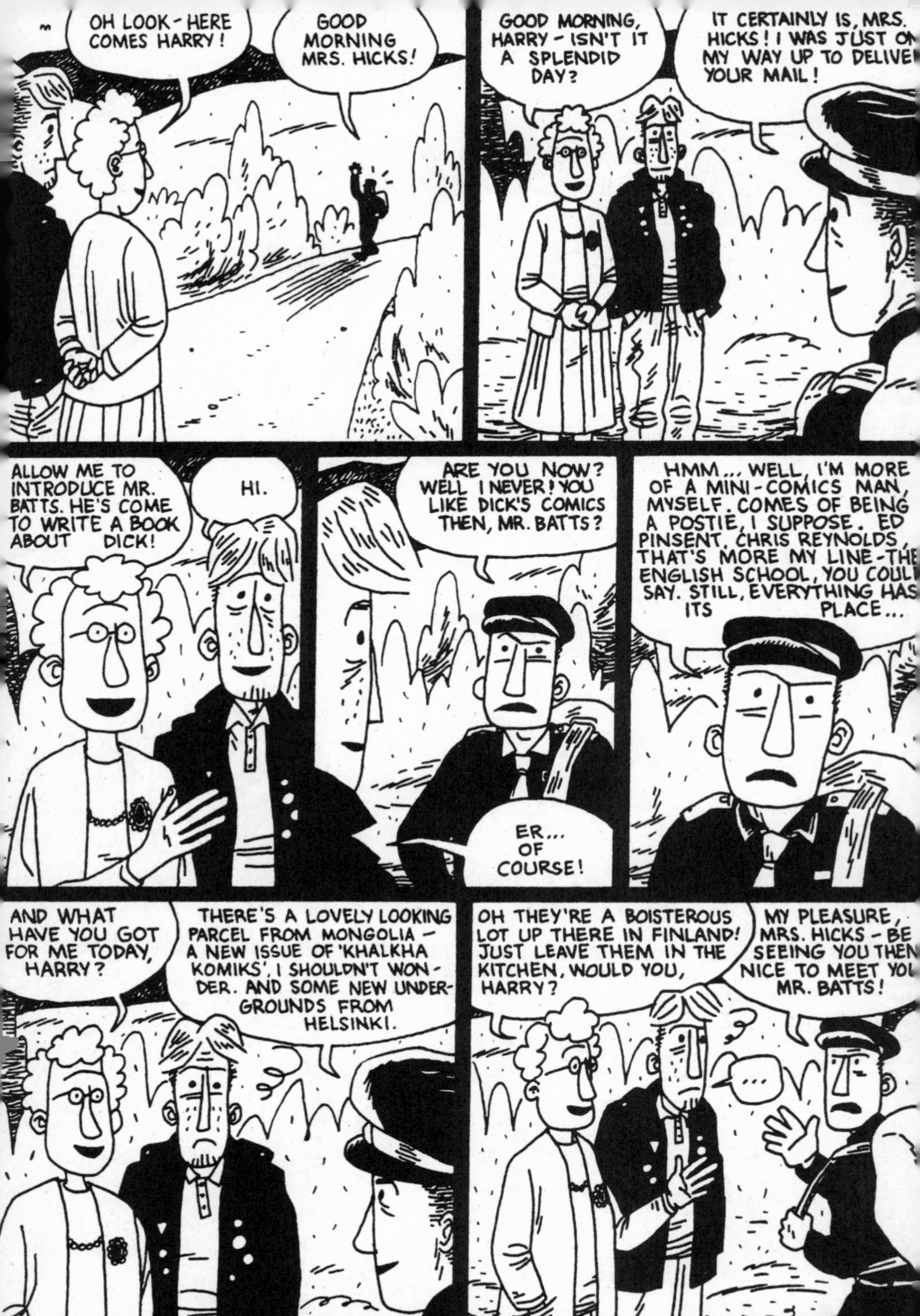

OH LOOK - HERE COMES HARRY!
GOOD MORNING MRS. HICKS!
GOOD MORNING, HARRY - ISN'T IT A SPLENDID DAY?
IT CERTAINLY IS, MRS. HICKS! I WAS JUST ON MY WAY UP TO DELIVER YOUR MAIL!
ALLOW ME TO INTRODUCE MR. BATTS. HE'S COME TO WRITE A BOOK ABOUT DICK!
HI.
ARE YOU NOW? WELL I NEVER! YOU LIKE DICK'S COMICS THEN, MR. BATTS?
ER... OF COURSE!
HMM... WELL, I'M MORE OF A MINI-COMICS MAN, MYSELF. COMES OF BEING A POSTIE, I SUPPOSE. ED PINSENT, CHRIS REYNOLDS, THAT'S MORE MY LINE - THE ENGLISH SCHOOL, YOU COULD SAY. STILL, EVERYTHING HAS ITS PLACE...
AND WHAT HAVE YOU GOT FOR ME TODAY, HARRY?
THERE'S A LOVELY LOOKING PARCEL FROM MONGOLIA - A NEW ISSUE OF 'KHALKHA KOMIKS', I SHOULDN'T WONDER. AND SOME NEW UNDERGROUNDS FROM HELSINKI.
OH THEY'RE A BOISTEROUS LOT UP THERE IN FINLAND! JUST LEAVE THEM IN THE KITCHEN, WOULD YOU, HARRY?
MY PLEASURE, MRS. HICKS - BE SEEING YOU THEN. NICE TO MEET YOU, MR. BATTS!
...

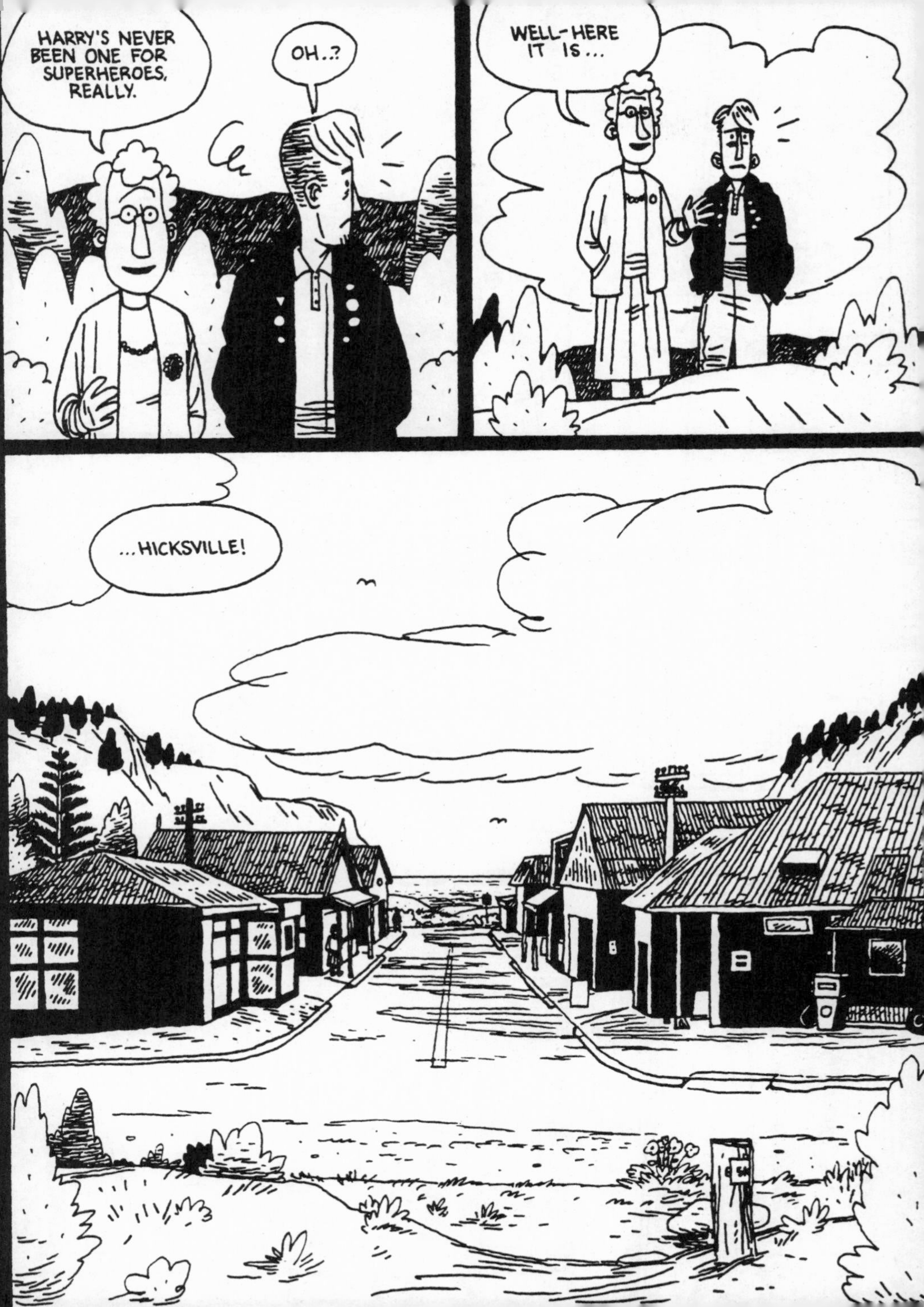
HARRY'S NEVER BEEN ONE FOR SUPERHEROES, REALLY.
OH..?
WELL-HERE IT IS...
...HICKSVILLE!

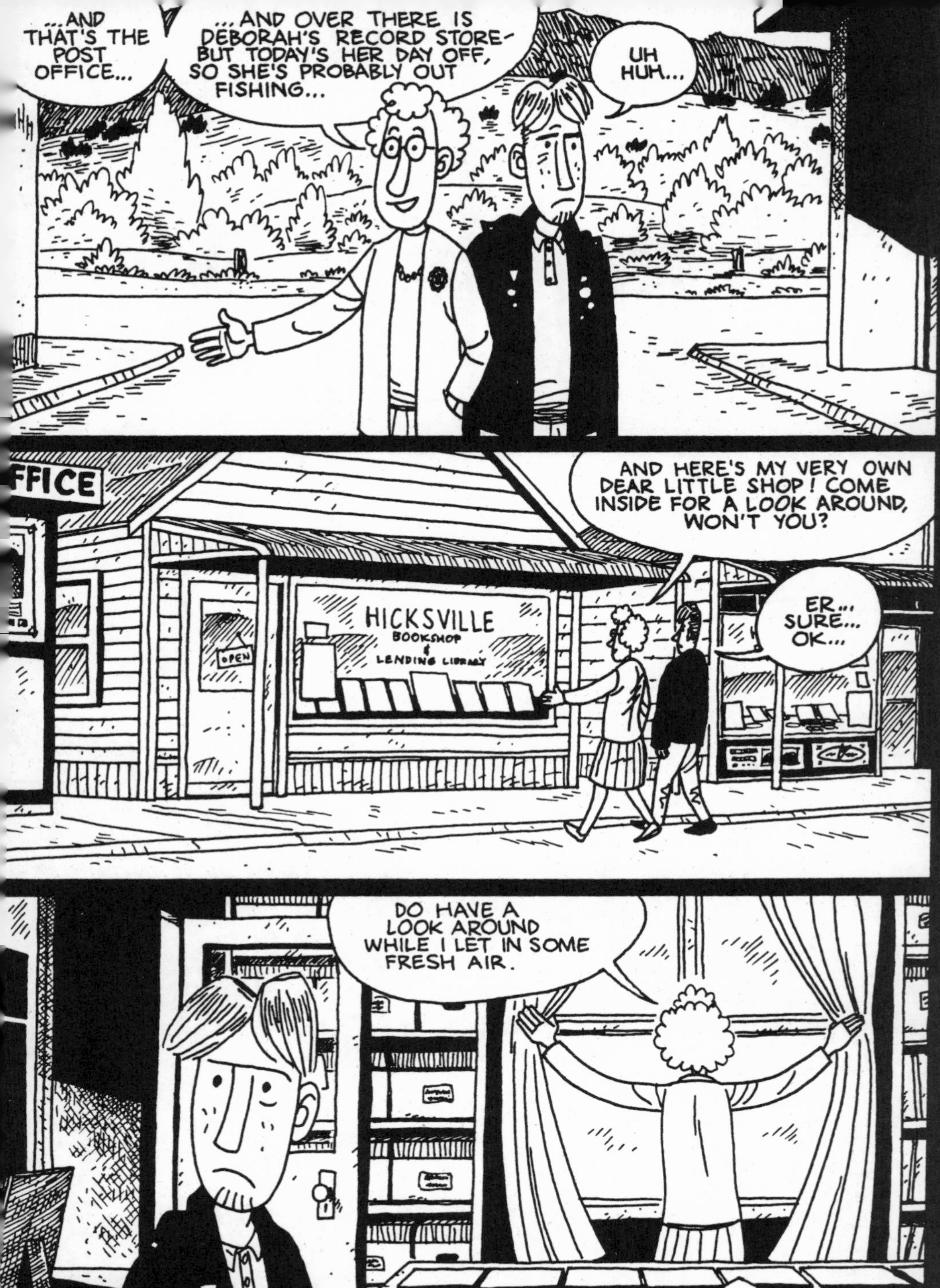
...AND THAT'S THE POST OFFICE...
...AND OVER THERE IS DEBORAH'S RECORD STORE- BUT TODAY'S HER DAY OFF, SO SHE'S PROBABLY OUT FISHING...
UH HUH...
FFICE
AND HERE'S MY VERY OWN DEAR LITTLE SHOP! COME INSIDE FOR A LOOK AROUND, WON'T YOU?
HICKSVILLE BOOKSHOP & LENDING LIBRARY
OPEN
ER... SURE... OK...
DO HAVE A LOOK AROUND WHILE I LET IN SOME FRESH AIR.

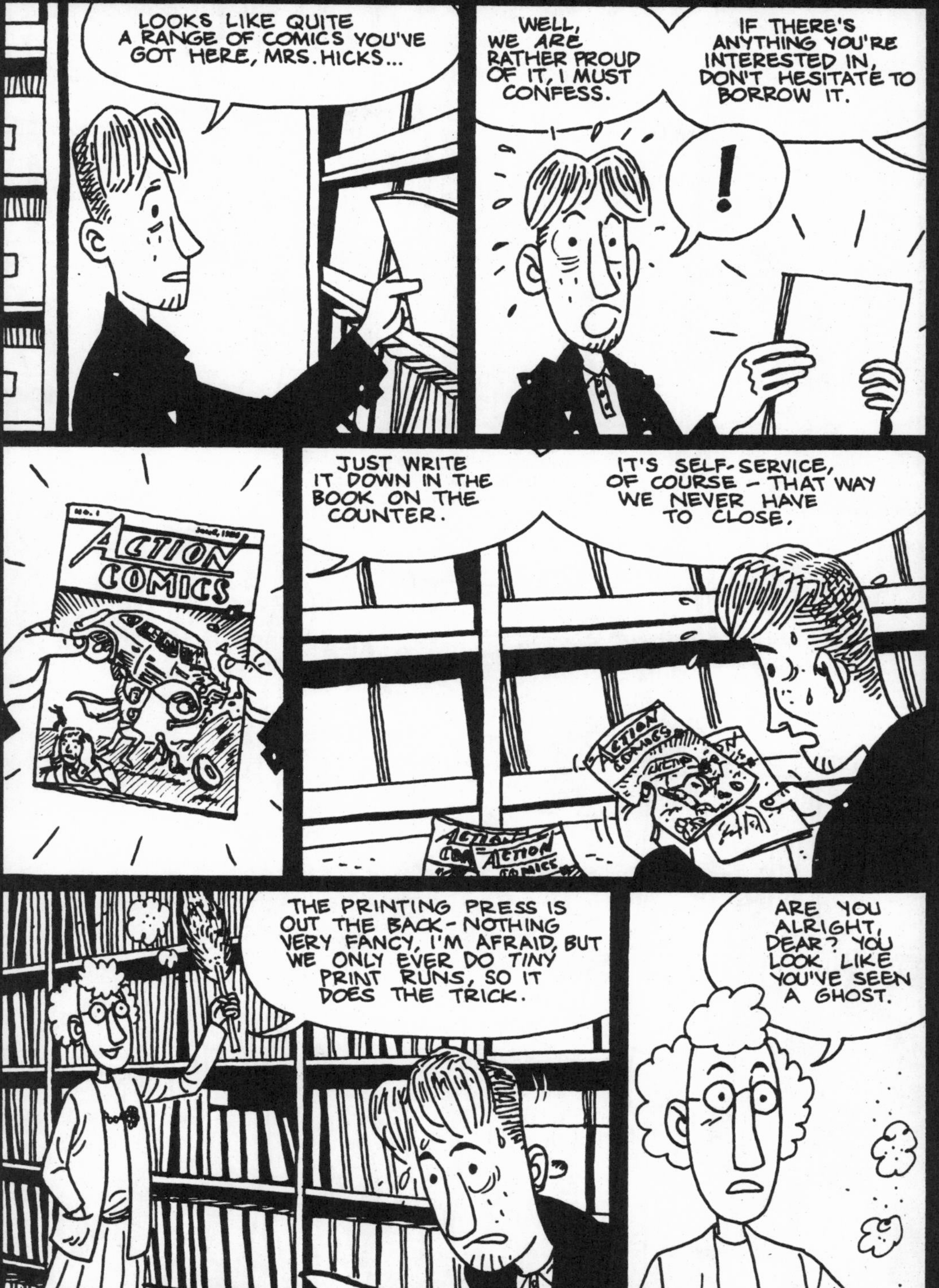
LOOKS LIKE QUITE A RANGE OF COMICS YOU'VE GOT HERE, MRS. HICKS...
WELL, WE ARE RATHER PROUD OF IT, I MUST CONFESS.
IF THERE'S ANYTHING YOU'RE INTERESTED IN, DON'T HESITATE TO BORROW IT.
!
ACTION COMICS
JUST WRITE IT DOWN IN THE BOOK ON THE COUNTER.
IT'S SELF-SERVICE, OF COURSE - THAT WAY WE NEVER HAVE TO CLOSE.
THE PRINTING PRESS IS OUT THE BACK - NOTHING VERY FANCY, I'M AFRAID, BUT WE ONLY EVER DO TINY PRINT RUNS, SO IT DOES THE TRICK.
ARE YOU ALRIGHT, DEAR? YOU LOOK LIKE YOU'VE SEEN A GHOST.

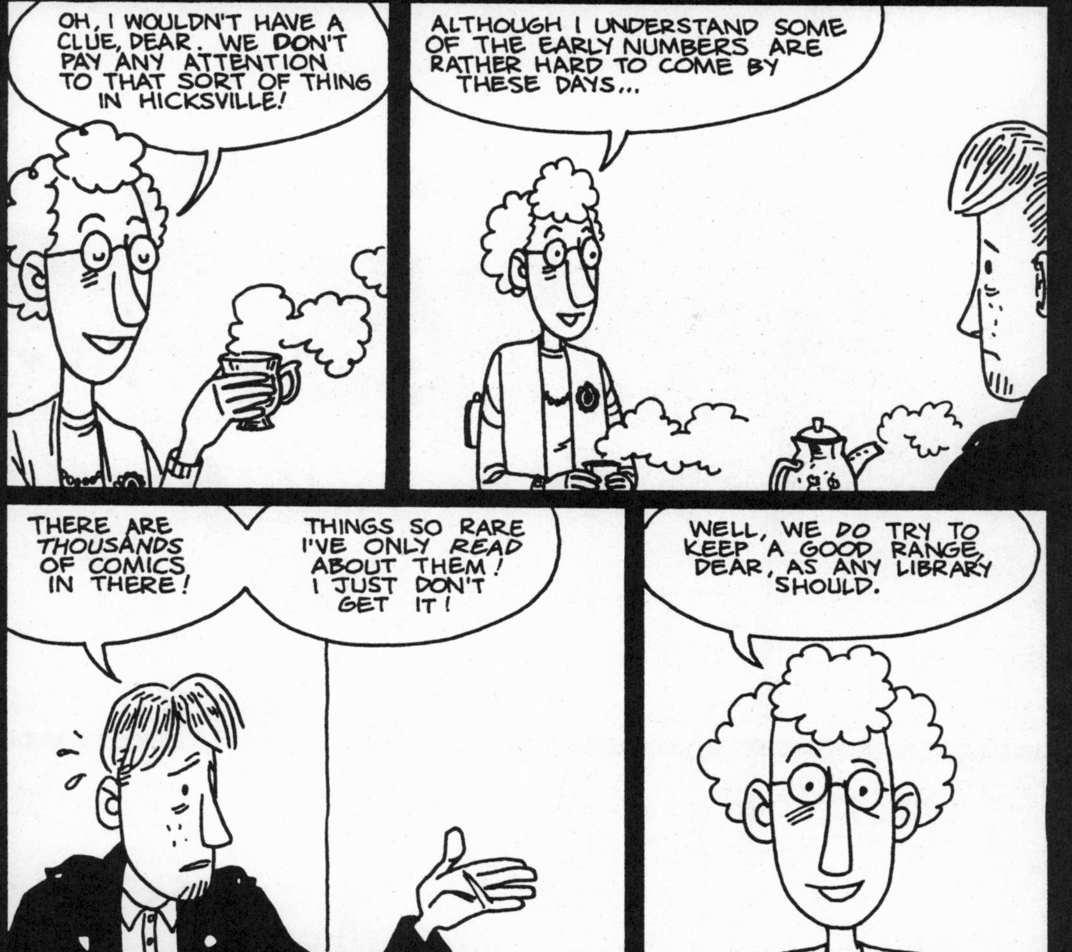
OH, I WOULDN'T HAVE A CLUE, DEAR. WE DON'T PAY ANY ATTENTION TO THAT SORT OF THING IN HICKSVILLE!
ALTHOUGH I UNDERSTAND SOME OF THE EARLY NUMBERS ARE RATHER HARD TO COME BY THESE DAYS...
THERE ARE THOUSANDS OF COMICS IN THERE!
THINGS SO RARE I'VE ONLY READ ABOUT THEM! I JUST DON'T GET IT!
WELL, WE DO TRY TO KEEP A GOOD RANGE, DEAR, AS ANY LIBRARY SHOULD.
LAMINGTON?

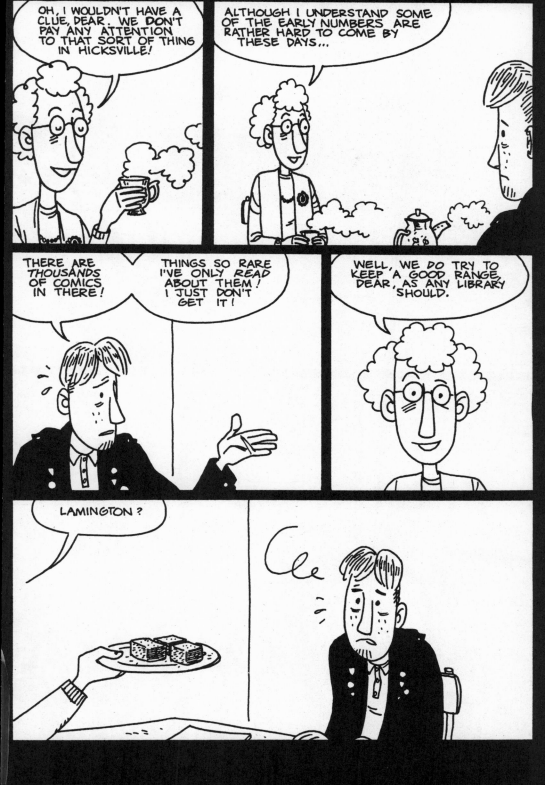

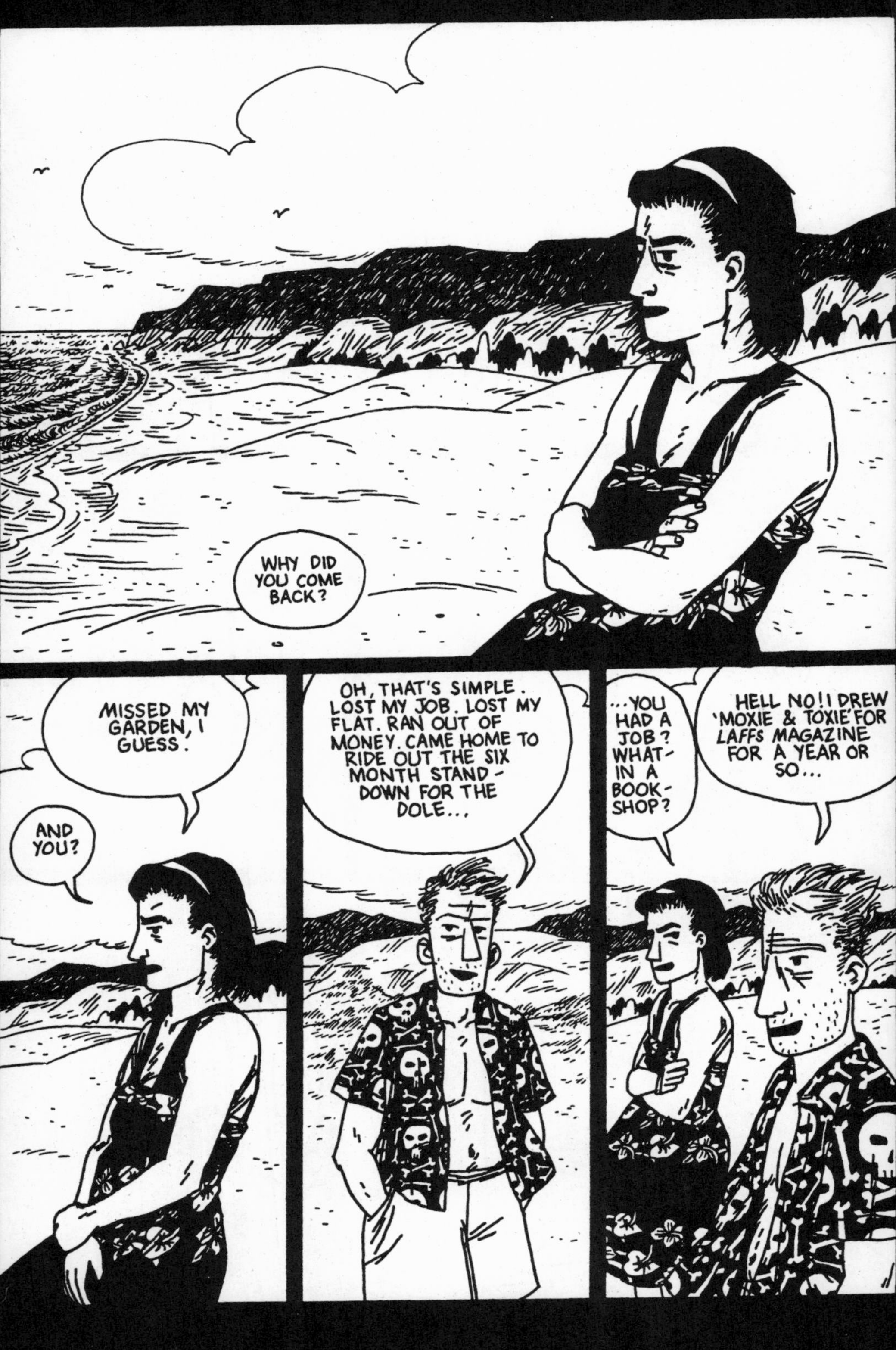
WHY DID YOU COME BACK?
MISSED MY GARDEN, I GUESS.
AND YOU?
OH, THAT'S SIMPLE. LOST MY JOB. LOST MY FLAT. RAN OUT OF MONEY. CAME HOME TO RIDE OUT THE SIX MONTH STAND-DOWN FOR THE DOLE...
...YOU HAD A JOB? WHAT- IN A BOOK-SHOP?
HELL NO!! DREW 'MOXIE & TOXIE' FOR LAFFS MAGAZINE FOR A YEAR OR SO...

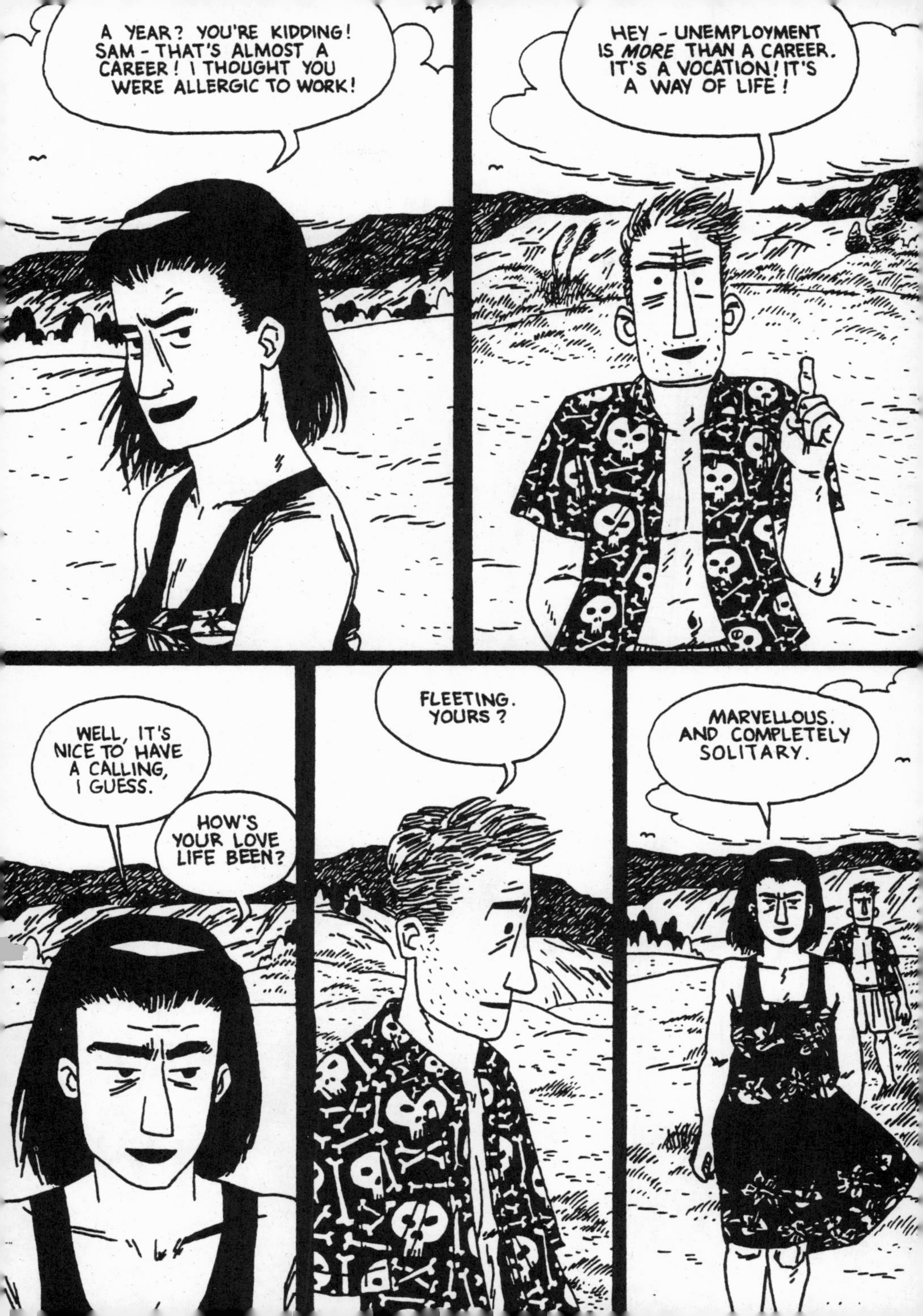

A YEAR? YOU'RE KIDDING! SAM - THAT'S ALMOST A CAREER! I THOUGHT YOU WERE ALLERGIC TO WORK!
HEY - UNEMPLOYMENT IS *MORE* THAN A CAREER. IT'S A VOCATION! IT'S A WAY OF LIFE!
WELL, IT'S NICE TO HAVE A CALLING, I GUESS.
HOW'S YOUR LOVE LIFE BEEN?
FLEETING. YOURS?
MARVELLOUS. AND COMPLETELY SOLITARY.

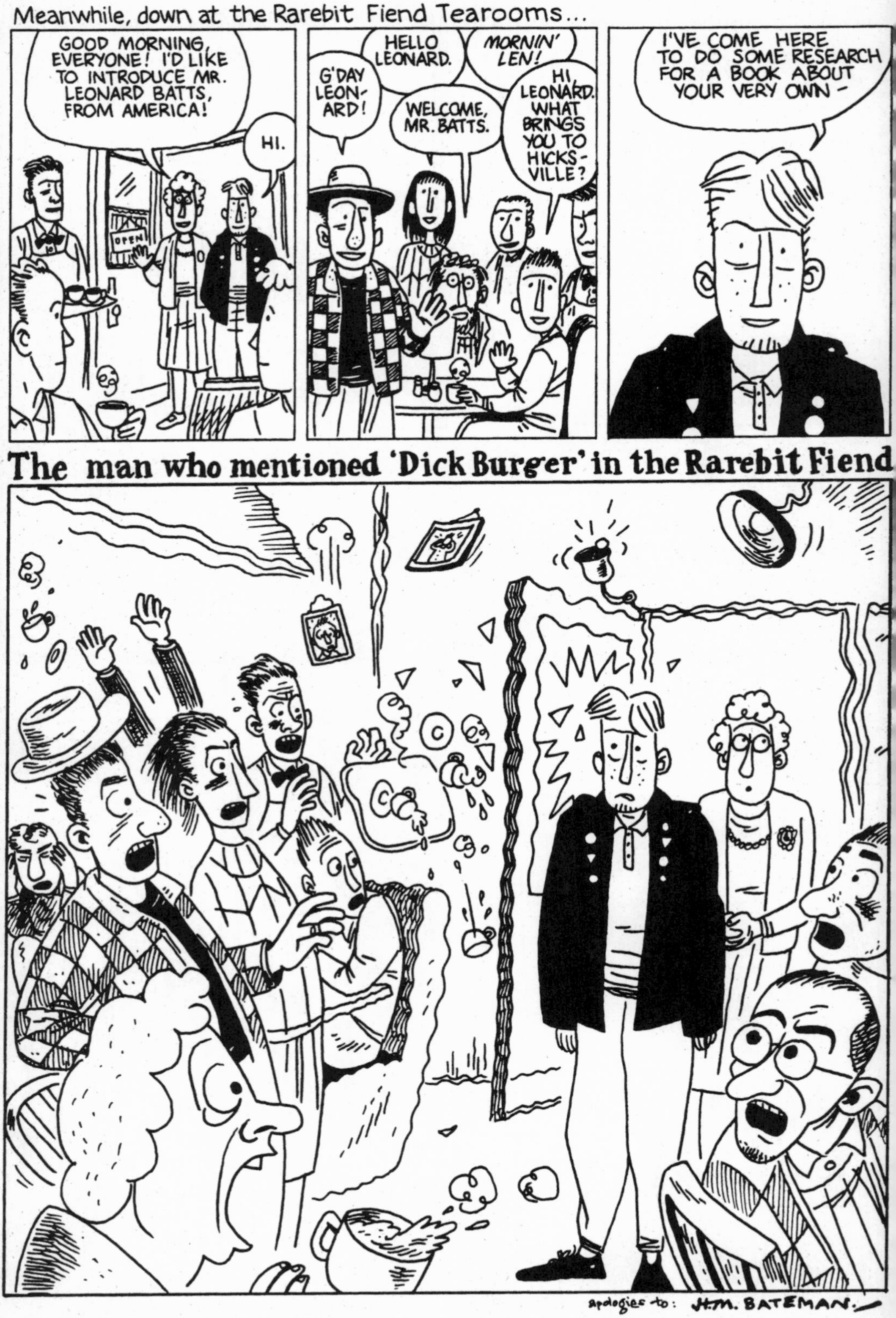
Meanwhile, down at the Rarebit Fiend Tearooms...
GOOD MORNING, EVERYONE! I'D LIKE TO INTRODUCE MR. LEONARD BATTS, FROM AMERICA!
HI.
OPEN
G'DAY LEON-ARD!
HELLO LEONARD.
MORNIN' LEN!
WELCOME, MR. BATTS.
HI LEONARD. WHAT BRINGS YOU TO HICKS-VILLE?
I'VE COME HERE TO DO SOME RESEARCH FOR A BOOK ABOUT YOUR VERY OWN -
The man who mentioned 'Dick Burger' in the Rarebit Fiend
apologies to: H.M. BATEMAN.

"Now we're in the age of 'comics as air.'"
Osamu Tezuka.

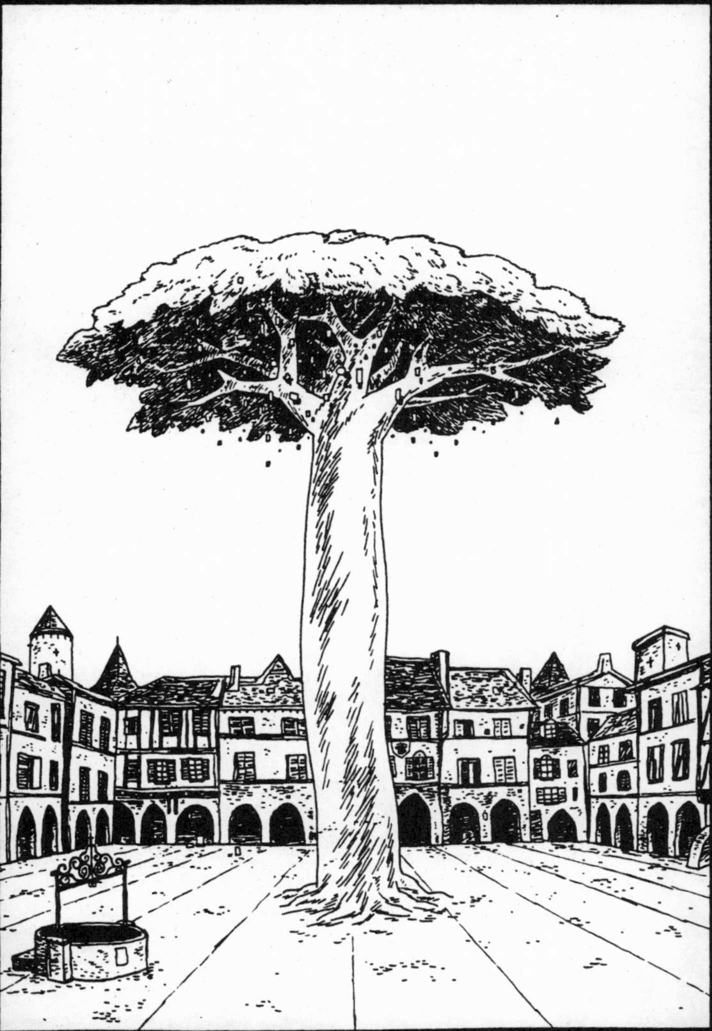

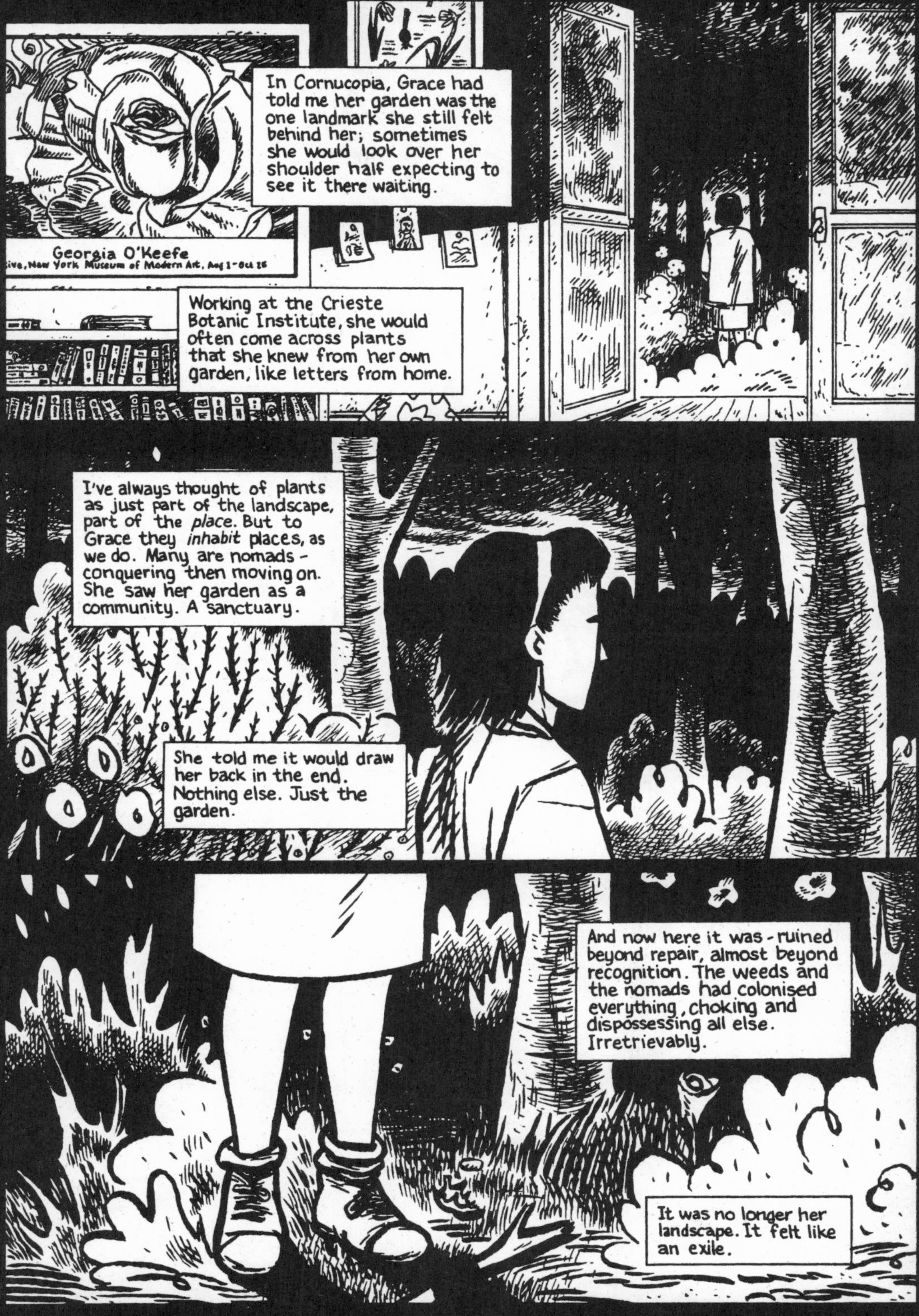
In Cornucopia, Grace had told me her garden was the one landmark she still felt behind her; sometimes she would look over her shoulder half expecting to see it there waiting.
Georgia O'Keefe
New York Museum of Modern Art, Aug 1 – Oct 26
Working at the Crieste Botanic Institute, she would often come across plants that she knew from her own garden, like letters from home.
I've always thought of plants as just part of the landscape, part of the *place*. But to Grace they *inhabit* places, as we do. Many are nomads - conquering then moving on. She saw her garden as a community. A sanctuary.
She told me it would draw her back in the end. Nothing else. Just the garden.
And now here it was - ruined beyond repair, almost beyond recognition. The weeds and the nomads had colonised everything, choking and dispossessing all else. Irretrievably.
It was no longer her landscape. It felt like an exile.

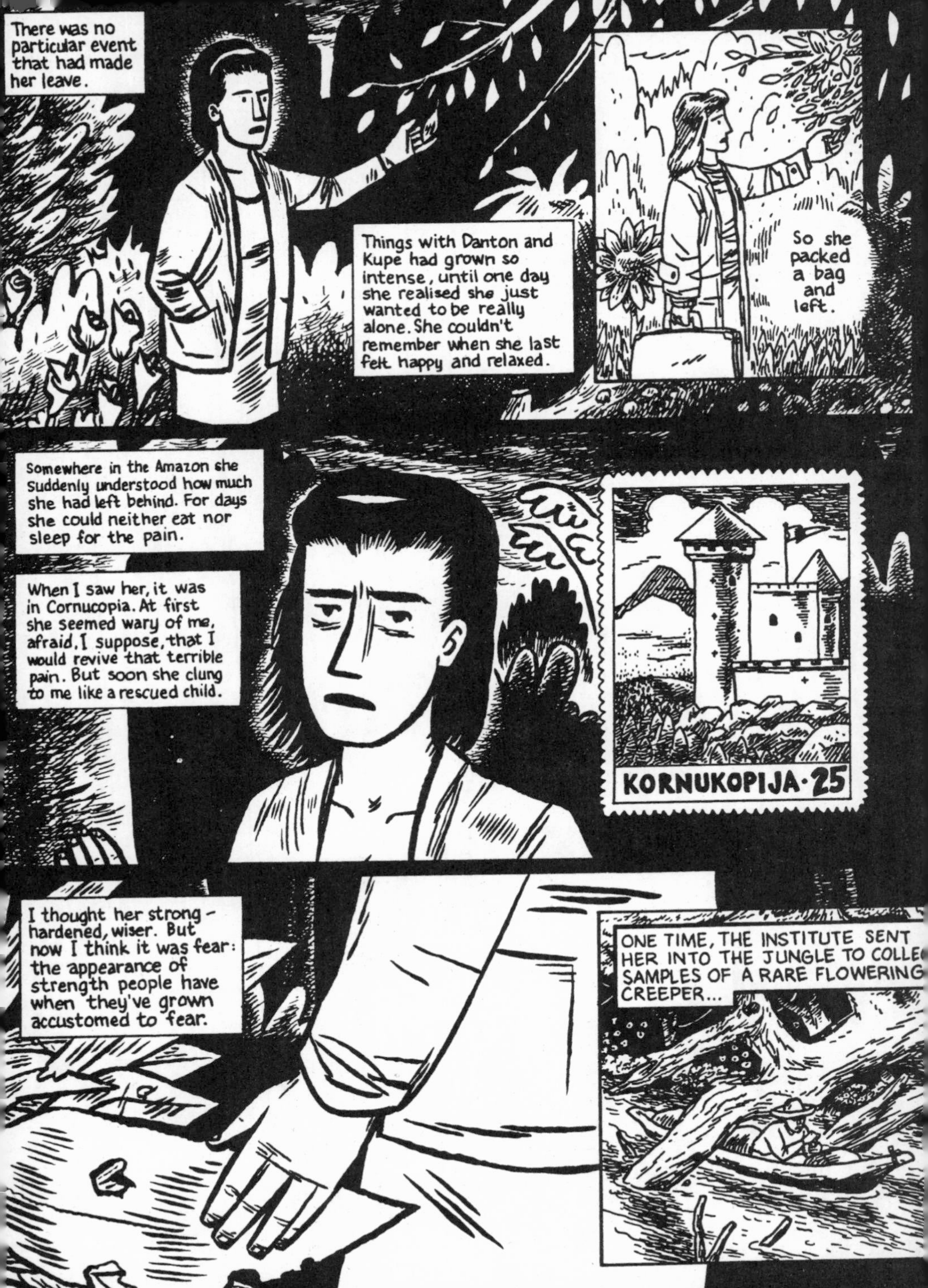

There was no particular event that had made her leave.
Things with Danton and Kupe had grown so intense, until one day she realised she just wanted to be really alone. She couldn't remember when she last felt happy and relaxed.
So she packed a bag and left.
Somewhere in the Amazon she suddenly understood how much she had left behind. For days she could neither eat nor sleep for the pain.
When I saw her, it was in Cornucopia. At first she seemed wary of me, afraid, I suppose, that I would revive that terrible pain. But soon she clung to me like a rescued child.
KORNUKOPIJA · 25
I thought her strong - hardened, wiser. But now I think it was fear: the appearance of strength people have when they've grown accustomed to fear.
ONE TIME, THE INSTITUTE SENT HER INTO THE JUNGLE TO COLLEC
SAMPLES OF A RARE FLOWERING CREEPER...

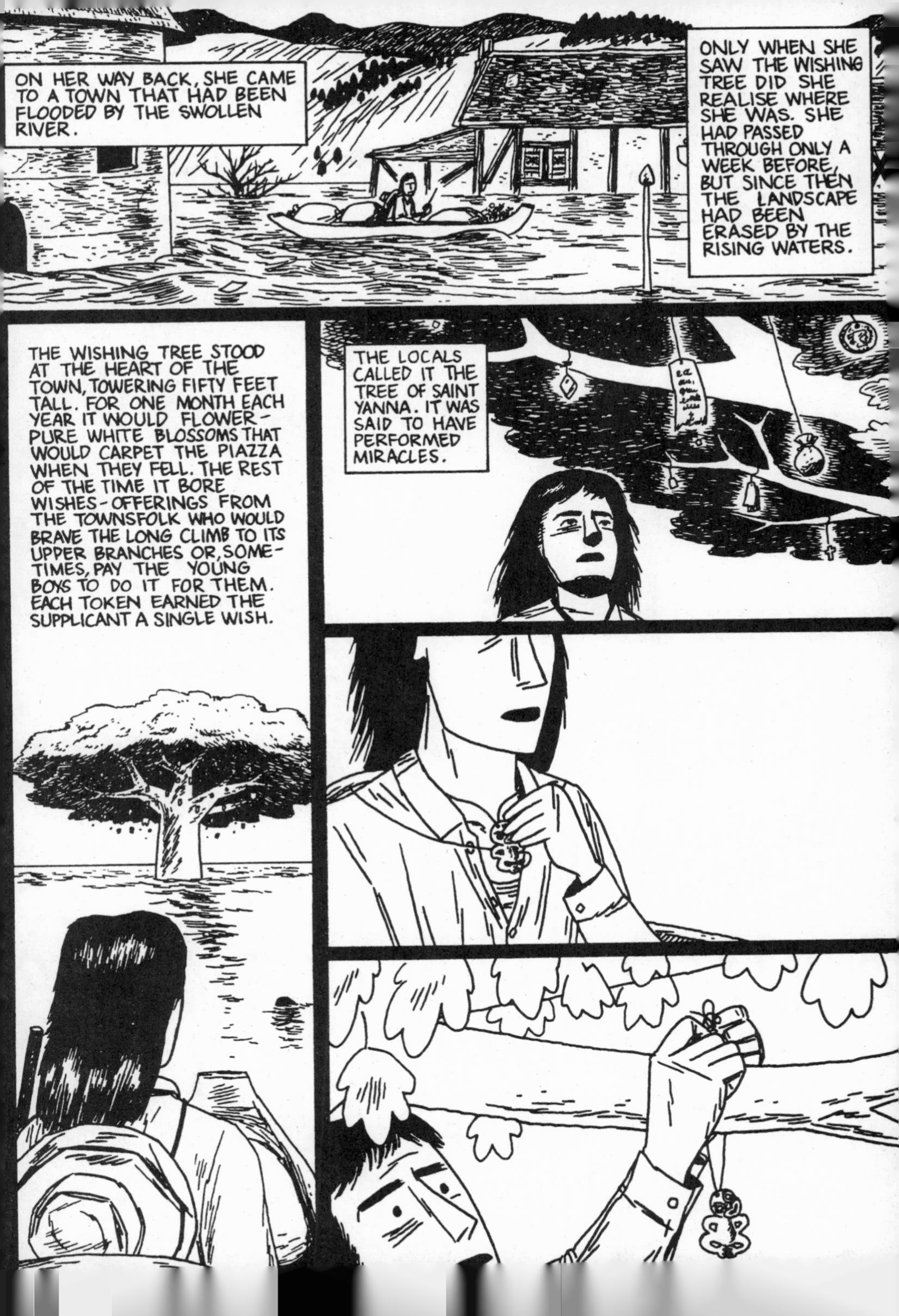
ON HER WAY BACK, SHE CAME TO A TOWN THAT HAD BEEN FLOODED BY THE SWOLLEN RIVER.
ONLY WHEN SHE SAW THE WISHING TREE DID SHE REALISE WHERE SHE WAS. SHE HAD PASSED THROUGH ONLY A WEEK BEFORE, BUT SINCE THEN THE LANDSCAPE HAD BEEN ERASED BY THE RISING WATERS.
THE WISHING TREE STOOD AT THE HEART OF THE TOWN, TOWERING FIFTY FEET TALL. FOR ONE MONTH EACH YEAR IT WOULD FLOWER-PURE WHITE BLOSSOMS THAT WOULD CARPET THE PIAZZA WHEN THEY FELL. THE REST OF THE TIME IT BORE WISHES-OFFERINGS FROM THE TOWNSFOLK WHO WOULD BRAVE THE LONG CLIMB TO ITS UPPER BRANCHES OR, SOMETIMES, PAY THE YOUNG BOYS TO DO IT FOR THEM. EACH TOKEN EARNED THE SUPPLICANT A SINGLE WISH.
THE LOCALS CALLED IT THE TREE OF SAINT YANNA. IT WAS SAID TO HAVE PERFORMED MIRACLES.

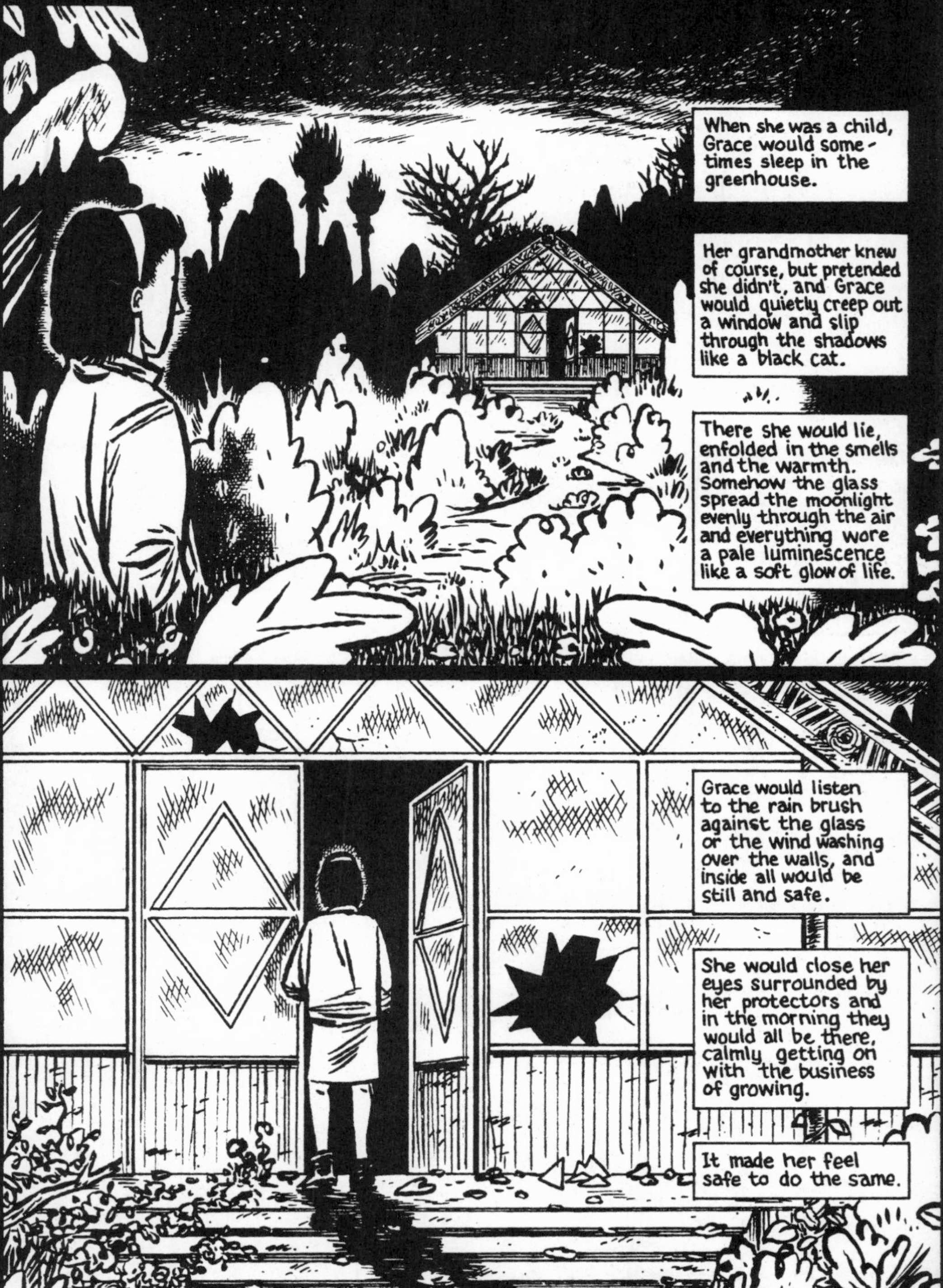
When she was a child, Grace would some-times sleep in the greenhouse.
Her grandmother knew of course, but pretended she didn't, and Grace would quietly creep out a window and slip through the shadows like a black cat.
There she would lie, enfolded in the smells and the warmth. Somehow the glass spread the moonlight evenly through the air and everything wore a pale luminescence like a soft glow of life.
Grace would listen to the rain brush against the glass or the wind washing over the walls, and inside all would be still and safe.
She would close her eyes surrounded by her protectors and in the morning they would all be there, calmly getting on with the business of growing.
It made her feel safe to do the same.

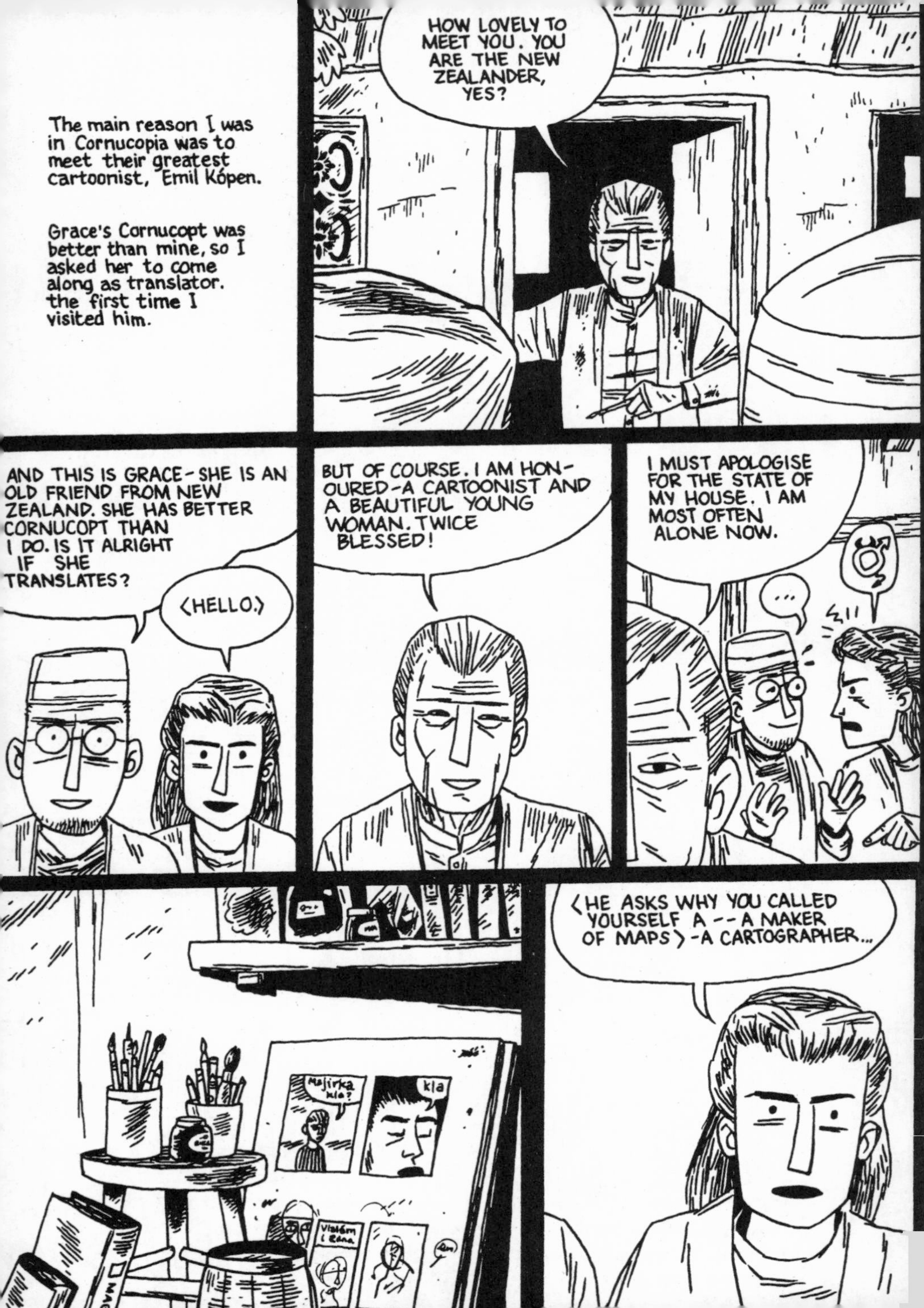
The main reason I was in Cornucopia was to meet their greatest cartoonist, Emil Kópen.
Grace's Cornucopt was better than mine, so I asked her to come along as translator. the first time I visited him.
HOW LOVELY TO MEET YOU. YOU ARE THE NEW ZEALANDER, YES?
AND THIS IS GRACE- SHE IS AN OLD FRIEND FROM NEW ZEALAND. SHE HAS BETTER CORNUCOPT THAN I DO. IS IT ALRIGHT IF SHE TRANSLATES?
<HELLO.>
BUT OF COURSE. I AM HONOURED-A CARTOONIST AND A BEAUTIFUL YOUNG WOMAN. TWICE BLESSED!
I MUST APOLOGISE FOR THE STATE OF MY HOUSE. I AM MOST OFTEN ALONE NOW.
...
kla
<HE ASKS WHY YOU CALLED YOURSELF A -- A MAKER OF MAPS> -A CARTOGRAPHER...

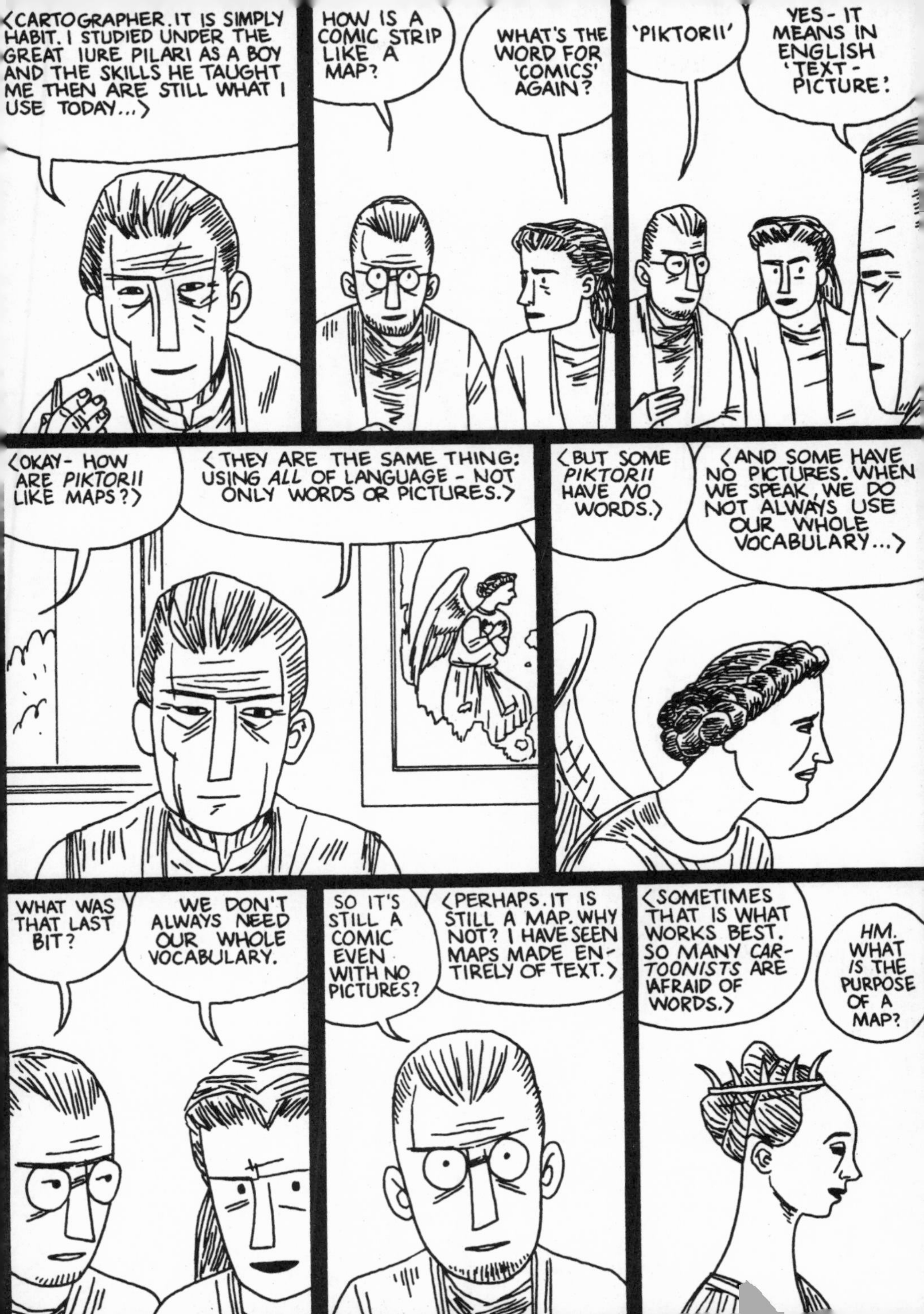
<CARTOGRAPHER. IT IS SIMPLY HABIT. I STUDIED UNDER THE GREAT IURE PILARI AS A BOY AND THE SKILLS HE TAUGHT ME THEN ARE STILL WHAT I USE TODAY...>
HOW IS A COMIC STRIP LIKE A MAP?
WHAT'S THE WORD FOR 'COMICS' AGAIN?
'PIKTORII'
YES - IT MEANS IN ENGLISH 'TEXT - PICTURE'.
<OKAY - HOW ARE *PIKTORII* LIKE MAPS?>
<THEY ARE THE SAME THING: USING *ALL* OF LANGUAGE - NOT ONLY WORDS OR PICTURES.>
<BUT SOME *PIKTORII* HAVE *NO* WORDS.>
<AND SOME HAVE NO PICTURES. WHEN WE SPEAK, WE DO NOT ALWAYS USE OUR WHOLE VOCABULARY...>
WHAT WAS THAT LAST BIT?
WE DON'T ALWAYS NEED OUR WHOLE VOCABULARY.
SO IT'S STILL A COMIC EVEN WITH NO PICTURES?
<PERHAPS. IT IS STILL A MAP. WHY NOT? I HAVE SEEN MAPS MADE ENTIRELY OF TEXT.>
<SOMETIMES THAT IS WHAT WORKS BEST. SO MANY *CARTOONISTS* ARE AFRAID OF WORDS.>
HM. WHAT *IS* THE PURPOSE OF A MAP?

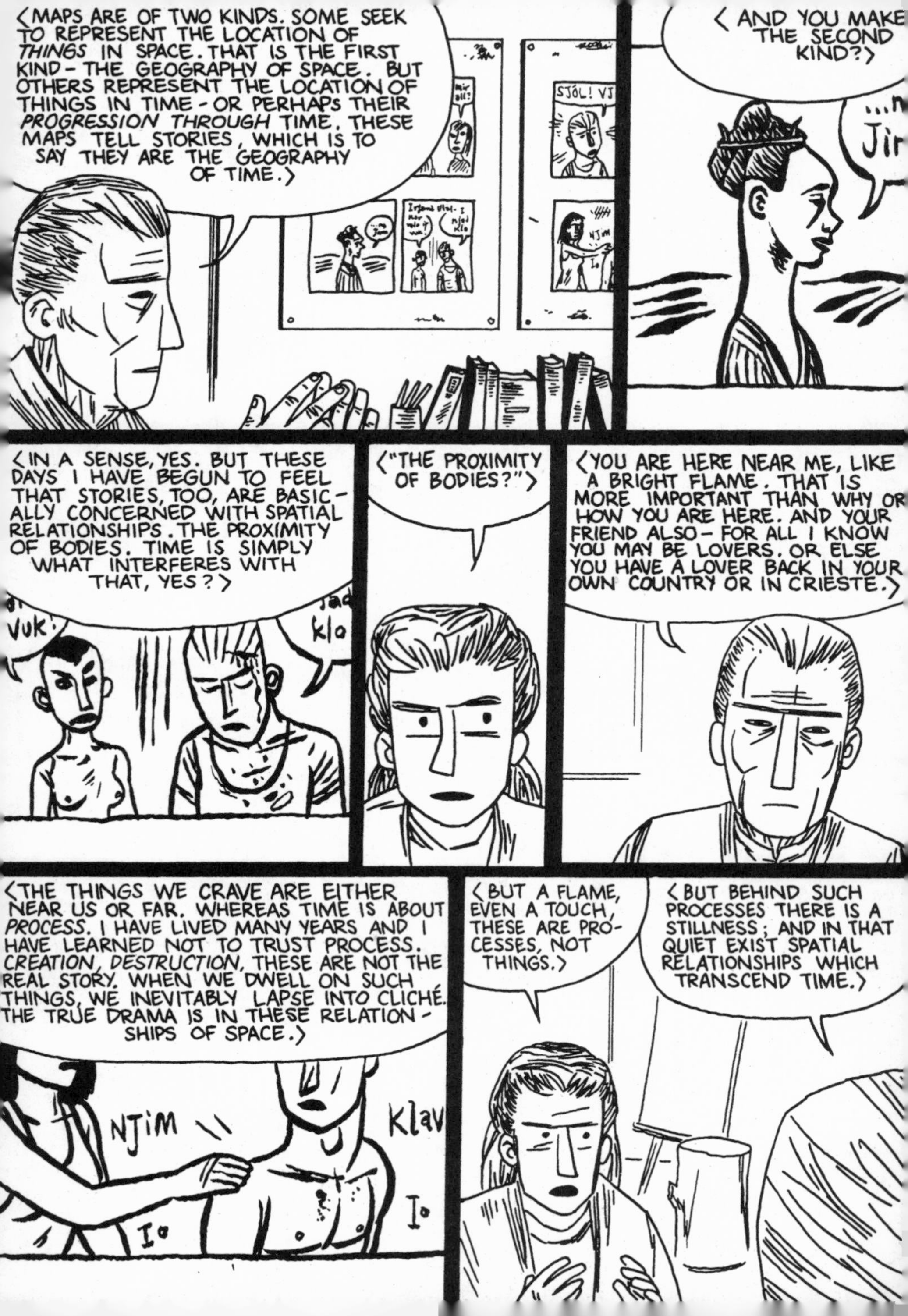
<MAPS ARE OF TWO KINDS. SOME SEEK TO REPRESENT THE LOCATION OF *THINGS* IN SPACE. THAT IS THE FIRST KIND – THE GEOGRAPHY OF SPACE. BUT OTHERS REPRESENT THE LOCATION OF THINGS IN TIME – OR PERHAPS THEIR *PROGRESSION THROUGH* TIME. THESE MAPS TELL STORIES, WHICH IS TO SAY THEY ARE THE GEOGRAPHY OF TIME.>
SJÓL! VJ
NJim
Io
< AND YOU MAKE THE SECOND KIND?>
...n
Jir
<IN A SENSE, YES. BUT THESE DAYS I HAVE BEGUN TO FEEL THAT STORIES, TOO, ARE BASICALLY CONCERNED WITH SPATIAL RELATIONSHIPS. THE PROXIMITY OF BODIES. TIME IS SIMPLY WHAT INTERFERES WITH THAT, YES?>
Vuk!
klo
<"THE PROXIMITY OF BODIES?">
<YOU ARE HERE NEAR ME, LIKE A BRIGHT FLAME. THAT IS MORE IMPORTANT THAN WHY OR HOW YOU ARE HERE. AND YOUR FRIEND ALSO – FOR ALL I KNOW YOU MAY BE LOVERS. OR ELSE YOU HAVE A LOVER BACK IN YOUR OWN COUNTRY OR IN CRIESTE.>
<THE THINGS WE CRAVE ARE EITHER NEAR US OR FAR. WHEREAS TIME IS ABOUT *PROCESS*. I HAVE LIVED MANY YEARS AND I HAVE LEARNED NOT TO TRUST PROCESS. *CREATION*, *DESTRUCTION*, THESE ARE NOT THE REAL STORY. WHEN WE DWELL ON SUCH THINGS, WE INEVITABLY LAPSE INTO CLICHÉ. THE TRUE DRAMA IS IN THESE RELATIONSHIPS OF SPACE.>
NJim
Klav
Io
Io
< BUT A FLAME, EVEN A TOUCH, THESE ARE PROCESSES, NOT THINGS.>
< BUT BEHIND SUCH PROCESSES THERE IS A STILLNESS; AND IN THAT QUIET EXIST SPATIAL RELATIONSHIPS WHICH TRANSCEND TIME.>

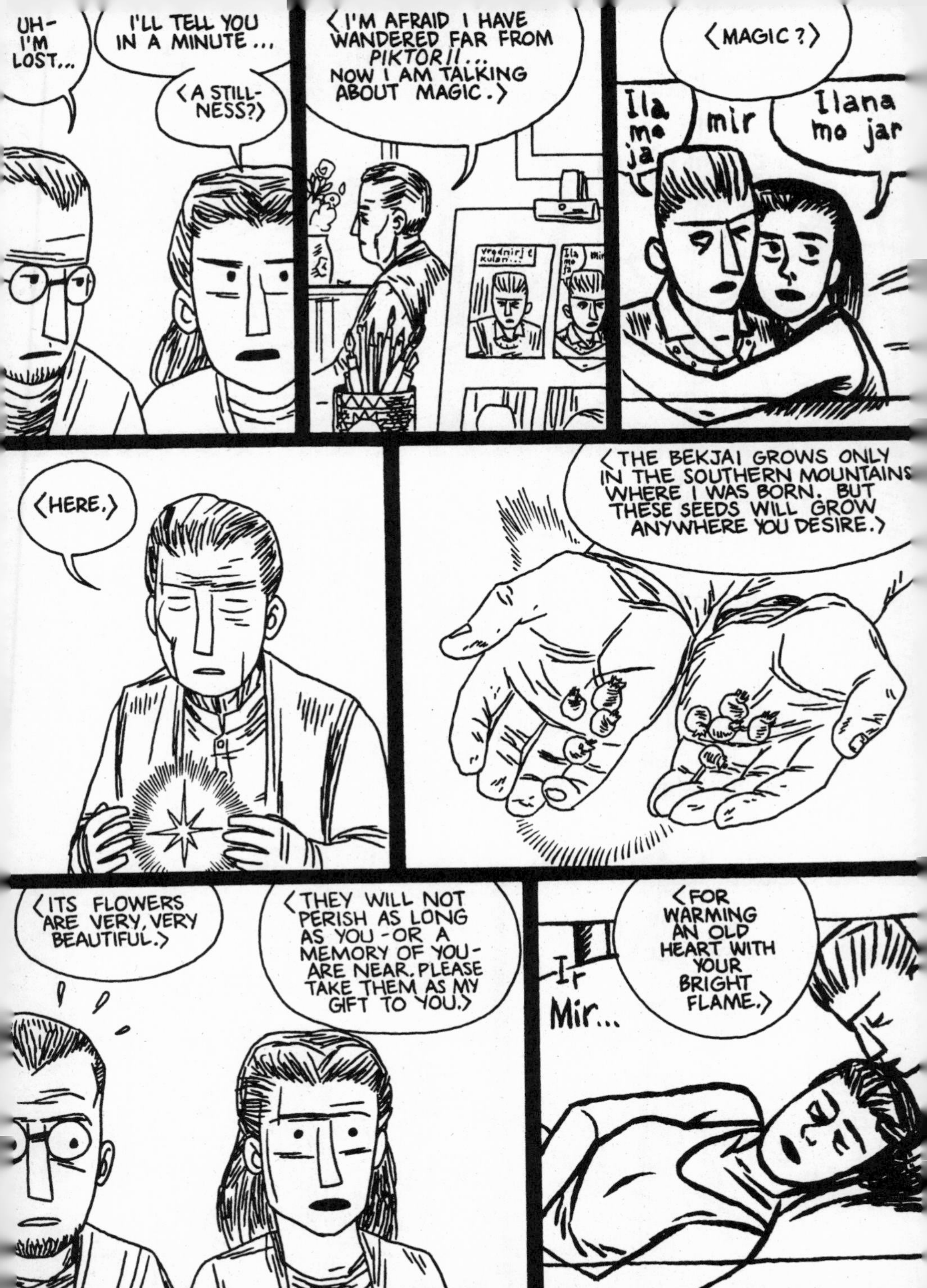
UH-
I'M
LOST...
I'LL TELL YOU
IN A MINUTE...
<A STILL-
NESS?>
<I'M AFRAID I HAVE
WANDERED FAR FROM
PIKTORII...
NOW I AM TALKING
ABOUT MAGIC.>
<MAGIC?>
Ila
mo
ja
mir
Ilana
mo jar
<HERE.>
<THE BEKJAI GROWS ONLY
IN THE SOUTHERN MOUNTAINS
WHERE I WAS BORN. BUT
THESE SEEDS WILL GROW
ANYWHERE YOU DESIRE.>
<ITS FLOWERS
ARE VERY, VERY
BEAUTIFUL.>
<THEY WILL NOT
PERISH AS LONG
AS YOU - OR A
MEMORY OF YOU -
ARE NEAR. PLEASE
TAKE THEM AS MY
GIFT TO YOU.>
Ir
Mir...
<FOR
WARMING
AN OLD
HEART WITH
YOUR
BRIGHT
FLAME.>

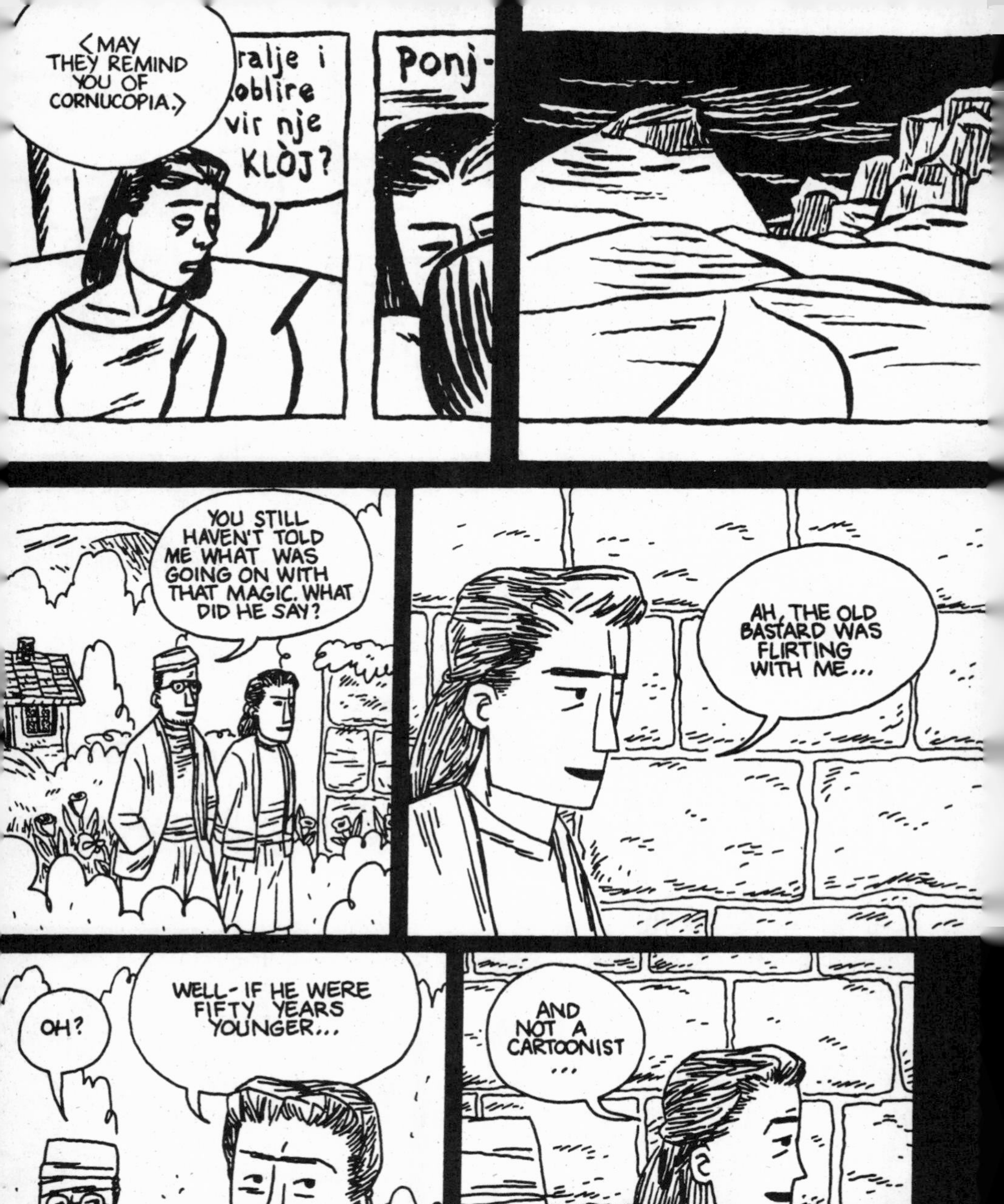
<MAY THEY REMIND YOU OF CORNUCOPIA.>
ralje i oblire vir nje KLÒJ?
Ponj-
YOU STILL HAVEN'T TOLD ME WHAT WAS GOING ON WITH THAT MAGIC. WHAT DID HE SAY?
AH, THE OLD BASTARD WAS FLIRTING WITH ME...
OH?
WELL- IF HE WERE FIFTY YEARS YOUNGER...
AND NOT A CARTOONIST ...

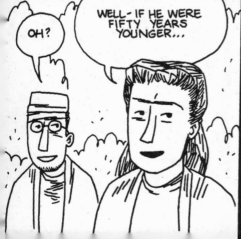

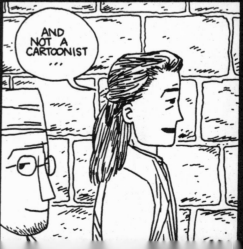

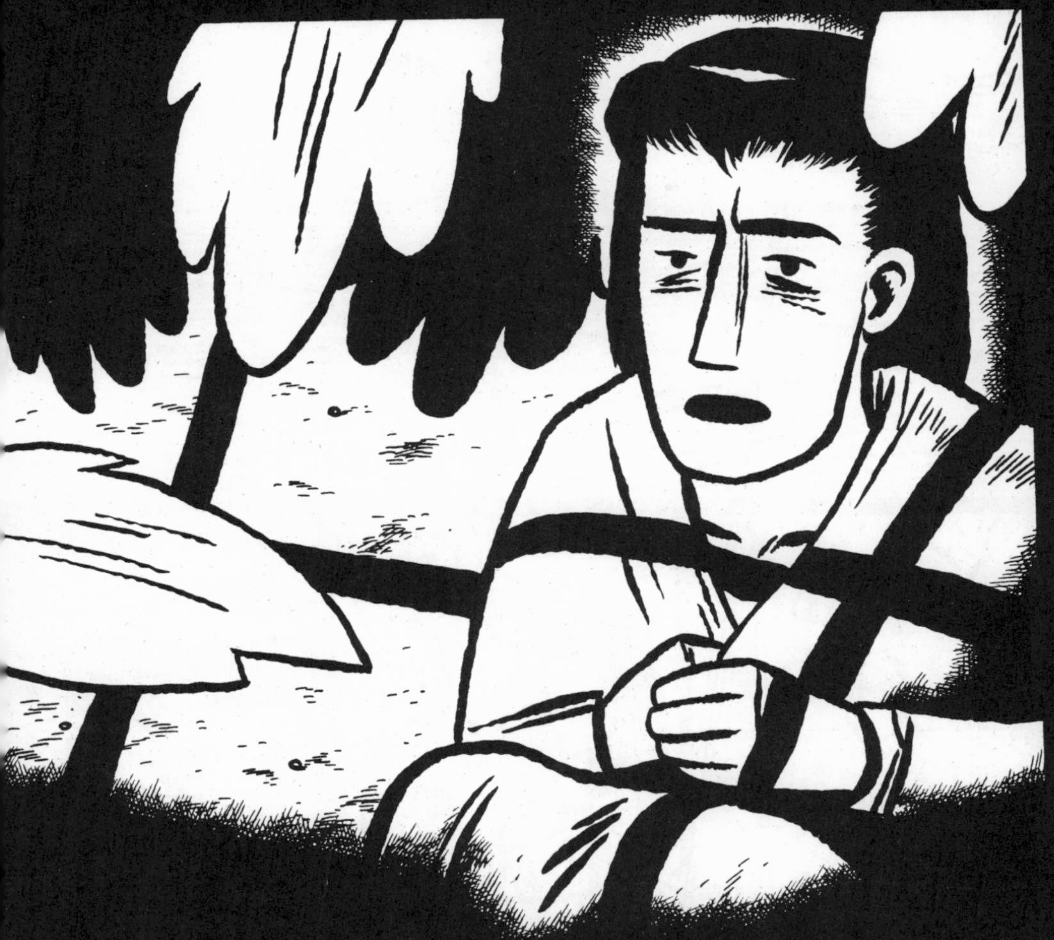

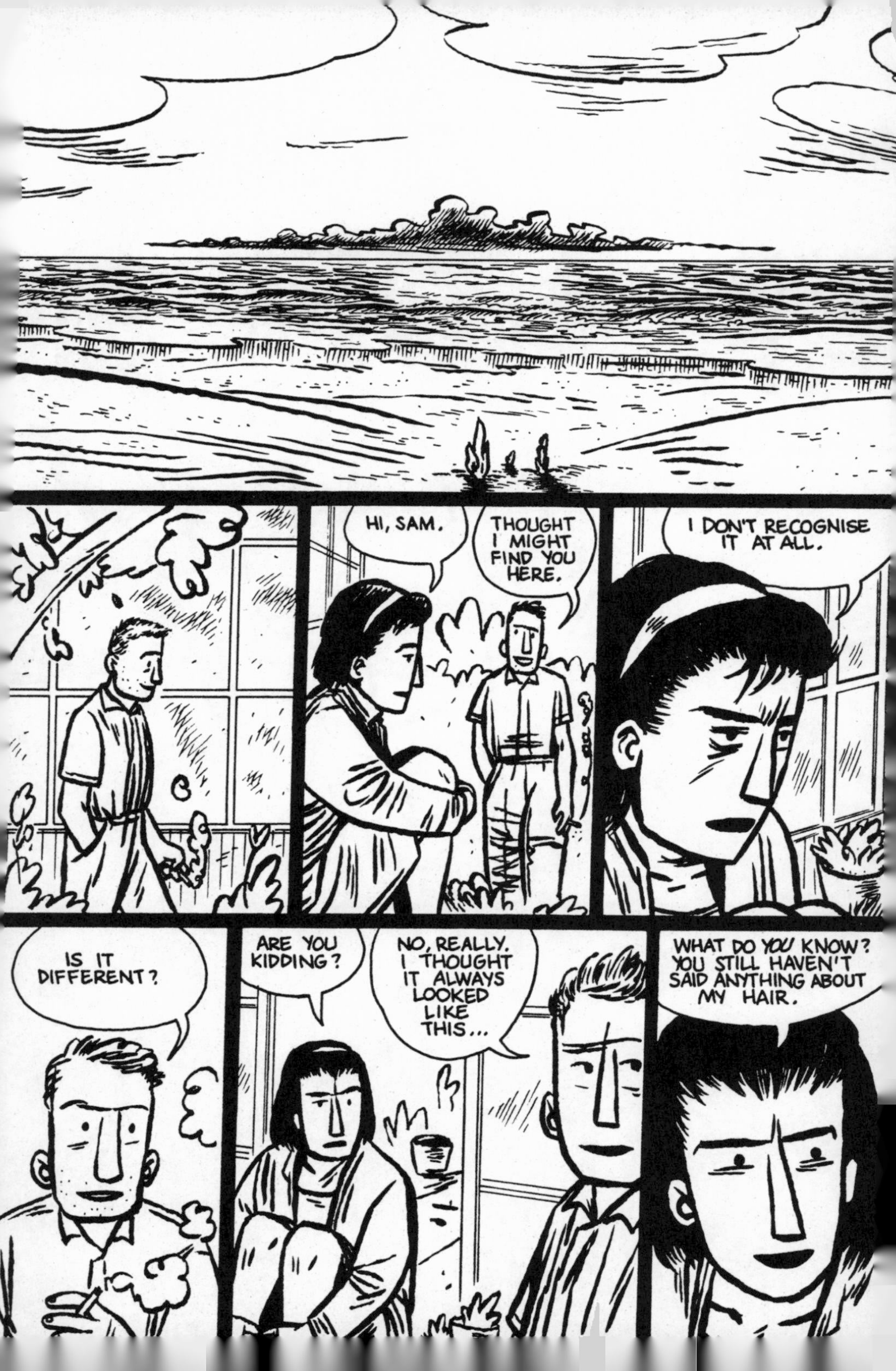
HI, SAM.
THOUGHT I MIGHT FIND YOU HERE.
I DON'T RECOGNISE IT AT ALL.
IS IT DIFFERENT?
ARE YOU KIDDING?
NO, REALLY. I THOUGHT IT ALWAYS LOOKED LIKE THIS...
WHAT DO *YOU* KNOW? YOU STILL HAVEN'T SAID ANYTHING ABOUT MY HAIR.

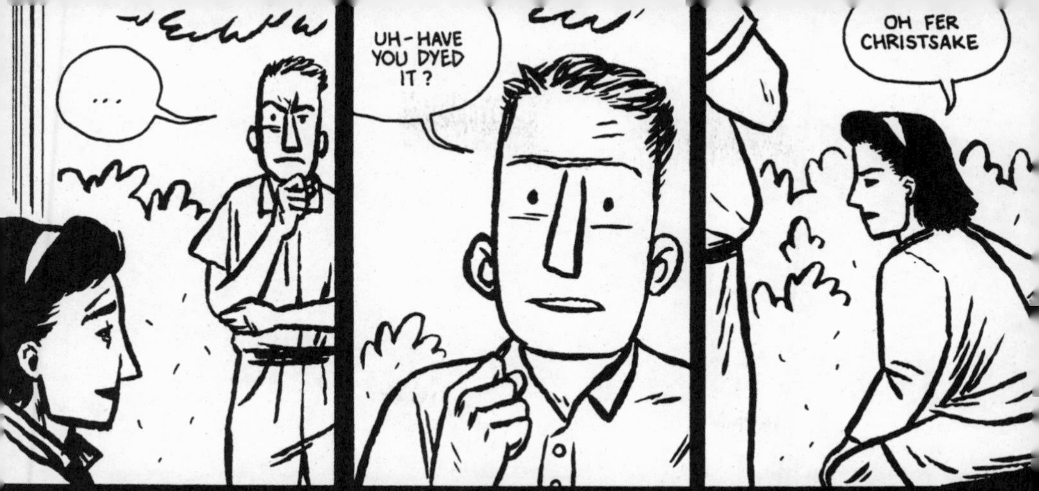
...
UH-HAVE YOU DYED IT?
OH FER CHRISTSAKE

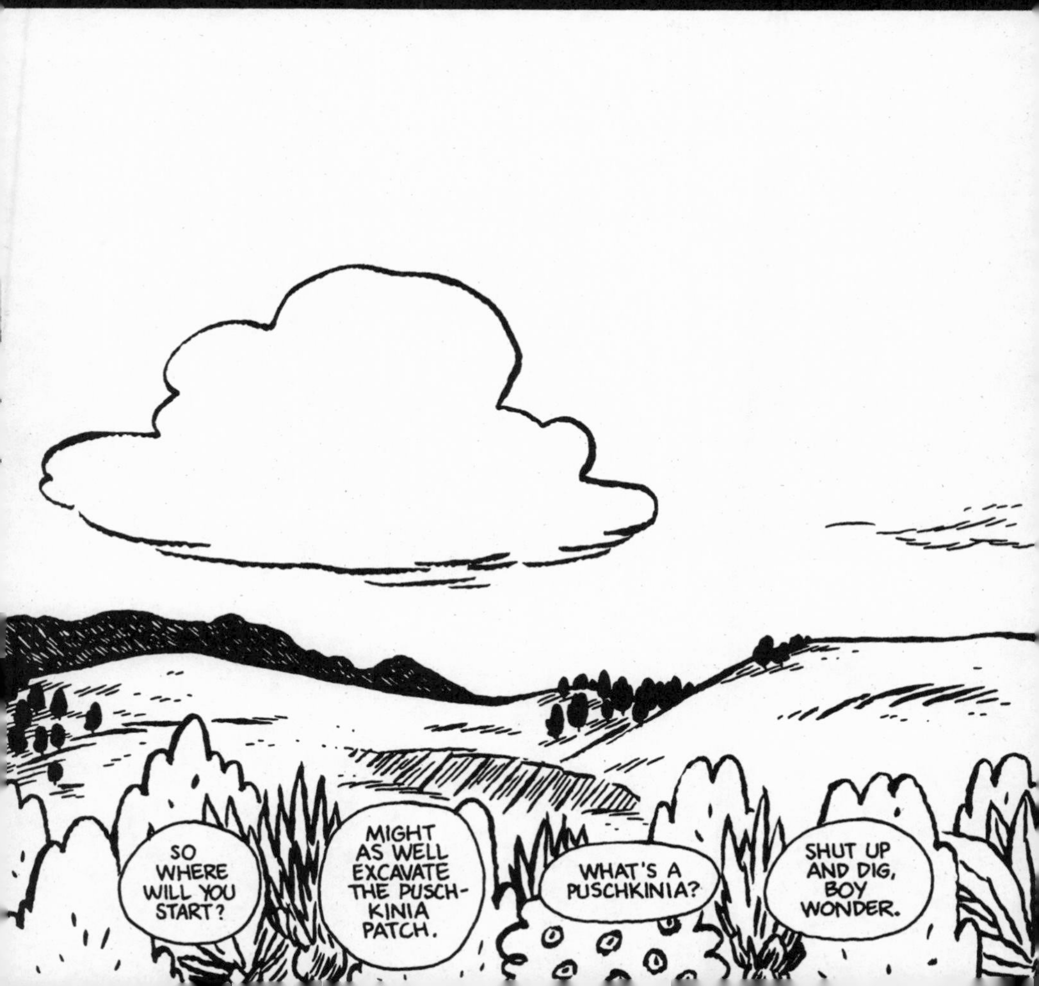
SO WHERE WILL YOU START?
MIGHT AS WELL EXCAVATE THE PUSCH-KINIA PATCH.
WHAT'S A PUSCHKINIA?
SHUT UP AND DIG, BOY WONDER.

Chapter Five

"We can't keep putting out this crap for very long."

Martin Goodman, founder of Marvel Comics, c. 1939.

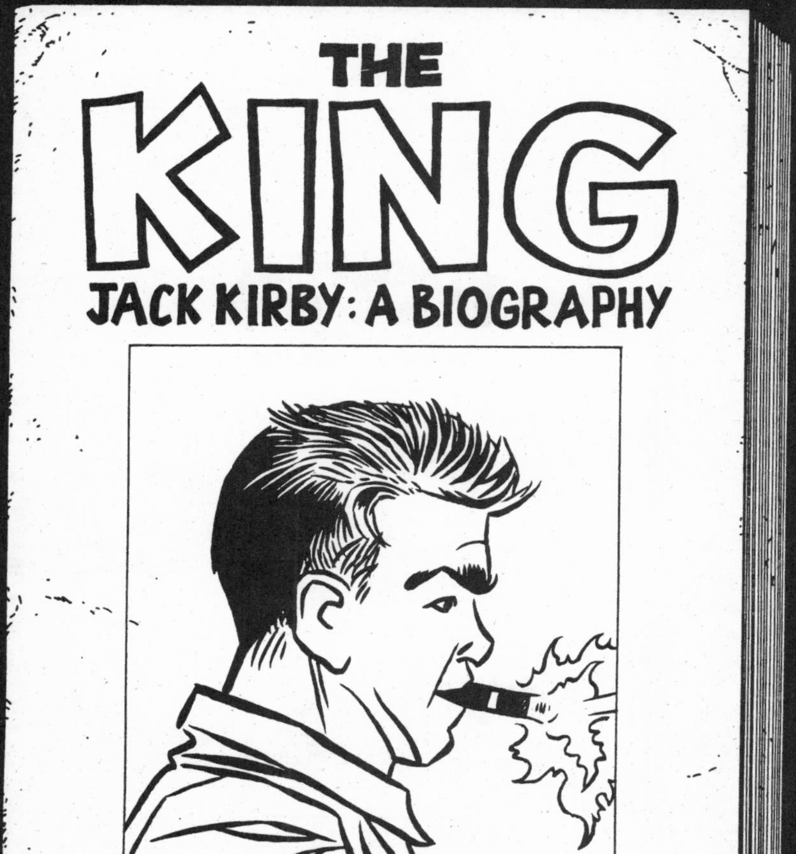
THE KING
JACK KIRBY: A BIOGRAPHY
LEONARD BATTS

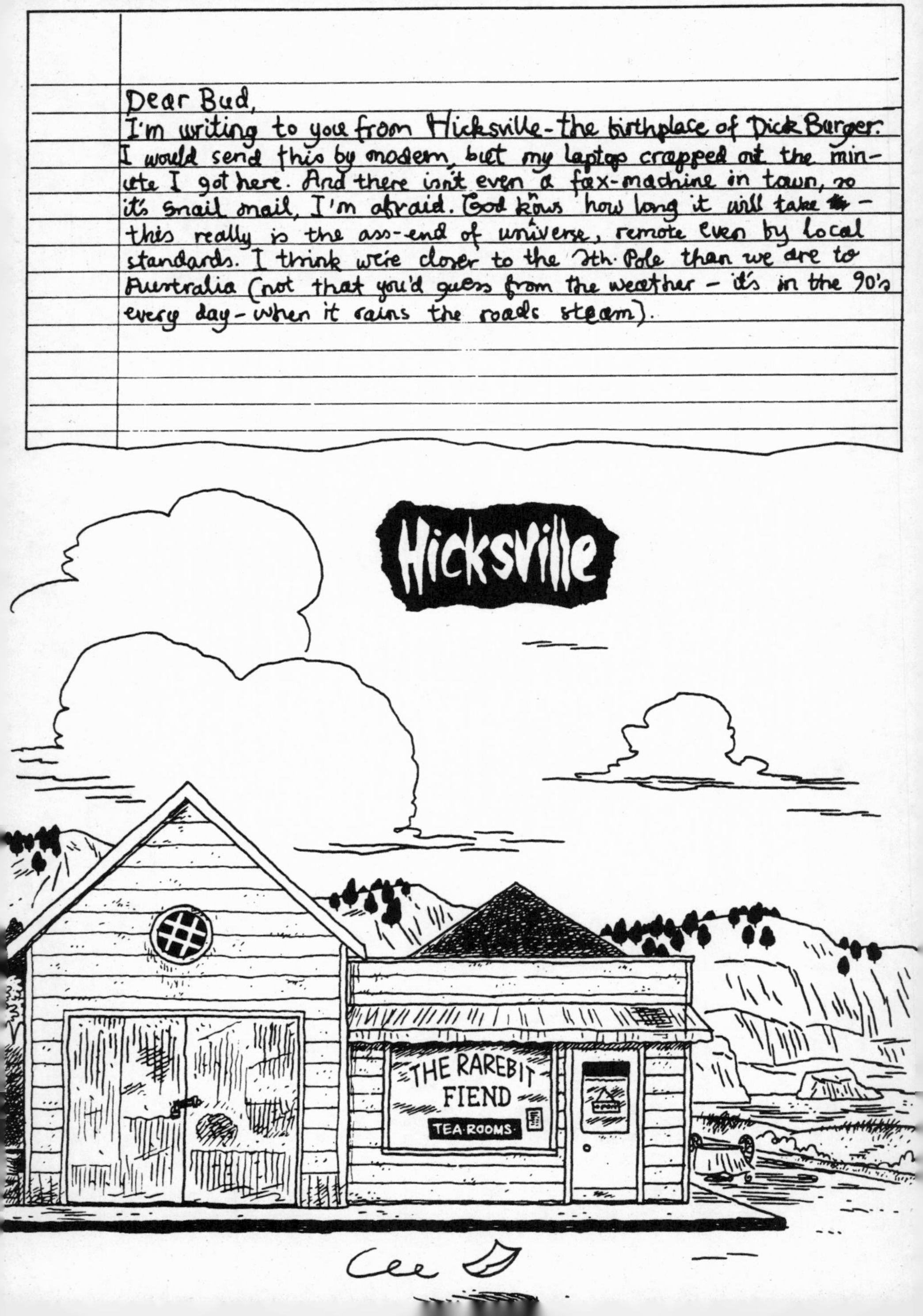
Dear Bud,
I'm writing to you from Hicksville - the birthplace of Dick Burger. I would send this by modem, but my laptop crapped out the minute I got here. And there isn't even a fax-machine in town, so it's snail mail, I'm afraid. God knows how long it will take - this really is the ass-end of universe, remote even by local standards. I think we're closer to the Sth. Pole than we are to Australia (not that you'd guess from the weather - it's in the 90's every day - when it rains the roads steam).
Hicksville
THE RAREBIT FIEND
TEA·ROOMS

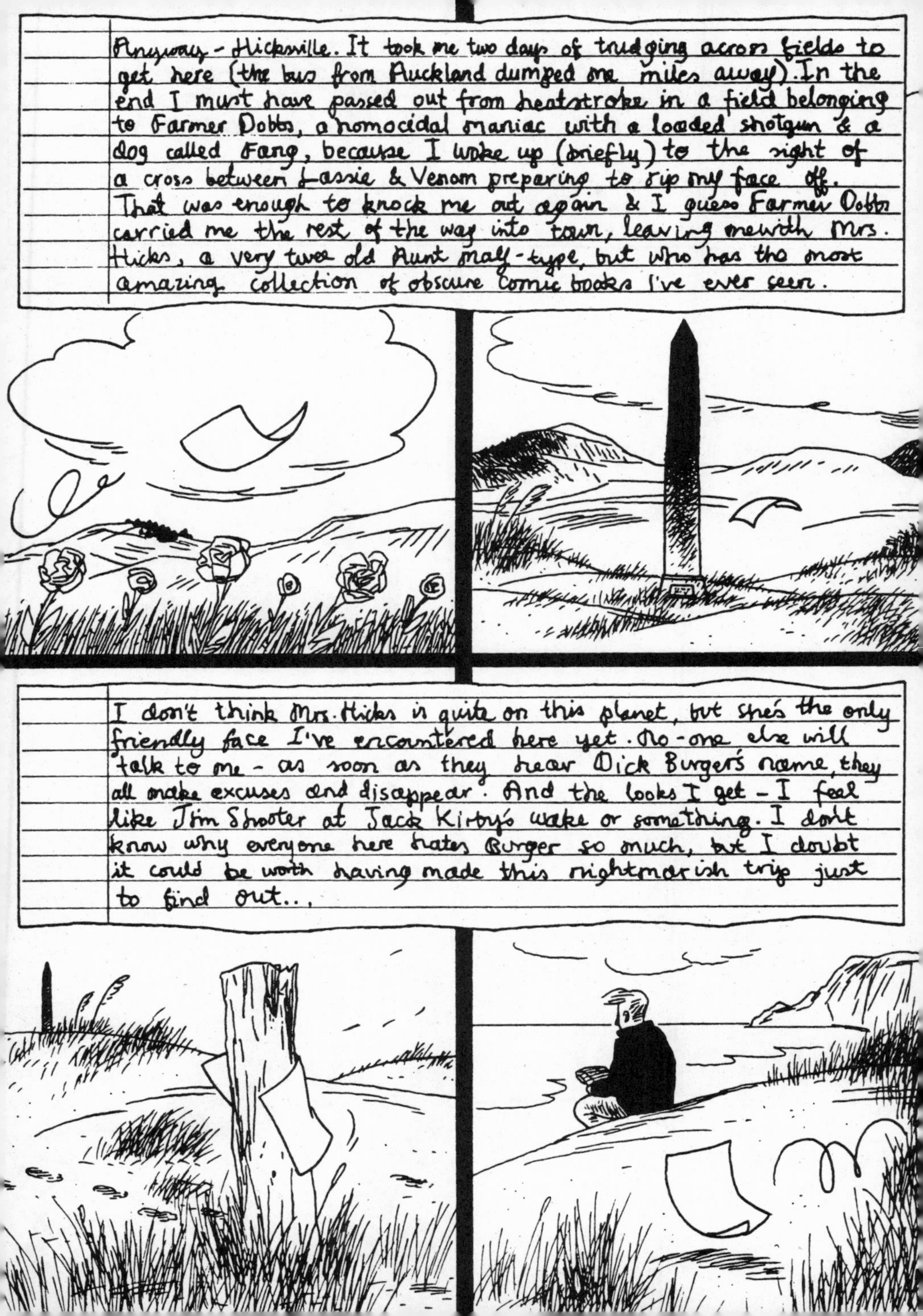
Anyway - Hicksville. It took me two days of trudging across fields to get here (the bus from Auckland dumped me miles away). In the end I must have passed out from heatstroke in a field belonging to Farmer Dobbs, a homocidal maniac with a loaded shotgun & a dog called Fang, because I woke up (briefly) to the sight of a cross between Lassie & Venom preparing to rip my face off. That was enough to knock me out again & I guess Farmer Dobbs carried me the rest of the way into town, leaving me with Mrs. Hicks, a very twee old Aunt May-type, but who has the most amazing collection of obscure comic books I've ever seen.
I don't think Mrs. Hicks is quite on this planet, but she's the only friendly face I've encountered here yet. No-one else will talk to me - as soon as they hear Dick Burger's name, they all make excuses and disappear. And the looks I get - I feel like Jim Shooter at Jack Kirby's wake or something. I don't know why everyone here hates Burger so much, but I doubt it could be worth having made this nightmarish trip just to find out...

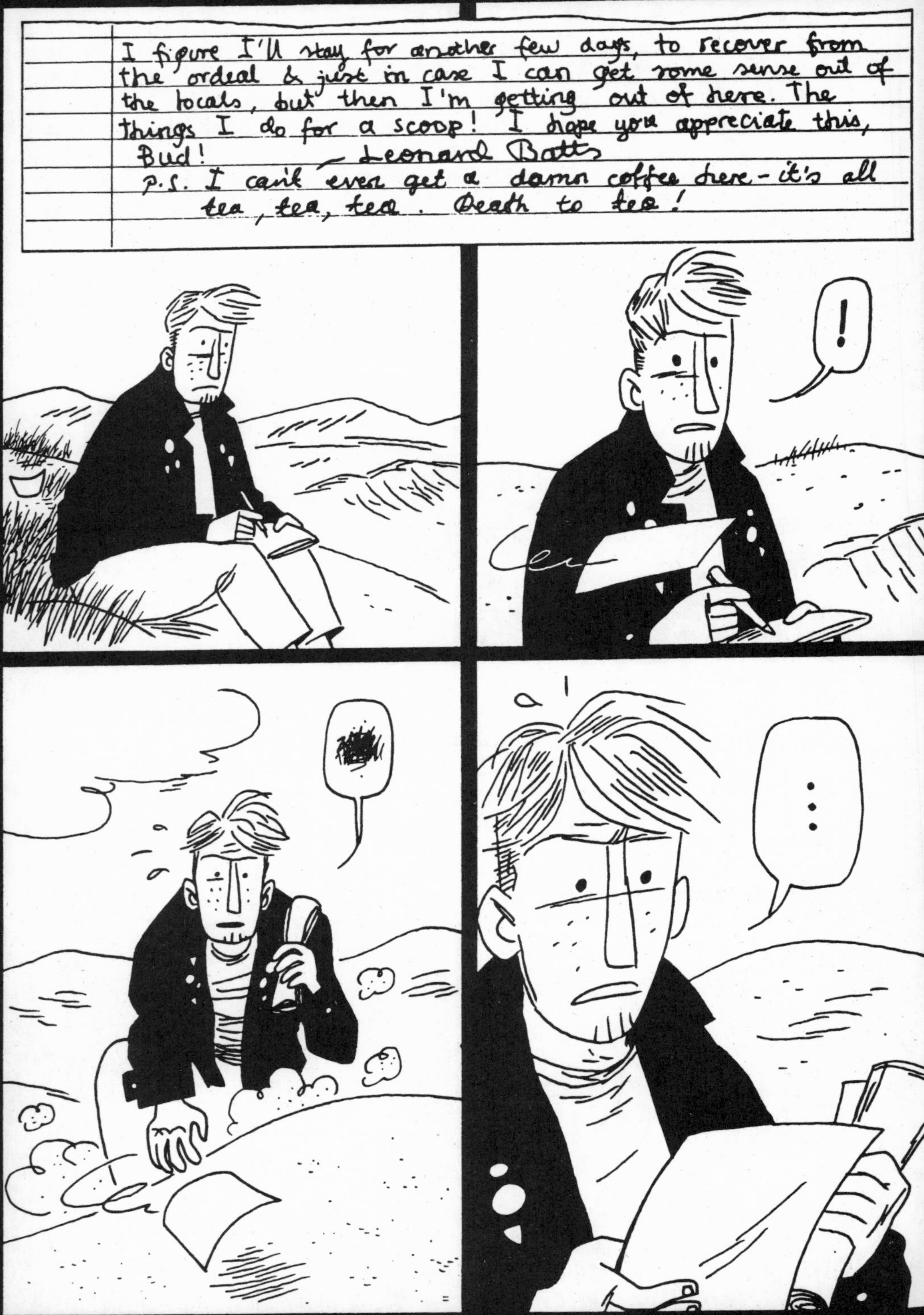
I figure I'll stay for another few days, to recover from the ordeal & just in case I can get some sense out of the locals, but then I'm getting out of here. The things I do for a scoop! I hope you appreciate this, Bud! — Leonard Batts
P.S. I can't even get a damn coffee here - it's all tea, tea, tea. Death to tea!
!
...

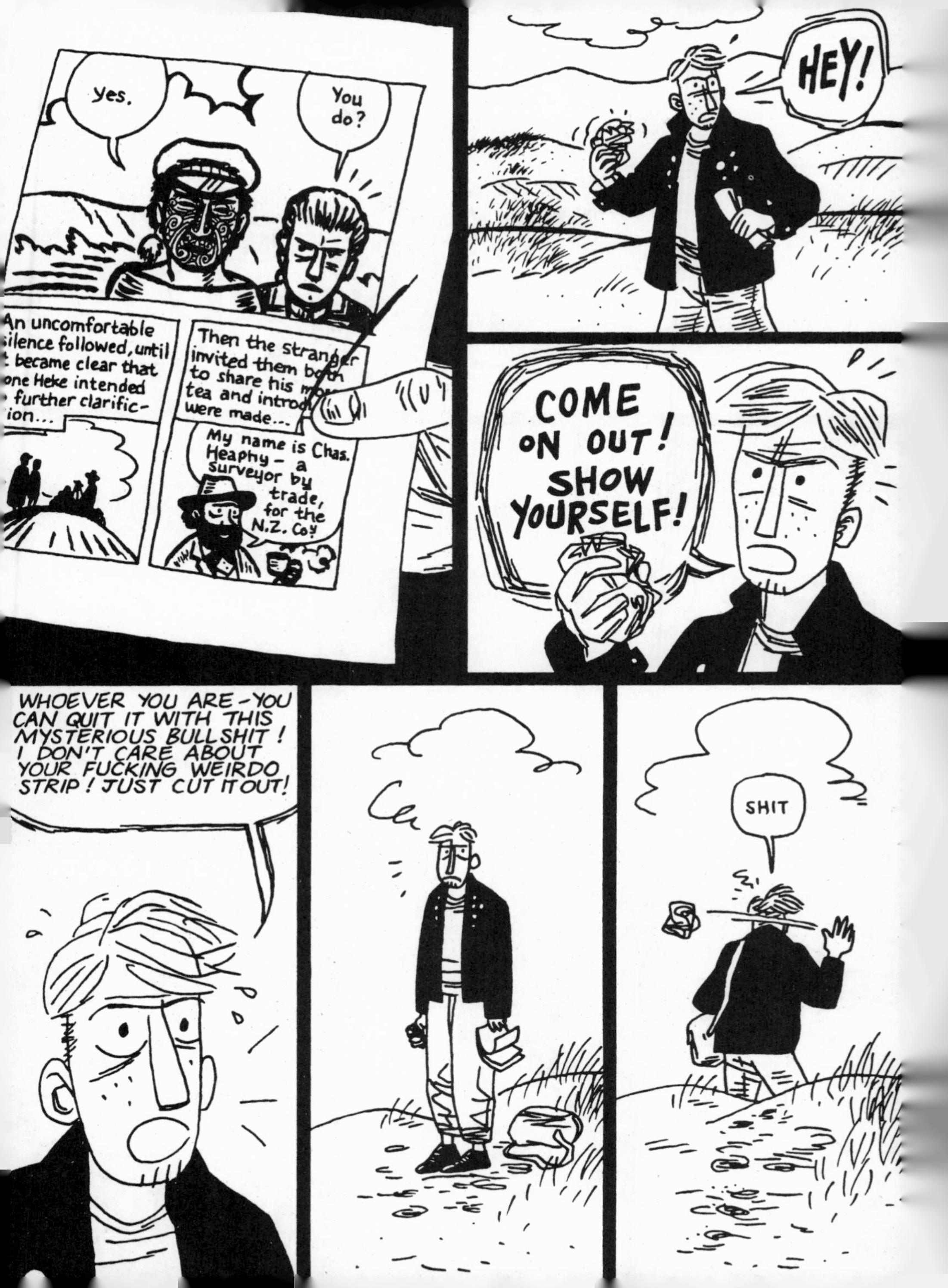
yes.
You do?
An uncomfortable
ilence followed, until
: became clear that
one Heke intended
further clarific-
ion...
Then the strang
invited them bo
to share his m
tea and introd
were made...
My name is Chas. Heaphy - a Surveyor by trade, for the N.Z. Coy
HEY!
COME ON OUT! SHOW YOURSELF!
WHOEVER YOU ARE - YOU CAN QUIT IT WITH THIS MYSTERIOUS BULLSHIT! I DON'T CARE ABOUT YOUR FUCKING WEIRDO STRIP! JUST CUT IT OUT!
SHIT

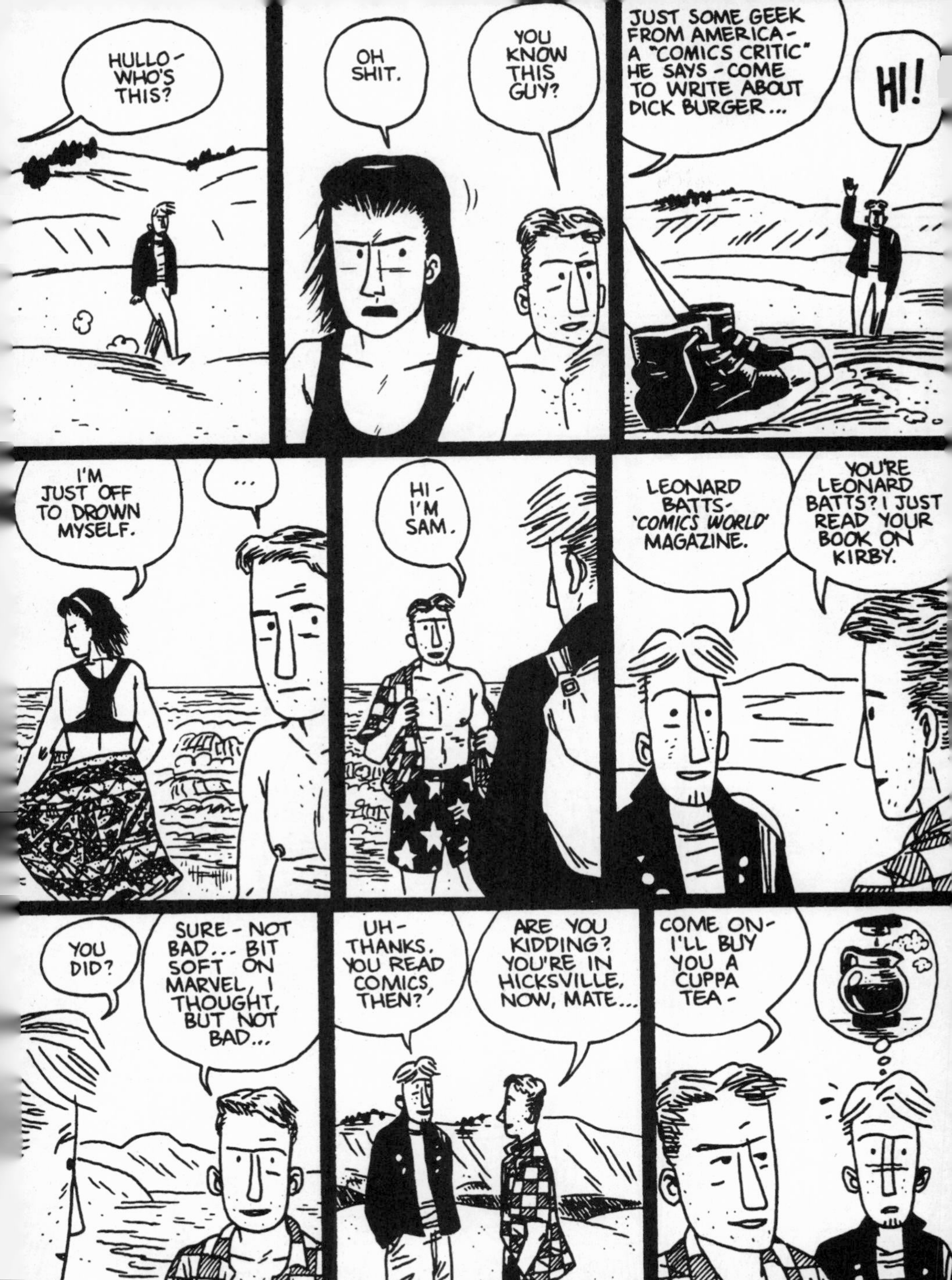
HULLO- WHO'S THIS?
OH SHIT.
YOU KNOW THIS GUY?
JUST SOME GEEK FROM AMERICA - A "COMICS CRITIC" HE SAYS - COME TO WRITE ABOUT DICK BURGER...
HI!
I'M JUST OFF TO DROWN MYSELF.
...
HI- I'M SAM.
LEONARD BATTS- 'COMICS WORLD' MAGAZINE.
YOU'RE LEONARD BATTS? I JUST READ YOUR BOOK ON KIRBY.
YOU DID?
SURE - NOT BAD... BIT SOFT ON MARVEL, I THOUGHT, BUT NOT BAD...
UH- THANKS. YOU READ COMICS, THEN?
ARE YOU KIDDING? YOU'RE IN HICKSVILLE, NOW, MATE...
COME ON- I'LL BUY YOU A CUPPA TEA -

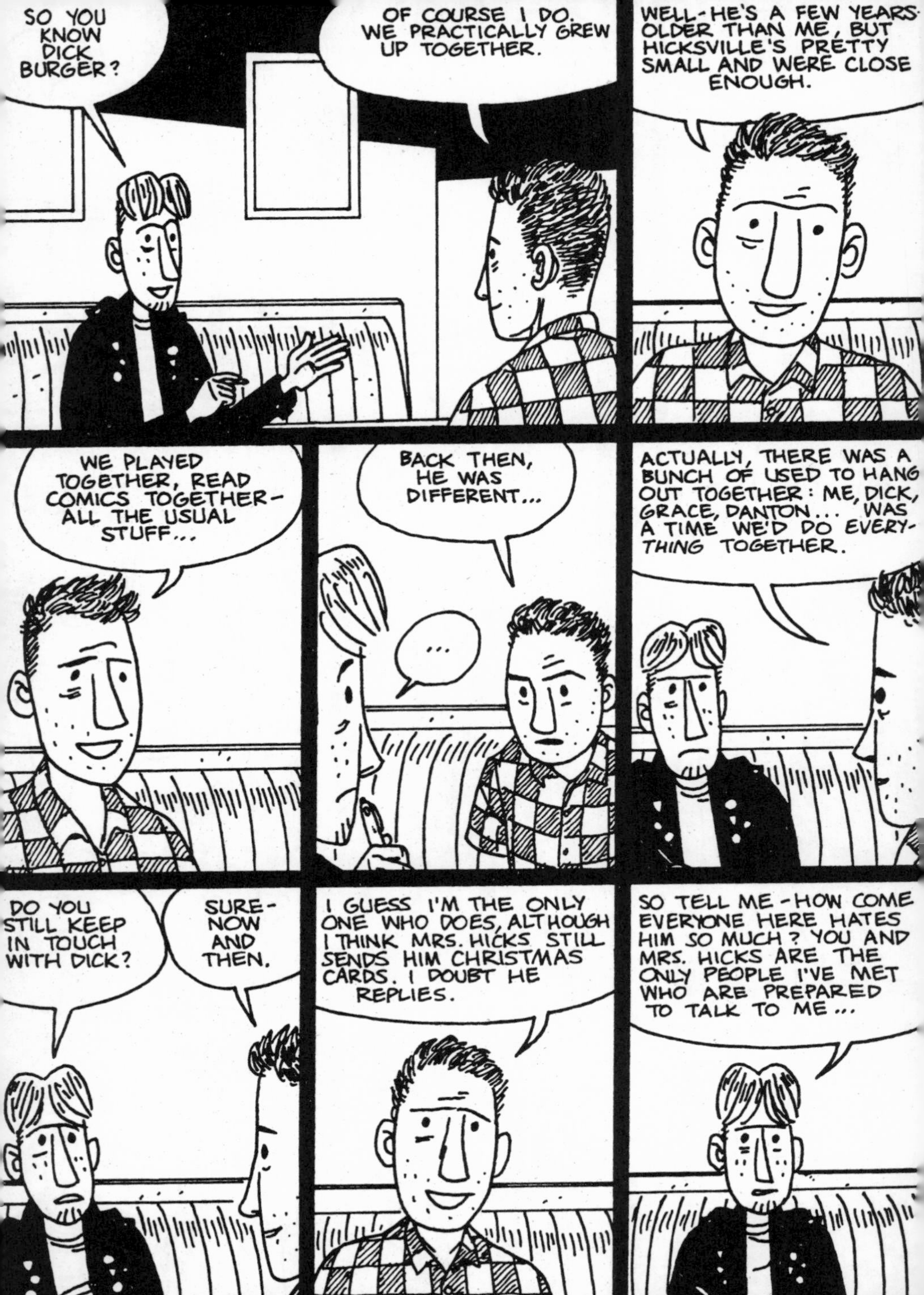
SO YOU KNOW DICK BURGER?
OF COURSE I DO. WE PRACTICALLY GREW UP TOGETHER.
WELL-HE'S A FEW YEARS OLDER THAN ME, BUT HICKSVILLE'S PRETTY SMALL AND WERE CLOSE ENOUGH.
WE PLAYED TOGETHER, READ COMICS TOGETHER-ALL THE USUAL STUFF...
BACK THEN, HE WAS DIFFERENT...
...
ACTUALLY, THERE WAS A BUNCH OF USED TO HANG OUT TOGETHER: ME, DICK, GRACE, DANTON... WAS A TIME WE'D DO EVERYTHING TOGETHER.
DO YOU STILL KEEP IN TOUCH WITH DICK?
SURE-NOW AND THEN.
I GUESS I'M THE ONLY ONE WHO DOES, ALTHOUGH I THINK MRS. HICKS STILL SENDS HIM CHRISTMAS CARDS. I DOUBT HE REPLIES.
SO TELL ME-HOW COME EVERYONE HERE HATES HIM SO MUCH? YOU AND MRS. HICKS ARE THE ONLY PEOPLE I'VE MET WHO ARE PREPARED TO TALK TO ME...

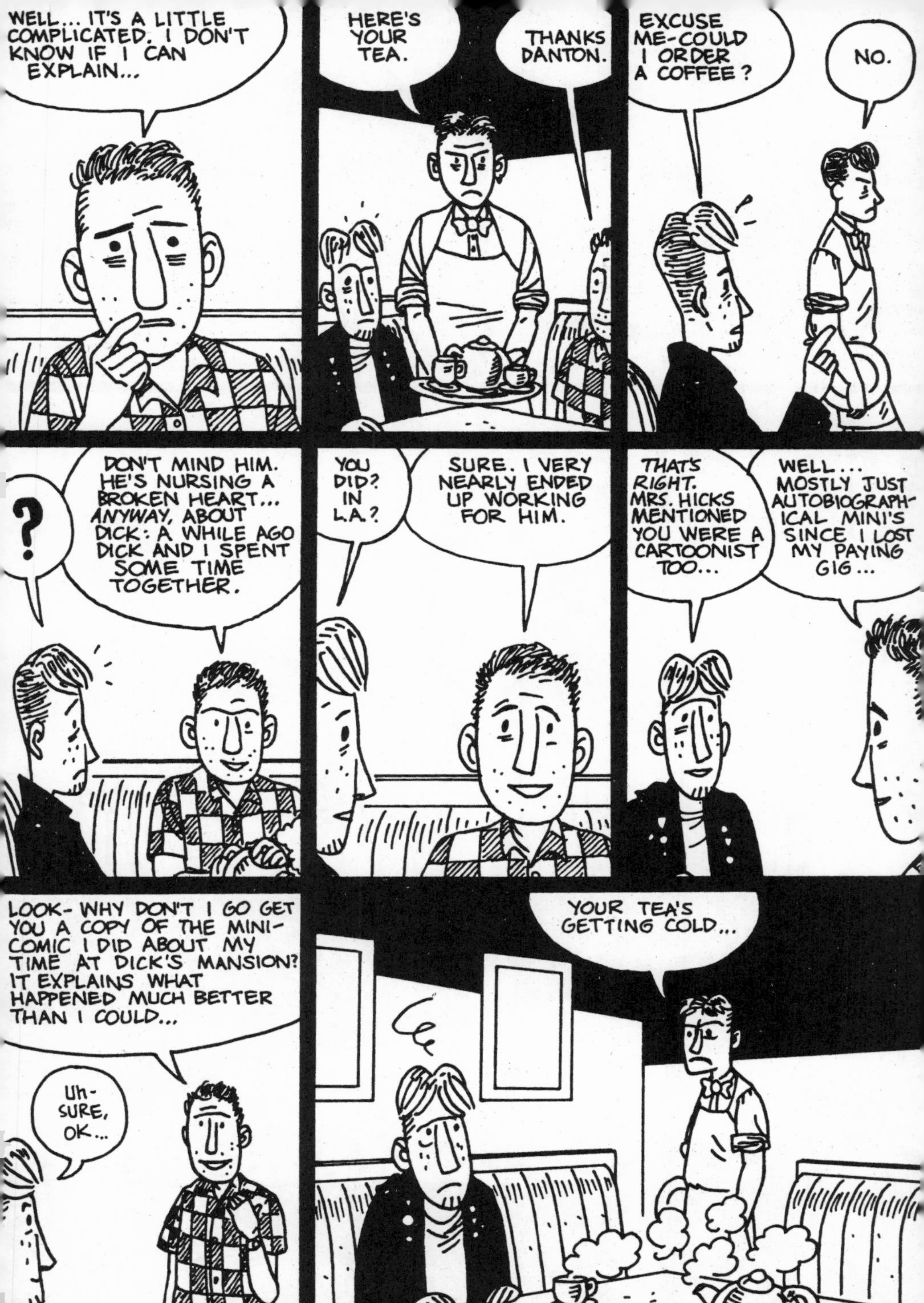
WELL... IT'S A LITTLE COMPLICATED. I DON'T KNOW IF I CAN EXPLAIN...
HERE'S YOUR TEA.
THANKS DANTON.
EXCUSE ME-COULD I ORDER A COFFEE?
NO.
?
DON'T MIND HIM. HE'S NURSING A BROKEN HEART... ANYWAY, ABOUT DICK: A WHILE AGO DICK AND I SPENT SOME TIME TOGETHER.
YOU DID? IN L.A.?
SURE. I VERY NEARLY ENDED UP WORKING FOR HIM.
THAT'S RIGHT. MRS. HICKS MENTIONED YOU WERE A CARTOONIST TOO...
WELL... MOSTLY JUST AUTOBIOGRAPHICAL MINI'S SINCE I LOST MY PAYING GIG...
LOOK- WHY DON'T I GO GET YOU A COPY OF THE MINI-COMIC I DID ABOUT MY TIME AT DICK'S MANSION? IT EXPLAINS WHAT HAPPENED MUCH BETTER THAN I COULD...
Uh-SURE, OK...
YOUR TEA'S GETTING COLD...

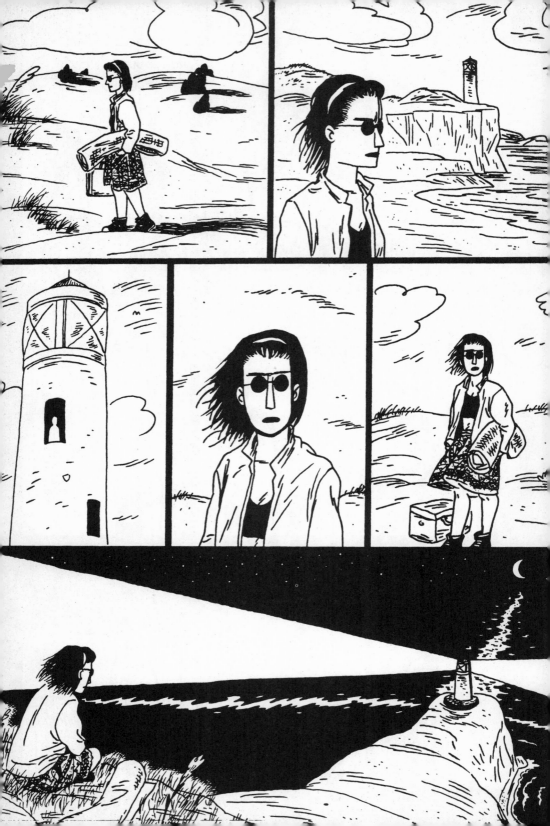

Chapter Six

"Even more than money,
an artist likes to be loved."
Joe Simon.

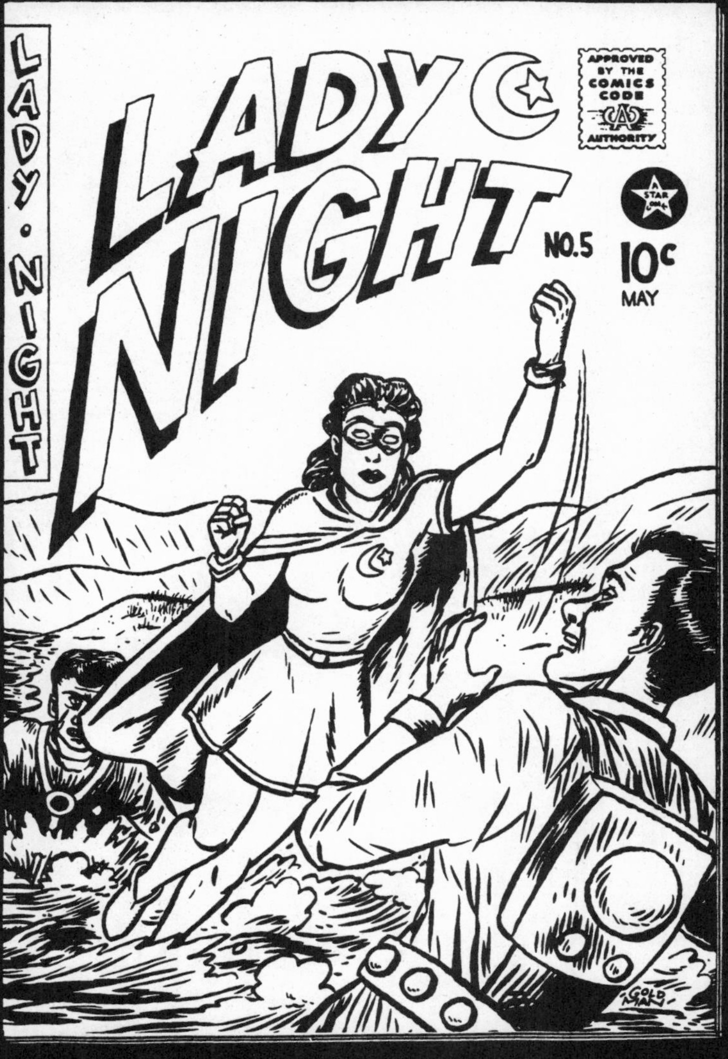
LADY NIGHT
LADY · NIGHT
APPROVED BY THE COMICS CODE AUTHORITY
NO.5
10¢
MAY
GOLDMAN

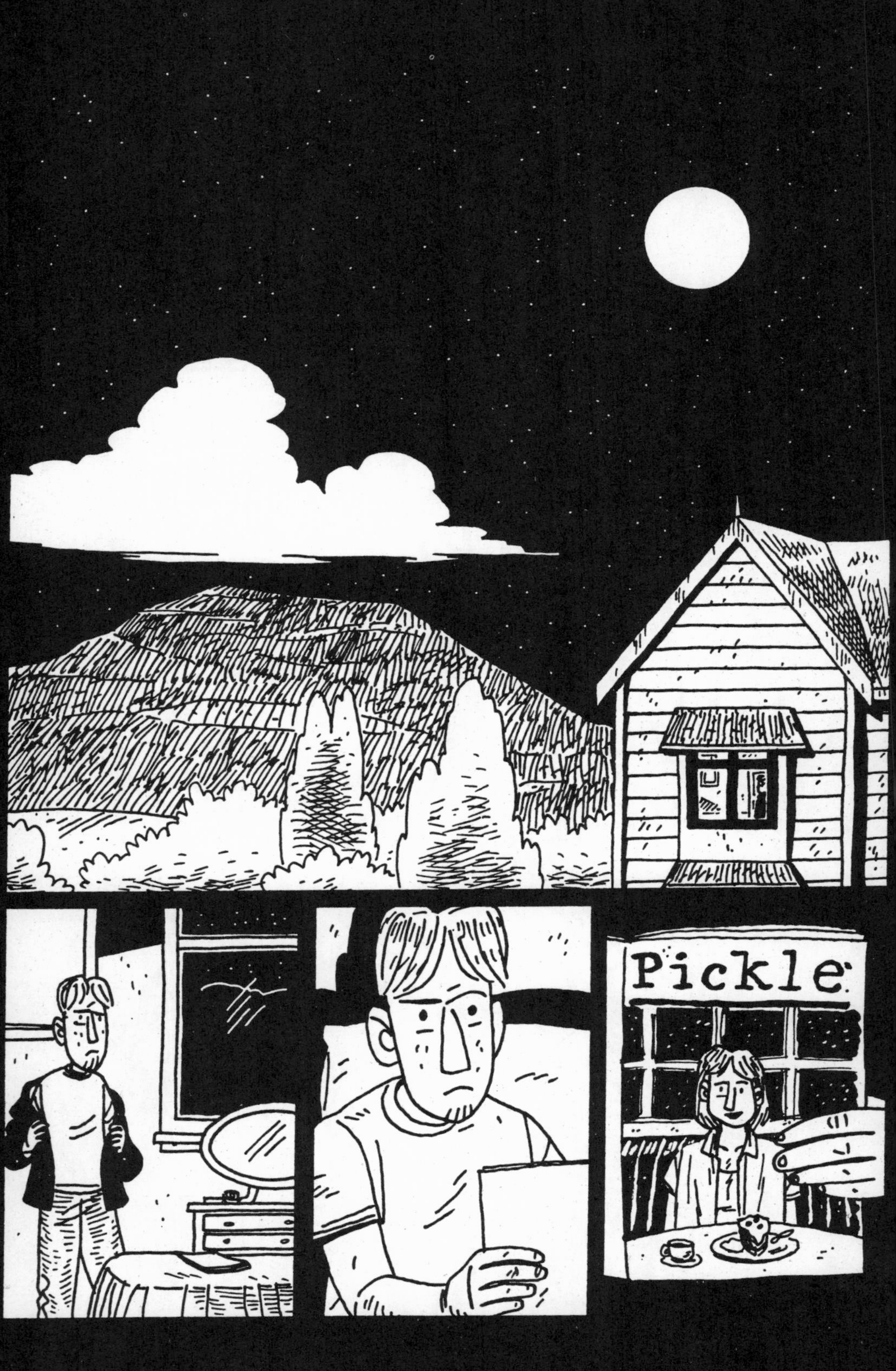
Pickle

Pickle

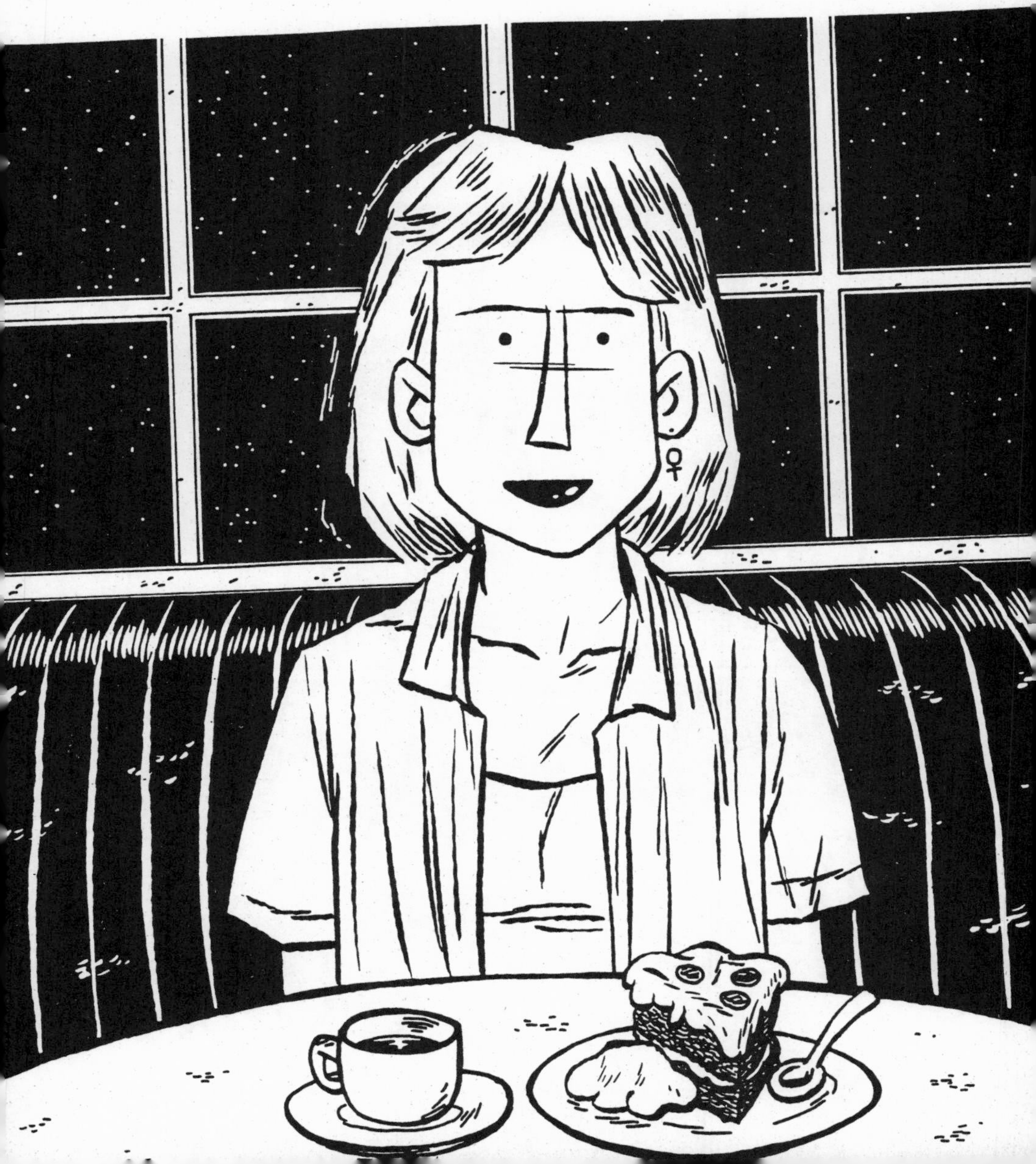

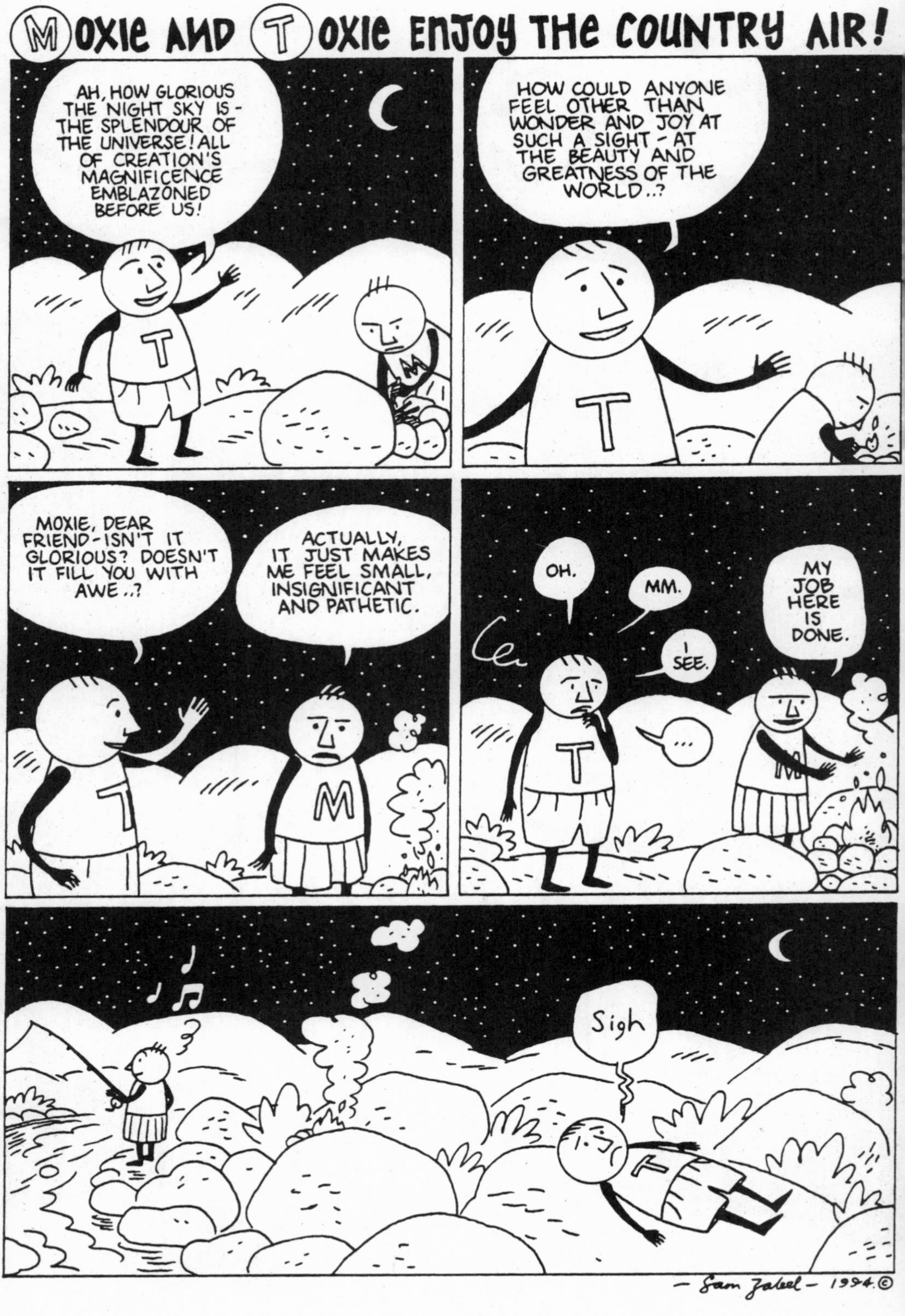
MOXIE AND TOXIE ENJOY THE COUNTRY AIR!
AH, HOW GLORIOUS THE NIGHT SKY IS - THE SPLENDOUR OF THE UNIVERSE! ALL OF CREATION'S MAGNIFICENCE EMBLAZONED BEFORE US!
HOW COULD ANYONE FEEL OTHER THAN WONDER AND JOY AT SUCH A SIGHT - AT THE BEAUTY AND GREATNESS OF THE WORLD..?
MOXIE, DEAR FRIEND - ISN'T IT GLORIOUS? DOESN'T IT FILL YOU WITH AWE..?
ACTUALLY, IT JUST MAKES ME FEEL SMALL, INSIGNIFICANT AND PATHETIC.
OH.
MM.
I SEE.
...
MY JOB HERE IS DONE.
Sigh
— Sam Zabel — 1994.©

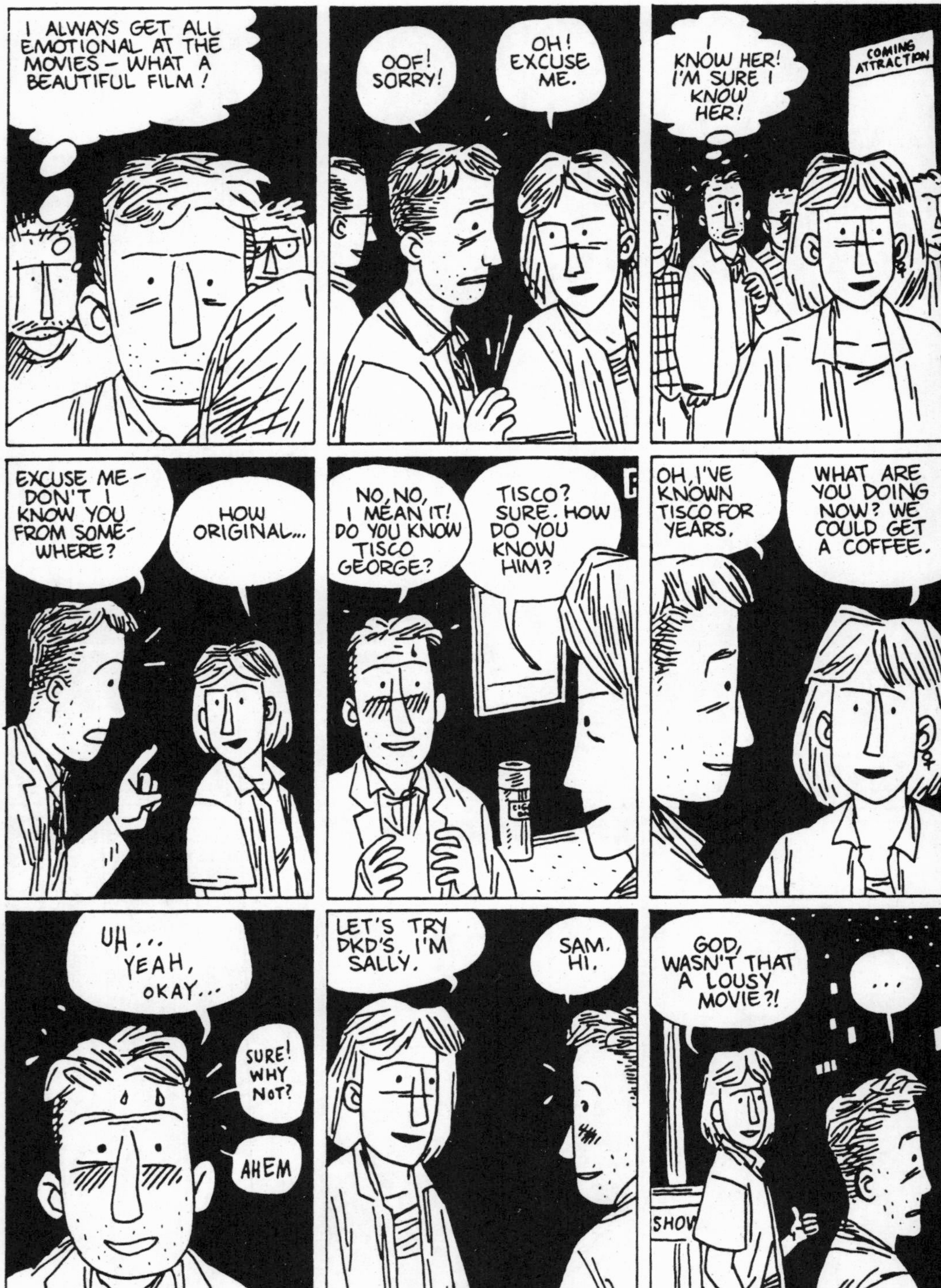
I ALWAYS GET ALL EMOTIONAL AT THE MOVIES – WHAT A BEAUTIFUL FILM!
OOF! SORRY!
OH! EXCUSE ME.
I KNOW HER! I'M SURE I KNOW HER!
COMING ATTRACTION
EXCUSE ME – DON'T I KNOW YOU FROM SOMEWHERE?
HOW ORIGINAL...
NO, NO, I MEAN IT! DO YOU KNOW TISCO GEORGE?
TISCO? SURE. HOW DO YOU KNOW HIM?
OH, I'VE KNOWN TISCO FOR YEARS.
WHAT ARE YOU DOING NOW? WE COULD GET A COFFEE.
UH... YEAH, OKAY...
SURE! WHY NOT?
AHEM
LET'S TRY DKD'S. I'M SALLY.
SAM. HI.
GOD, WASN'T THAT A LOUSY MOVIE?!
...
SHOW

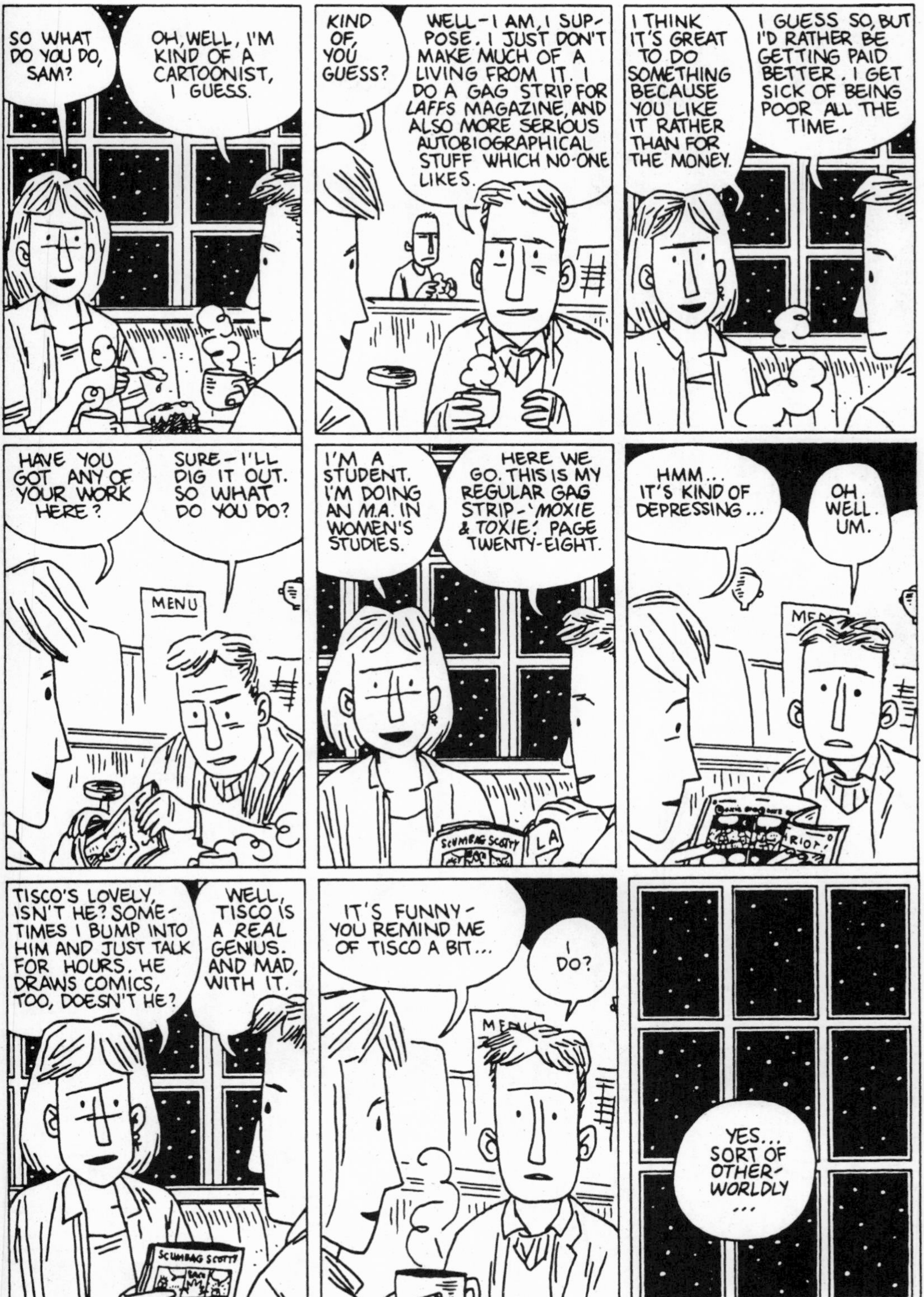
SO WHAT DO YOU DO, SAM?
OH, WELL, I'M KIND OF A CARTOONIST, I GUESS.
KIND OF, YOU GUESS?
WELL - I AM, I SUPPOSE. I JUST DON'T MAKE MUCH OF A LIVING FROM IT. I DO A GAG STRIP FOR LAFFS MAGAZINE, AND ALSO MORE SERIOUS AUTOBIOGRAPHICAL STUFF WHICH NO-ONE LIKES.
I THINK IT'S GREAT TO DO SOMETHING BECAUSE YOU LIKE IT RATHER THAN FOR THE MONEY.
I GUESS SO, BUT I'D RATHER BE GETTING PAID BETTER. I GET SICK OF BEING POOR ALL THE TIME.
HAVE YOU GOT ANY OF YOUR WORK HERE?
SURE - I'LL DIG IT OUT. SO WHAT DO YOU DO?
MENU
I'M A STUDENT. I'M DOING AN M.A. IN WOMEN'S STUDIES.
HERE WE GO. THIS IS MY REGULAR GAG STRIP - 'MOXIE & TOXIE.' PAGE TWENTY-EIGHT.
SCUMBAG SCOTTY
HMM... IT'S KIND OF DEPRESSING...
OH. WELL. UM.
TISCO'S LOVELY, ISN'T HE? SOMETIMES I BUMP INTO HIM AND JUST TALK FOR HOURS. HE DRAWS COMICS, TOO, DOESN'T HE?
WELL, TISCO IS A REAL GENIUS. AND MAD, WITH IT.
SCUMBAG SCOTTY
IT'S FUNNY - YOU REMIND ME OF TISCO A BIT...
I DO?
YES... SORT OF OTHER-WORLDLY...

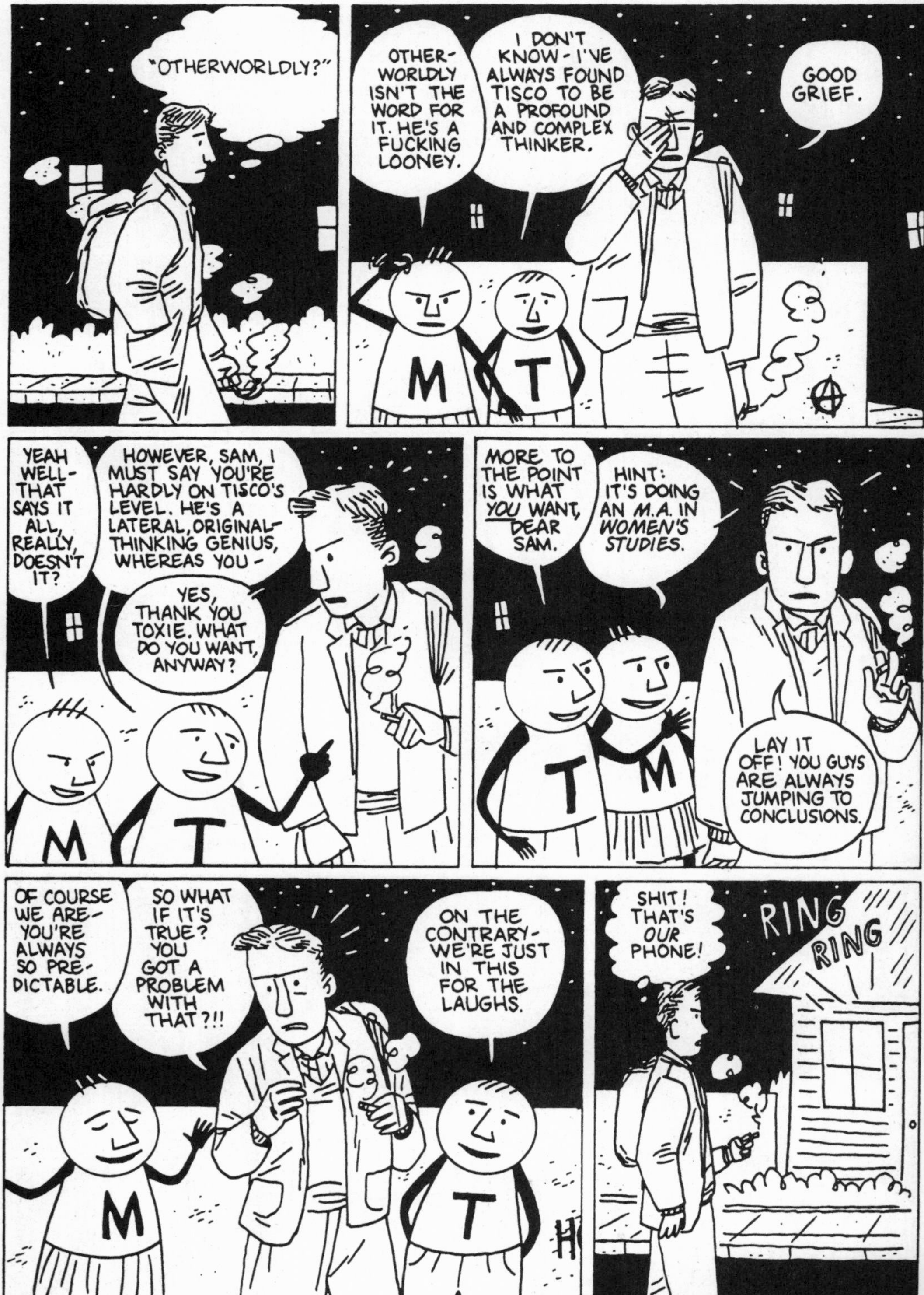
"OTHERWORLDLY?"
OTHER-WORLDLY ISN'T THE WORD FOR IT. HE'S A FUCKING LOONEY.
I DON'T KNOW - I'VE ALWAYS FOUND TISCO TO BE A PROFOUND AND COMPLEX THINKER.
GOOD GRIEF.
M
T
YEAH WELL- THAT SAYS IT ALL, REALLY, DOESN'T IT?
HOWEVER, SAM, I MUST SAY YOU'RE HARDLY ON TISCO'S LEVEL. HE'S A LATERAL, ORIGINAL-THINKING GENIUS, WHEREAS YOU -
YES, THANK YOU TOXIE. WHAT DO YOU WANT, ANYWAY?
MORE TO THE POINT IS WHAT YOU WANT, DEAR SAM.
HINT: IT'S DOING AN M.A. IN WOMEN'S STUDIES.
LAY IT OFF! YOU GUYS ARE ALWAYS JUMPING TO CONCLUSIONS.
OF COURSE WE ARE- YOU'RE ALWAYS SO PRE-DICTABLE.
SO WHAT IF IT'S TRUE? YOU GOT A PROBLEM WITH THAT?!!
ON THE CONTRARY- WE'RE JUST IN THIS FOR THE LAUGHS.
SHIT! THAT'S OUR PHONE!
RING
RING

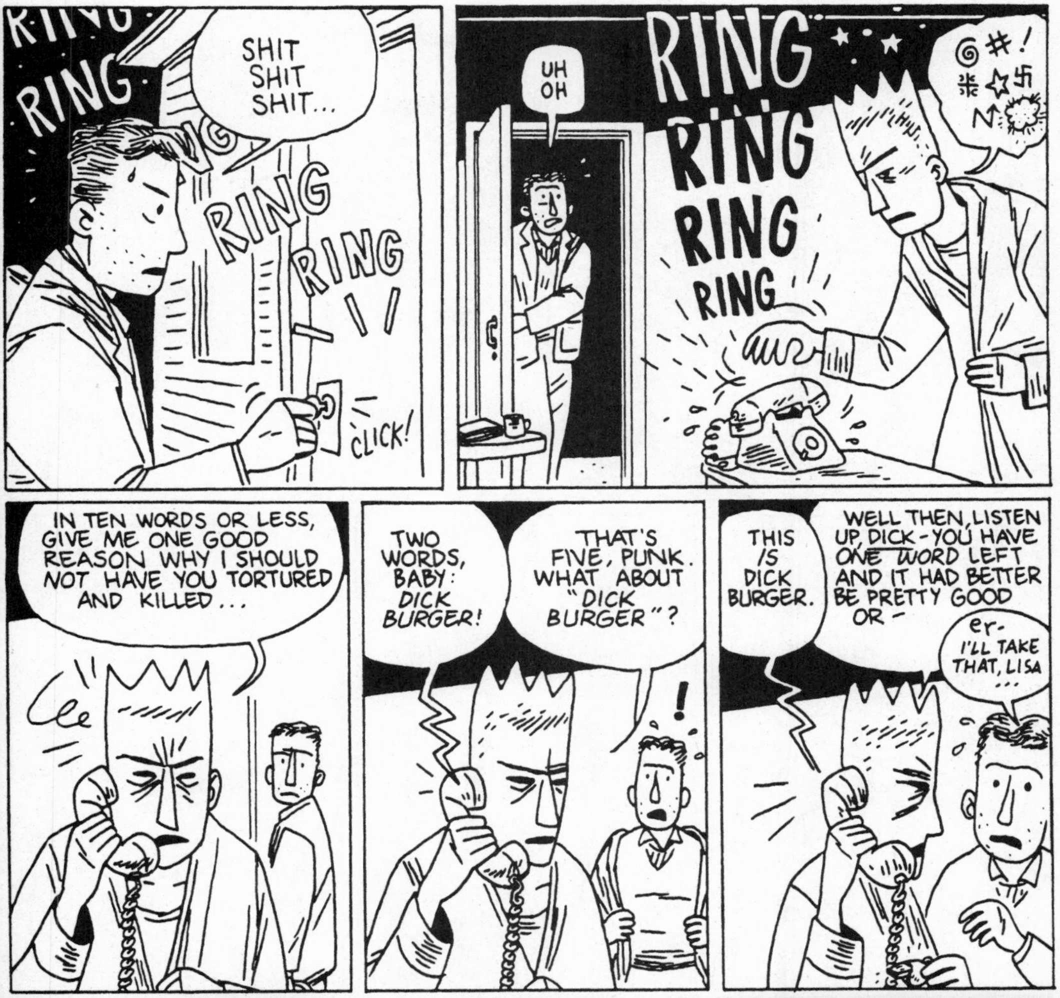
RING
RING
SHIT SHIT SHIT...
RING
RING
CLICK!
UH OH
RING
RING
RING
RING
IN TEN WORDS OR LESS, GIVE ME ONE GOOD REASON WHY I SHOULD NOT HAVE YOU TORTURED AND KILLED...
TWO WORDS, BABY: DICK BURGER!
THAT'S FIVE, PUNK. WHAT ABOUT "DICK BURGER"?
!
THIS IS DICK BURGER.
WELL THEN, LISTEN UP, DICK - YOU HAVE ONE WORD LEFT AND IT HAD BETTER BE PRETTY GOOD OR -
er- I'LL TAKE THAT, LISA ...
SORRY, LISA...
...
MORD
HELLO? DICK?
SAM?

SAM - WHAT THE HELL ARE YOU DOING CHATTING TO THE BOUNCERS WHEN THERE'S A ROOMFUL OF PUBLISHERS AND BABES TO CRUISE?!

I'M SORRY MR. BURGER SIR-WE DIDN'T REALISE THIS MAN WAS A FRIEND OF YOURS...

...

THAT'S OKAY BOYS! JUST KEEP UP THE GOOD WORK!

Thank you, sir...

JESUS, DICK! YOU COULD'VE SENT ME AN INVITE OR SOMETHING.

INVITES ARE FOR NOBODIES, SAM. I DON'T BOTHER WITH THAT SHIT WITH MY FRIENDS! NOW SHUT UP AND GET YOURSELF A DRINK, HERE!

BOLLINGER, SIR?

AH... TA.

SO, UH, DICK- HOW'VE YOU BEEN?

WELL, CAPTAIN TOMORROW JUST PASSED THE 3 MILLION MARK, ETERNAL'S MARKET SHARE KEEPS CLIMBING, AND WE JUST CLINCED A NEW DEAL FOR 2 MOVIES! I'VE BEEN OKAY!!

SIR, THERE'S A MR. McFARLANE ON THE PHONE FOR YOU...

TELL HIM I'M BUSY!

?

SO WHAT ABOUT YOU, SAM? STILL DRAWING MISERABLE CARTOONS ABOUT BEING BROKE ALL THE TIME?

I GUESS SO. AND ALSO A WEEKLY MOXIE AND TOXIE STRIP FOR 'LAFFS' MAGAZINE.

OH YEAH? SO WHAT DOES LAFFS PAY?

UH- THIRTY DOLLARS FOR ONE PAGE.

HA HA HA HA- MAN, THAT HURTS!

...BEFORE TAX.

DICK! HOWAYA, DICK?! ...er...

YEAH YEAH GREAT, STAN. GOTTA DASH. CATCH YA LATER, SAM.

B-BUT DICK- WHAT ABOUT MY PROPOSAL, DICK? HAVE YOU HAD A CHANCE TO...

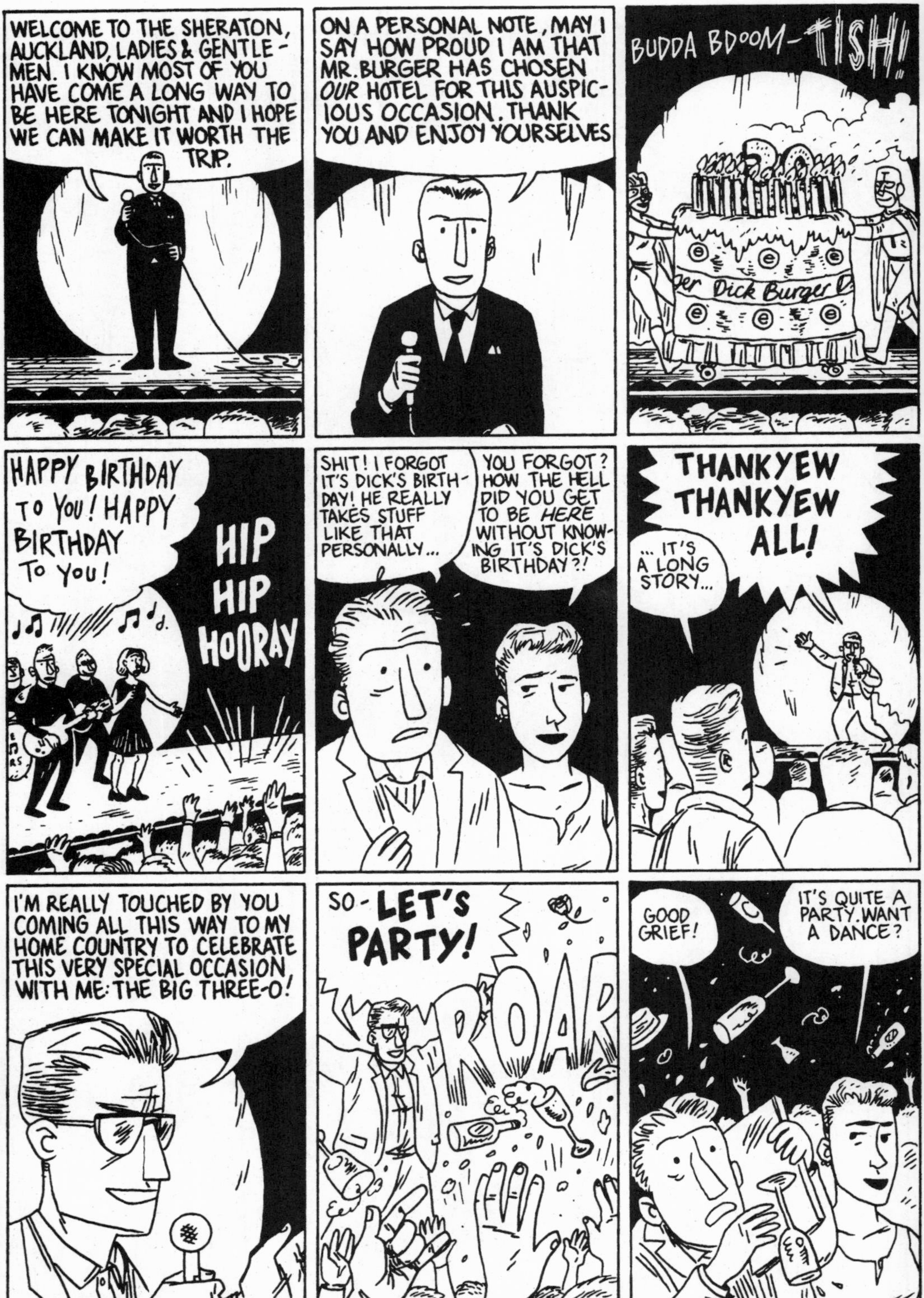
WELCOME TO THE SHERATON, AUCKLAND, LADIES & GENTLE-MEN. I KNOW MOST OF YOU HAVE COME A LONG WAY TO BE HERE TONIGHT AND I HOPE WE CAN MAKE IT WORTH THE TRIP.
ON A PERSONAL NOTE, MAY I SAY HOW PROUD I AM THAT MR. BURGER HAS CHOSEN OUR HOTEL FOR THIS AUSPICIOUS OCCASION. THANK YOU AND ENJOY YOURSELVES
BUDDA BDOOM-TISH!
Dick Burger
HAPPY BIRTHDAY TO YOU! HAPPY BIRTHDAY TO YOU!
HIP HIP HOORAY
SHIT! I FORGOT IT'S DICK'S BIRTHDAY! HE REALLY TAKES STUFF LIKE THAT PERSONALLY...
YOU FORGOT? HOW THE HELL DID YOU GET TO BE HERE WITHOUT KNOWING IT'S DICK'S BIRTHDAY?!
THANKYEW THANKYEW ALL!
... IT'S A LONG STORY...
I'M REALLY TOUCHED BY YOU COMING ALL THIS WAY TO MY HOME COUNTRY TO CELEBRATE THIS VERY SPECIAL OCCASION WITH ME: THE BIG THREE-O!
SO-LET'S PARTY!
ROAR
GOOD GRIEF!
IT'S QUITE A PARTY. WANT A DANCE?

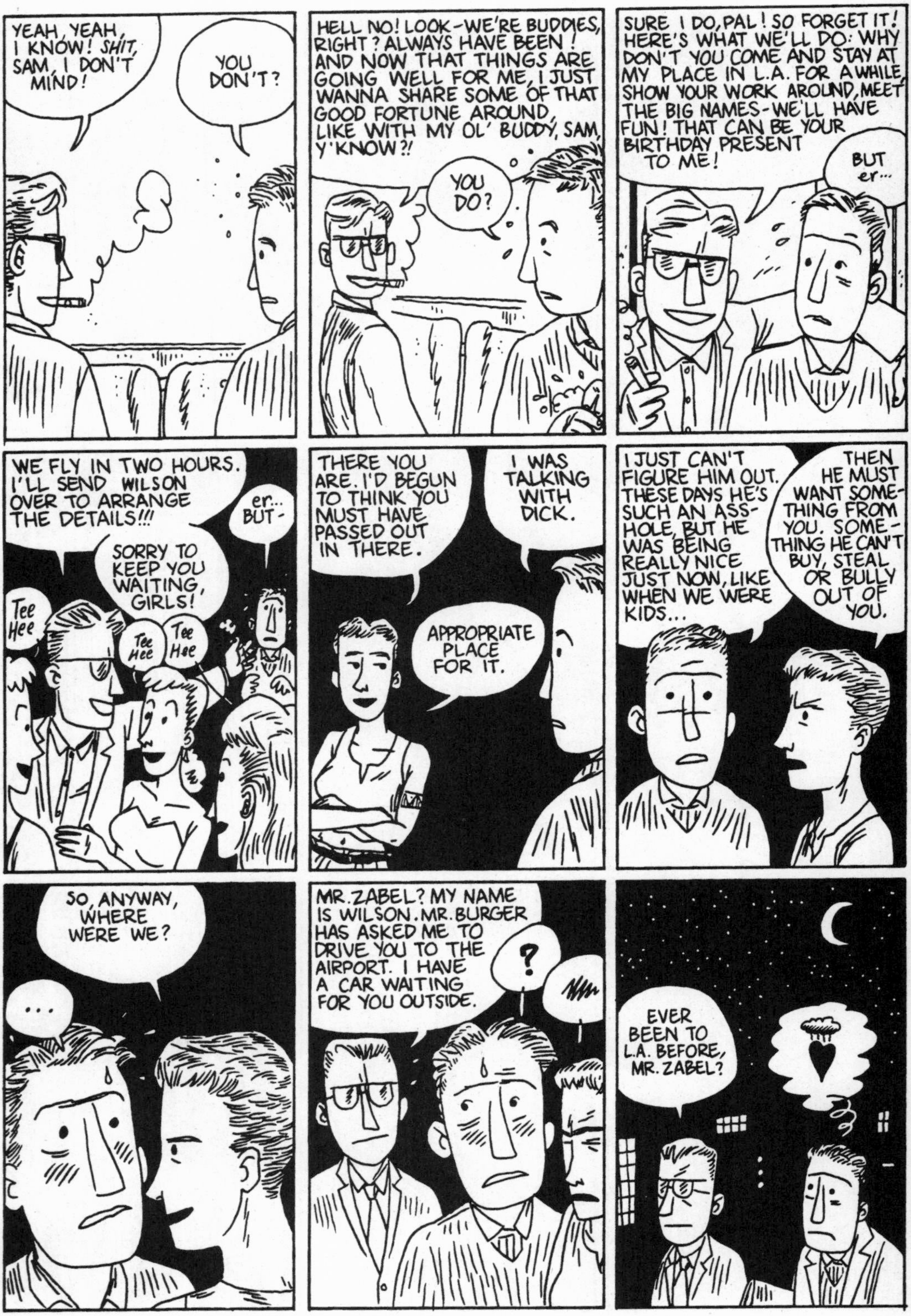
YEAH, YEAH, I KNOW! SHIT, SAM, I DON'T MIND!
YOU DON'T?
HELL NO! LOOK-WE'RE BUDDIES, RIGHT? ALWAYS HAVE BEEN! AND NOW THAT THINGS ARE GOING WELL FOR ME, I JUST WANNA SHARE SOME OF THAT GOOD FORTUNE AROUND, LIKE WITH MY OL' BUDDY, SAM, Y'KNOW?!
YOU DO?
SURE I DO, PAL! SO FORGET IT! HERE'S WHAT WE'LL DO: WHY DON'T YOU COME AND STAY AT MY PLACE IN L.A. FOR A WHILE, SHOW YOUR WORK AROUND, MEET THE BIG NAMES-WE'LL HAVE FUN! THAT CAN BE YOUR BIRTHDAY PRESENT TO ME!
BUT er...
WE FLY IN TWO HOURS. I'LL SEND WILSON OVER TO ARRANGE THE DETAILS!!!
er... BUT-
SORRY TO KEEP YOU WAITING, GIRLS!
Tee Hee
Tee Hee
Tee Hee
THERE YOU ARE. I'D BEGUN TO THINK YOU MUST HAVE PASSED OUT IN THERE.
I WAS TALKING WITH DICK.
APPROPRIATE PLACE FOR IT.
I JUST CAN'T FIGURE HIM OUT. THESE DAYS HE'S SUCH AN ASS-HOLE, BUT HE WAS BEING REALLY NICE JUST NOW, LIKE WHEN WE WERE KIDS...
THEN HE MUST WANT SOME-THING FROM YOU. SOME-THING HE CAN'T BUY, STEAL OR BULLY OUT OF YOU.
SO, ANYWAY, WHERE WERE WE?
...
MR. ZABEL? MY NAME IS WILSON. MR. BURGER HAS ASKED ME TO DRIVE YOU TO THE AIRPORT. I HAVE A CAR WAITING FOR YOU OUTSIDE.
?
EVER BEEN TO L.A. BEFORE, MR. ZABEL?

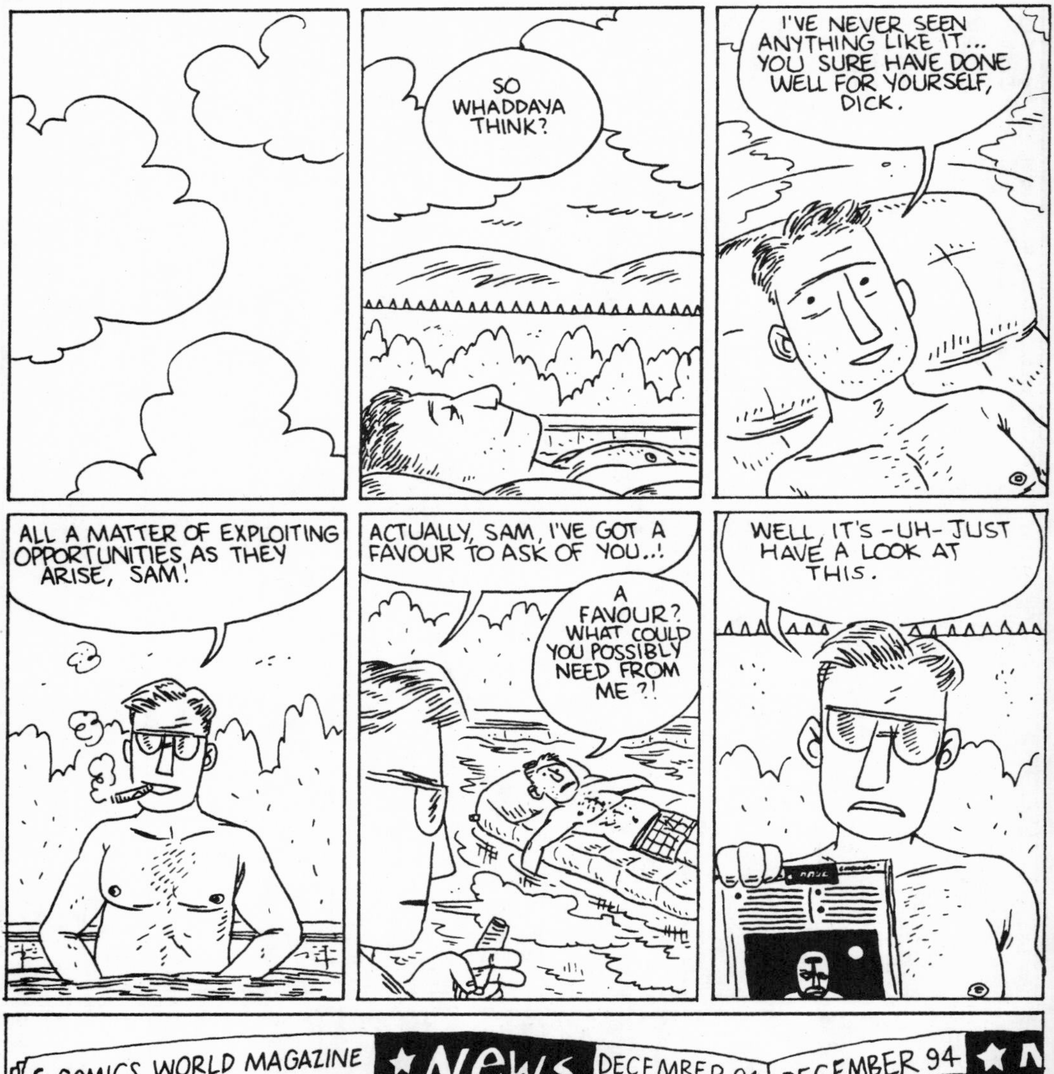
SO WHADDAYA THINK?
I'VE NEVER SEEN ANYTHING LIKE IT... YOU SURE HAVE DONE WELL FOR YOURSELF, DICK.
ALL A MATTER OF EXPLOITING OPPORTUNITIES AS THEY ARISE, SAM!
ACTUALLY, SAM, I'VE GOT A FAVOUR TO ASK OF YOU..!
A FAVOUR? WHAT COULD YOU POSSIBLY NEED FROM ME?!
WELL, IT'S -UH- JUST HAVE A LOOK AT THIS.
6 COMICS WORLD MAGAZINE
News
DECEMBER 94
DECEMBER 94
Dick Burger for Comic Book Hall of Fame.
BY LEONARD BATTS (L.A)
Eternal Comics and creator of the best-selling Captain Tomorrow, Lady Night and Smashfist graphic novels, Dick Burger is to be admitted to the Comic Book Hall of Fame in a special ceremony in New York on Saturday 25 February. The awards committee of the American Comics Creators Guild announced their decision last week, saying: "At only 30 years of age, Dick has already made such an impact on the industry and medium that we saw little point in waiting until he's as old as us before honoring him."
Burger's career began a mere years ago when he sold
The ceremony honouring Burger will be by invitatio only and will feature spee by such luminaries as Sta Lee, Joe Lumpen and Glor Vixenburg and also a childhood friend of Burger from New Zealand, who will tell the hitherto untold st of Burger's early years in that isolated tiny country

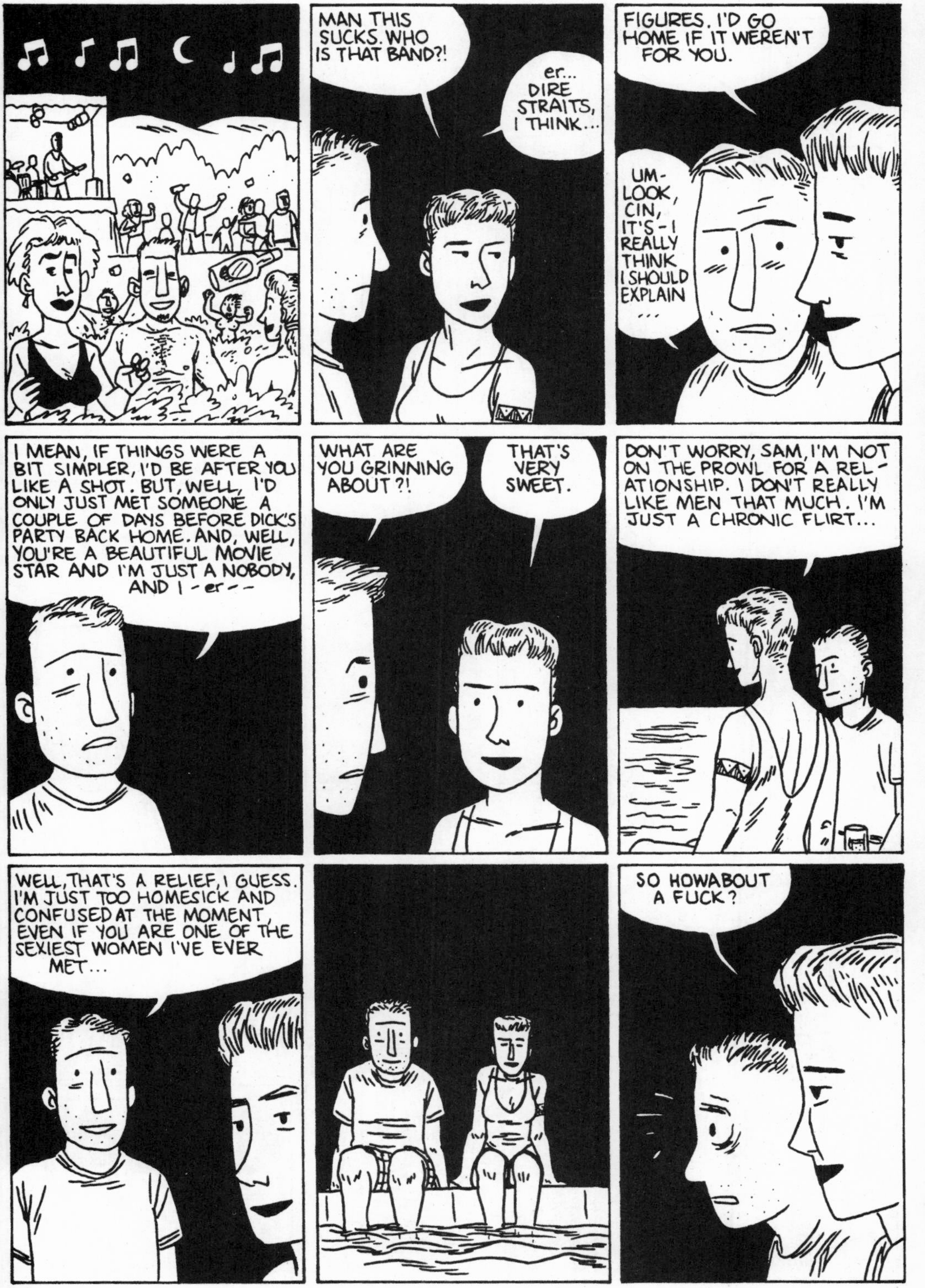
MAN THIS SUCKS. WHO IS THAT BAND?!
er... DIRE STRAITS, I THINK...
FIGURES. I'D GO HOME IF IT WEREN'T FOR YOU.
UM- LOOK, CIN, IT'S - I REALLY THINK I SHOULD EXPLAIN ...
I MEAN, IF THINGS WERE A BIT SIMPLER, I'D BE AFTER YOU LIKE A SHOT. BUT, WELL, I'D ONLY JUST MET SOMEONE A COUPLE OF DAYS BEFORE DICK'S PARTY BACK HOME. AND, WELL, YOU'RE A BEAUTIFUL MOVIE STAR AND I'M JUST A NOBODY, AND I - er - -
WHAT ARE YOU GRINNING ABOUT?!
THAT'S VERY SWEET.
DON'T WORRY, SAM, I'M NOT ON THE PROWL FOR A REL-ATIONSHIP. I DON'T REALLY LIKE MEN THAT MUCH. I'M JUST A CHRONIC FLIRT...
WELL, THAT'S A RELIEF, I GUESS. I'M JUST TOO HOMESICK AND CONFUSED AT THE MOMENT, EVEN IF YOU ARE ONE OF THE SEXIEST WOMEN I'VE EVER MET...
SO HOWABOUT A FUCK?

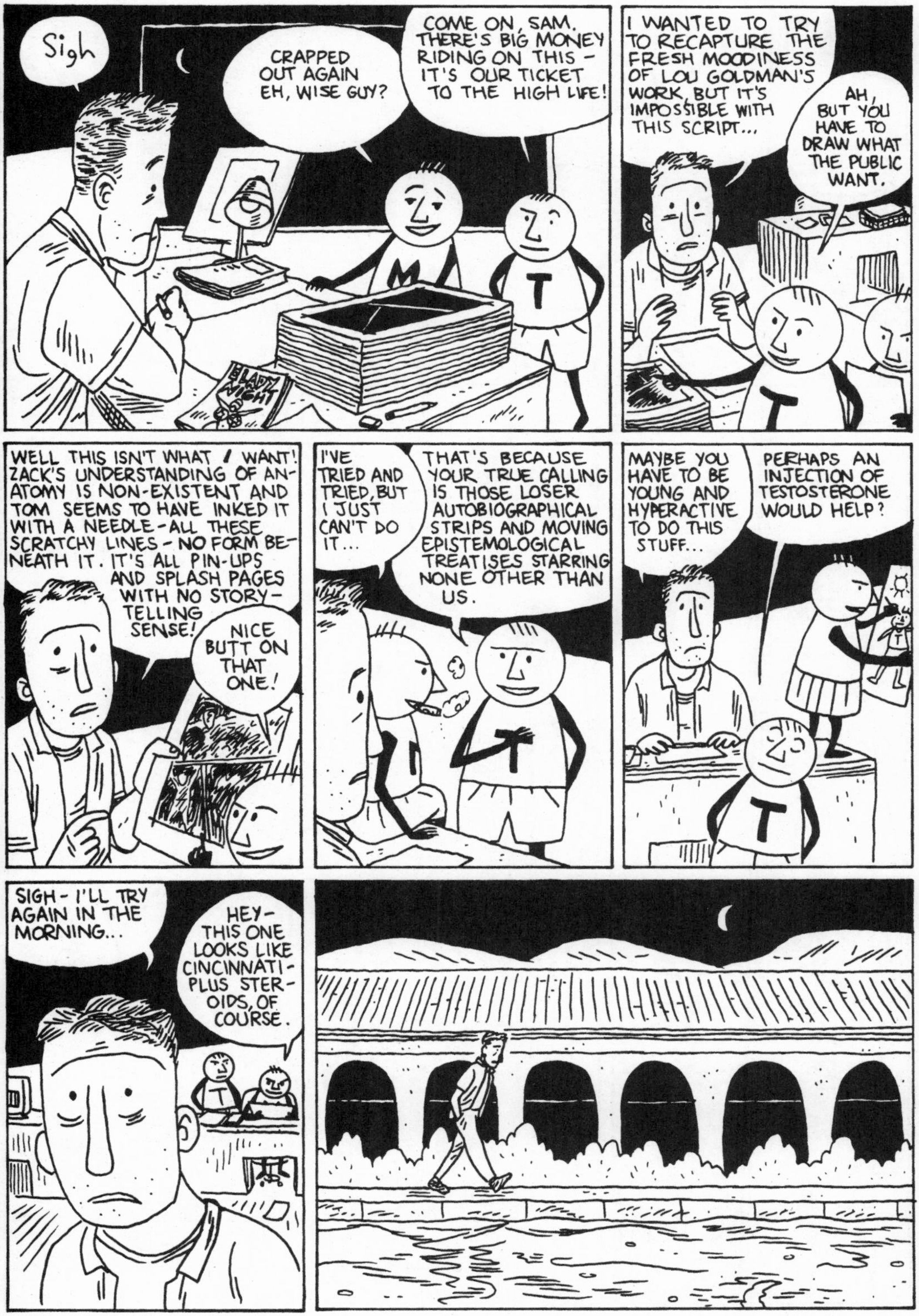
Sigh
CRAPPED OUT AGAIN EH, WISE GUY?
COME ON, SAM. THERE'S BIG MONEY RIDING ON THIS - IT'S OUR TICKET TO THE HIGH LIFE!
LADY NIGHT
I WANTED TO TRY TO RECAPTURE THE FRESH MOODINESS OF LOU GOLDMAN'S WORK, BUT IT'S IMPOSSIBLE WITH THIS SCRIPT...
AH, BUT YOU HAVE TO DRAW WHAT THE PUBLIC WANT.
WELL THIS ISN'T WHAT I WANT! ZACK'S UNDERSTANDING OF ANATOMY IS NON-EXISTENT AND TOM SEEMS TO HAVE INKED IT WITH A NEEDLE - ALL THESE SCRATCHY LINES - NO FORM BENEATH IT. IT'S ALL PIN-UPS AND SPLASH PAGES WITH NO STORY-TELLING SENSE!
NICE BUTT ON THAT ONE!
I'VE TRIED AND TRIED, BUT I JUST CAN'T DO IT...
THAT'S BECAUSE YOUR TRUE CALLING IS THOSE LOSER AUTOBIOGRAPHICAL STRIPS AND MOVING EPISTEMOLOGICAL TREATISES STARRING NONE OTHER THAN US.
MAYBE YOU HAVE TO BE YOUNG AND HYPERACTIVE TO DO THIS STUFF...
PERHAPS AN INJECTION OF TESTOSTERONE WOULD HELP?
SIGH - I'LL TRY AGAIN IN THE MORNING...
HEY - THIS ONE LOOKS LIKE CINCINNATI - PLUS STEROIDS, OF COURSE.

SATURDAY...

SAM, I JUST WANTED TO SAY THANKS FOR DOING THIS.

LOOK, DICK, I —

THERE'S NO HOT CHOCOLATE, SO I GOT YOU A VODKA.

HI, CINCIN! GLAD YOU COULD COME!

WOULDN'T MISS THIS FOR THE WORLD, DICK.

HA HA — WELL, I'D BETTER GO GET CHANGED! TOUCH-DOWN IN TWO HOURS!

ASS-HOLE.

I CAN'T UNDERSTAND HOW THE GUILD CAN PUT *DICK* IN THEIR STUPID HALL OF FAME, BUT NOT LOU GOLD-MAN.

LOU WHO?

HE CREATED 'LADY NIGHT'! SURELY YOU'VE —

HMPH. I DON'T READ COMICS, SAM, I JUST DRESS UP LIKE 'EM FOR A LIVING.

LOU WAS ONE OF THE BEST CARTOONISTS OF THE FIFTIES. HIS 'LADY NIGHT' WAS COM-PLETELY DIFFERENT TO DICK'S. IT WAS EXCITING, A BIT SAD AND VERY MORAL AND HUMANE. BUT HE'S NEVER BEEN TREATED WELL BY THE INDUSTRY.

STILL, HE SHOULD DO ALRIGHT OUT OF THE MOVIE.

I DOUBT IT. HE'S NEVER OWNED THE COPYRIGHT TO LADY NIGHT. HE'D BE LUCKY EVEN TO GET A CREDIT.

OH. AND THIS IS HIS LADY NIGHT? CAN I READ IT?

SURE. YOUR DIRECTOR MIGHT NOT APPROVE, THOUGH.

FUCK MY DIRECTOR. OR ON SECOND THOUGHTS, DON'T— HE'D PROBABLY GIVE YOU A PART IN HIS NEXT MOVIE.

YOU DON'T MEAN YOU—

HEY-GIVE ME SOME CREDIT— WHAT DO YOU THINK I'VE GOT AN AGENT FOR?

SHEEIT! THIS AIN'T THE DAUGHTER OF DARKNESS I KNOW! PAGE 5 AND NOBODY'S DEAD YET! AND HER CHEST— WHY, IT'S ALMOST BELIEVABLE!

HA! YOU'RE READING A REAL COMIC NOW, MATE!

WHAT POWER THE ORB HOLDS! COULD IT BE THAT THIS IS WHAT TURNED ARLON TO EVIL? AND WHAT MAY IT DO TO KYROS... OR TO ME?!

LADY NIGHT! HAVE YOU THE ORB?!

HAVE PATIENCE, KYROS!

HERE!

LET ME HAVE IT!! WITHOUT IT WE ARE BOTH LOST!!

YOU ARE ALREADY LOST, KYROS- LOST TO EVIL AND DARKNESS! I CANNOT ALLOW YOU TO GAIN THE ORB OF ARLON AND ITS POWER!

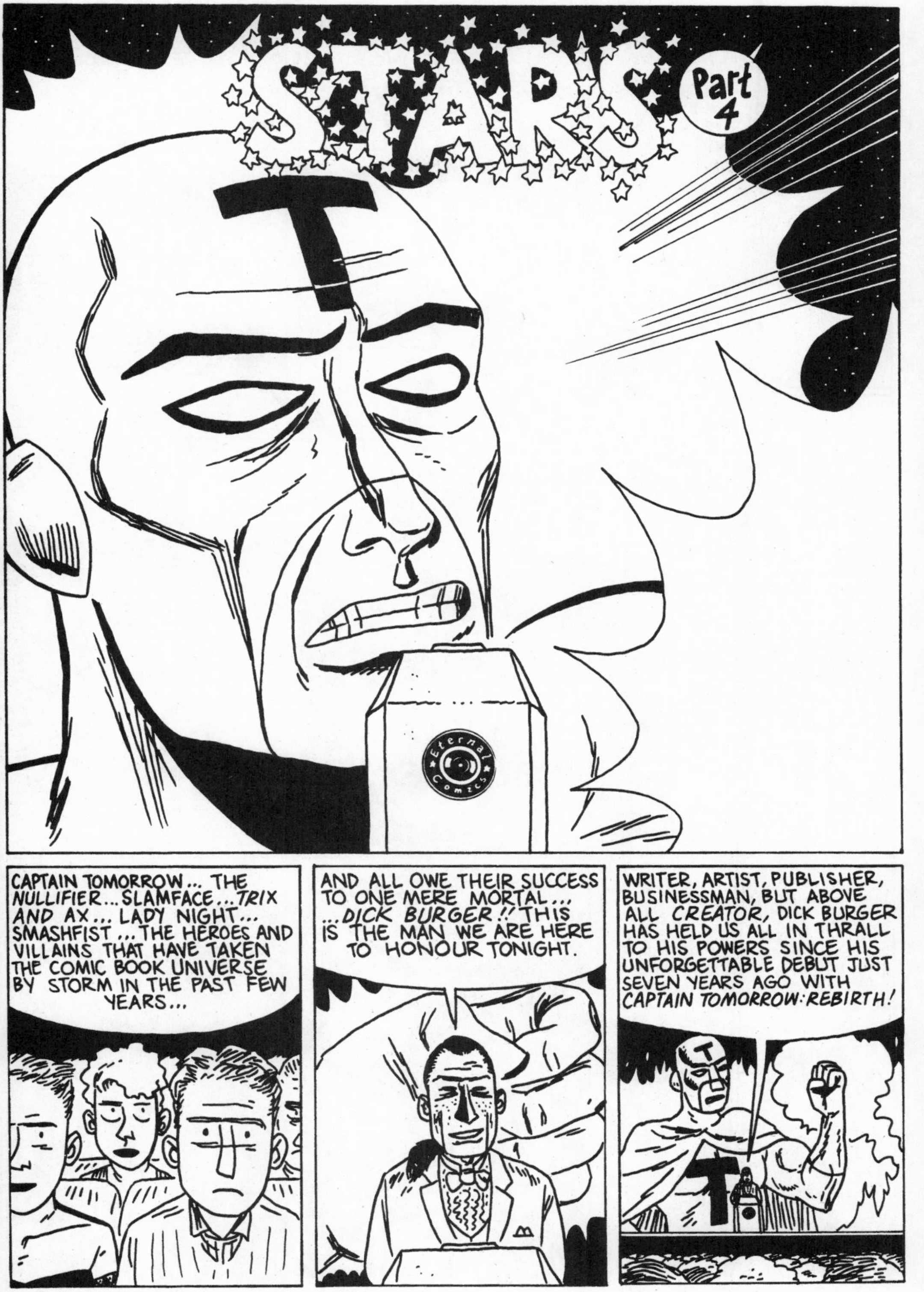

STARS
Part 4
Eternal Comics
CAPTAIN TOMORROW... THE NULLIFIER... SLAMFACE... TRIX AND AX... LADY NIGHT... SMASHFIST... THE HEROES AND VILLAINS THAT HAVE TAKEN THE COMIC BOOK UNIVERSE BY STORM IN THE PAST FEW YEARS...
AND ALL OWE THEIR SUCCESS TO ONE MERE MORTAL... ...DICK BURGER!! THIS IS THE MAN WE ARE HERE TO HONOUR TONIGHT.
WRITER, ARTIST, PUBLISHER, BUSINESSMAN, BUT ABOVE ALL CREATOR, DICK BURGER HAS HELD US ALL IN THRALL TO HIS POWERS SINCE HIS UNFORGETTABLE DEBUT JUST SEVEN YEARS AGO WITH CAPTAIN TOMORROW: REBIRTH!

...DICK'S THE BEST! HE'S A GREAT GUY! IF I'D HAD A GUY LIKE *HIM* IN THE *BULLPEN* THIRTY YEARS AGO, JUST THINK WHERE WE'D BE TODAY! OF COURSE I *DID* HAVE A GUY LIKE A GUY BACK THEN ... AND HIS NAME WAS *JACK KIRBY!!*

I USED TO THINK NO-ONE COULD EVER REACH JACK'S LEVEL OF GENIUS, BUT THAT WAS BEFORE DICK CAME ALONG. *DICK -- YOU ARE THE GREATEST GUY* I'VE EVER KNOWN ... AND, DICK, DON'T FORGET TO SPELL MY NAME RIGHT ON THE CHECK!

HAHAHAHAH

EVER SINCE THE LAUNCH OF *CAPTAIN TOMORROW: REBIRTH,* DICK BURGER HAS BEEN *THE* CREATIVE FORCE IN COMICS. MORE RECENTLY HE WENT ON TO BECOME THE MOST IMPORTANT FIGURE IN THE *BUSINESS* OF COMICS AS WELL.

IT IS MY BELIEF THAT DICK WILL LEAD US INTO THE NEXT CENTURY AND BEYOND -- INTO A NEW AND UNPRECEDENTED ERA IN COMIC BOOK HISTORY, IN TERMS OF POPULARITY, FINANCIAL GROWTH AND MOST IMPORTANTLY, CREATIVE SUCCESS NEVER DREAMED OF...

WITH THE RELEASE OF THE FORTHCOMING *LADY NIGHT* MOTION PICTURE, I AM SURE DICK BURGER WILL USHER IN A NEW GOLDEN AGE FOR AMERICAN COMIC ART.

AND OUR NEXT SPEAKER IS NONE OTHER THAN THE CREATOR OF THE GOLDEN AGE LADY NIGHT HIMSELF --- *LOU GOLDMAN!!*

CLAP CLAP CLAP CLAP

!

-AH-HEM! ...THE FIRST TIME I SAW DICK BURGER WAS UP AT THE ETERNAL OFFICES. I WAS DROP-PING IN A JOB AND THERE WAS DICK, KIDDING AROUND WITH ED TOGLIANI, ACTING OUT A CAPTAIN TOMORROW FIGHT SCENE. AND I THOUGHT TO MYSELF: WHO *IS* THIS IDIOT?

YOU'RE NEXT, MR. ZABEL.

HA HA HAHAHA HA HA

SO NOW I KNOW.

HAHAHAHA HAHAH

CONGRATULATIONS DICK...

CLAP CLAP CLAP CLAP CLAP

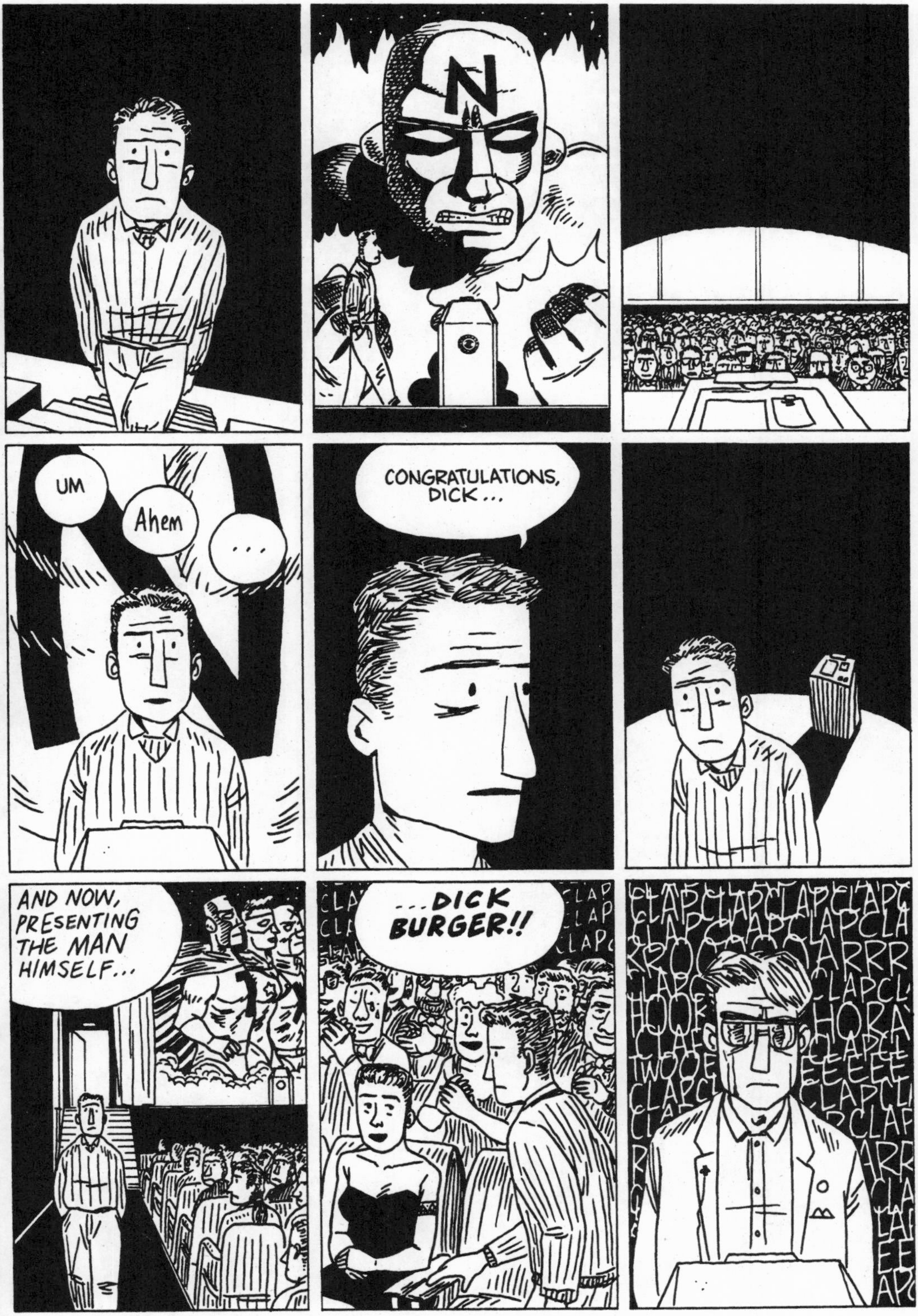
UM
Ahem
...
CONGRATULATIONS, DICK...
AND NOW, PRESENTING THE MAN HIMSELF...
...DICK BURGER!!
CLAP
CLAP
CLAPCLAPCLAPCLAPC
CLAPCLAPCLAPCLA
ARRR
HOOR
HORA
TWOOEEEEEE
CLAPCL
CLAP

SO WHICH SPEECH WAS THAT?

...

NEW YORK'S KINDA PRETTY AT NIGHT, HUH?

HM...

HOMESICK?

I GUESS. AUCKLAND'S NOT MUCH OF A CITY, BUT SOMETIMES I THINK THAT'S WHY I LIKE IT.

I THINK I'M OUT OF MY LEAGUE.

...

I GOT YOU A PRESENT.

WHA-?

DON'T OPEN IT NOW. NOT HERE.

IT'S JUST A LITTLE SOMETHING TO USE WHEN YOU NEED IT.

ANYWAY, CATCH YA LATER. I GOTTA GO SCHMOOZE.

MR. GOLDMAN?

WHO ARE YOU?

er- MY NAME'S SAM ZABEL. I'M FROM HICKSVILLE.

HICKSVILLE, EH? NO SHIT--- YEAH, I'VE HEARD OF HICKSVILLE...

I KNEW YOU WOULD HAVE.

OLD MORT MOLSON USED TO TALK ABOUT HICKSVILLE- SAID HE'D BEEN THERE A COUPLE A TIMES, BUT YOU KNOW I ALWAYS FIGURED IT WAS LIKE A META-PHOR...

I CAN ASSURE YOU IT'S QUITE REAL, MR. GOLDMAN.

WELL WHADDAYA KNOW? HICKSVILLE, EH? MAN, THAT'S REALLY SOME-THING...

ARE YOU A CARTOONIST THEN, SAM?

OH WELL, I DUNNO... DICK HAD HIRED ME TO PENCIL LADY NIGHT, BUT AFTER TONIGHT I GUESS I'M PROBABLY UNEM-PLOYED AGAIN. ANYWAY, NO-ONE COULD EVER DO LADY NIGHT LIKE YOU DID, SIR.

THAT'S KIND OF YOU, SON, BUT I DOUBT MOST OF THE KIDS TODAY SEE IT THAT WAY.

I DON'T THINK THAT'S NECESSAR-ILY TRUE, SIR. I MEAN MAYBE IT COULDN'T LOOK THE SAME NOW, BUT IF THE STORIES YOU WROTE AND THE CARE YOU TOOK WITH THE DRAWING- I BELIEVE THEY WOULD BE A REVELATION TO MOST KIDS TODAY.

I WISH THAT WERE TRUE, SAM. BUT I'M JUST AN OLD MAN - I DON'T UNDERSTAND THESE VIDEO GAMES AND SPLATTER MOVIES AND SO ON. I ALWAYS TRIED TO WRITE ABOUT GOOD AND EVIL AND HOW EASILY WE BECOME EVIL. THESE DAYS I LOOK AT THE COMICS AND I CAN'T TELL WHO IS THE GOOD GUY. EVERYBODY'S EVIL TODAY.

LOU.

SAM.

...

HI DICK.

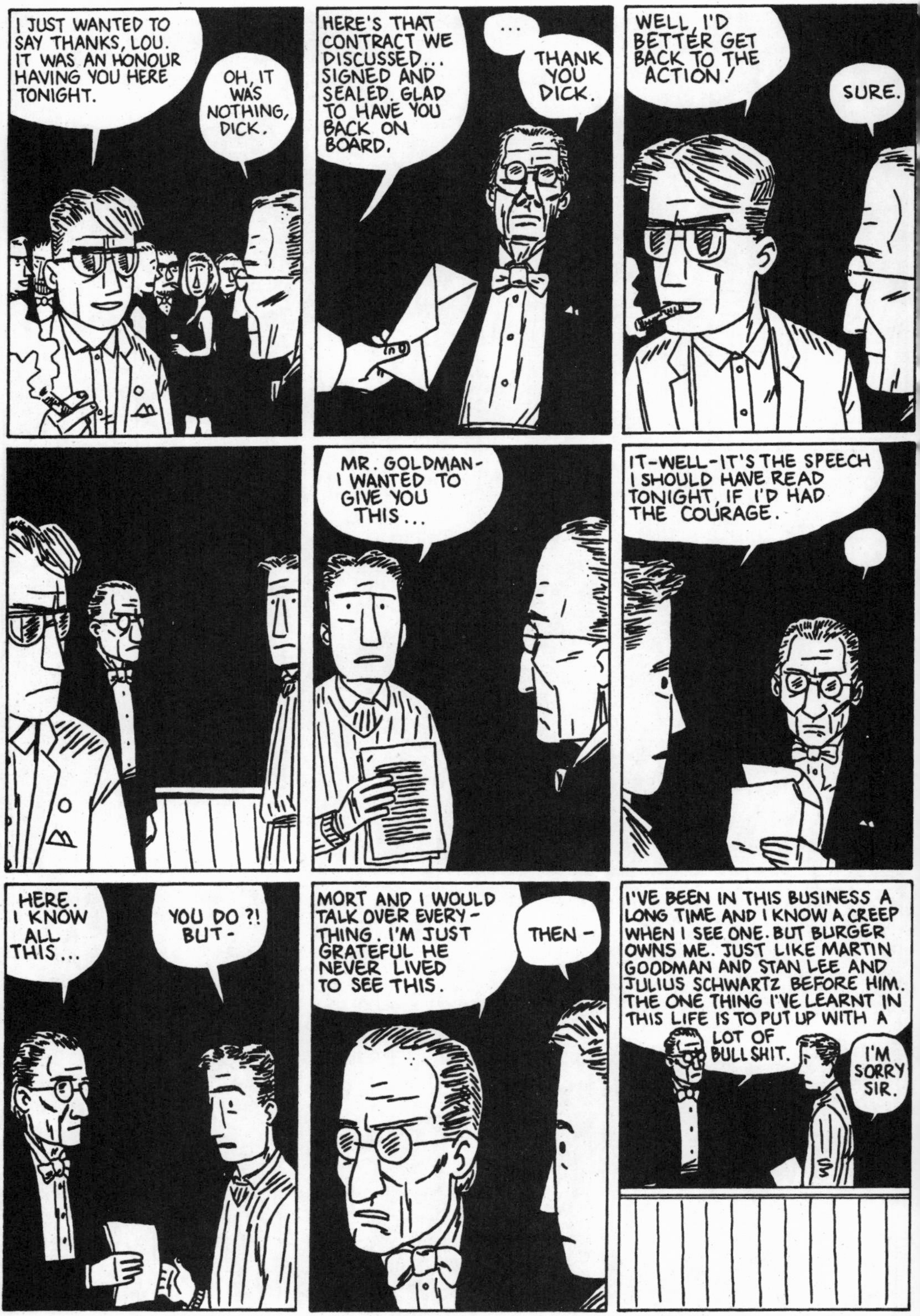
I JUST WANTED TO SAY THANKS, LOU. IT WAS AN HONOUR HAVING YOU HERE TONIGHT.
OH, IT WAS NOTHING, DICK.
HERE'S THAT CONTRACT WE DISCUSSED... SIGNED AND SEALED. GLAD TO HAVE YOU BACK ON BOARD.
...
THANK YOU DICK.
WELL, I'D BETTER GET BACK TO THE ACTION!
SURE.
MR. GOLDMAN- I WANTED TO GIVE YOU THIS...
IT-WELL-IT'S THE SPEECH I SHOULD HAVE READ TONIGHT, IF I'D HAD THE COURAGE.
HERE. I KNOW ALL THIS...
YOU DO?! BUT-
MORT AND I WOULD TALK OVER EVERY-THING. I'M JUST GRATEFUL HE NEVER LIVED TO SEE THIS.
THEN-
I'VE BEEN IN THIS BUSINESS A LONG TIME AND I KNOW A CREEP WHEN I SEE ONE. BUT BURGER OWNS ME. JUST LIKE MARTIN GOODMAN AND STAN LEE AND JULIUS SCHWARTZ BEFORE HIM. THE ONE THING I'VE LEARNT IN THIS LIFE IS TO PUT UP WITH A
LOT OF BULLSHIT.
I'M SORRY SIR.

LOOK, SON, DON'T SWEAT IT OVER *LADY NIGHT.* ALL THE BEST CARTOONISTS THESE DAYS ARE ON WELFARE.

THANK YOU, SIR!

HEY- CALL ME LOU. YOU'RE MAKING ME FEEL A MILLION YEARS OLD HERE.

THAT YOUR GIRL, SAM?

CINCINATTI? OH NO, SHE'S- WELL - SHE'S A GOOD FRIEND.

HMM. SHE REMINDS ME OF MY FIRST WIFE, GOD REST HER SOUL. SHE WAS A BEAUTIFUL WOMAN... CARRIED HERSELF *SO*... KNOW WHAT SHE SAID TO ME THE NIGHT I PROPOSED?

"YOU'VE MADE THE STARS SHINE."

THERE'S NOTHING BETTER THAN DESERVING LOVE. WHEN SOMEONE CAN SEE THE GOOD IN YOU, THAT'S THE BEST THING THERE IS.

OF COURSE, FIVE YEARS LATER SHE LEFT ME FOR A SHOE SALESMAN, SO GO FIGURE...

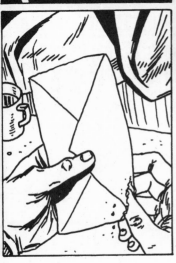

SUNDAY...

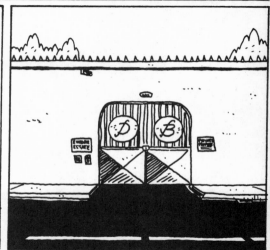

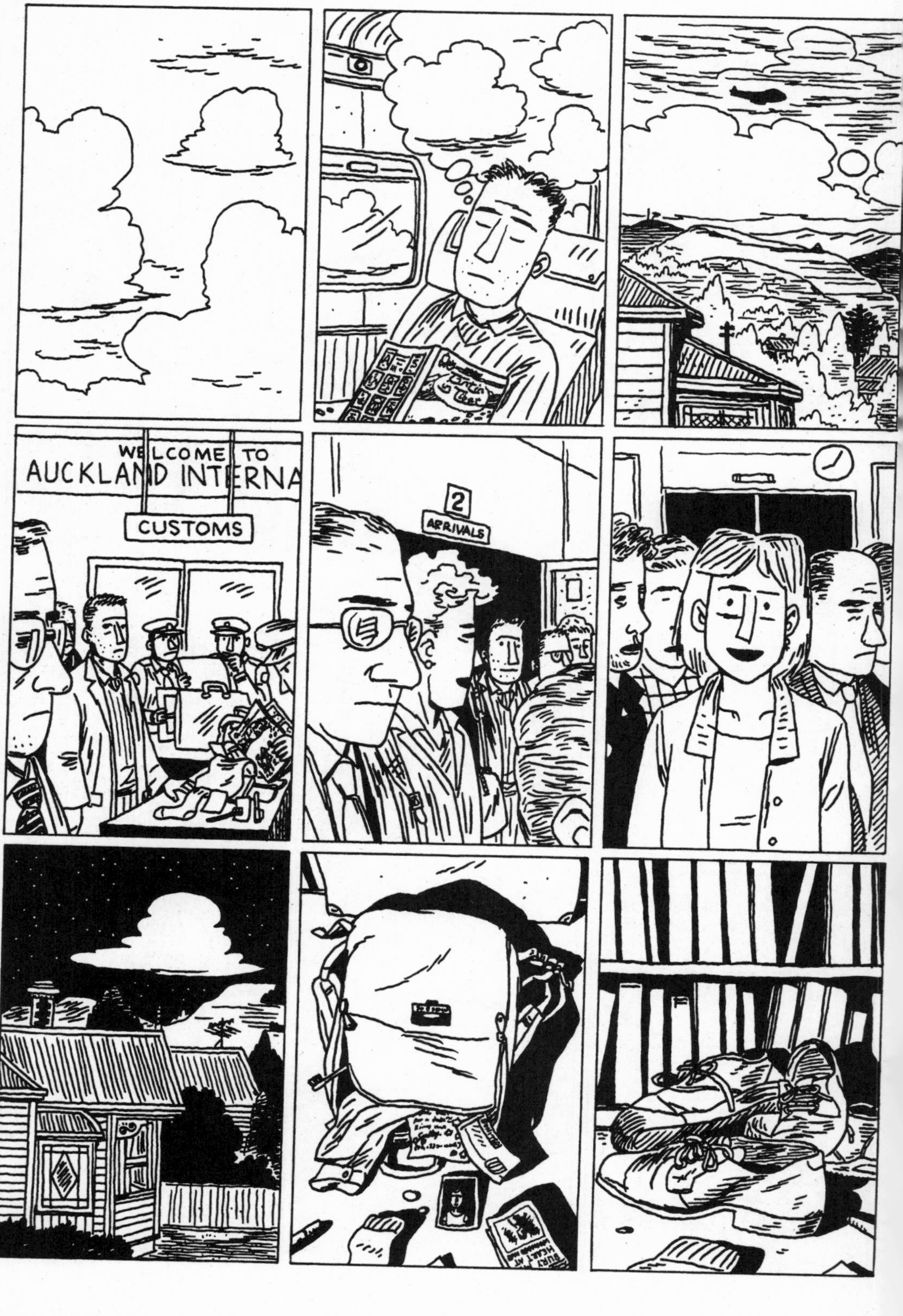

WELCOME TO
AUCKLAND INTERNA
CUSTOMS
2
ARRIVALS
BURY MY HEART AT

I HAVE TO ADMIT— WHEN YOU SAID YOU WANTED TO SHOW ME YOUR BEDROOM CEILING, I DIDN'T THINK YOU ACTUALLY MEANT...

BE PATIENT. THEY'RE SOAKING UP LIGHT.

WHAT?

OKAY, THAT'LL DO. SWITCH OFF THE LAMP.

CLICK

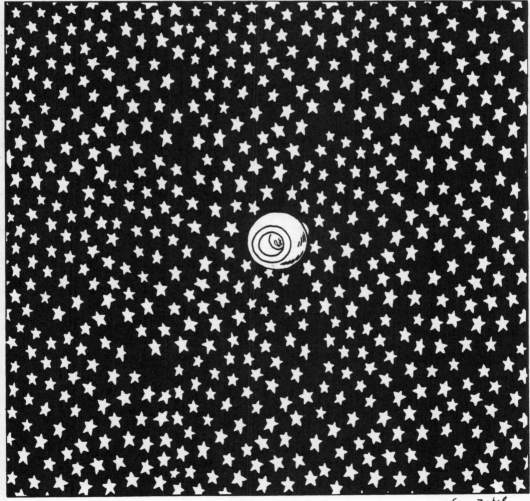

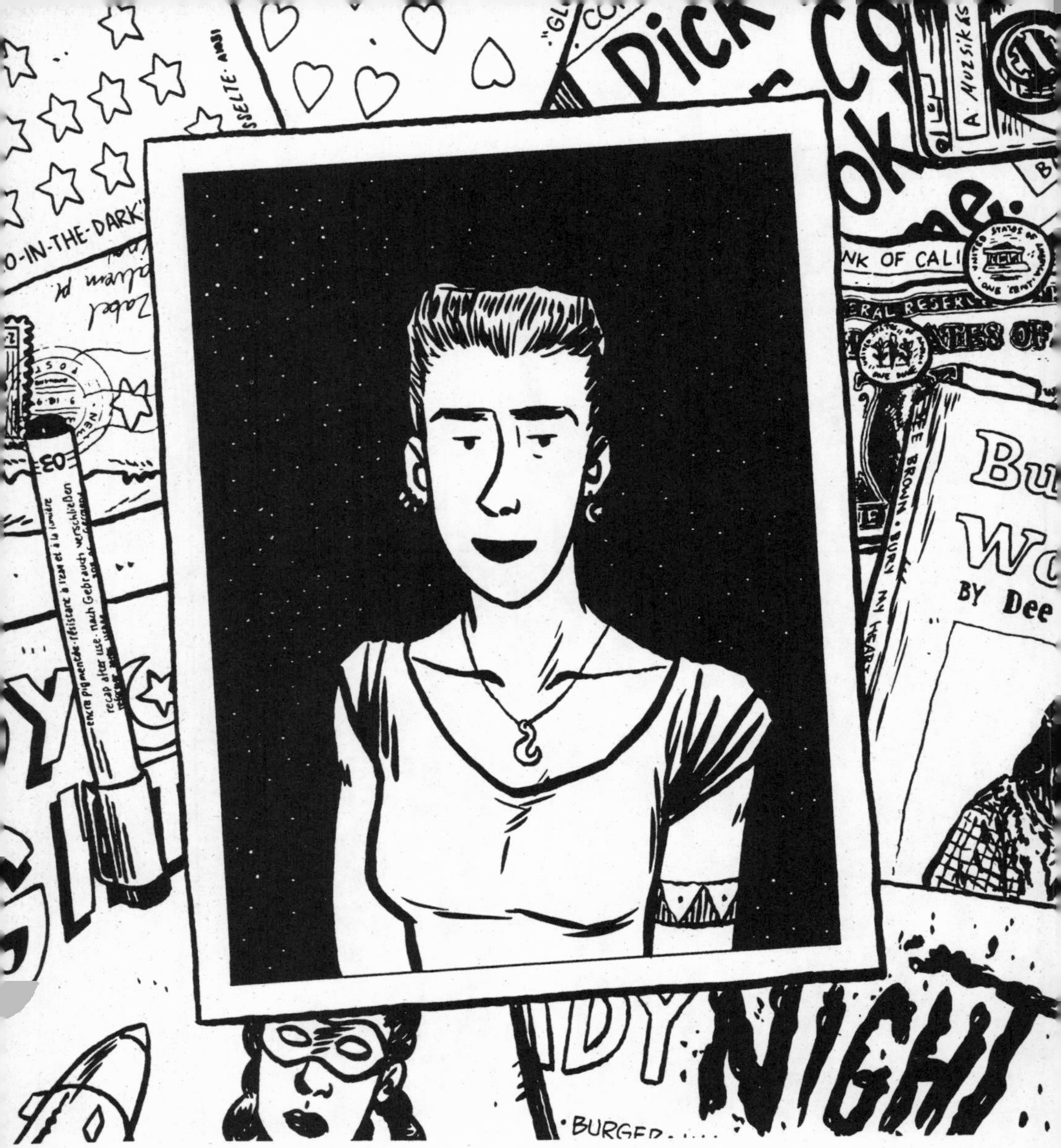
Dick
O-IN-THE-DARK
NK OF CALI
BROWN
BY Dee
DY
NIGHT
BURGER

Hicksville Press

Chapter Seven

"The medium of exchange in the comics business is guilt; it's not money."
Steve Englehart.

MARCH 1996
VOL. XII NO. 3
$2.95
LONG MAY HE RULE ETERNAL!!
COMICS WORLD
SPECIAL TRIBUTE ISSUE!!
ALL HAIL THE KING!!
DICK BURGER ENTERS THE HALL OF FAME
Eternal

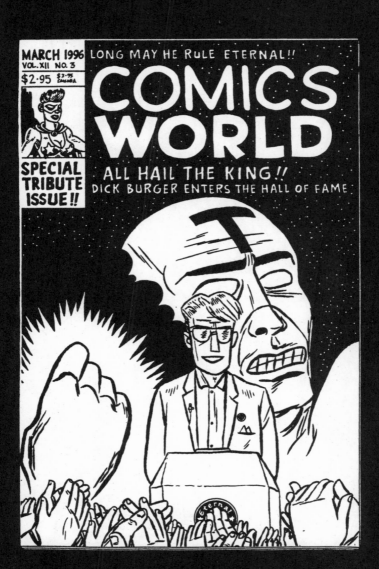

I had been charting this region for four months, when two weeks ago, a strange phenomenon occurred. I awoke one morning to find the landscape around me had inexplicably changed.

A hill had moved several leagues to the West; another had doubled in height. A gorge had become a valley, and a gentle brook was now a precipitous waterfall.

Since then I have been attempting to get my bearings and so to rectify my maps, but to no avail. The land is constantly in flux!

The land has never been still like a corpse. How do you map a man's life? The earth is playing a joke on you ...

Then we must find another way to determine our location.

But how, when there are no fixed landmarks against which to measure?

Simple. By using the stars and the compass. It is called *navigation*, sir.

But that is a mariner's art, good Captain, and as you can plainly tell, we are not at sea!

Hush. Did you hear that?

HOW ARE YOU FEELING NOW DEAR?

MUCH BETTER, THANKS MRS. HICKS. WOULD YOU MIND IF I MADE A TOLL CALL TO THE STATES? I CAN GIVE YOU CASH FOR IT.

WHY OF COURSE, DEAR, GO RIGHT AHEAD. THE PHONE'S IN THE HALL. *NOW*... HAVE YOU THOUGHT ABOUT WHAT YOU'D LIKE TO WEAR TO THE PARTY ON SATURDAY, DEAR. IF I START YOUR COSTUME TONIGHT, I SHOULD HAVE PLENTY OF TIME...

ACTUALLY, I HAVE, YES...

I'LL PUT YOU THROUGH NOW, MR. BAT *CRCKLLEE*

THANKS.

HELLO?

HELLO- IS THAT CINCINNATI WALKER?

...MIGHT BE. WHO ARE YOU?

MY NAME'S LEONARD BATTS, MS. WALKER. I WRITE FOR *COMICS WORLD* MAGAZINE. I'M CALLING FROM NEW ZEALAND TO CONFIRM A STORY GIVEN ME BY SAM ZABEL.

UH HUH...

er...DO YOU KNOW SAM ZABEL MS. WALKER...?

SURE. TELL HIM HE OWES ME A POSTCARD. WHAT'S HE TOLD YOU?

HE SAYS HE SPENT A WEEK AT DICK BURGER'S MANSION IN L.A. IN FEBRUARY '95 - THAT'S WHEN YOU WERE FILMING LADY NIGHT.

YEAH, I REMEMBER. WHAT DO YOU WANT TO KNOW?

DID SAM EVER TALK ABOUT DICK'S PAST? ABOUT SOMETHING TERRIBLE HE HAD DONE IN NEW ZEALAND?

...MMM...

DID HE TELL YOU WHAT THAT THING WAS?

...

MS. WALKER?

CRACKLE

I'M SORRY- THIS IS A TERRIBLE LINE- I DIDN'T GET THAT LAST BIT-

CRRRR CCRRAACCC HISSSPOP CCCRR

HELLO?

SCRRKKK

...

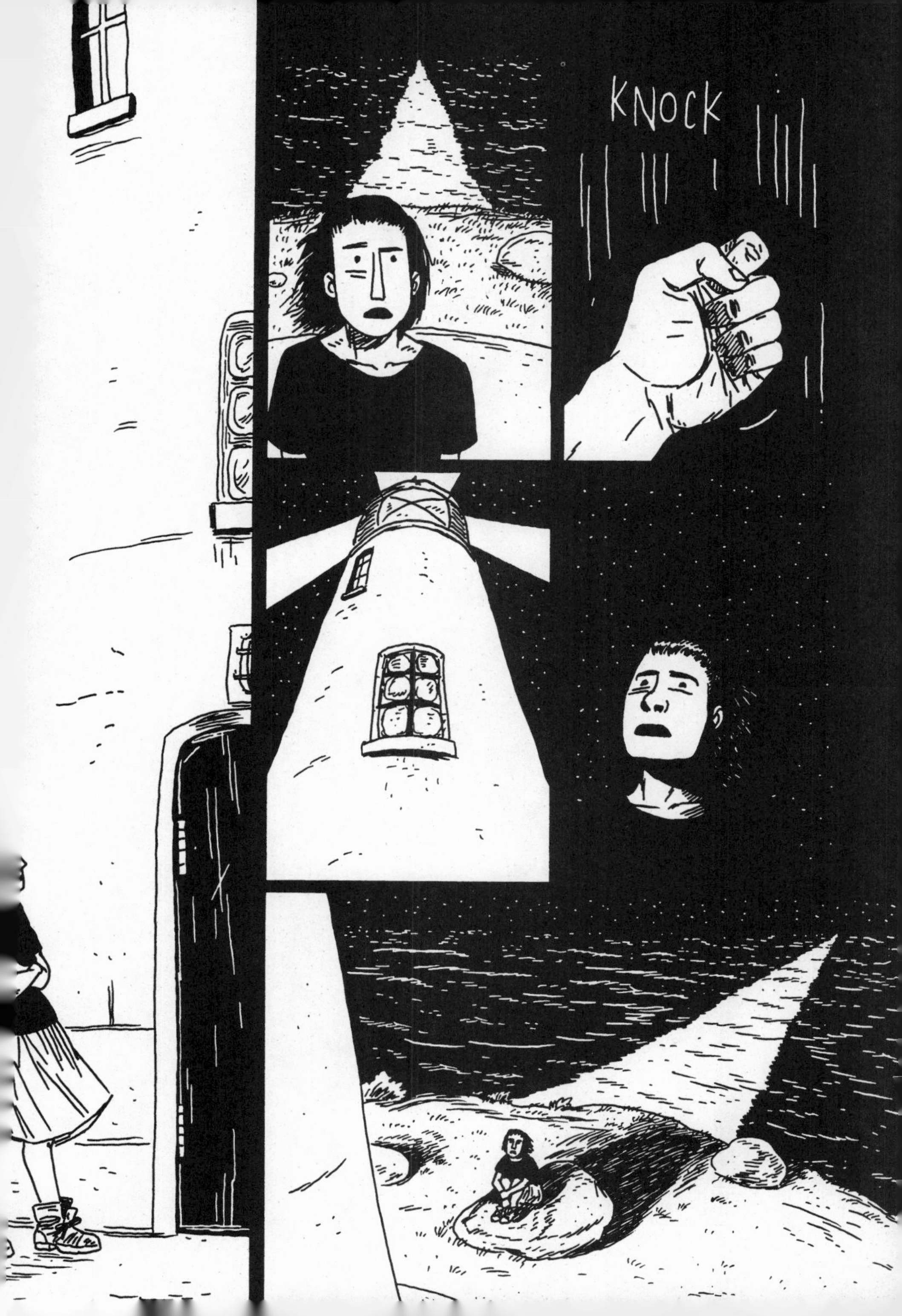
KNOCK

Chapter Eight

"I've seen recent examples of superheroes being pushed around and made fun of and I don't go along with it. Nobody ever pushed me around in those serials. The world needs heroes today."

Kirk Alyn, star of Superman (1948)
and Atom Man vs. Superman (1952).

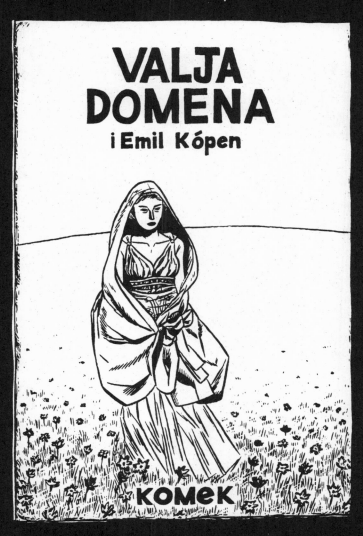

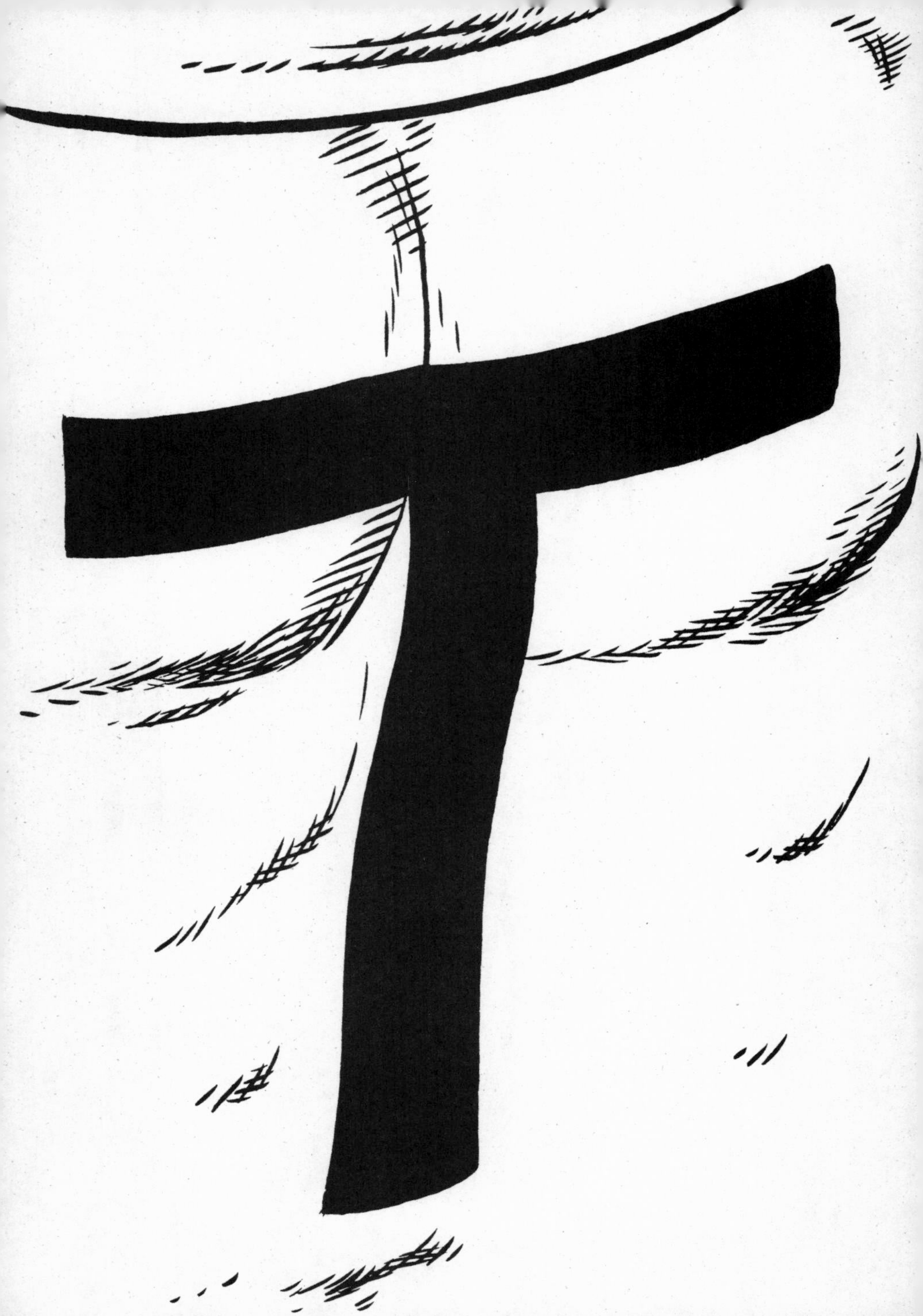

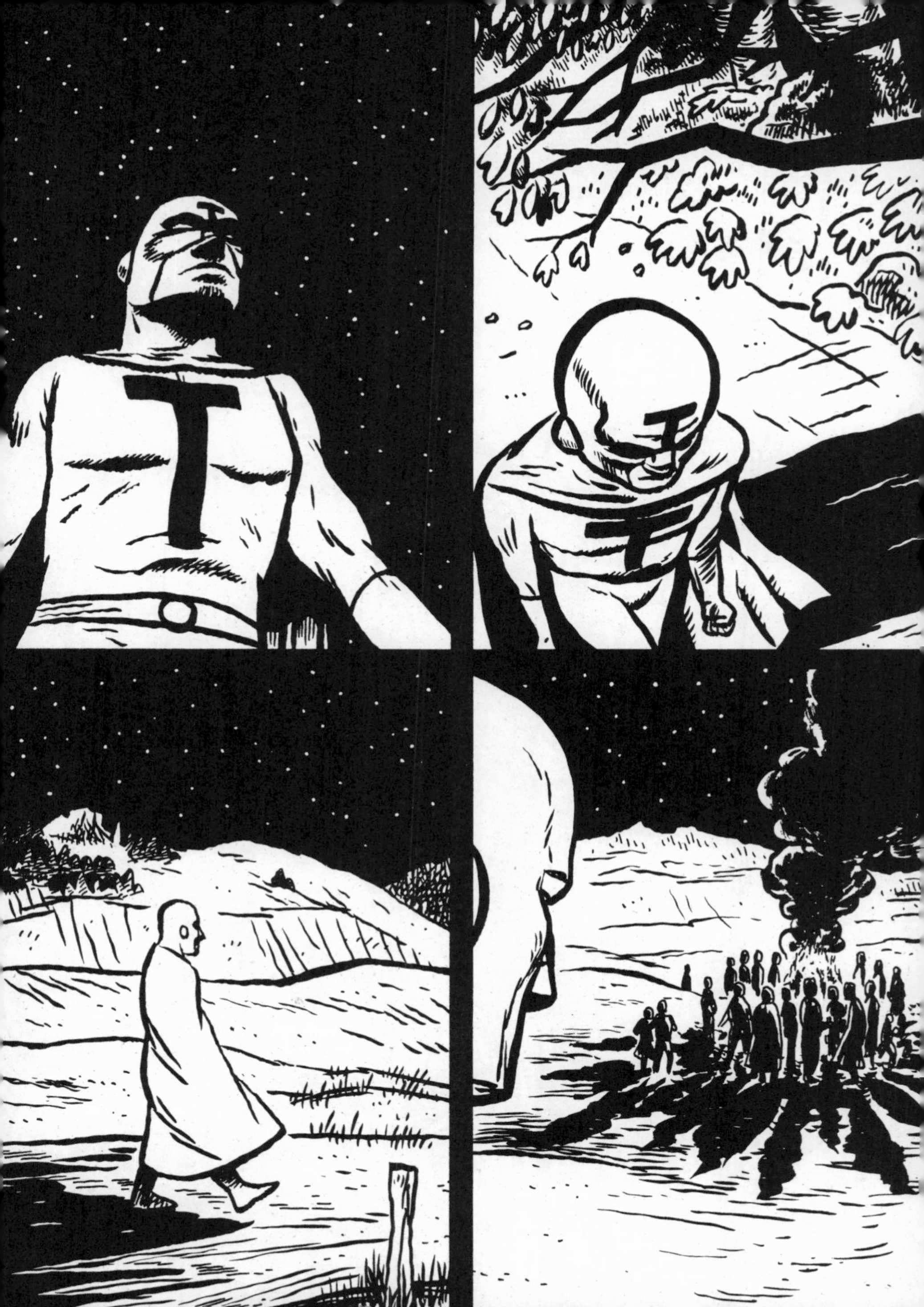

YEAH, WELL, GRACE THINKS I'M TOO FAT NOW FOR ROBIN.

OH GOOD HEAVENS, I WOULDN'T SAY THAT! I EXPECT SHE'S JUST BEING A LITTLE IRREVERENT!

HULLO YOU TWO!

OH MY, HOW IMPRESSIVE, HARRY DEAR!

THANK YOU, MRS. HICKS. JUST A LITTLE SOMETHING I THREW TOGETHER, YOU KNOW! HOW'S YOUR VISITOR FROM AMERICA GETTING ON?

LEONARD? WELL, TO BE QUITE HONEST, I'M A LITTLE WORRIED ABOUT HIM, THE POOR DEAR...

WORRIED?

er... I DON'T KNOW HOW MUCH I SHOULD SAY... I SUPPOSE YOU'LL SEE FOR YOURSELVES SOON ENOUGH...

SO HE IS COMING DOWN FOR THE PARTY? WHAT'S HE DOING FOR A COSTUME?

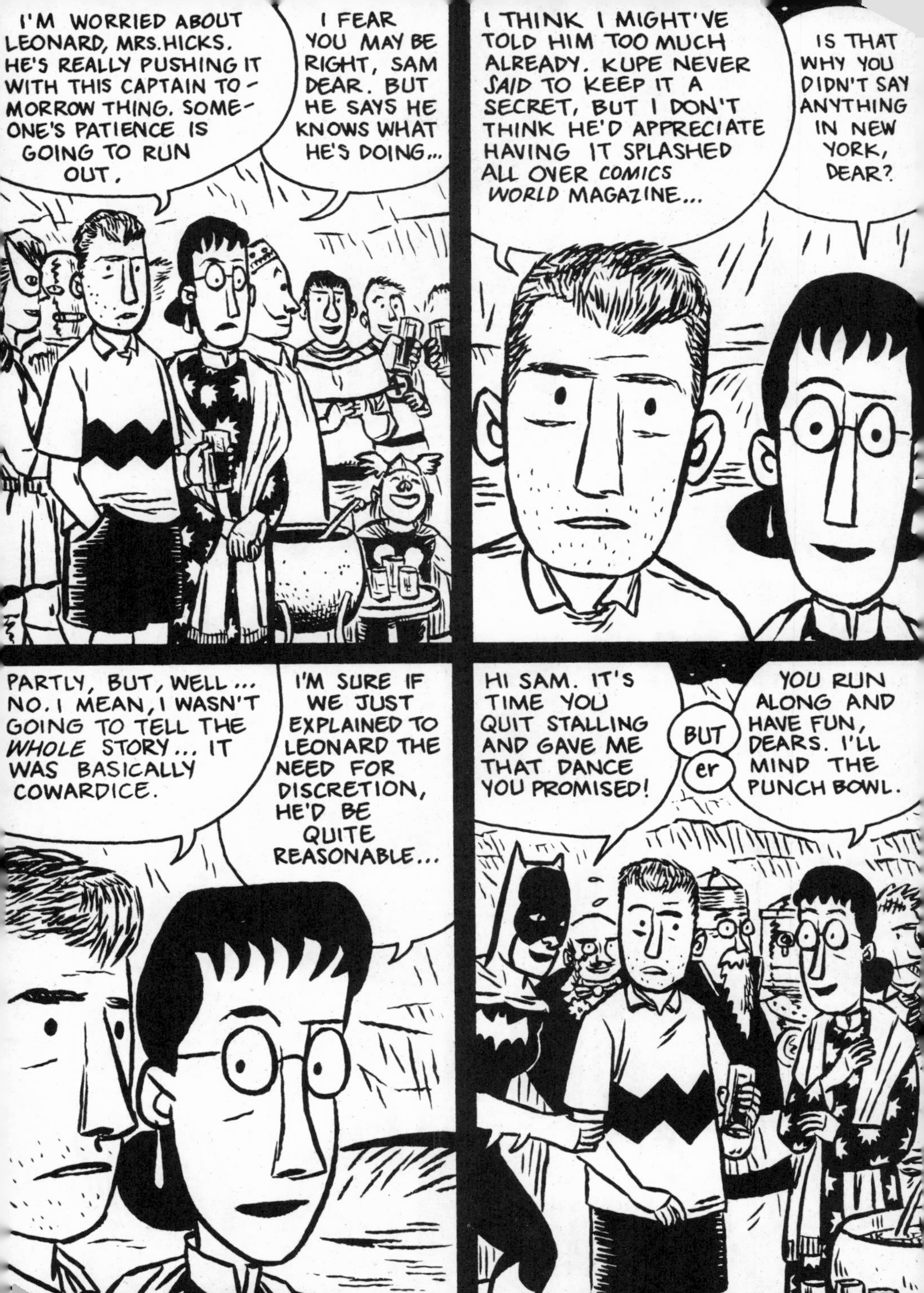
I'M WORRIED ABOUT LEONARD, MRS. HICKS. HE'S REALLY PUSHING IT WITH THIS CAPTAIN TO-MORROW THING. SOME-ONE'S PATIENCE IS GOING TO RUN OUT.
I FEAR YOU MAY BE RIGHT, SAM DEAR. BUT HE SAYS HE KNOWS WHAT HE'S DOING...
I THINK I MIGHT'VE TOLD HIM TOO MUCH ALREADY. KUPE NEVER SAID TO KEEP IT A SECRET, BUT I DON'T THINK HE'D APPRECIATE HAVING IT SPLASHED ALL OVER COMICS WORLD MAGAZINE...
IS THAT WHY YOU DIDN'T SAY ANYTHING IN NEW YORK, DEAR?
PARTLY, BUT, WELL... NO. I MEAN, I WASN'T GOING TO TELL THE WHOLE STORY... IT WAS BASICALLY COWARDICE.
I'M SURE IF WE JUST EXPLAINED TO LEONARD THE NEED FOR DISCRETION, HE'D BE QUITE REASONABLE...
HI SAM. IT'S TIME YOU QUIT STALLING AND GAVE ME THAT DANCE YOU PROMISED!
BUT
er
YOU RUN ALONG AND HAVE FUN, DEARS. I'LL MIND THE PUNCH BOWL.

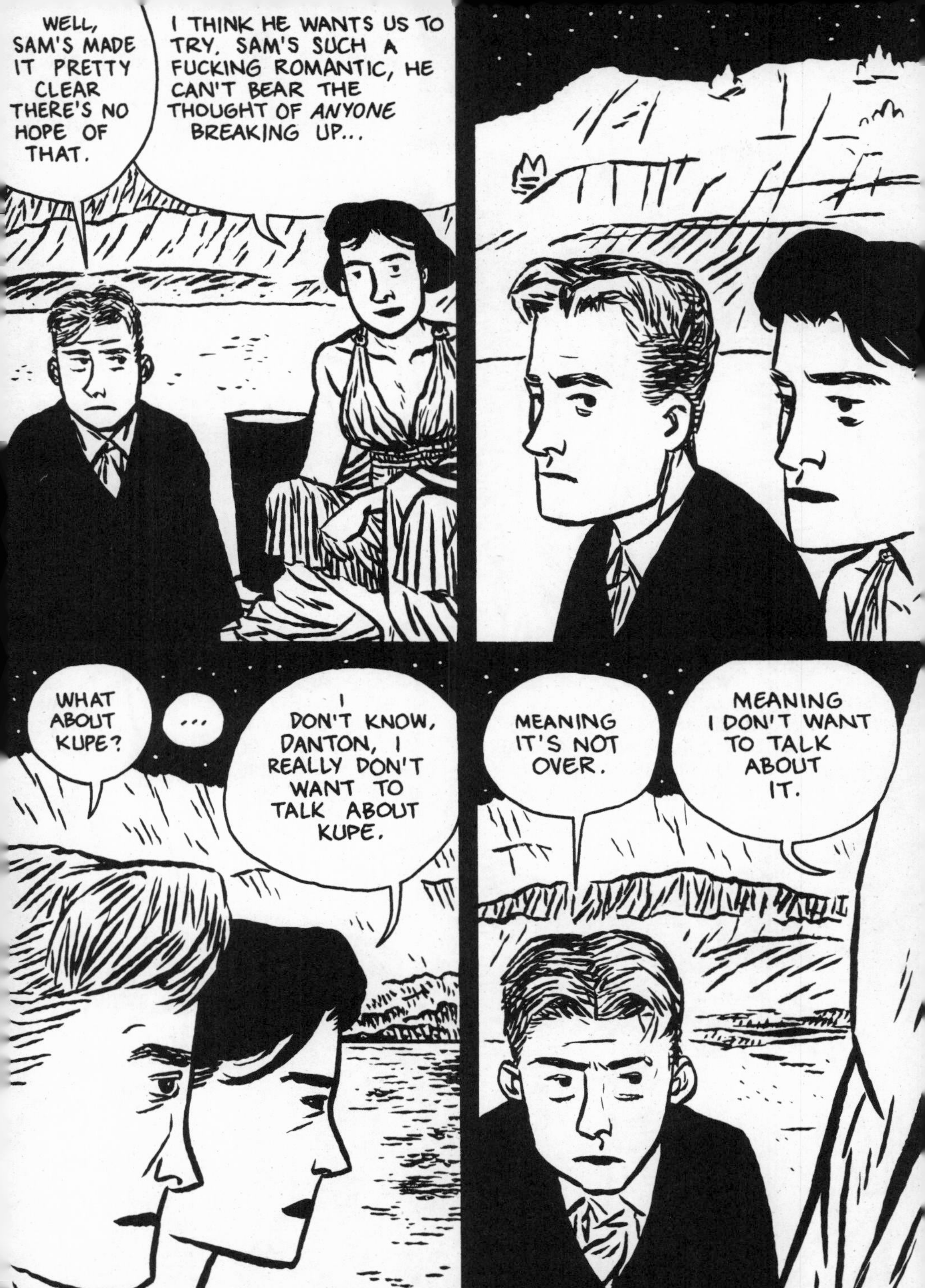

WELL, SAM'S MADE IT PRETTY CLEAR THERE'S NO HOPE OF THAT.
I THINK HE WANTS US TO TRY. SAM'S SUCH A FUCKING ROMANTIC, HE CAN'T BEAR THE THOUGHT OF *ANYONE* BREAKING UP...
WHAT ABOUT KUPE?
...
I DON'T KNOW, DANTON, I REALLY DON'T WANT TO TALK ABOUT KUPE.
MEANING IT'S NOT OVER.
MEANING I DON'T WANT TO TALK ABOUT IT.

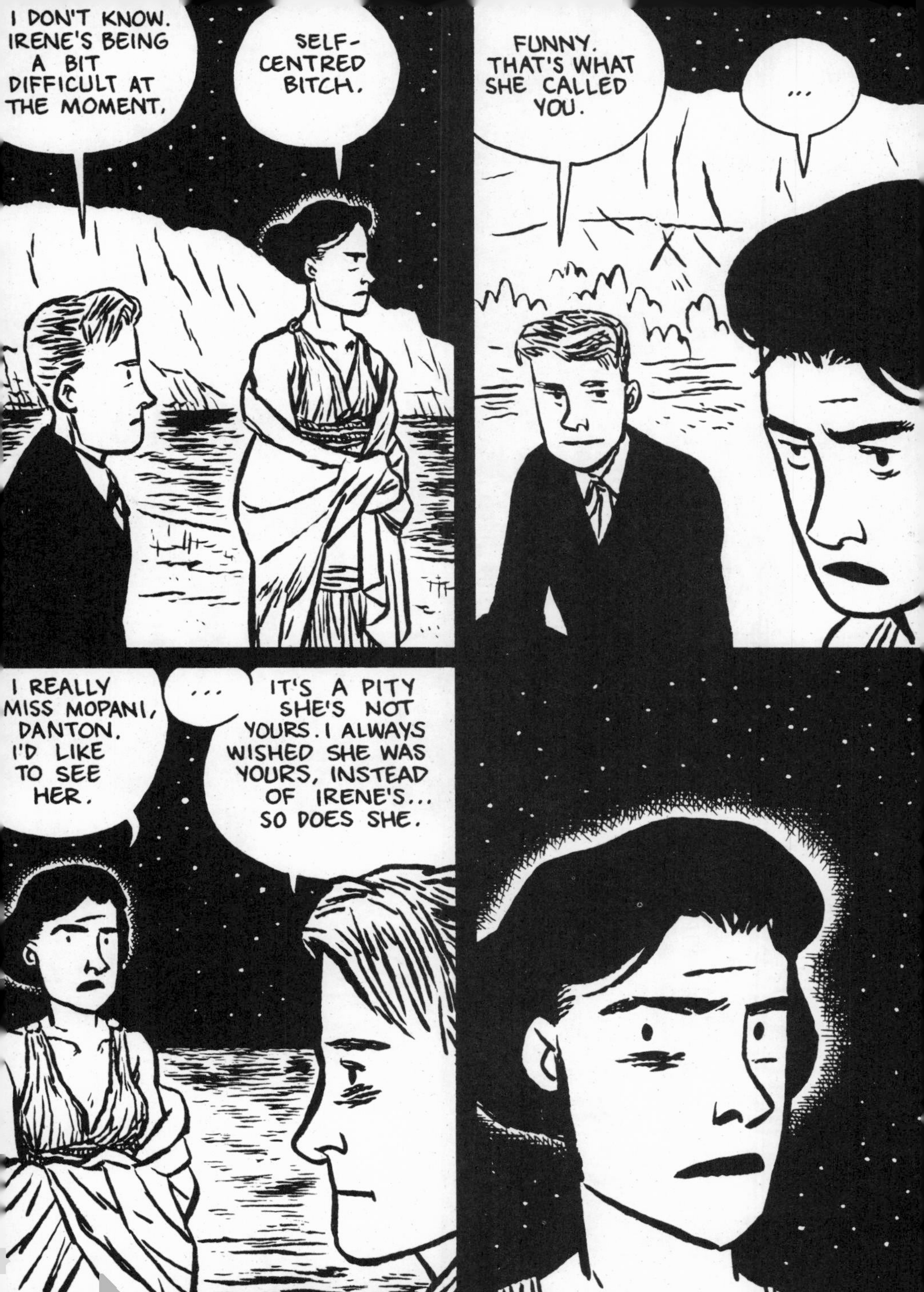
I DON'T KNOW. IRENE'S BEING A BIT DIFFICULT AT THE MOMENT.
SELF-CENTRED BITCH.
FUNNY. THAT'S WHAT SHE CALLED YOU.
...
I REALLY MISS MOPANI, DANTON. I'D LIKE TO SEE HER.
...
IT'S A PITY SHE'S NOT YOURS. I ALWAYS WISHED SHE WAS YOURS, INSTEAD OF IRENE'S... SO DOES SHE.

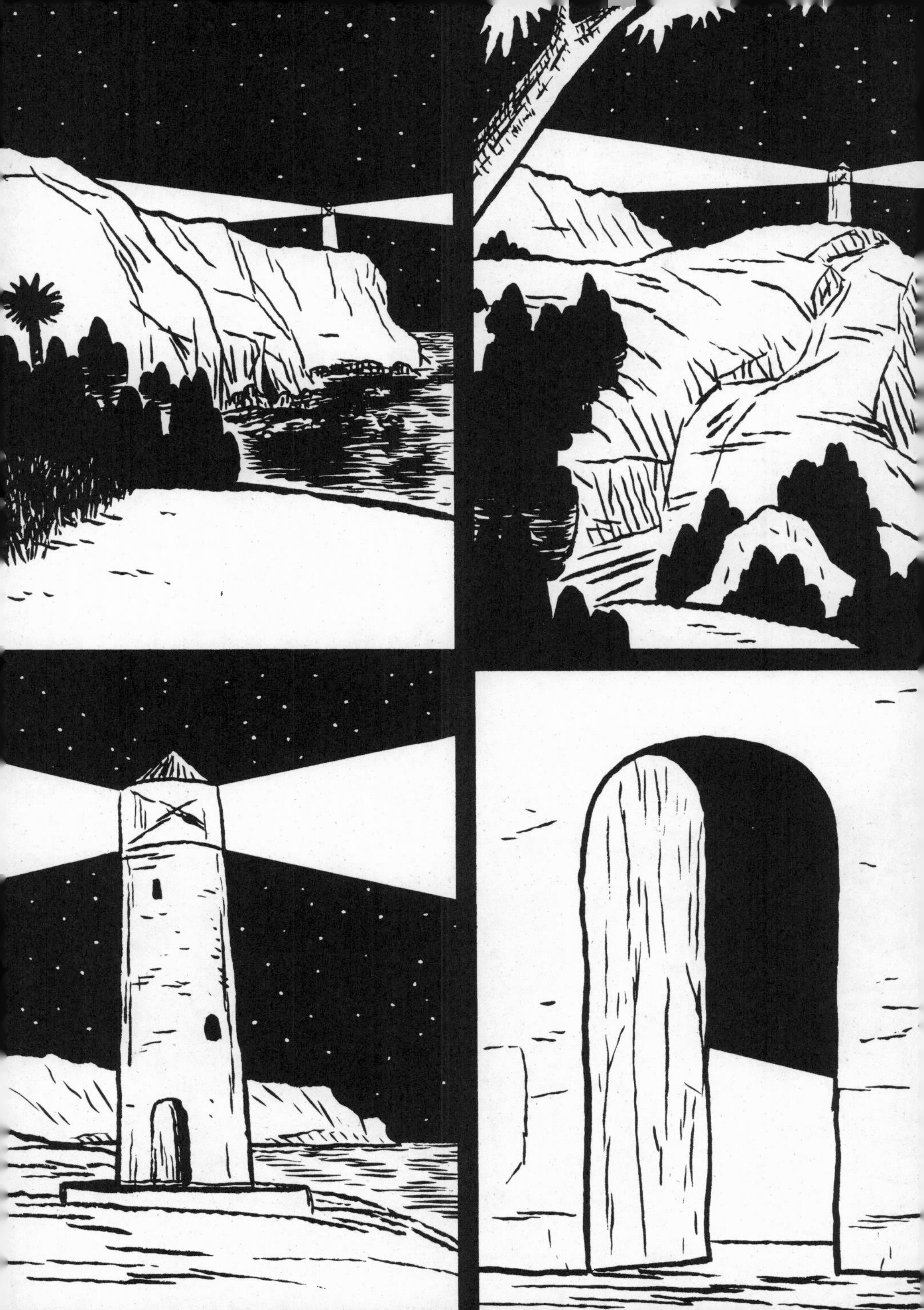

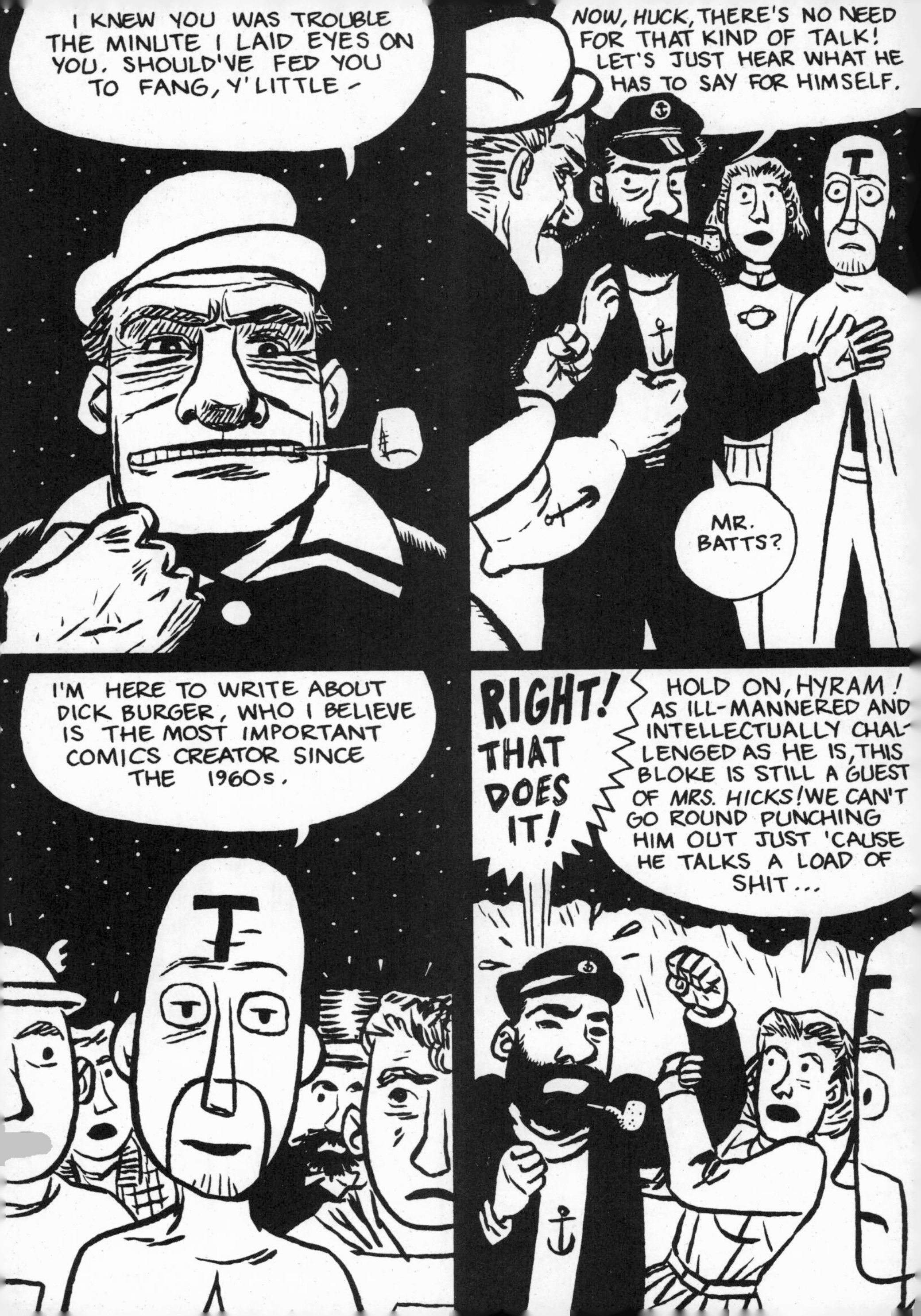

I KNEW YOU WAS TROUBLE THE MINUTE I LAID EYES ON YOU. SHOULD'VE FED YOU TO FANG, Y'LITTLE -
NOW, HUCK, THERE'S NO NEED FOR THAT KIND OF TALK! LET'S JUST HEAR WHAT HE HAS TO SAY FOR HIMSELF.
MR. BATTS?
I'M HERE TO WRITE ABOUT DICK BURGER, WHO I BELIEVE IS THE MOST IMPORTANT COMICS CREATOR SINCE THE 1960s.
RIGHT! THAT DOES IT!
HOLD ON, HYRAM! AS ILL-MANNERED AND INTELLECTUALLY CHALLENGED AS HE IS, THIS BLOKE IS STILL A GUEST OF MRS. HICKS! WE CAN'T GO ROUND PUNCHING HIM OUT JUST 'CAUSE HE TALKS A LOAD OF SHIT...

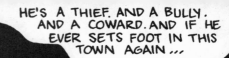

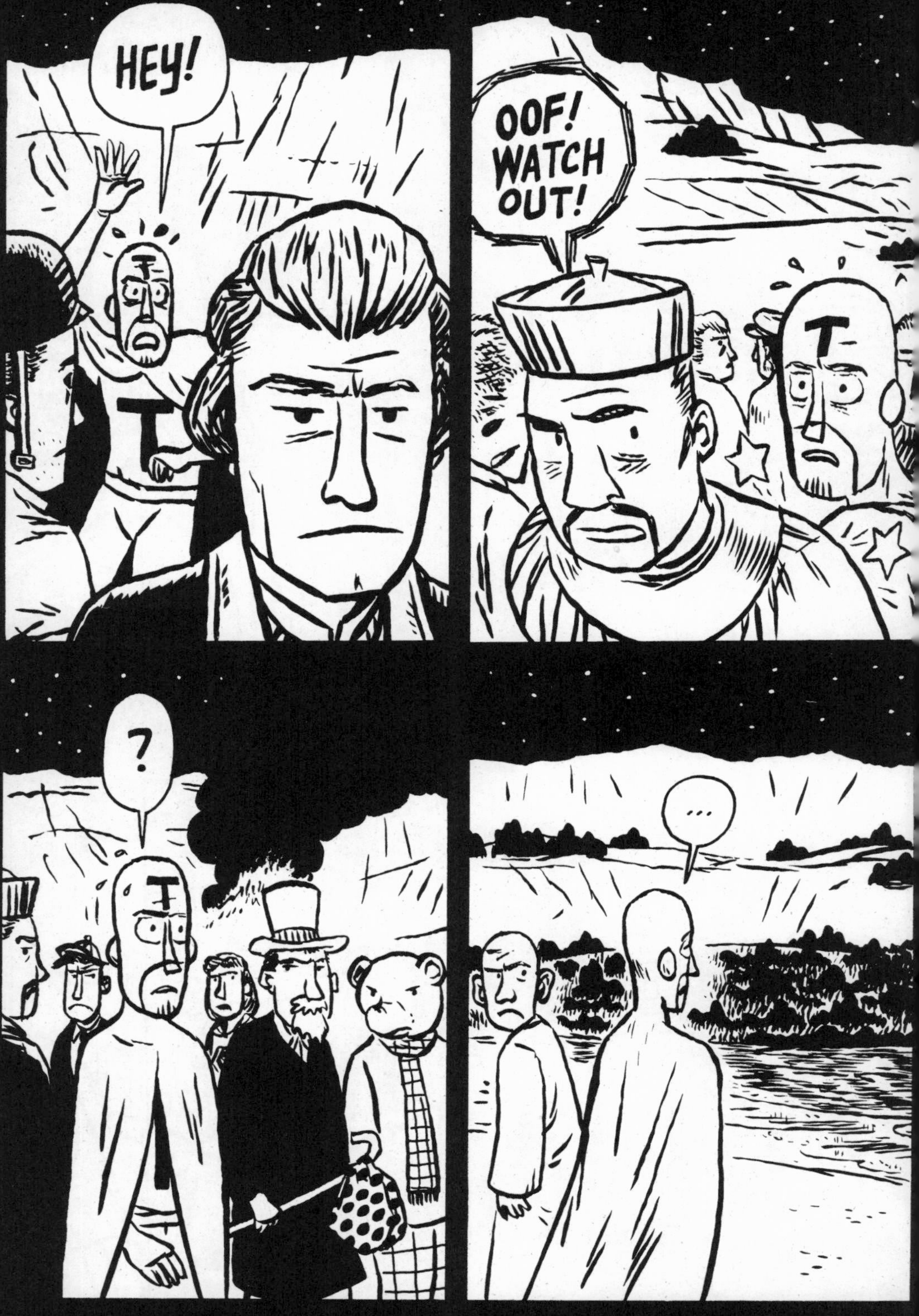
HEY!
OOF! WATCH OUT!
?
...

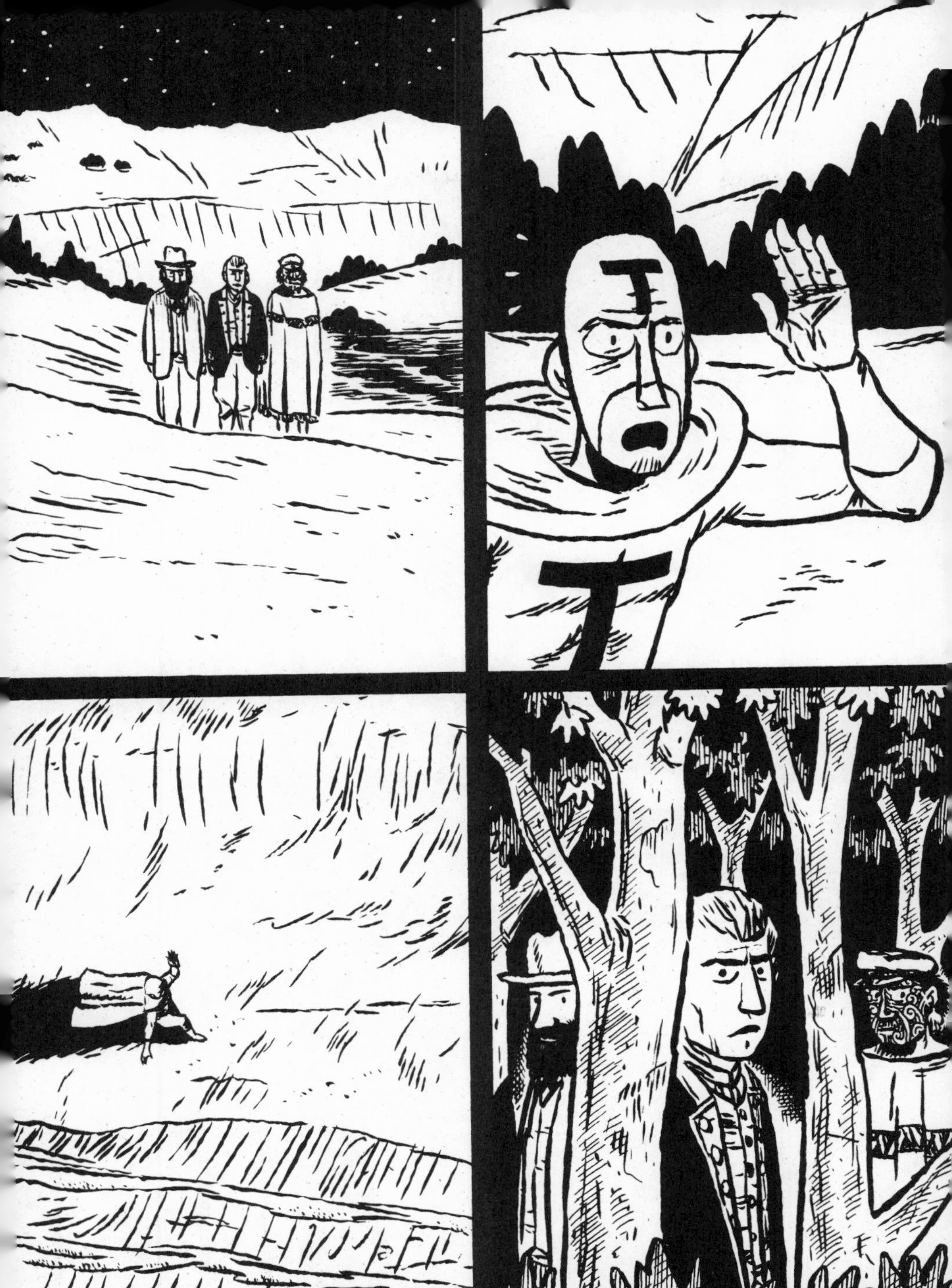

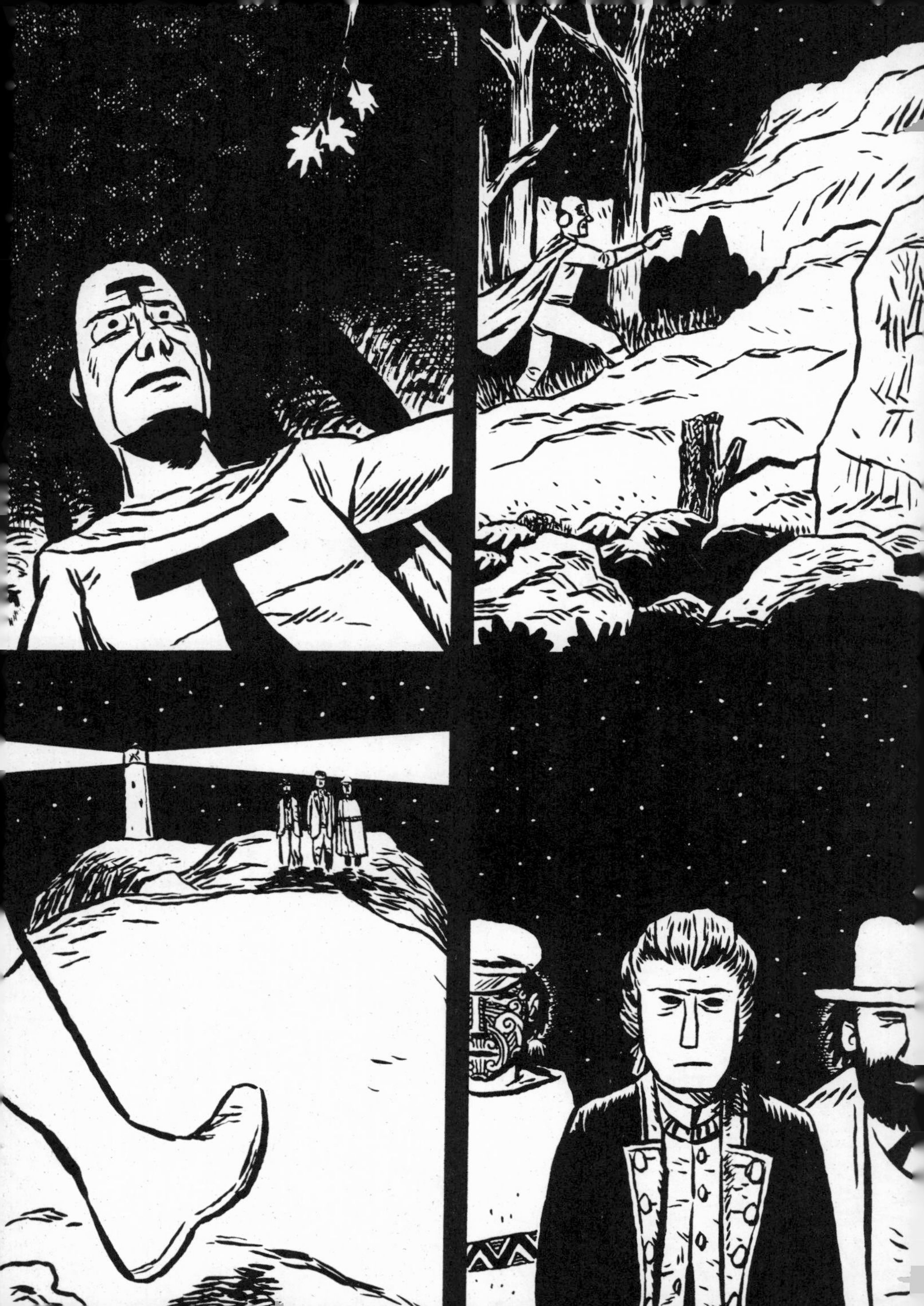

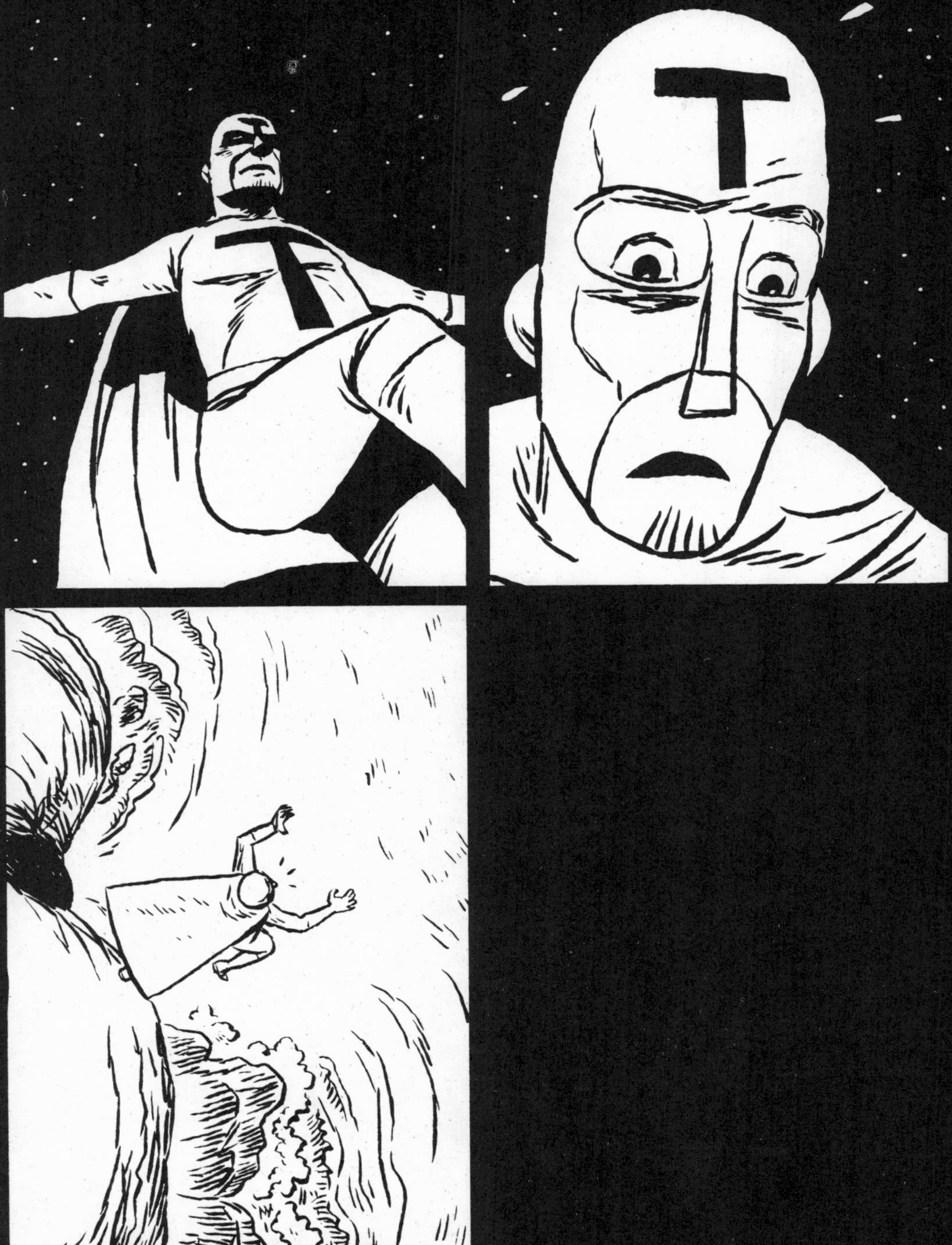

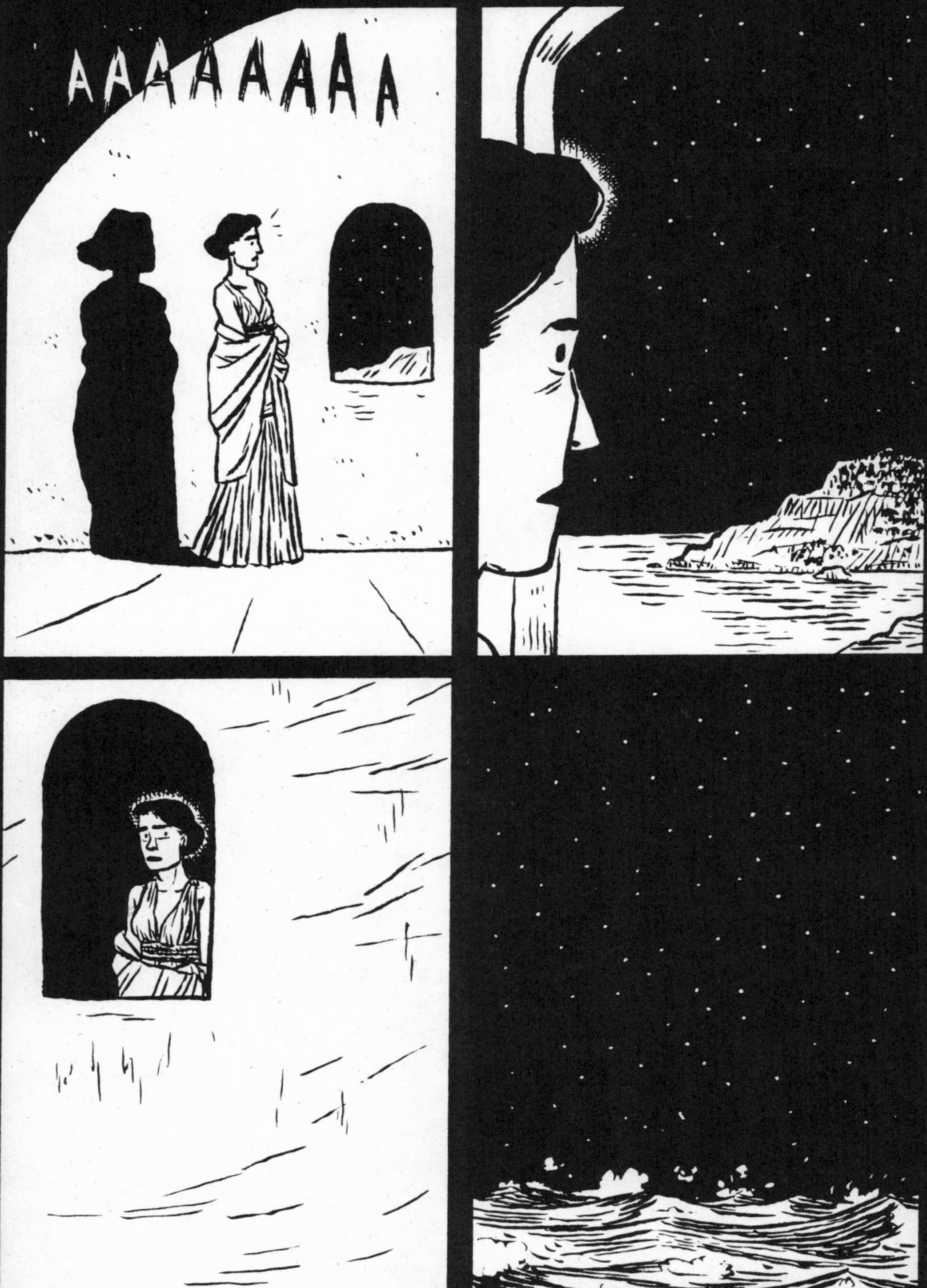
AAAAAAAA

Chapter Nine

"Inspiration! Who ever heard of
a comic artist being inspired?"
George Herriman, c.1902.

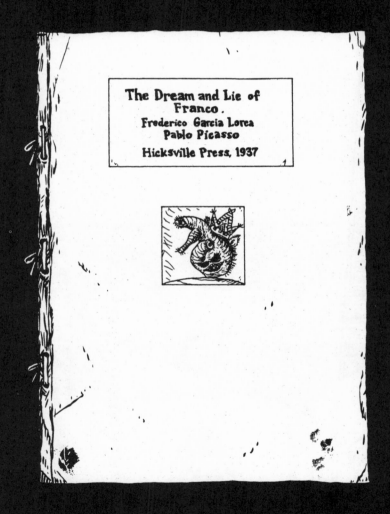

The Dream and Lie of
Franco.
Frederico Garcia Lorca
Pablo Picasso

Hicksville Press, 1937

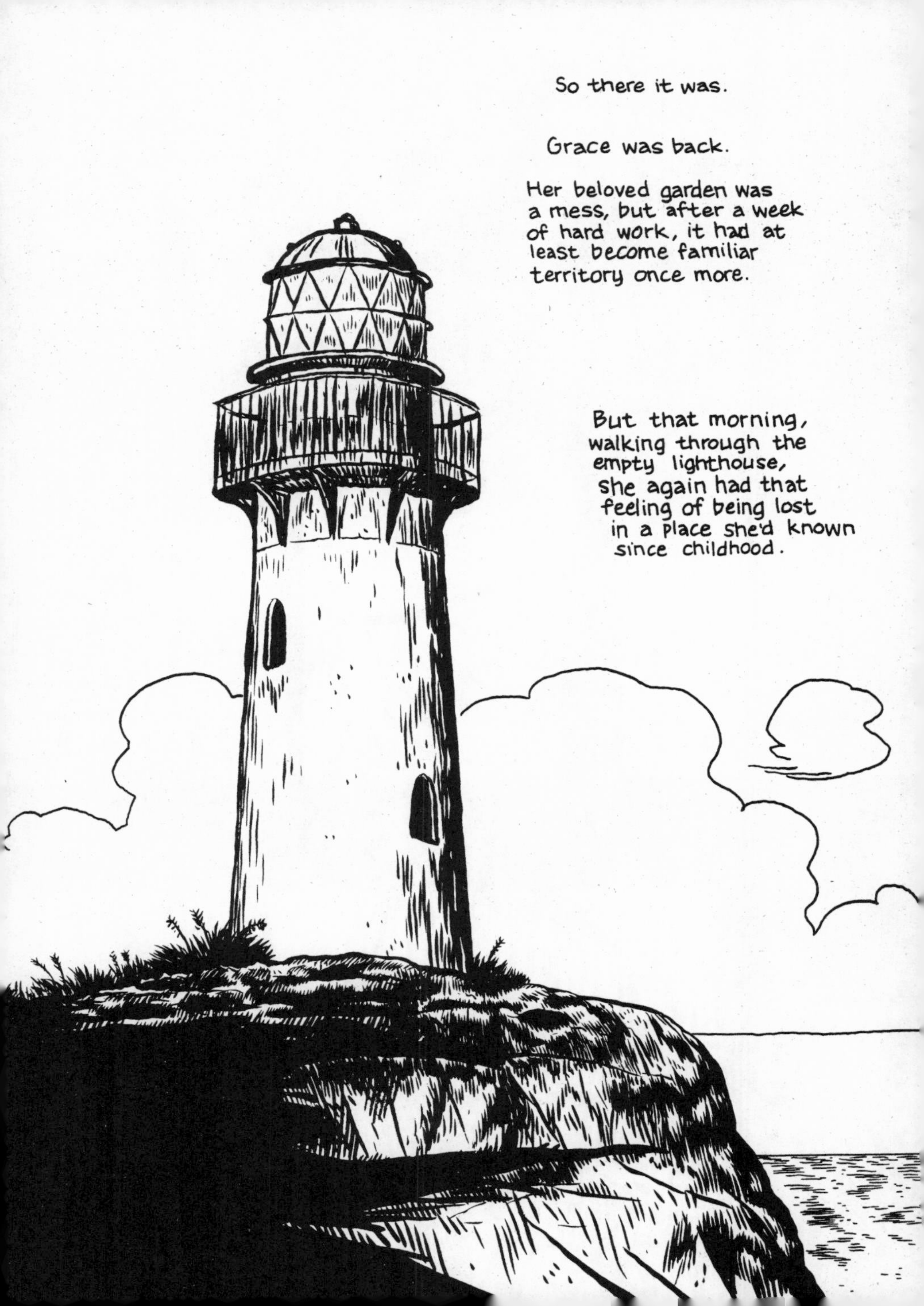
So there it was.
Grace was back.
Her beloved garden was a mess, but after a week of hard work, it had at least become familiar territory once more.
But that morning, walking through the empty lighthouse, she again had that feeling of being lost in a place she'd known since childhood.

There was another time
she'd come to the lighthouse,
looking for Kupe...

Walking barefoot over
the cold stone floor

into the dark tunnels

That time,
she'd known
where to
find him

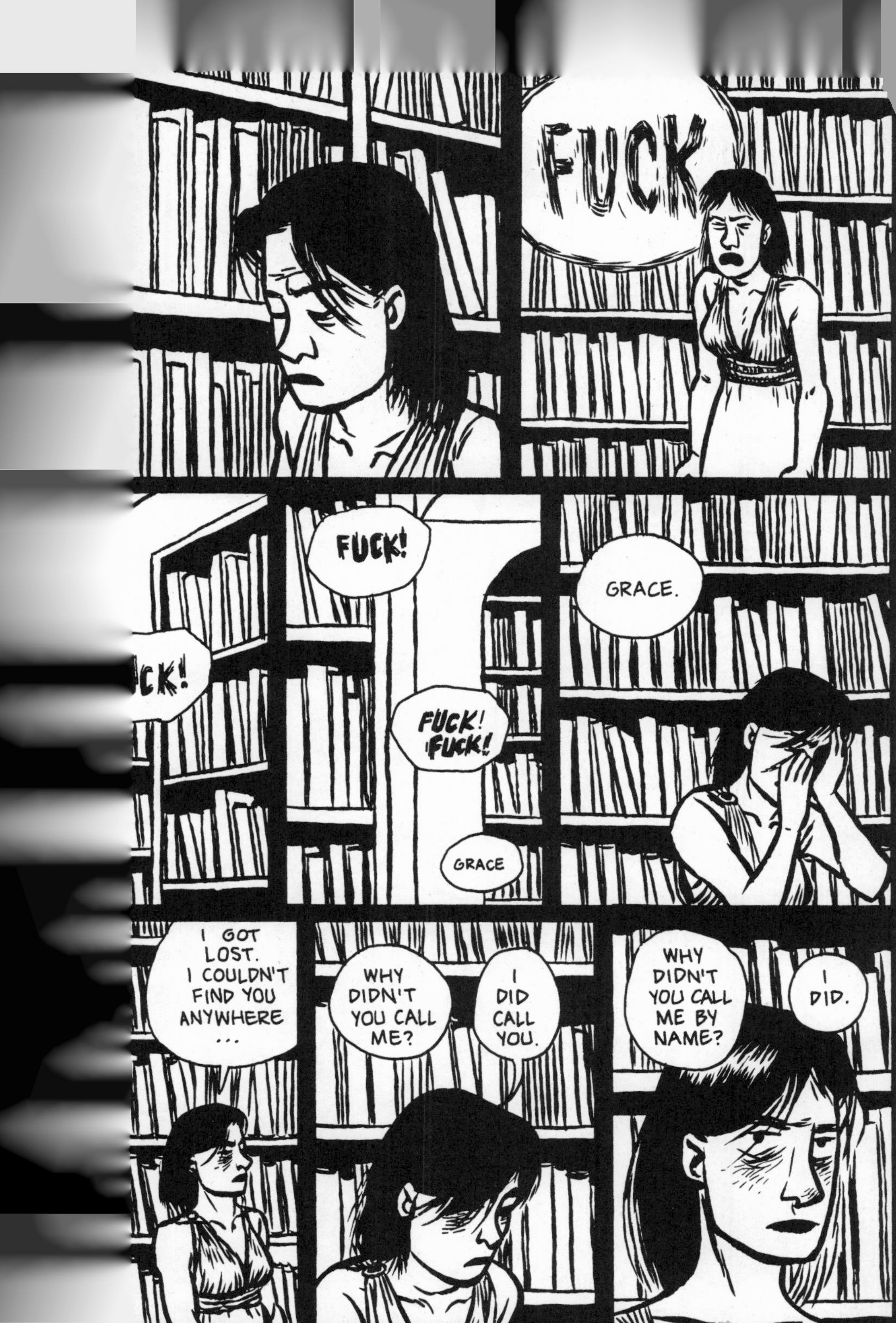
FUCK
FUCK!
CK!
FUCK! FUCK!
GRACE
GRACE.
I GOT LOST. I COULDN'T FIND YOU ANYWHERE ...
WHY DIDN'T YOU CALL ME?
I DID CALL YOU.
WHY DIDN'T YOU CALL ME BY NAME?
I DID.

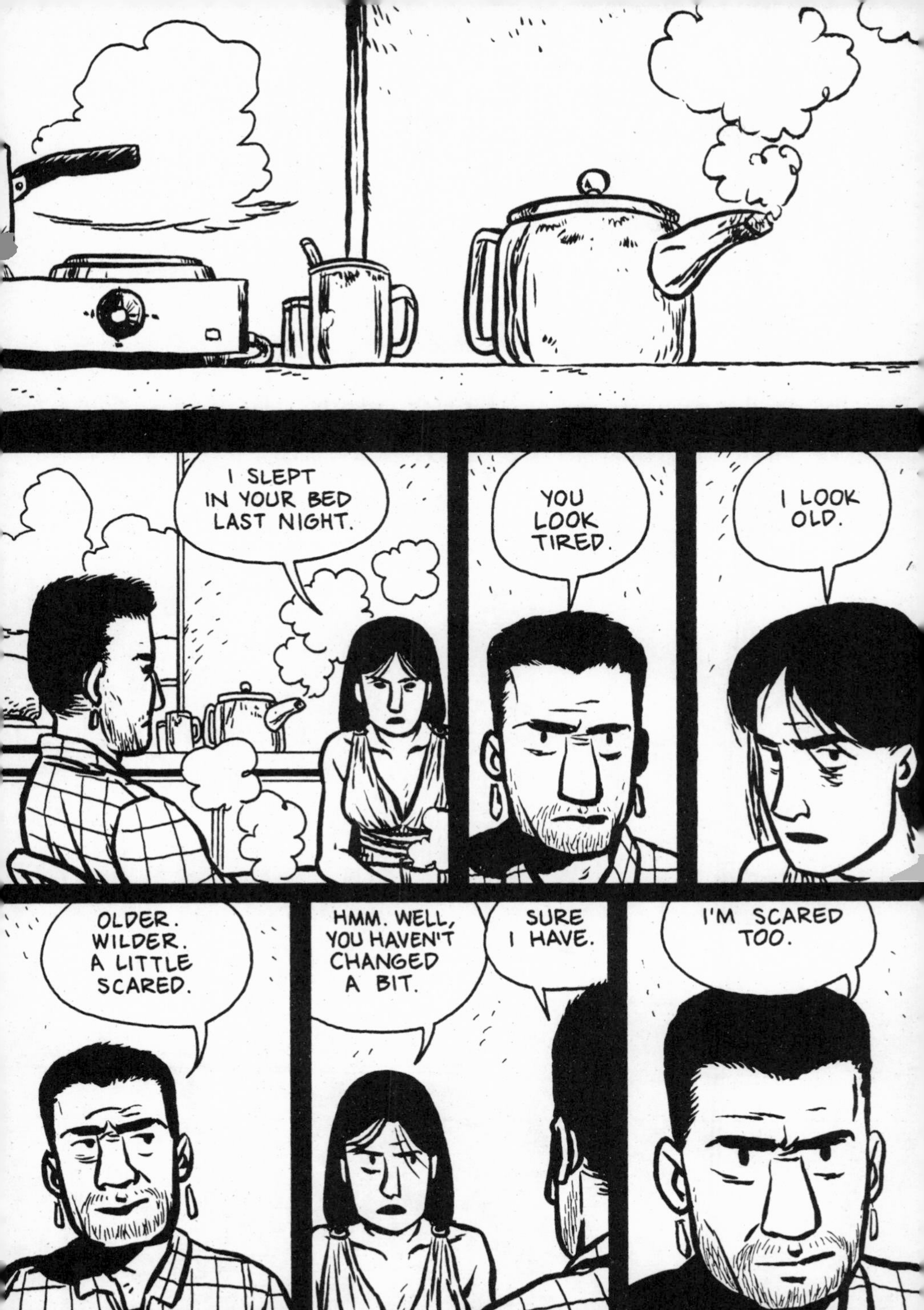
I SLEPT IN YOUR BED LAST NIGHT.
YOU LOOK TIRED.
I LOOK OLD.
OLDER. WILDER. A LITTLE SCARED.
HMM. WELL, YOU HAVEN'T CHANGED A BIT.
SURE I HAVE.
I'M SCARED TOO.

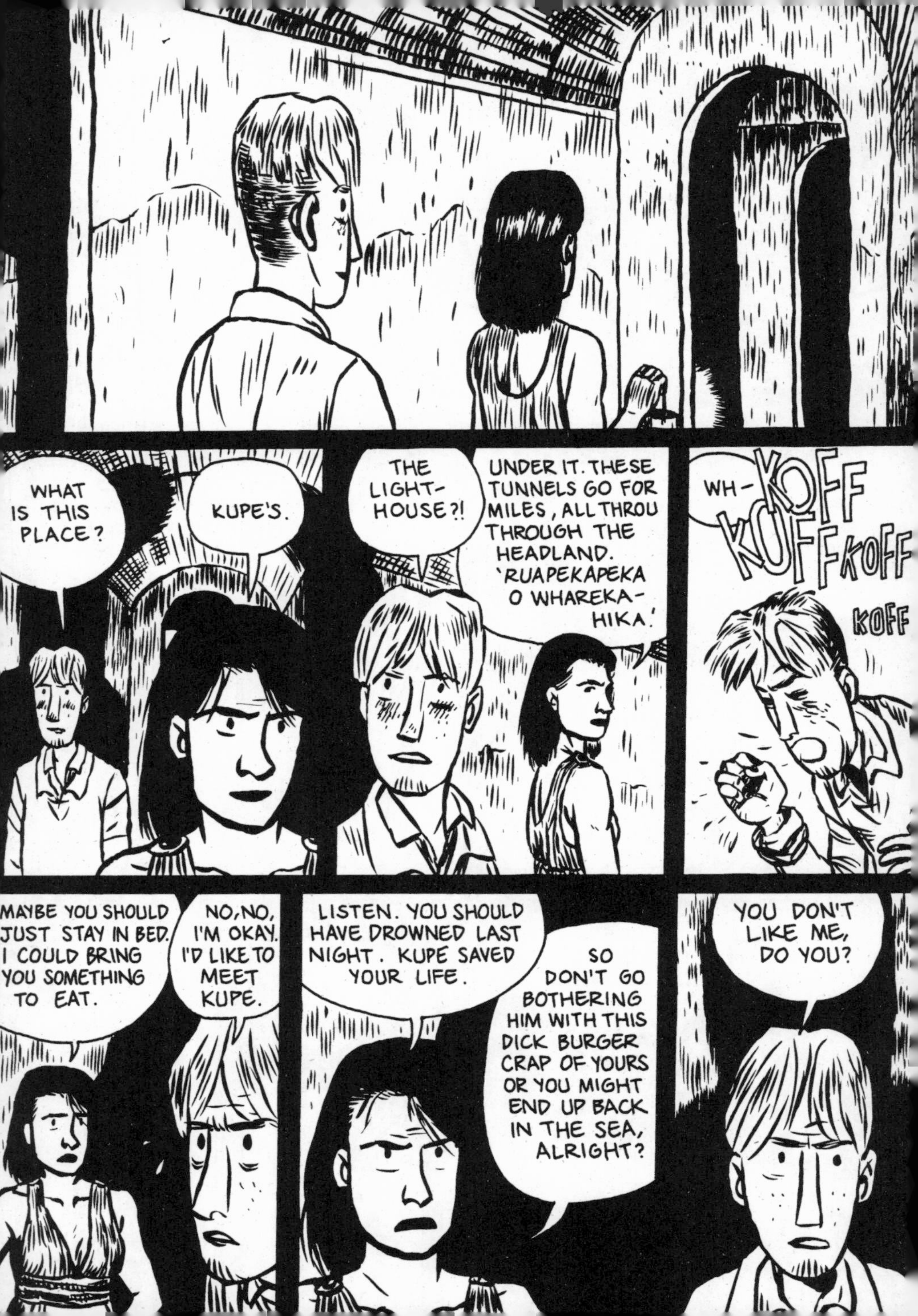
WHAT IS THIS PLACE?
KUPE'S.
THE LIGHT-HOUSE?!
UNDER IT. THESE TUNNELS GO FOR MILES, ALL THROU THROUGH THE HEADLAND. 'RUAPEKAPEKA O WHAREKAHIKA.'
WH-KOFF
KOFF KOFF KOFF
KOFF
MAYBE YOU SHOULD JUST STAY IN BED. I COULD BRING YOU SOMETHING TO EAT.
NO, NO, I'M OKAY. I'D LIKE TO MEET KUPE.
LISTEN. YOU SHOULD HAVE DROWNED LAST NIGHT. KUPE SAVED YOUR LIFE.
SO DON'T GO BOTHERING HIM WITH THIS DICK BURGER CRAP OF YOURS OR YOU MIGHT END UP BACK IN THE SEA, ALRIGHT?
YOU DON'T LIKE ME, DO YOU?

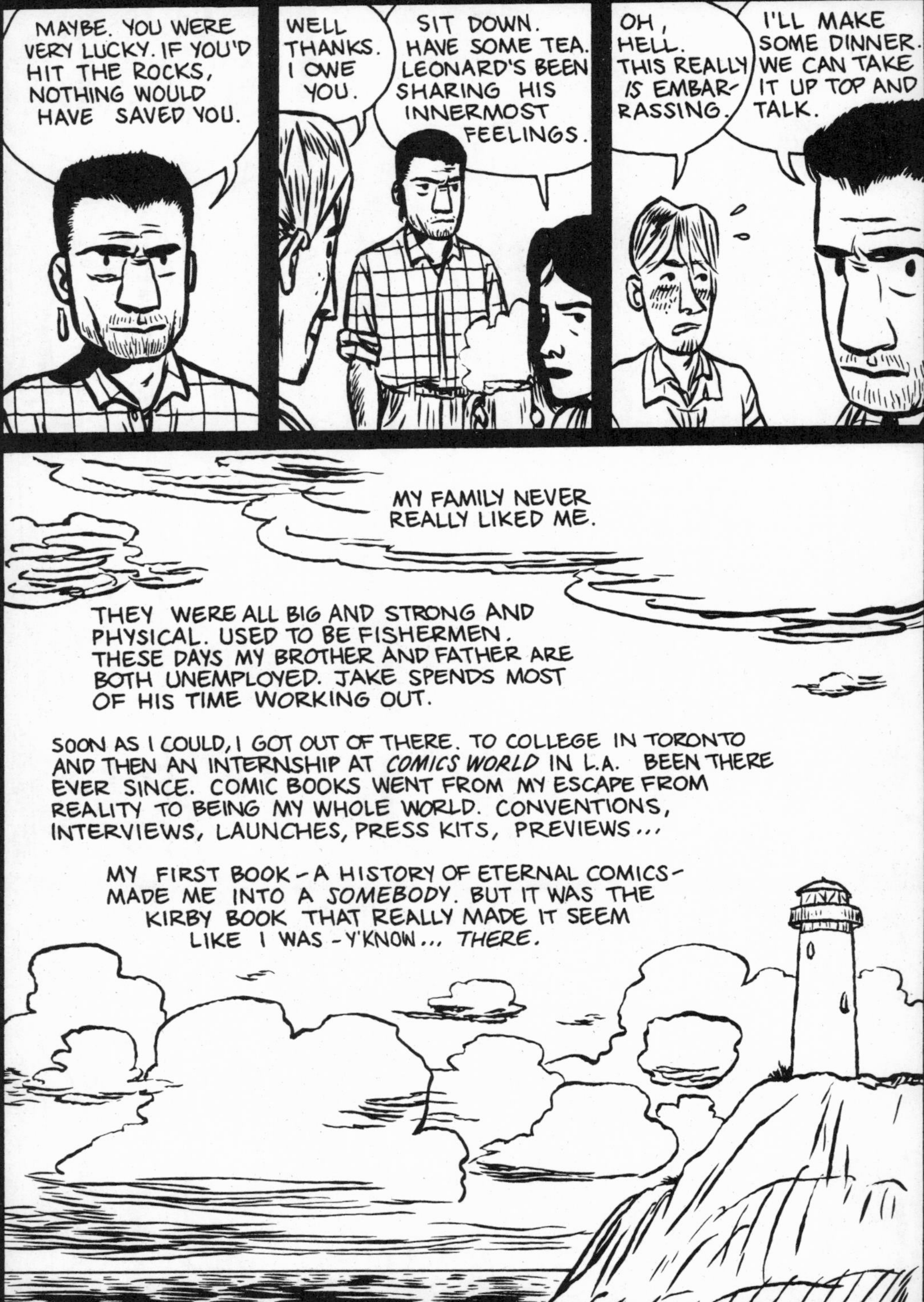
MAYBE. YOU WERE VERY LUCKY. IF YOU'D HIT THE ROCKS, NOTHING WOULD HAVE SAVED YOU.
WELL THANKS. I OWE YOU.
SIT DOWN. HAVE SOME TEA. LEONARD'S BEEN SHARING HIS INNERMOST FEELINGS.
OH, HELL. THIS REALLY IS EMBARRASSING.
I'LL MAKE SOME DINNER. WE CAN TAKE IT UP TOP AND TALK.
MY FAMILY NEVER REALLY LIKED ME.
THEY WERE ALL BIG AND STRONG AND PHYSICAL. USED TO BE FISHERMEN. THESE DAYS MY BROTHER AND FATHER ARE BOTH UNEMPLOYED. JAKE SPENDS MOST OF HIS TIME WORKING OUT.
SOON AS I COULD, I GOT OUT OF THERE. TO COLLEGE IN TORONTO AND THEN AN INTERNSHIP AT COMICS WORLD IN L.A. BEEN THERE EVER SINCE. COMIC BOOKS WENT FROM MY ESCAPE FROM REALITY TO BEING MY WHOLE WORLD. CONVENTIONS, INTERVIEWS, LAUNCHES, PRESS KITS, PREVIEWS...
MY FIRST BOOK - A HISTORY OF ETERNAL COMICS - MADE ME INTO A SOMEBODY. BUT IT WAS THE KIRBY BOOK THAT REALLY MADE IT SEEM LIKE I WAS - Y'KNOW... THERE.

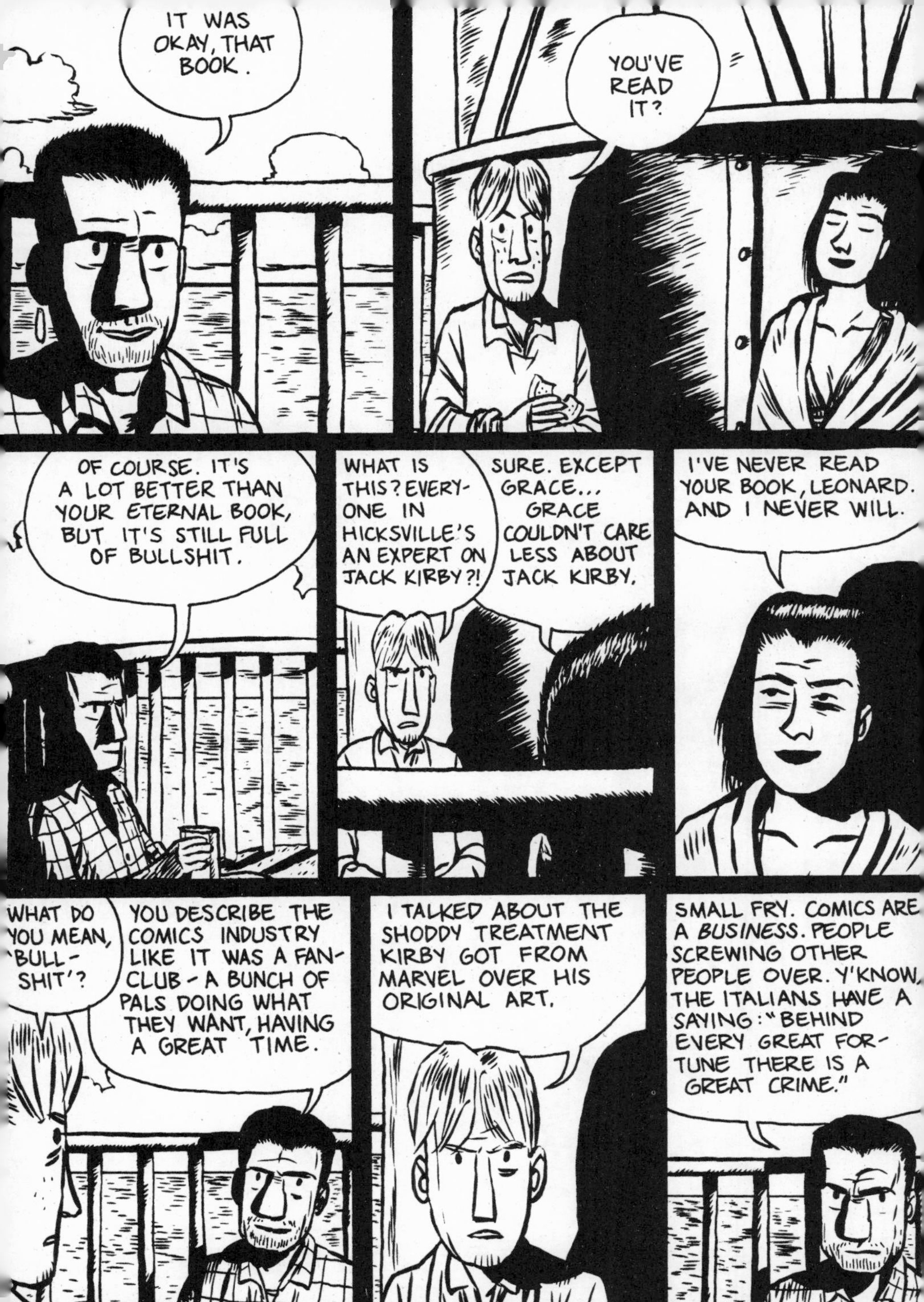
IT WAS OKAY, THAT BOOK.
YOU'VE READ IT?
OF COURSE. IT'S A LOT BETTER THAN YOUR ETERNAL BOOK, BUT IT'S STILL FULL OF BULLSHIT.
WHAT IS THIS? EVERY-ONE IN HICKSVILLE'S AN EXPERT ON JACK KIRBY?!
SURE. EXCEPT GRACE... GRACE COULDN'T CARE LESS ABOUT JACK KIRBY.
I'VE NEVER READ YOUR BOOK, LEONARD. AND I NEVER WILL.
WHAT DO YOU MEAN, 'BULL-SHIT'?
YOU DESCRIBE THE COMICS INDUSTRY LIKE IT WAS A FAN-CLUB - A BUNCH OF PALS DOING WHAT THEY WANT, HAVING A GREAT TIME.
I TALKED ABOUT THE SHODDY TREATMENT KIRBY GOT FROM MARVEL OVER HIS ORIGINAL ART.
SMALL FRY. COMICS ARE A *BUSINESS*. PEOPLE SCREWING OTHER PEOPLE OVER. Y'KNOW, THE ITALIANS HAVE A SAYING: "BEHIND EVERY GREAT FOR-TUNE THERE IS A GREAT CRIME."

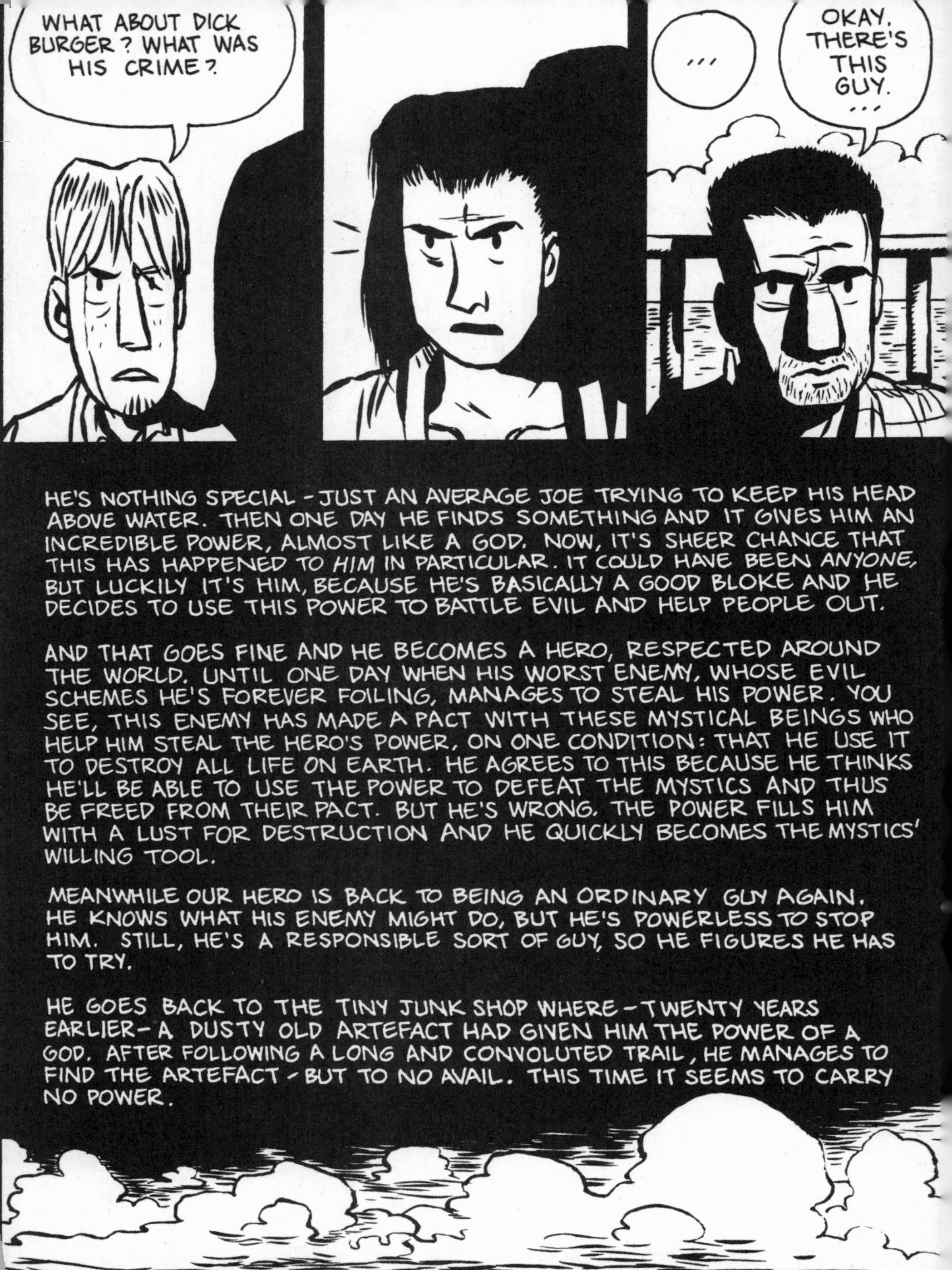
WHAT ABOUT DICK BURGER? WHAT WAS HIS CRIME?
...
OKAY. THERE'S THIS GUY. ...
HE'S NOTHING SPECIAL - JUST AN AVERAGE JOE TRYING TO KEEP HIS HEAD ABOVE WATER. THEN ONE DAY HE FINDS SOMETHING AND IT GIVES HIM AN INCREDIBLE POWER, ALMOST LIKE A GOD. NOW, IT'S SHEER CHANCE THAT THIS HAS HAPPENED TO *HIM* IN PARTICULAR. IT COULD HAVE BEEN *ANYONE*, BUT LUCKILY IT'S HIM, BECAUSE HE'S BASICALLY A GOOD BLOKE AND HE DECIDES TO USE THIS POWER TO BATTLE EVIL AND HELP PEOPLE OUT.
AND THAT GOES FINE AND HE BECOMES A HERO, RESPECTED AROUND THE WORLD. UNTIL ONE DAY WHEN HIS WORST ENEMY, WHOSE EVIL SCHEMES HE'S FOREVER FOILING, MANAGES TO STEAL HIS POWER. YOU SEE, THIS ENEMY HAS MADE A PACT WITH THESE MYSTICAL BEINGS WHO HELP HIM STEAL THE HERO'S POWER, ON ONE CONDITION: THAT HE USE IT TO DESTROY ALL LIFE ON EARTH. HE AGREES TO THIS BECAUSE HE THINKS HE'LL BE ABLE TO USE THE POWER TO DEFEAT THE MYSTICS AND THUS BE FREED FROM THEIR PACT. BUT HE'S WRONG. THE POWER FILLS HIM WITH A LUST FOR DESTRUCTION AND HE QUICKLY BECOMES THE MYSTICS' WILLING TOOL.
MEANWHILE OUR HERO IS BACK TO BEING AN ORDINARY GUY AGAIN. HE KNOWS WHAT HIS ENEMY MIGHT DO, BUT HE'S POWERLESS TO STOP HIM. STILL, HE'S A RESPONSIBLE SORT OF GUY, SO HE FIGURES HE HAS TO TRY.
HE GOES BACK TO THE TINY JUNK SHOP WHERE - TWENTY YEARS EARLIER - A DUSTY OLD ARTEFACT HAD GIVEN HIM THE POWER OF A GOD. AFTER FOLLOWING A LONG AND CONVOLUTED TRAIL, HE MANAGES TO FIND THE ARTEFACT - BUT TO NO AVAIL. THIS TIME IT SEEMS TO CARRY NO POWER.

BUT OUR HERO CANNOT GIVE UP. HE RETRACES HIS OWN STEPS DURING
THE YEARS FOLLOWING THAT FIRST VISIT TO THE OLD JUNK SHOP, AND
AS THE STORY OF HIS CAREER AS A SUPERHERO UNFOLDS, HE BEGINS
TO DISCERN PATTERNS AND NOTICE DETAILS THAT HE HAD PREVIOUSLY
TAKEN FOR GRANTED. AND GRADUALLY THE SECRETS OF HIS LOST
POWER.

ALL THIS TIME HE'S BEING PURSUED BY HIS ENEMIES, BUT HE MANAGES
TO STAY ONE STEP AHEAD OF THEM, JUST BY THINKING AHEAD AND
ACCEPTING THE HELP OF GOOD PEOPLE. BUT FINALLY, HIS LUCK RUNS
OUT. HIS ENEMY FINDS HIM AND HE'S TRAPPED. AS HIS ENEMY
PREPARES TO DESTROY HIM, OUR HERO HOLDS THE OLD ARTEFACT
BEFORE HIM, AS A FUTILE SHIELD...

THE ENEMY UNLEASHES THE POWER — AND AS IT STRIKES THE ARTEFACT,
THERE IS A HUGE, CATACLYSMIC EXPLOSION.

THEN EVERYTHING FALLS QUIET.

AFTER WHAT SEEMS LIKE AN ETERNITY, OUR HERO AWAKES, AMAZED
THAT HE'S STILL ALIVE. HIS ENEMY HAS BEEN KILLED, AND THE POWER
SNUFFED OUT FOREVER AFTER DESTROYING ITS OWN SOURCE. THE
WORLD HAS BEEN SAVED.

AND SO OUR HERO RETURNS TO HIS ORDINARY LIFE, MORE CONTENTED
THAN HE HAS EVER BEEN. HE MARRIES, RAISES CHILDREN, RETIRES,
GROWS OLD.

NOW AND THEN, HE MISSES THE DAYS WHEN HE HAD THE POWER OF
A GOD. BUT FOR THE MOST PART, HE'S HAPPY WITH HIS LIFE.

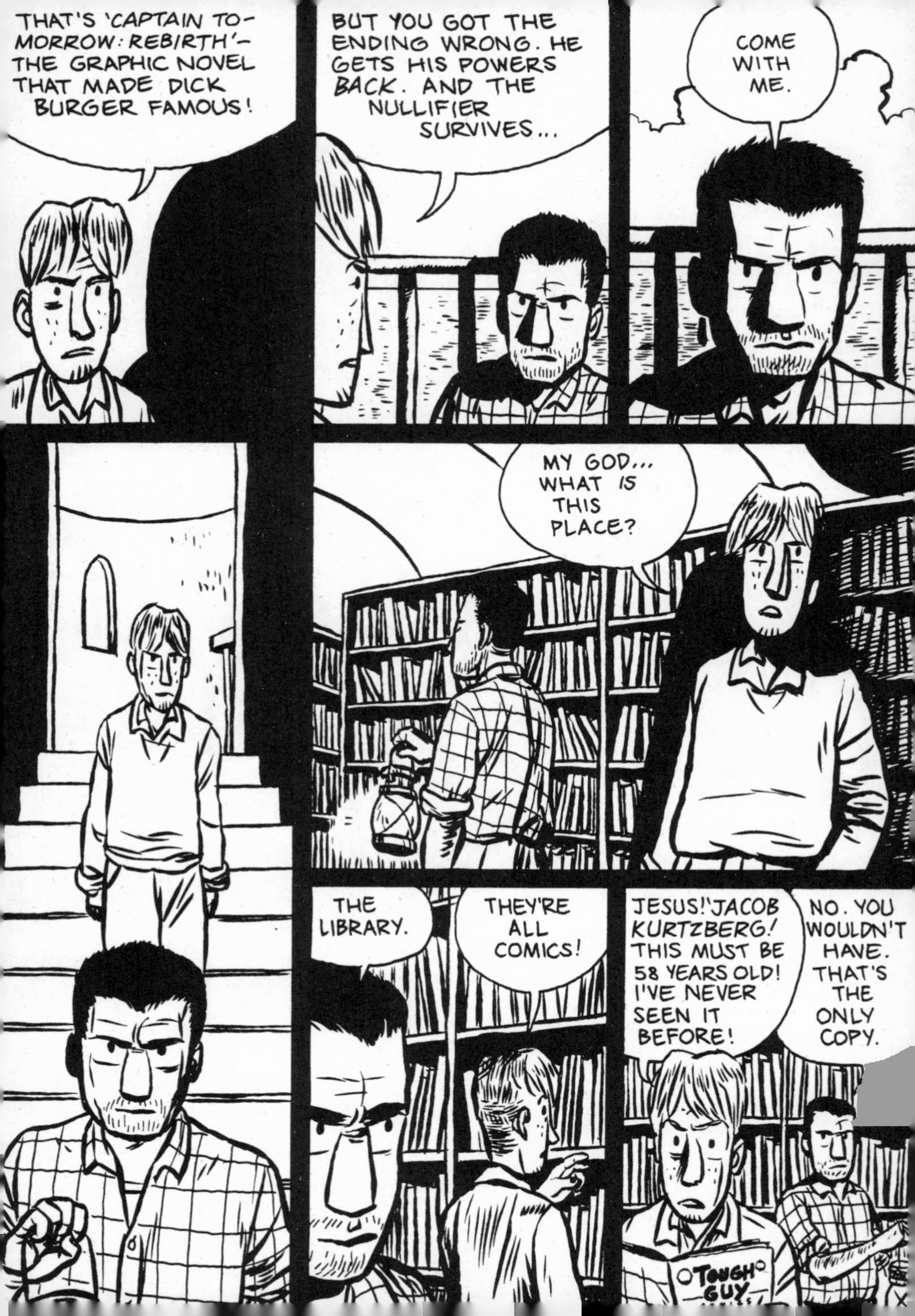
THAT'S 'CAPTAIN TO-MORROW: REBIRTH'– THE GRAPHIC NOVEL THAT MADE DICK BURGER FAMOUS!
BUT YOU GOT THE ENDING WRONG. HE GETS HIS POWERS BACK. AND THE NULLIFIER SURVIVES...
COME WITH ME.
MY GOD... WHAT IS THIS PLACE?
THE LIBRARY.
THEY'RE ALL COMICS!
JESUS! 'JACOB KURTZBERG'! THIS MUST BE 58 YEARS OLD! I'VE NEVER SEEN IT BEFORE!
NO. YOU WOULDN'T HAVE. THAT'S THE ONLY COPY.
TOUGH GUY

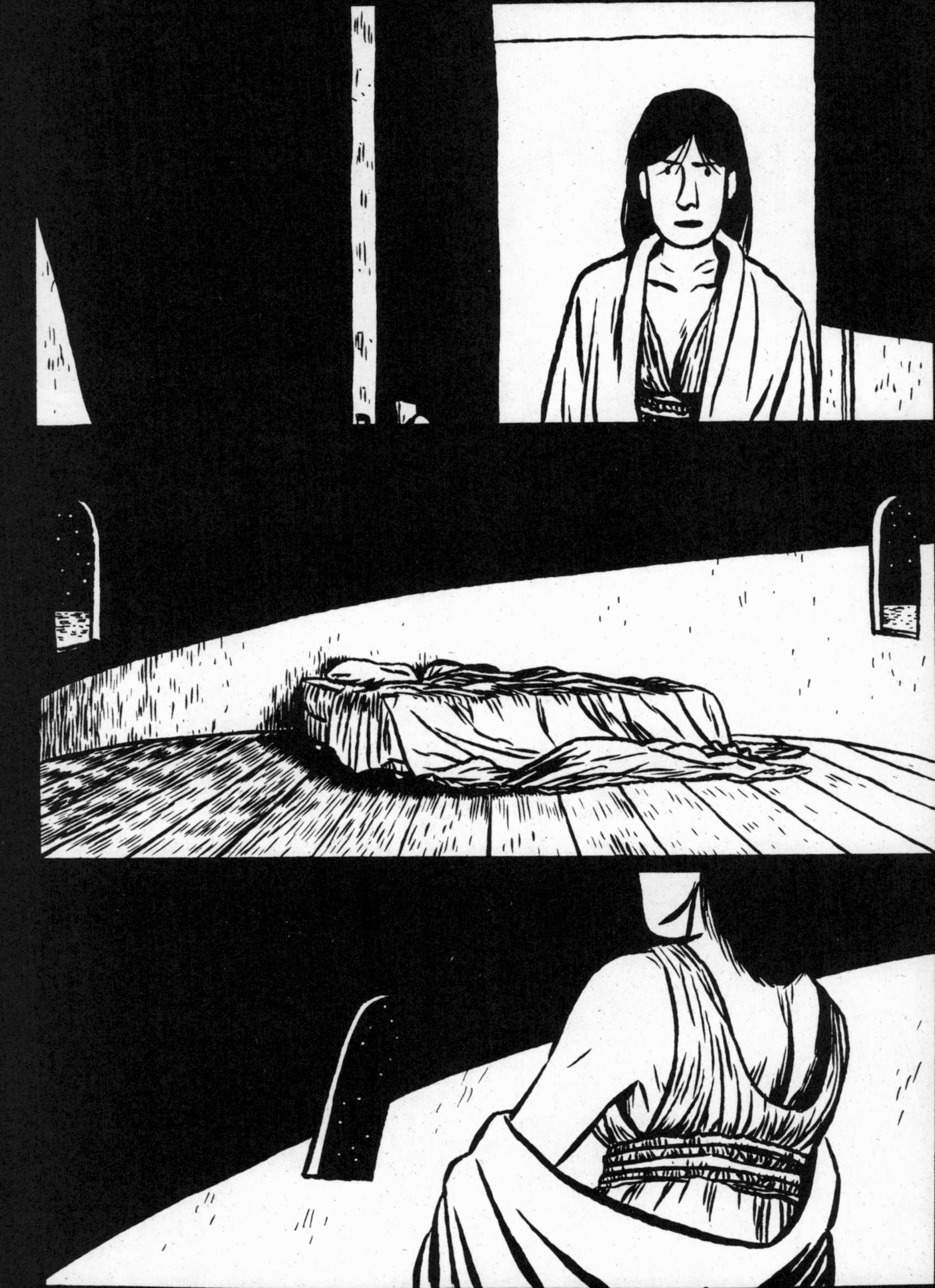

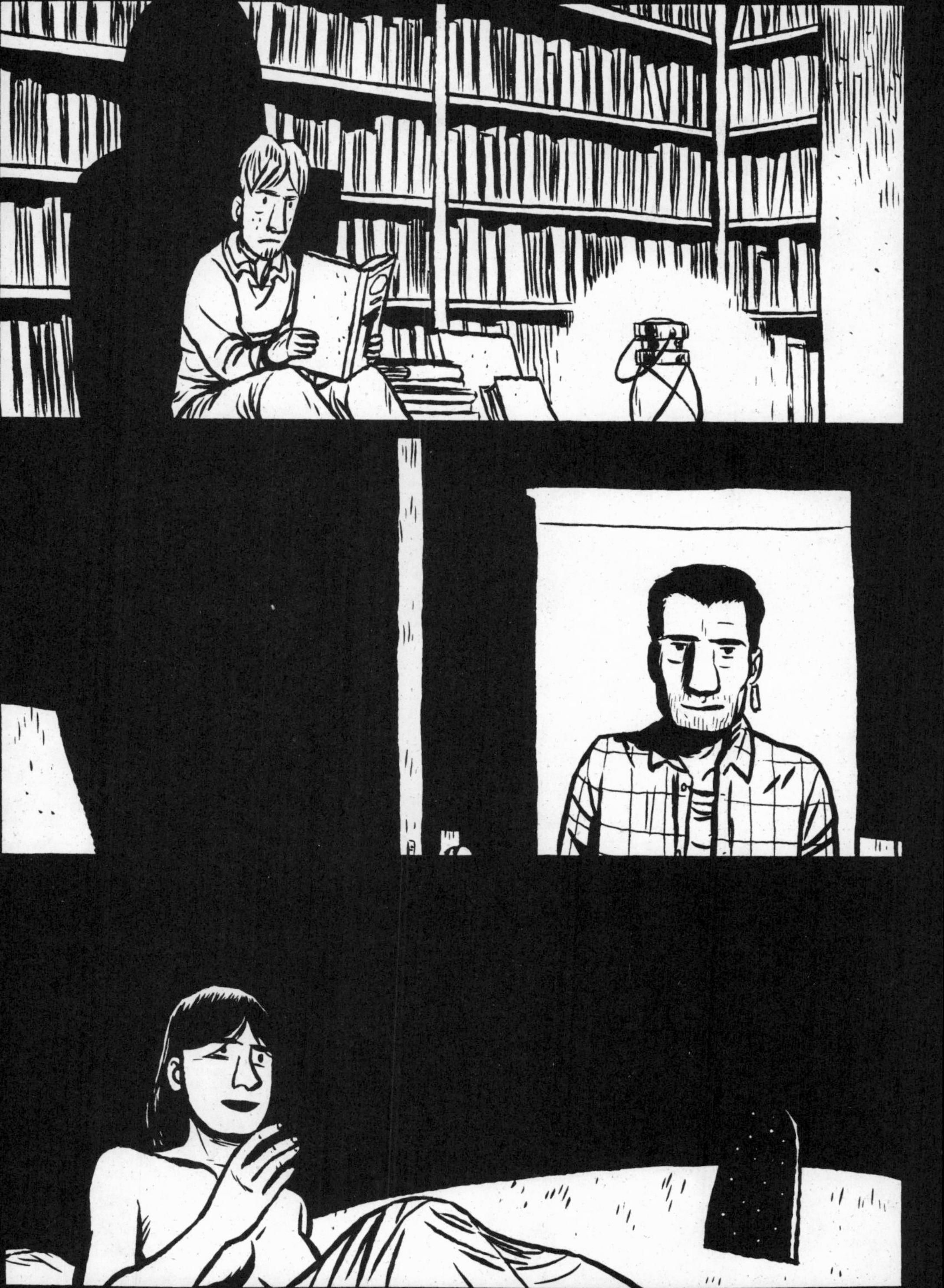

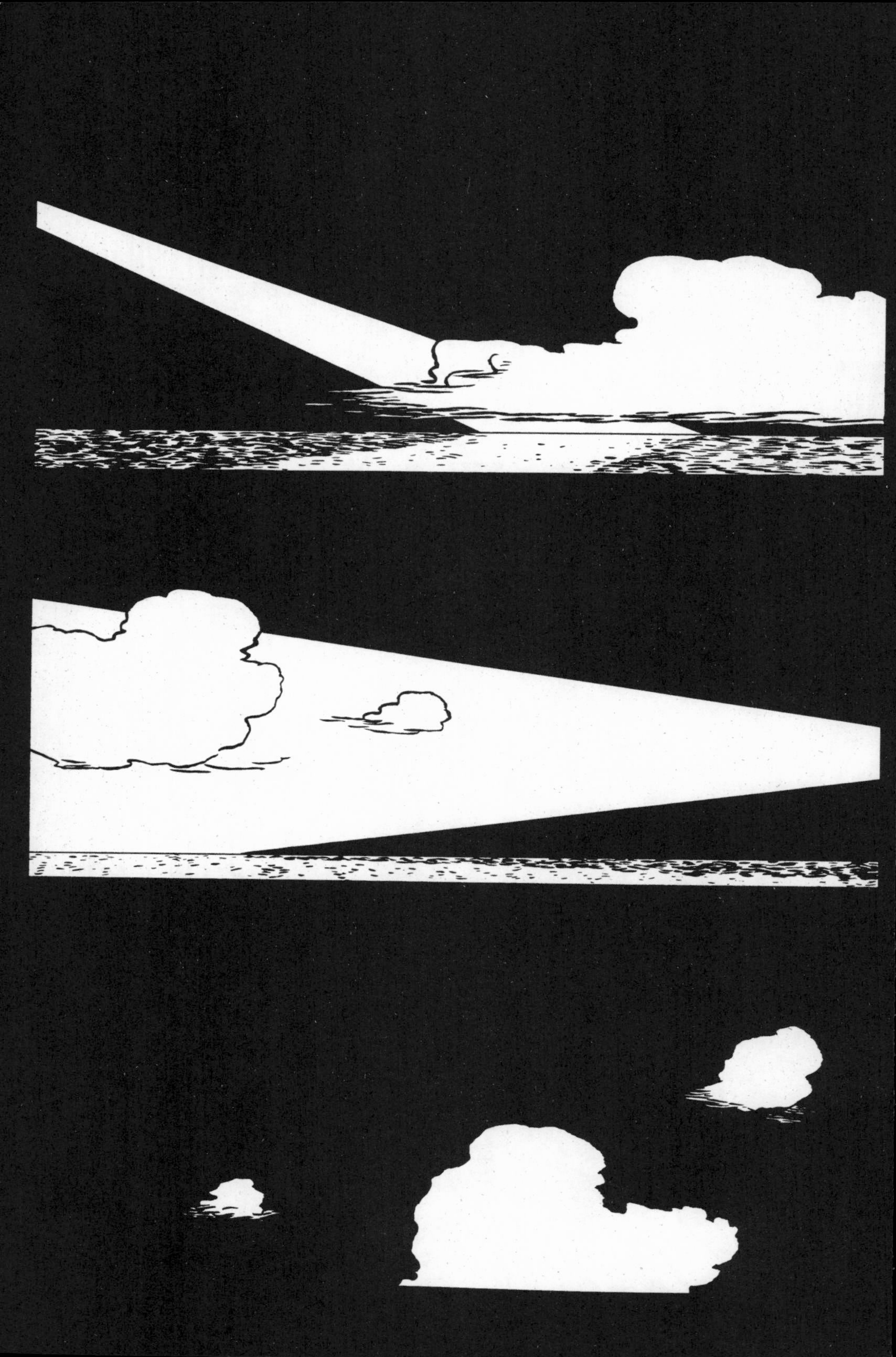

Chapter Ten

"Good is better than evil
because it's nicer."

Milton Caniff.

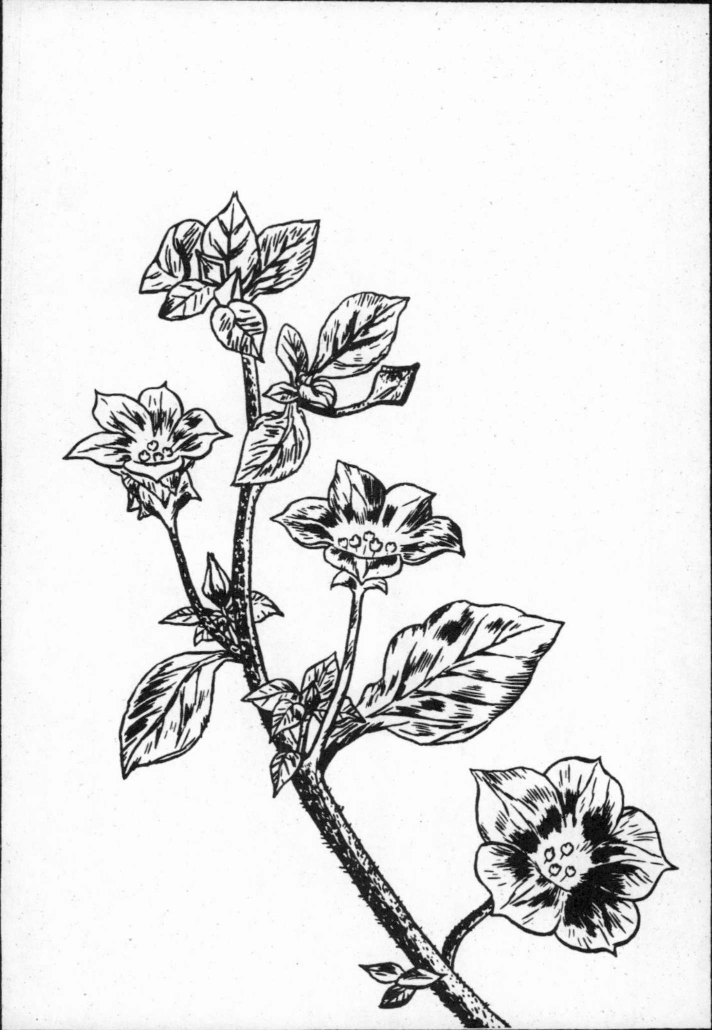

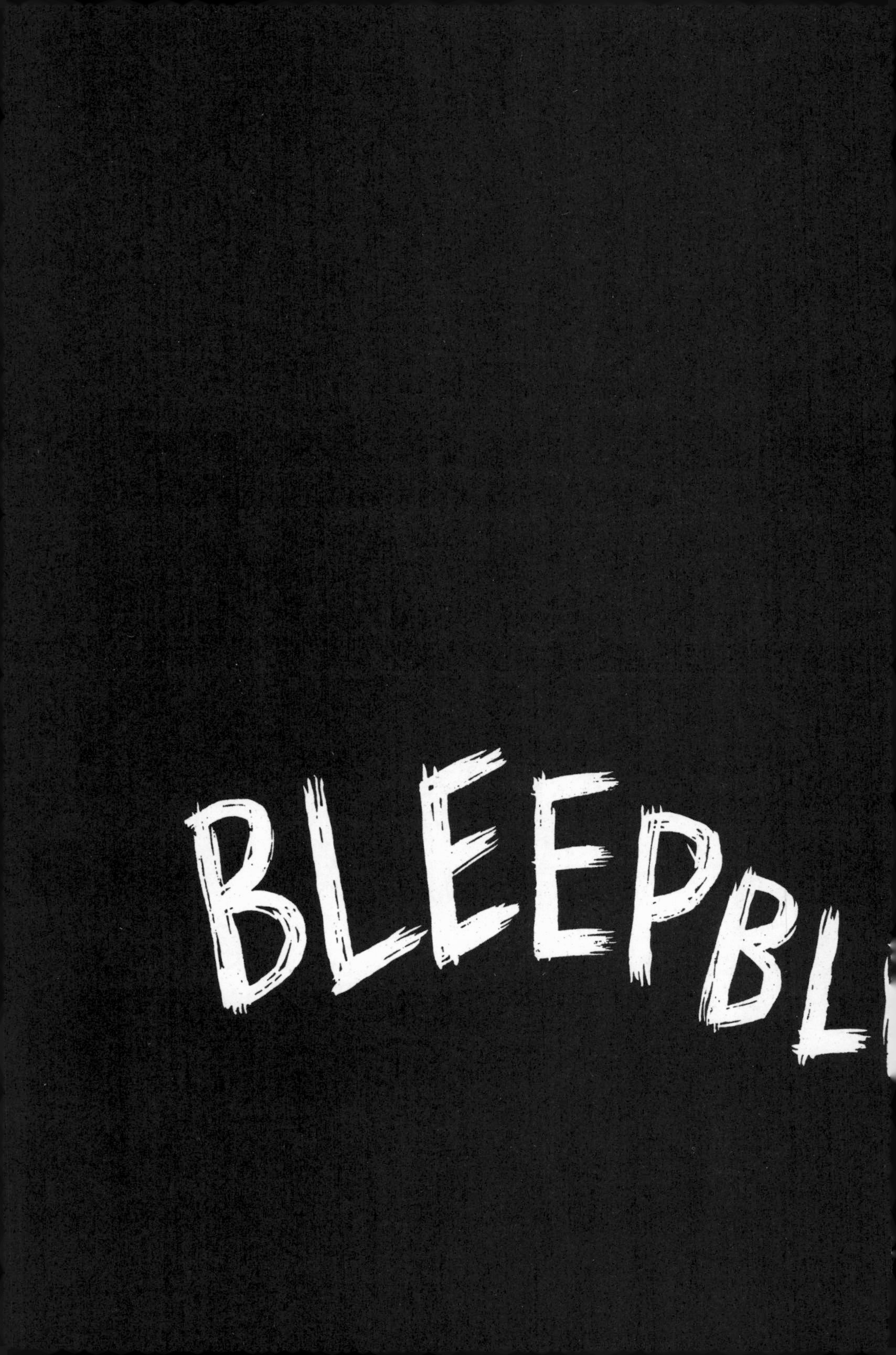
BLEEPBL

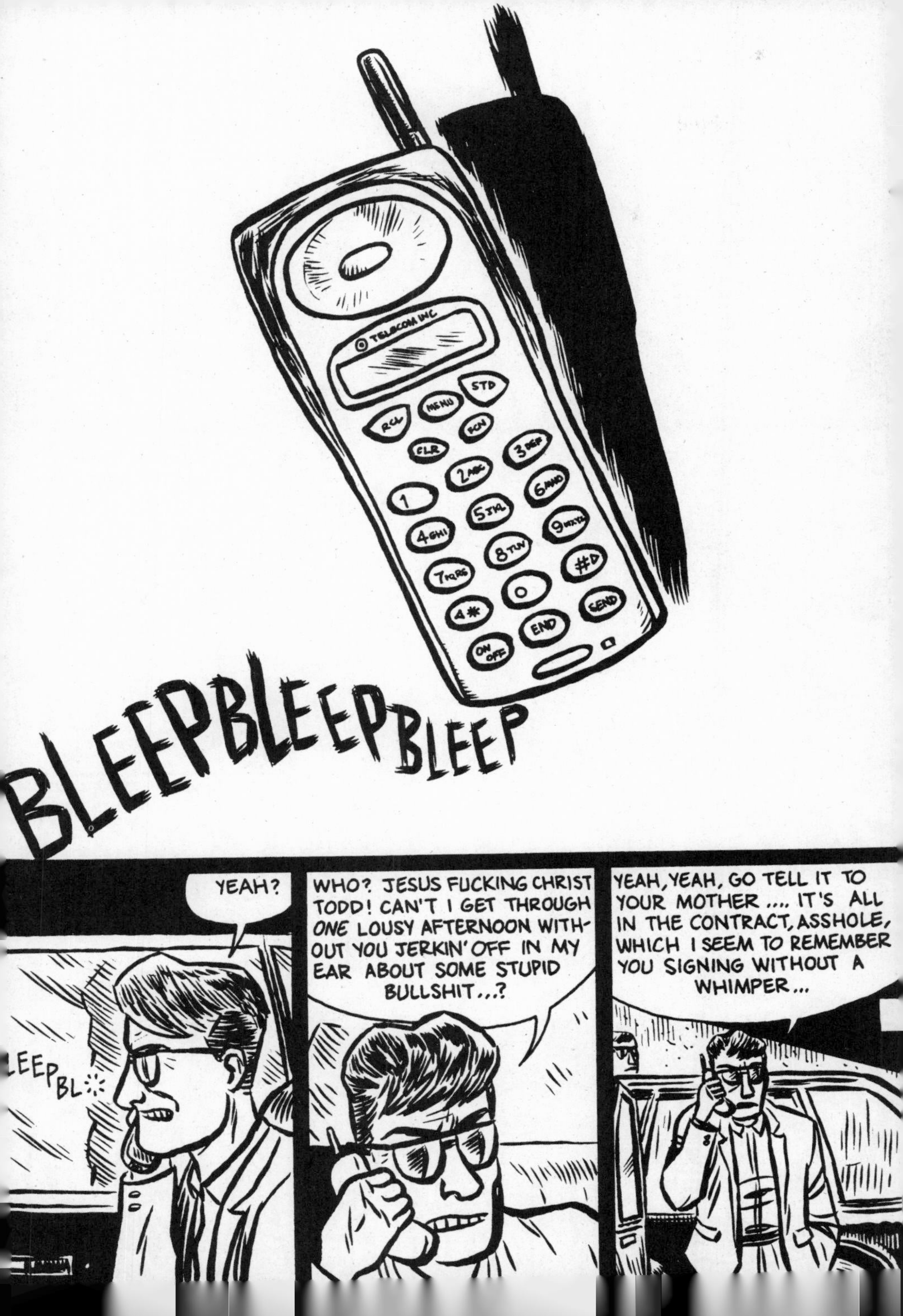
© TELECOM INC
STD
MENU
RCL
FCN
CLR
1
2ABC
3DEF
4GHI
5JKL
6MNO
7PQRS
8TUV
9WXYZ
#D
0
SEND
END
ON OFF
BLEEPBLEEPBLEEP
YEAH?
LEEPBL
WHO? JESUS FUCKING CHRIST TODD! CAN'T I GET THROUGH *ONE* LOUSY AFTERNOON WITHOUT YOU JERKIN' OFF IN MY EAR ABOUT SOME STUPID BULLSHIT...?
YEAH, YEAH, GO TELL IT TO YOUR MOTHER .... IT'S ALL IN THE CONTRACT, ASSHOLE, WHICH I SEEM TO REMEMBER YOU SIGNING WITHOUT A WHIMPER...

NOW SHUT UP AND GO AWAY — I'M ABOUT TO BE MOBBED BY THOUSANDS OF SWEATY FANBOYS HERE...

ROOARRR

ROOARRR

OARRO

CK BURGER

CAPTAIN TOMORROW: KAOS $12.95

signatures $15 ea

DY

Captain

QUE
HER

MR. BURGER, SIR — I WONDER IF YOU COULD TAKE A LOOK AT MY PORTFOLIO — I - er -

YEAH, YEAH, JUST ADD IT TO THE PILE...

DON'T CALL US, WE'LL CALL YOU...

IF YOU WOULDN'T MIND SIGNING THESE, DICK... I - er - I REALLY ADMIRE YOUR WORK ...REALLY...

COOL!

aptain MOR

LADY NIGHT

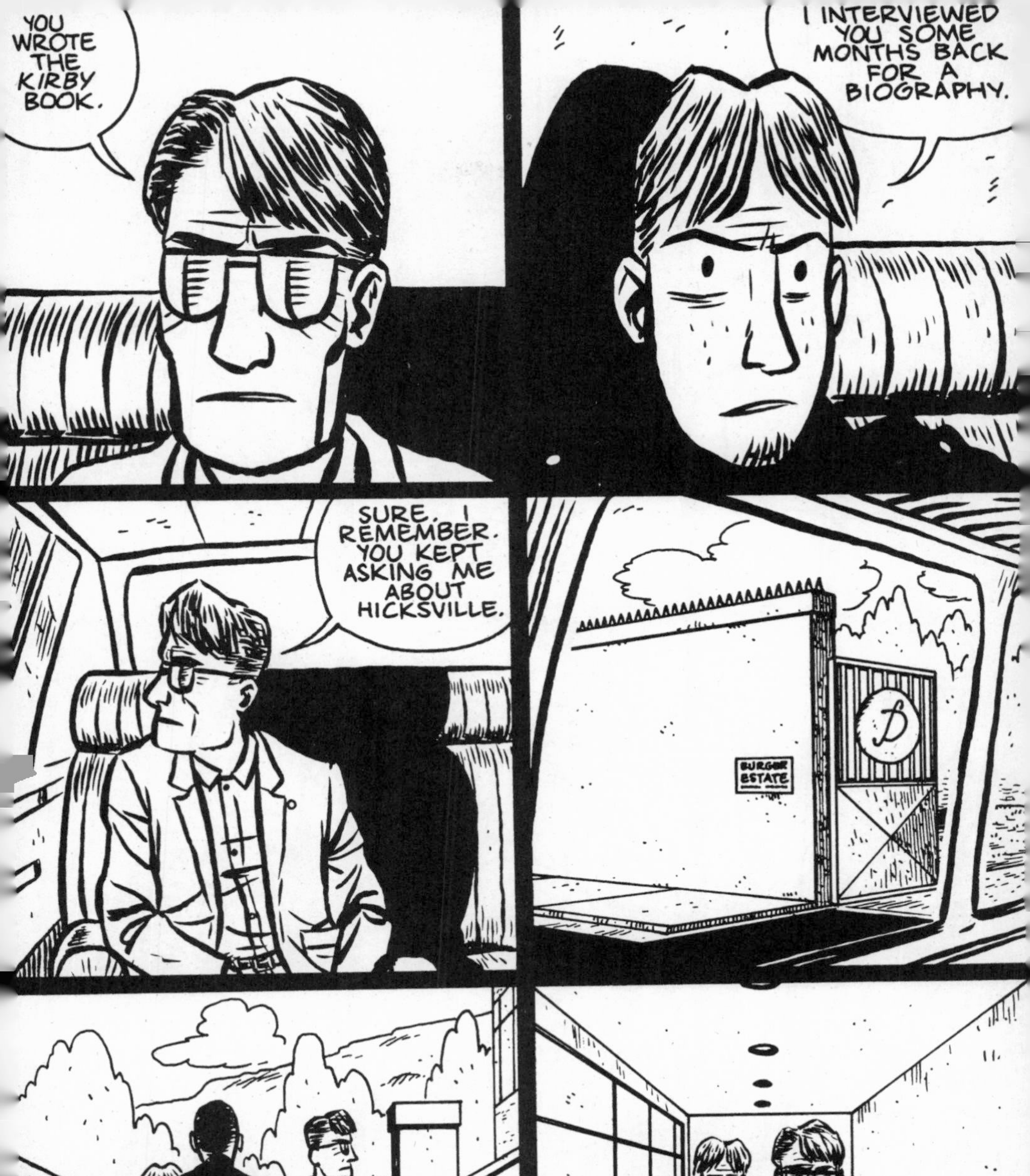
YOU WROTE THE KIRBY BOOK.
I INTERVIEWED YOU SOME MONTHS BACK FOR A BIOGRAPHY.
SURE. I REMEMBER. YOU KEPT ASKING ME ABOUT HICKSVILLE.
BURGER ESTATE

SIT DOWN, LEONARD.

...

WHAT DO YOU WANT, LEONARD?

THE ORIGINALS. KUPE WANTS THEM BACK.

...

CAPTAIN TOMORROW
REBIRTH ALEX ROLSON

YOU'LL SCREW ME. I'M FUCKED.

I'M JUST HERE FOR THE ART, MR. BURGER.

WHAT IF I TOLD YOU THIS IS A FORGERY? A TRICK? DONE **AFTER** MY BOOK...?

SHIT... Y'KNOW, I COULD BURY YOU, LEONARD, YOU DO KNOW THAT, DON'T YOU? I COULD FUCKING BURY YOU.

I'D LIKE TO HEAR THE STORY FROM YOU, I'D LIKE TO KNOW WHY YOU DID IT...

SURE YOU WOULD.

SURE YOU WOULD.

Y'KNOW, I MET MORT MOLSON WHEN I WAS A KID. HE SPENT SOME TIME IN HICKSVILLE IN THE EARLY SEVENTIES...

... WORKING ON THIS

...VILLE PRESS

CAPTAIN TOMORROW: REBIRTH

by MORT MOLSON

HE WAS LIKE A GOD TO ME: THE CREATOR OF CAPTAIN TOMORROW! I'D SIT IN THE BACK OF THE RAREBIT FIEND WHILE HE TOLD EVERYONE STORIES OF HIM AND LOU GOLDMAN AND JACK KIRBY IN THE '40S AND '50S...

ONE DAY I SUMMONED UP THE COURAGE TO SHOW HIM SOME OF MY OWN COMICS- FIREBOY, THE SEEKER, THE BLACK EAGLE.... I'D POURED MY HEART INTO THOSE STORIES... ALL THE LONELINESS AND FEAR OF HAVING NO PARENTS... THE CRAVING FOR LOVE AND RESPECT... THE LONGING TO REALLY BE SOMEBODY.

IT'S TIME TO BEGIN.

WITH ME, LUCA!

AT THE LAST MINUTE...

FIREBOT, NO!!

HE LOOKED THROUGH THEM ALL WITHOUT SAYING A WORD... I SAT THERE NERVOUS AS HELL, A REAL FANBOY, FOR ABOUT AN HOUR ... THEN FINALLY HE STACKED THEM NEATLY IN A TIDY PILE AND LOOKED AT ME...

THIS IS PRETTY SERIOUS STUFF, SON, YOU GOT TROUBLE AT HOME?

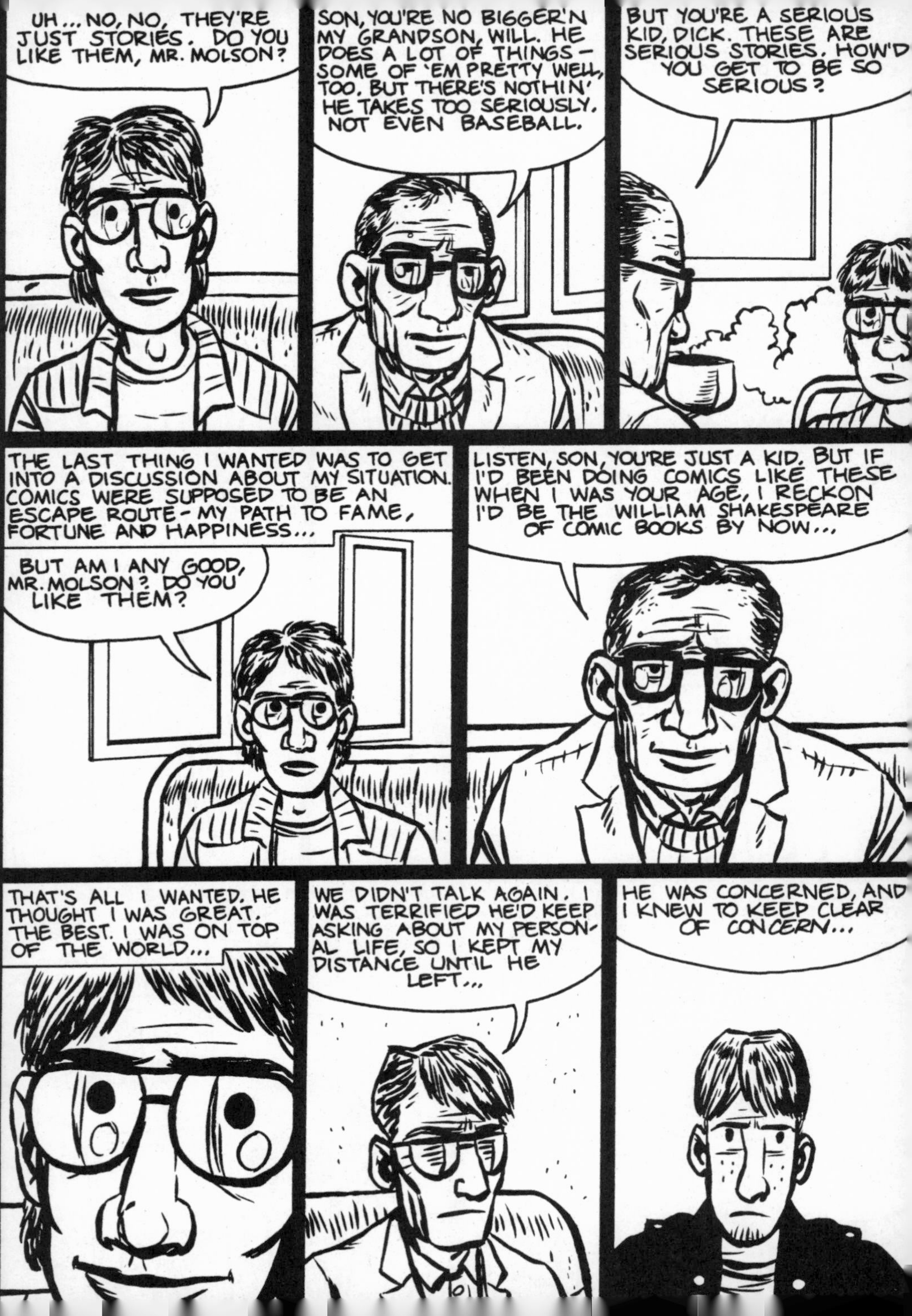
UH... NO, NO, THEY'RE JUST STORIES. DO YOU LIKE THEM, MR. MOLSON?
SON, YOU'RE NO BIGGER'N MY GRANDSON, WILL. HE DOES A LOT OF THINGS - SOME OF 'EM PRETTY WELL, TOO. BUT THERE'S NOTHIN' HE TAKES TOO SERIOUSLY. NOT EVEN BASEBALL.
BUT YOU'RE A SERIOUS KID, DICK. THESE ARE SERIOUS STORIES. HOW'D YOU GET TO BE SO SERIOUS?
THE LAST THING I WANTED WAS TO GET INTO A DISCUSSION ABOUT MY SITUATION. COMICS WERE SUPPOSED TO BE AN ESCAPE ROUTE - MY PATH TO FAME, FORTUNE AND HAPPINESS...
BUT AM I ANY GOOD, MR. MOLSON? DO YOU LIKE THEM?
LISTEN, SON, YOU'RE JUST A KID. BUT IF I'D BEEN DOING COMICS LIKE THESE WHEN I WAS YOUR AGE, I RECKON I'D BE THE WILLIAM SHAKESPEARE OF COMIC BOOKS BY NOW...
THAT'S ALL I WANTED. HE THOUGHT I WAS GREAT. THE BEST. I WAS ON TOP OF THE WORLD...
WE DIDN'T TALK AGAIN. I WAS TERRIFIED HE'D KEEP ASKING ABOUT MY PERSONAL LIFE, SO I KEPT MY DISTANCE UNTIL HE LEFT...
HE WAS CONCERNED, AND I KNEW TO KEEP CLEAR OF CONCERN...

PEOPLE WOULD DIG ALL THE HURT AND FEAR UP OUT OF YOU TO SATISFY THEIR OWN CURIOSITY... AND THEN LEAVE YOU TO BURY IT ALL AGAIN AS BEST YOU COULD BY YOURSELF...
SO WHAT HAPPENED?
I LOST IT. MOLSON WAS RIGHT - THOSE COMICS WERE SERIOUS. AFTER A WHILE I GOT SCARED OF WHERE THEY WERE TAKING ME. FOR A FEW YEARS I COULDN'T DRAW ANYTHING...
BUT THE AMBITION WAS STILL THERE... I WAS DESPERATE TO BE SOMEBODY BIG-'THE GREATEST COMICS CREATOR IN HISTORY'!
SO EVERYONE WOULD KNOW I WAS WORTH SOMETHING. PEOPLE WOULD RESPECT ME. ADMIRE ME. ESPECIALLY IN HICKSVILLE...
SO I COPIED STUFF. OTHER PEOPLE'S COMICS WEREN'T AS DANGEROUS. AND I FOUND I COULD TAKE A FORTY YEAR OLD STORY AND MAKE IT LOOK MODERN...
AT FIRST IT WAS JUST FOR FUN AND PRACTICE... I ONLY EVER SHOWED THEM TO SAM. I NEVER DREAMED OF PUBLISHING THEM. BUT AFTER A WHILE, IT WAS ALL I COULD DO...
...
DID YOU MEET GRACE?
MHM.

WHAT... HOW IS SHE?

UH... SHE... SHE WASN'T VERY FRIENDLY. AND SHE DOESN'T LIKE YOU VERY MUCH...

HA... ..YEAH...

I STOPPED LIKING YOU A LONG TIME AGO.

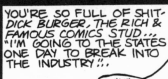

YOU'RE SO FULL OF SHIT, DICK BURGER, THE RICH & FAMOUS COMICS STUD... "I'M GOING TO THE STATES ONE DAY TO BREAK INTO THE INDUSTRY"...

YEAH, YEAH — WELL WHY DON'T YOU JUST FUCKING GO ?!

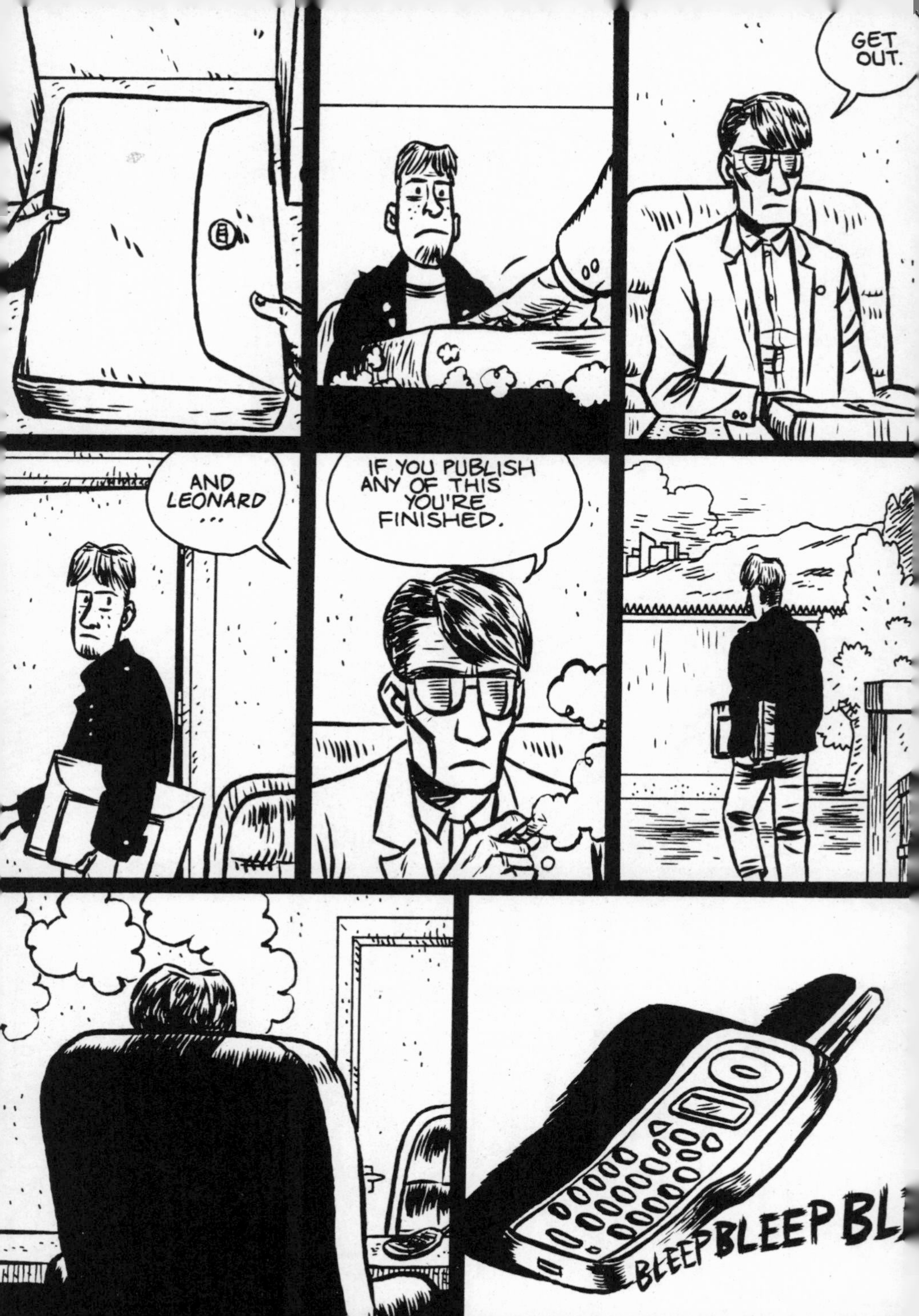
GET OUT.
AND LEONARD ...
IF YOU PUBLISH ANY OF THIS YOU'RE FINISHED.
BLEEP BLEEP BL

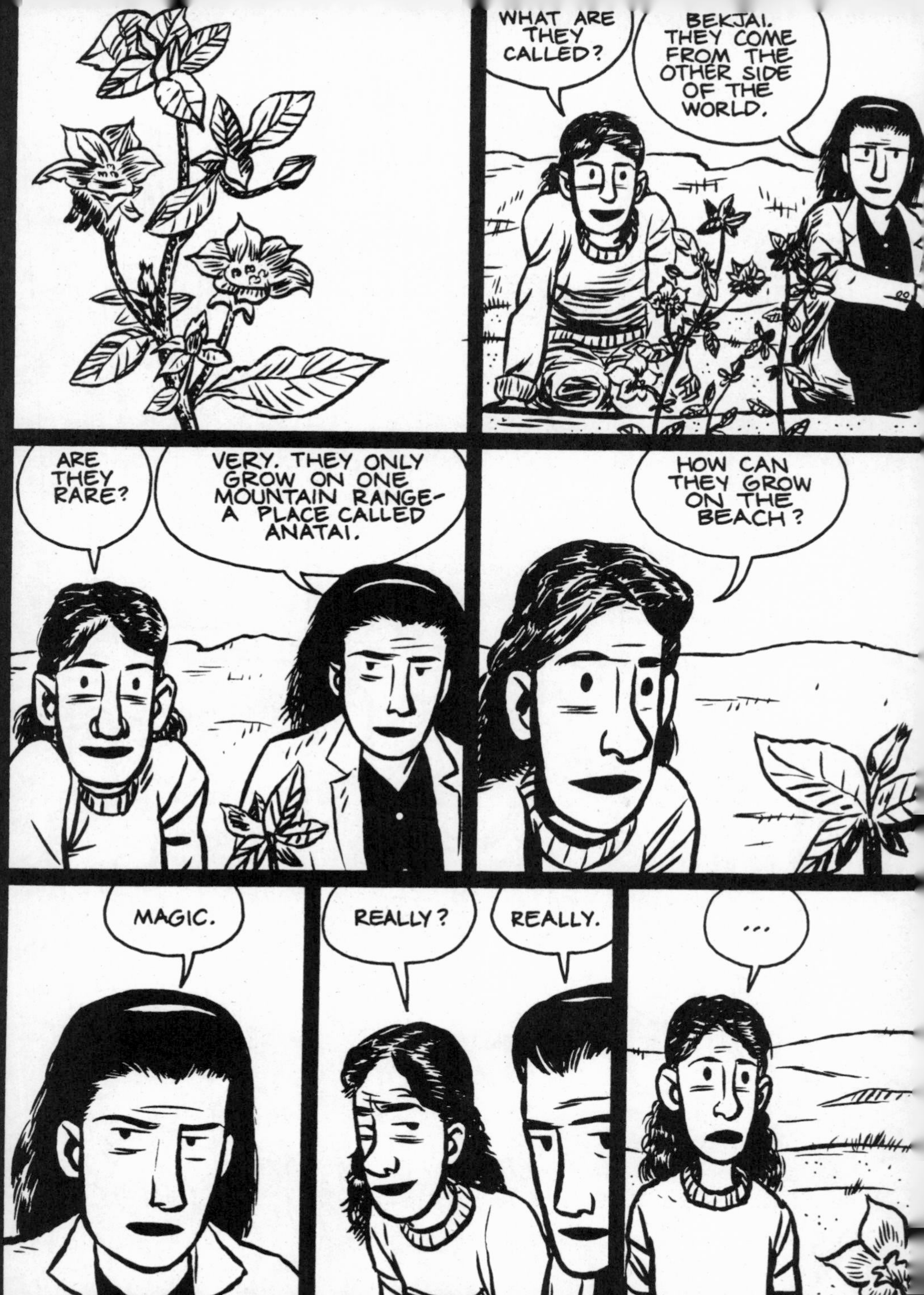
WHAT ARE THEY CALLED?
BEKJAI. THEY COME FROM THE OTHER SIDE OF THE WORLD.
ARE THEY RARE?
VERY. THEY ONLY GROW ON ONE MOUNTAIN RANGE- A PLACE CALLED ANATAI.
HOW CAN THEY GROW ON THE BEACH?
MAGIC.
REALLY?
REALLY.
...

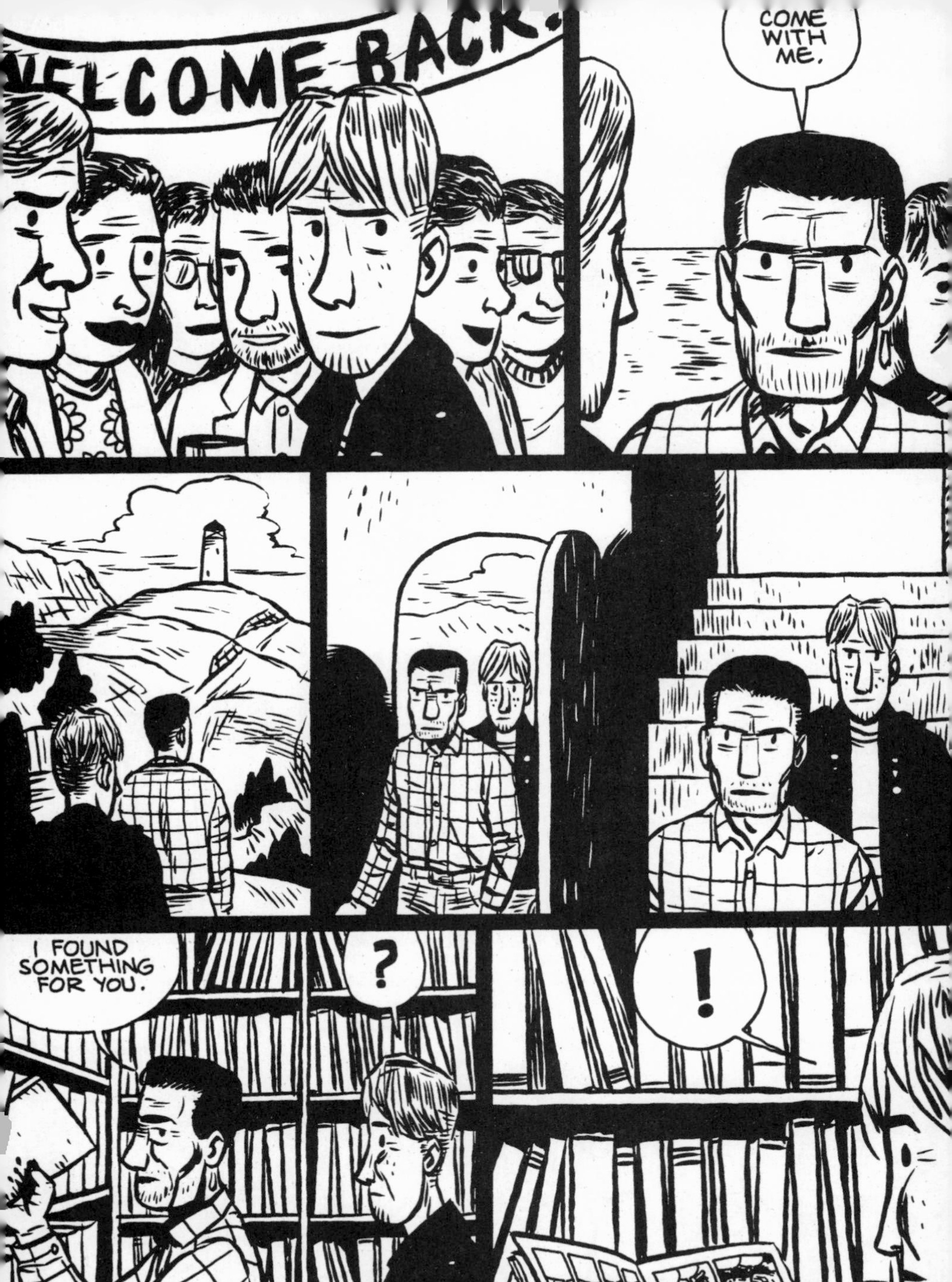
WELCOME BACK.
COME WITH ME.
I FOUND SOMETHING FOR YOU.
?
!

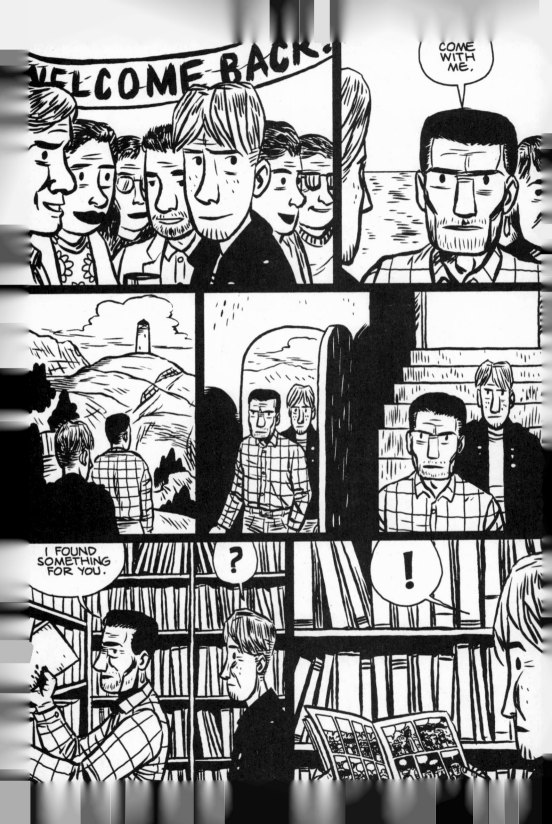

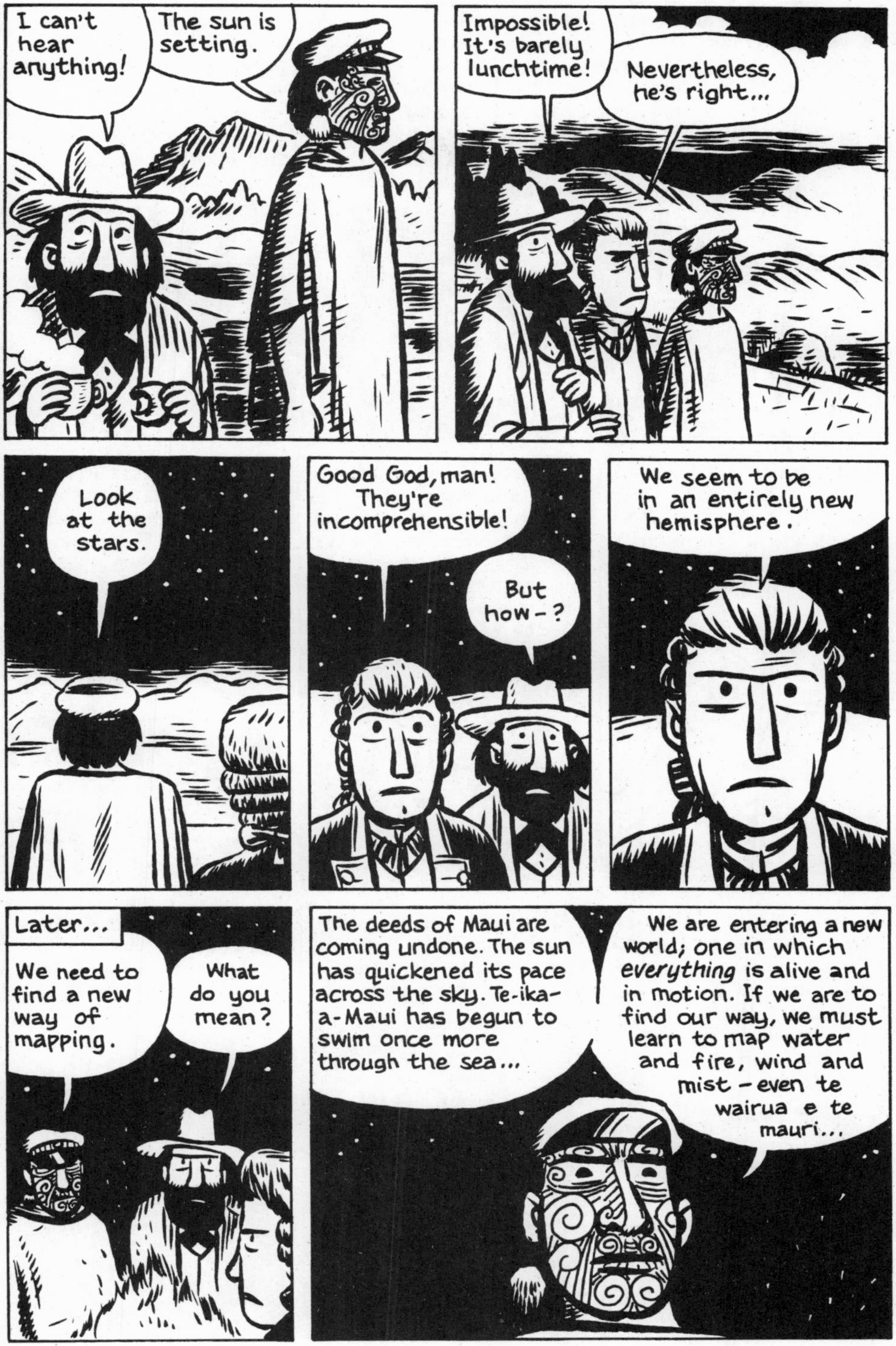

I can't hear anything!
The sun is setting.
Impossible! It's barely lunchtime!
Nevertheless, he's right...
Look at the stars.
Good God, man! They're incomprehensible!
But how-?
We seem to be in an entirely new hemisphere.
Later...
We need to find a new way of mapping.
What do you mean?
The deeds of Maui are coming undone. The sun has quickened its pace across the sky. Te-ika-a-Maui has begun to swim once more through the sea...
We are entering a new world; one in which *everything* is alive and in motion. If we are to find our way, we must learn to map water and fire, wind and mist - even te wairua e te mauri...

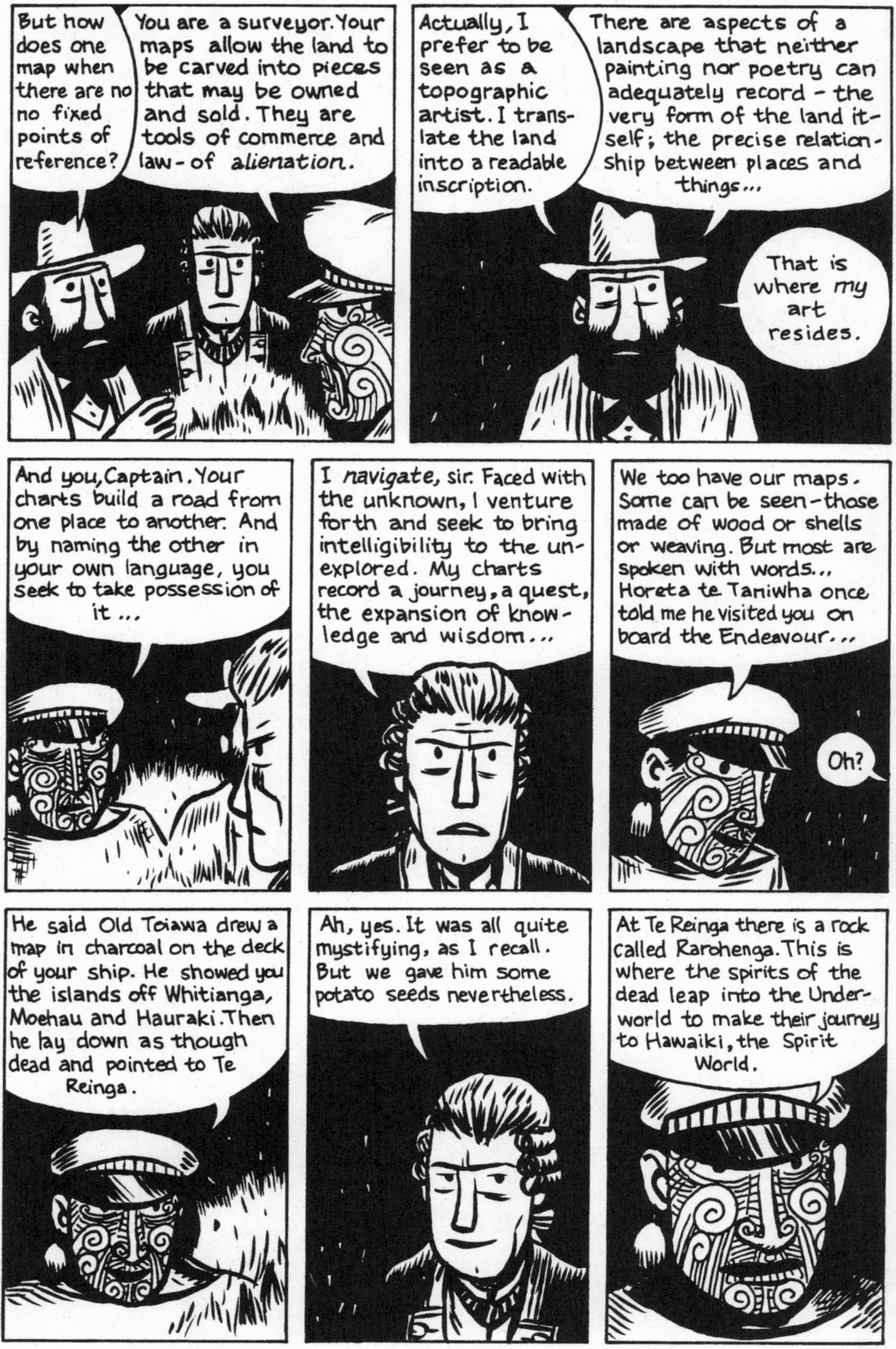

But how does one map when there are no no fixed points of reference?
You are a surveyor. Your maps allow the land to be carved into pieces that may be owned and sold. They are tools of commerce and law - of *alienation*.
Actually, I prefer to be seen as a topographic artist. I translate the land into a readable inscription.
There are aspects of a landscape that neither painting nor poetry can adequately record - the very form of the land itself; the precise relationship between places and things...
That is where *my* art resides.
And you, Captain. Your charts build a road from one place to another. And by naming the other in your own language, you seek to take possession of it ...
I *navigate*, sir. Faced with the unknown, I venture forth and seek to bring intelligibility to the unexplored. My charts record a journey, a quest, the expansion of knowledge and wisdom...
We too have our maps. Some can be seen - those made of wood or shells or weaving. But most are spoken with words... Horeta te Taniwha once told me he visited you on board the Endeavour...
Oh?
He said Old Toiawa drew a map in charcoal on the deck of your ship. He showed you the islands off Whitianga, Moehau and Hauraki. Then he lay down as though dead and pointed to Te Reinga.
Ah, yes. It was all quite mystifying, as I recall. But we gave him some potato seeds nevertheless.
At Te Reinga there is a rock called Rarohenga. This is where the spirits of the dead leap into the Underworld to make their journey to Hawaiki, the Spirit World.

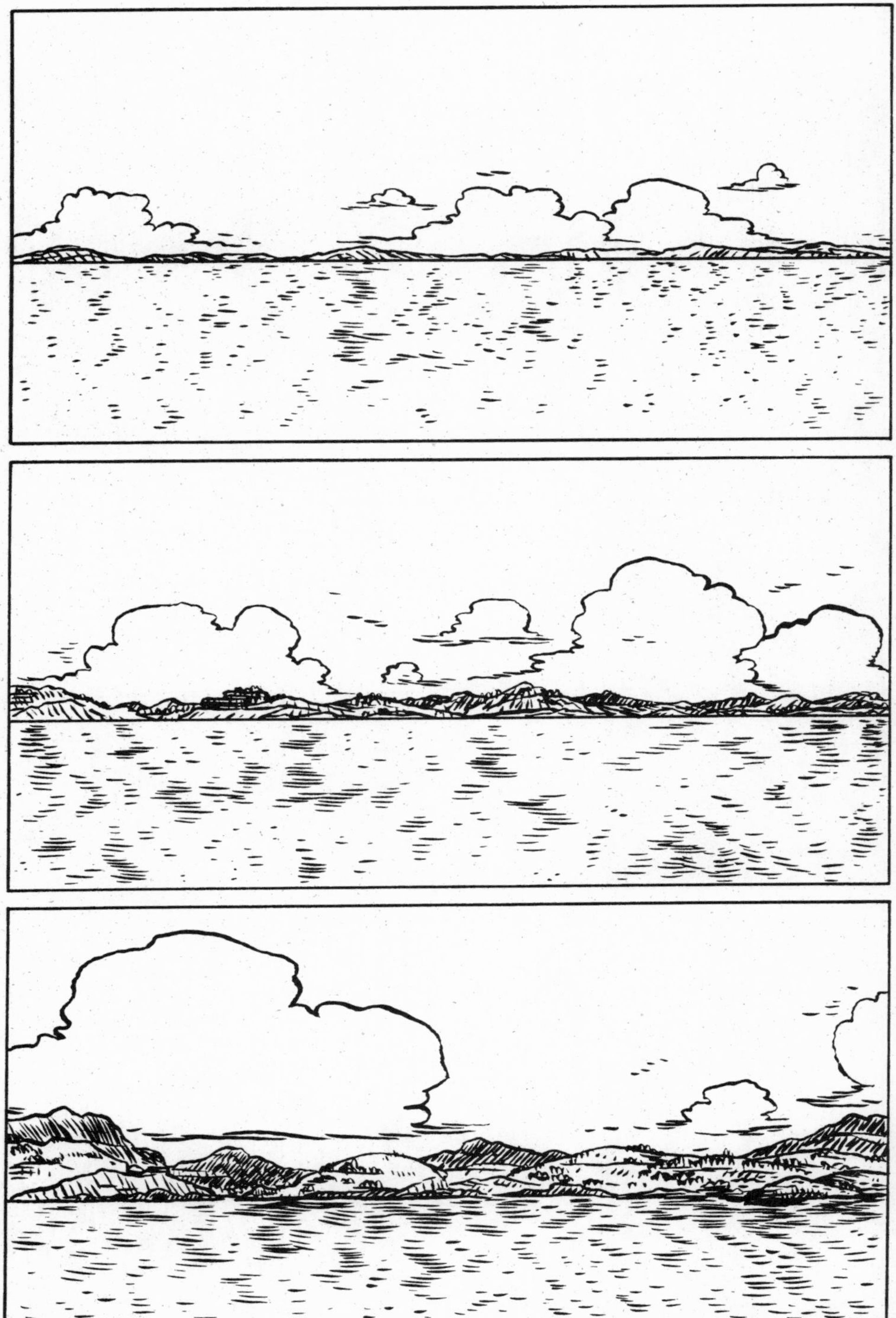

"Real or not - fact or unfact -
it was a beautiful vision."

George Herriman,
Krazy Kat.

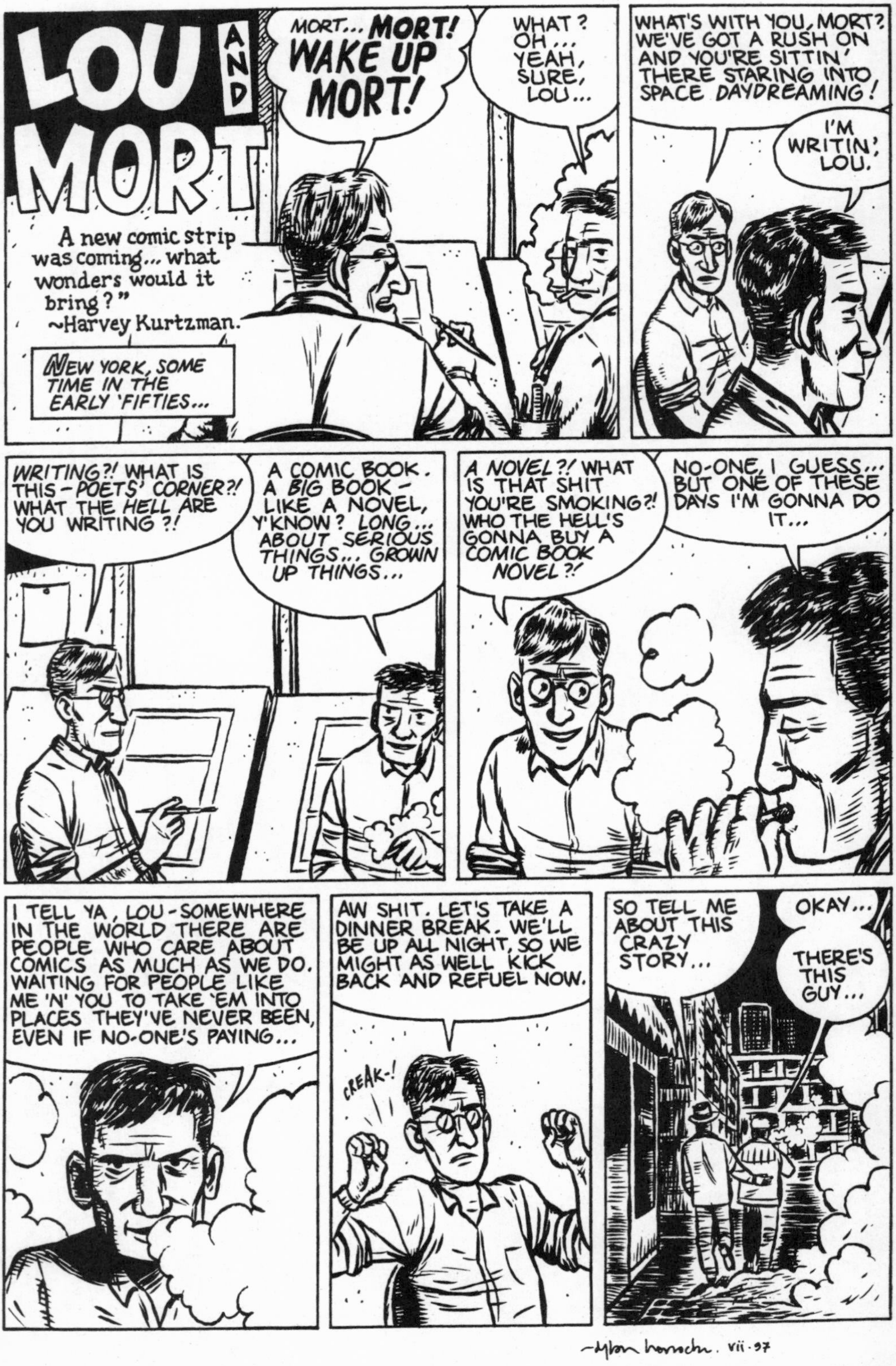
LOU AND MORT
"A new comic strip was coming... what wonders would it bring?" ~Harvey Kurtzman.
NEW YORK, SOME TIME IN THE EARLY 'FIFTIES...
MORT... MORT! WAKE UP MORT!
WHAT? OH... YEAH, SURE, LOU...
WHAT'S WITH YOU, MORT? WE'VE GOT A RUSH ON AND YOU'RE SITTIN' THERE STARING INTO SPACE DAYDREAMING!
I'M WRITIN', LOU.
WRITING?! WHAT IS THIS - POETS' CORNER?! WHAT THE HELL ARE YOU WRITING?!
A COMIC BOOK. A BIG BOOK - LIKE A NOVEL, Y'KNOW? LONG... ABOUT SERIOUS THINGS... GROWN UP THINGS...
A NOVEL?! WHAT IS THAT SHIT YOU'RE SMOKING?! WHO THE HELL'S GONNA BUY A COMIC BOOK NOVEL?!
NO-ONE, I GUESS... BUT ONE OF THESE DAYS I'M GONNA DO IT...
I TELL YA, LOU - SOMEWHERE IN THE WORLD THERE ARE PEOPLE WHO CARE ABOUT COMICS AS MUCH AS WE DO. WAITING FOR PEOPLE LIKE ME 'N' YOU TO TAKE 'EM INTO PLACES THEY'VE NEVER BEEN, EVEN IF NO-ONE'S PAYING...
AW SHIT. LET'S TAKE A DINNER BREAK. WE'LL BE UP ALL NIGHT, SO WE MIGHT AS WELL KICK BACK AND REFUEL NOW.
CREAK-!
SO TELL ME ABOUT THIS CRAZY STORY...
OKAY...
THERE'S THIS GUY...
vii.97

GLOSSARY

Action Comics: Issue #1 (June 1938) contains Superman's first appearance (by Jerry Siegel and Joe Schuster) and in 1996 was worth US$145,000.00.

Ae: (pronounced "Aye") "Yes" (Maori).

Anatai: a range of mountains in Cornucopia.

Aotearoa: (pr 'Ah-oh-tee-ah-roe-ah') Maori name for New Zealand; lit. 'Land of the long white cloud.'

Sergio Aragones (1937-) Spanish-born cartoonist, famous for his work in *Mad* magazine and his creation *Groo the Wanderer*. Once described as "the world's fastest cartoonist."

Arohanui: (pr 'Ah-roh-hah-noo-ee') literally big love (Maori).

Auckland: Largest city in New Zealand (population c. 1 million), situated on an isthmus and dominated by its harbours and a series of extinct volcanic cones. Also called 'Tamaki Makaurau' — "Tamaki of a thousand lovers."

Bach: (pr 'Batch') New Zealand term for a seaside holiday shack (derived from 'bachelor').

H. M. Bateman: (1887-1970) Cartoonist and social satirist, famous for a series of cartoons in the British magazine *Tatler* depicting social gaffes, entitled 'The Man Who....'

Bekjai: a rare alpine flower from the Anatai mountains.

Jack Cole: (1918-1958) Cartoonist, known for his manic inventiveness and practical jokes, who reportedly wept when other artists were assigned to draw his creation *Plastic Man*. He inexplicably took his own life at the pinnacle of his career.

Captain James Cook, R.N.: (1728-1779) Earliest english discoverer of New Zealand, who first circumnavigated the country in 1769-70 in the *Endeavour*. Earned a reputation as one of the greatest explorers and cartographers of all time before being slain in Hawaii.

Cornucopia: a country once famous for cartography and magic. During the middle ages, travellers were reluctant to enter its borders for fear of sorcery and witchcraft, but Cornucopian cartographers were highly sought after for their skill. The landscape has remained largely unchanged since the Enlightenment. Its towns, roads and fields often seem designed to suit occult geomantic purposes rather than practical ones.

Crieste: Capital city of Cornucopia.

Eisner Award: American award for comics. Named for Will Eisner, creator of *The Spirit* and a series of groundbreaking graphic novels including *A Contract With God* (1978).

Eternal Comics: publisher of *Captain Tomorrow*, now owned by Dick Burger.

Lou Goldman: (1920-) American cartoonist, famous for his creation *Lady Night*.

Martin Goodman: (1908-1992) Founder, publisher and managing editor of Marvel Comics until 1971.

Harvey Award: American award for comics named after Harvey Kurtzman.

Hauraki: (pr 'Hoe-rah-kee') "Northern wind" — the North Island's Hauraki gulf, beside which sits New Zealand's largest city Auckland.

Hawaiki: (pr 'Hah-why-ee-kee') The Spirit World and also the ancestral home of the Maori.

Charles Heaphy: (1820-1881) Painter, draughtsman and surveyor employed by the New Zealand Company in 1839. Heaphy's paintings were used to promote New Zealand to potential settlers and he was involved in the surveying of the first British colonies at Port Nicholson and Nelson. During the Waikato War (1863-64), Heaphy became the only member of the colonial militia to receive the Victoria Cross. He later held various positions of public influence — including the Surveyor General at Auckland — and briefly entered politics.

George Herriman: (1880-1944) American cartoonist; creator of the newspaper strip *Krazy Kat*, which ran from 1913 until his death and numbered among its fans e. e. cummings, Pablo Picasso, Robert Graves and Jack Kerouac, who called it an immediate progenitor of the Beat Generation.

Hick's Bay: Also called 'Wharekahika' — sparsely settled bay near the tip of East Cape, New Zealand. Named after Lt. Zachary Hicks, one of Captain Cook's crew.

Hogan's Alley: American newspaper comic by R. F. Outcault which was instrumental in beginning the 'funny pages' boom at the turn of the century.

Hone Heke: (pronounced 'Hoh-nay Hay-kay') (1810-1850) Leading chief of the Nga Puhi tribe; the first to sign the Treaty of Waitangi in 1840. Five years later he fought a successful war of independence against the British, which began when he cut down the British flagpole at Kororareka. His ally Kawiti has been credited with inventing modern trench warfare.

Edgar P. Jacobs: (1904-1987) Belgian cartoonist and opera singer. In 1944 Jacobs entered a partnership with Hergé (Georges Remi) as colourist (and co-creator) on *Tintin*. In 1947, however, Hergé ended their partnership after Jacobs demanded equal billing. Jacobs went on to achieve fame in his own right with his own series *Blake & Mortimer*.

Justice League: *The Justice League of America*, a popular superhero-team comic published by DC Comics.

Jack "the King" Kirby: (1917-1994: born Jacob Kurtzberg) Cartoonist credited by many with the success of Marvel Comics in the 1960s and the creation of many famous characters like *Captain America* (co-created with Joe Simon), *the Hulk, the Fantastic Four*, etc. In the 1980s a controversy erupted over Marvel withholding his original artwork.

Emil Kópen: (1914-) Cornucopia's most popular cartoonist, whose work has appeared in Cornucopian newspapers, magazines and books since he was a teenager. It is a mark of the popular esteem in which Kópen is held in Cornucopia that his obscure and erotic comic strip *Irjan vir Pidz* is still printed in the otherwise highly conservative newspaper *Criesti Njad*. Outside his native country, however, he is almost completely unknown.

Kupe: (pronounced "Koo-pay") According to some oral traditions, the original Kupe was the first polynesian navigator to discover Aotearoa. After exploring the coasts and naming many landmarks, he returned to Hawaiki to tell of his discovery. There followed a series of larger migrations — the Maori settlement of Aotearoa.

Kupenga: (pr 'koo-payngah') nets (Maori).

Harvey Kurtzman: (1924-1993) American cartoonist; creator of *Mad, Frontline Combat* and *Two-Fisted Tales*, among others. His war comics are famous for their meticulous research and commitment to historical accuracy.

Lady Night: Superhero comic created by Lou Goldman in the 1950s and repopularised in the 1990s by Dick Burger.

Lamington: A cube of sponge cake coated in chocolate and dried coconut.

Stan Lee: (1922- Born Stanley Lieber) Editor, writer and publisher of Marvel Comics, who headed their rise to dominance of the market during the 1960s and 1970s. Is credited with the creation of such classic Marvel icons as *The Hulk, The Fantastic Four* and *The Silver Surfer*. Debate still rages, however, over the extent of Lee's contribution to these and other characters, compared with that of collaborator Jack Kirby.

Frederico Garcia Lorca: (1899-1936) Spanish poet and dramatist, executed by fascists during the Spanish Civil War.

Winsor McCay: (1867?-1934) Pioneer American newspaper cartoonist and animator; creator of *Little Nemo in Slumberland*, *Dreams of a Rarebit Fiend* and *Pilgrim's Progress*, among others.

Maori: (pr 'Maah-oh-ree') The indigenous people (or 'Tangata Whenua' — "people of the land") of Aotearoa/New Zealand.

Maui: (pronounced 'Mow-ee') a significant figure in Maori legend; a trickster-hero and demi-god whose feats included forcing the sun to slow its journey across the skies and fishing up the North Island from the sea. His story is told in a graphic novel by Chris Slane and Robert Sullivan, *Maui: Legends of the Outcast*, published by Godwit Press, P.O. Box 34-683, Birkenhead, Auckland, New Zealand).

"Me he korokoro tui": (pr 'May hay koroh-koroh too-ee') "The throat of a tui" — Maori proverb used to describe one who speaks beautifully. The tui is a native bird, whose throat bears a white crest.

Moehau: (pronounced 'Moh-ay-hoe') "Windy resting place" — a hill at the tip of the Coromandel Peninsula, where Tama-te-Kapua, captain of the Arawa canoe was buried.

Mort Molson: (1916-1978) American cartoon-ist, active from 1938 until his death.

Mopani: (pr 'Moe-pah-nee') African species of bee, and also a tree favoured by them.

New Zealand Company: Private company formed in 1839 to found British colonies in New Zealand.

Pakeha: (pr 'Pah-kay-ha') Maori term for European settlers in New Zealand (origin obscure).

Pekapeka: (pr 'Payck-ah-payck-ah') Native bat of New Zealand.

Pablo Picasso: (1881-1973) Spanish painter and fan of George Herriman's newspaper strip *Krazy Kat*.

Ed Pinsent: (1960-) British cartoonist, once described as "the Philip Larkin of comics," whose work has appeared in *Escape*, *Fox Comics*, *Fast Fiction* and countless self-published mini-comics. Several collections of his work are available from Slab-o-Concrete publishers.

Placentia Bay: Bay in Newfoundland, Canada.

Puriri: (pr 'Poo-ree-ree') New Zealand native bird.

Puschkinia: Flowering plant.

Chris Reynolds: (1960-) British cartoonist, whose work has appeared in *Escape* magazine, *Mauretania Comics*, *Fast Fiction*, and various mini-comics. His graphic novel, *Mauretania*, was published by Penguin Books.

Ruapekapeka o Wharekahika: (pr 'Roo-ah-peck-ah-peck-ah oh Far-ay-kah-heekah') "The Bat's Nest at Wharekahika." Affectionately known to some locals as 'the Bat Cave.'

Julius Schwartz: (1915-) Influential editor and writer at National Periodicals and D.C. Comics.

William Shakespeare: (1564-1616) The 'George Herriman' of the stage.

Jim Shooter: (1951-) Managing-editor at Marvel Comics during the controversy-filled years of the 1980s, when cartoonists were agi-tating for royalties, creative control and greater recognition. Shooter gained a reputa-tion as a loyal 'company man' and conse-quently became unpopular with creators' rights advocates. He was Marvel's most prominent spokesperson during the dispute over the return of Jack Kirby artwork.

Gertrude Stein: (1874-1946) American-born poet, who, with partner Alice B. Toklas, host-ed legendary parties for the bohemian set in Paris.

Taonga: (pr 'Tah-ongah') "Treasure, posses-sion" (Maori).

Tapu: (pr 'Tah-poo') "Holy, sacred; under rit-ual restriction or prohibition" (Maori).

Te Araroa: (pr 'Tay Ah-rah-roe-ah') "The long path." A town on the East Cape (near Hicks Bay), nestled between Whetumatarau mountain and the long sweeping beach of Kawakawa Bay.

Te-Ika-a-Maui: (pronounced 'Tay Ee-kah ah Mow-ee') "The fish of Maui." Maori name for the North Island.

Te Reinga: (pronounced 'Tay Ray-eengah') Also called Te Rerenga Wairua, "the Leaping Place of the Spirits." The northernmost point of New Zealand, from which the spirits of the dead leap on their journey to Hawaiki.

Horeta te Taniwha: (pronounced 'Ho-ray-tah tay Tah-nee-fah') Member of the Ngaati Whanaunga tribe who was a boy when Captain Cook first visited New Zealand. Later grew to become a famous chief.

"Te Wairua e te Mauri": (pronounced 'Tay Why-roo-ah ay tay Mah-ooree') "the spirit and the life-force" (Maori). 'Mauri' is the force that binds together the body and the spirit.

Te Waka-o-Maui: (pr 'Tay Wah-kah oh Mow-ee') "The canoe of Maui." A Maori name for New Zealand's South Island.

"Tena koe": (pr 'Tay-nah Koh-ay') Maori welcome.

Tipuna: (pr 'Tee-poo-nah') "Ancestors" (Maori).

Toiawa: (pr 'Toy-ah-wah') Eighteenth century rangatira (chief), probably of the Ngaati Pou (or Te Uri-o-Pou) tribe of the Hauraki Gulf.

Rodolphe Töpffer: (1799-1846) Swiss writer, artist and educator who wrote and drew a series of extremely inventive 'picture stories' admired by Goethe. Sometimes called 'the father of the modern comic strip.'

Valja Domena: (pr 'Vah-lyah Dom-ay-nah') Comic by Cornucopian cartoonist Emil Kópen, telling the story of a *Bethgemani* (or member of the order of witches).

Waka: (pr 'Wah-kah') Maori canoe.

Cincinatti Walker: (1975-) American movie actress.

Whitianga: (pr 'Fee-tee-ahng-ah') "the crossing or ford." Beautiful bay in the Coromandel Peninsula.

Wally Wood: (1927-1981) Cartoonist, one of the EC Comics greats. Three years before he took his own life, Wood said that "working in comics is like sentencing yourself to a life at hard labour in solitary confinement. If I had to do it all over again, I wouldn't do it... and yet, I'm not sorry for where I am."

NOTE

The map on page 19 was drawn by Lt. (later Captain) James Cook, R.N., based on his first circumnavigation of New Zealand, 1769-1770.

The map of Aotearoa/New Zealand on page 22 was drawn in 1793 by Tuki Tahua and Ngahuruhuru, two Northland Maori abducted and taken to Norfolk Island on the request of its governor, who hoped they could train the island's convict labourers to dress flax. Being men, however, the two Maori knew little about the women's task of flax-processing. Tuki and Ngahuruhuru stayed on Norfolk Island for some six months, as guests of the governor. Their map was first drawn in chalk on the floor of the governor's mansion and then copied onto paper. The governor's secretary then annotated the map based on Tuki Tahua and Ngahuruhuru's descriptions. Running the length of Te Ika-a-Maui (the North Island) is the road taken by the spirits of the dead on their journey to Te Reinga and thence to Hawaiki.

Tuki and Ngahuruhuru's map is now held at the Public Record Office, London, England, as MPG 532(5). There are good accounts of it in Kelly, J. 'Tuki's Map of New Zealand,' *NZ Map Society Journal*, 1995; McKinnon, M. (ed) *New Zealand Historical Atlas*, Bateman (Auckland, 1997); Barton, P. 'Maori Cartography and the European Encounter' in D. Woodward and G. M. Lewis (ed's) *Traditional Cartography in African, American, Arctic, Australian and Pacific Societies*, University of Chicago Press (Chicago, 1998).

ABOUT THE AUTHOR

Dylan Horrocks is 32 and lives by the sea at
Omana Beach near Auckland, New Zealand,
with his partner Terry and their sons Louis
and Abram. *(illustration by Teresa Fleming)*

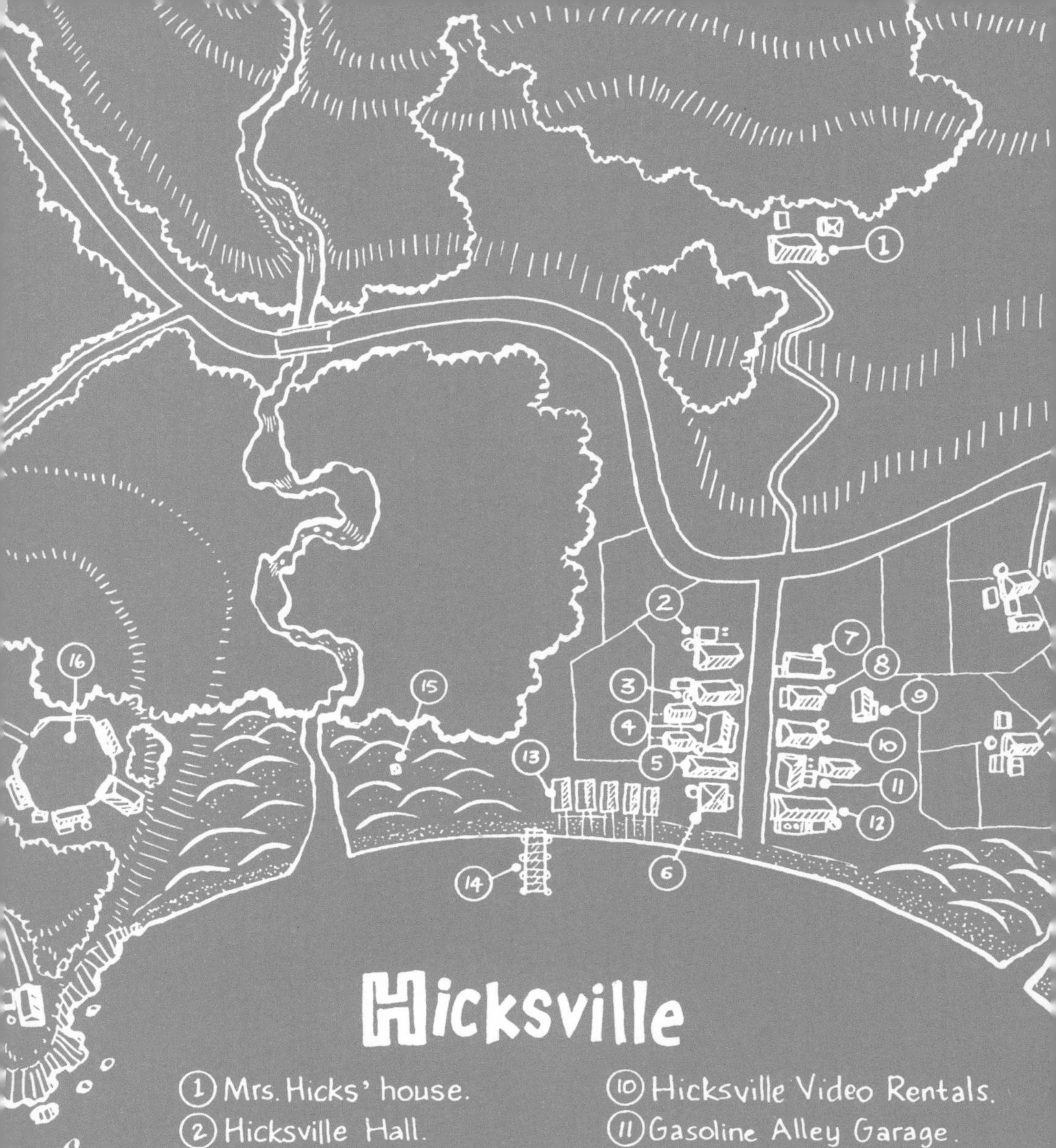
1
2
3
4
5
6
7
8
9
10
11
12
13
14
15
16

Hicksville

1. Mrs. Hicks' house.
2. Hicksville Hall.
3. Hicksville Dairy.
4. School.
5. Hicksville Record Shop.
6. Dr. Ropata's surgery.
7. Post Office & Stationers.
8. Hicksville Bookshop & Lending Library.
9. Hicksville Press.
10. Hicksville Video Rentals.
11. Gasoline Alley Garage.
12. The Rarebit Fiend Tea-Rooms.
13. Boat Sheds.
14. Jetty.
15. War Memorial.
16. Marae (Pakiwaituhi).
17. Kupe's Lighthouse.
18. Cave (Ruapekapeka o Wharekahika).
19. Grace's house & garden.